THE SCOTTISH TRADES UNION CONGRESS
The First Eighty Years

THE SCOTTISH TRADES UNION CONGRESS

THE FIRST 80 YEARS 1897 - 1977

Angela Tuckett

in conjunction with
THE SCOTTISH TRADES UNION CONGRESS

First published 1986 by

MAINSTREAM PUBLISHING COMPANY (EDINBURGH) LTD.
7 Albany Street
Edinburgh EH1 3UG

in conjunction with

THE SCOTTISH TRADES UNION CONGRESS
Middleton House
16 Woodlands Terrace
Glasgow G3 6DF

ISBN 1 85158 023 9 (cloth)
ISBN 1 85158 024 7 (paperback)

10 pt Century Schoolbook by
Pennart Typesetting (Edinburgh) Ltd

Printed by McCorquodale (Scotland) Ltd., Glasgow

CONTENTS

I Am The Common Man

Joe Corrie

I am the Common Man.
I am the brute and the slave,
I am the fool, the despised
From the cradle to the grave.

I am the hewer of coal,
I am the tiller of soil,
I am serf of the seas
Born to bear and to toil.

I am the builder of halls,
I am the dweller of slums,
I am the filth and the scourge
When winter's depression comes.

I am the fighter of wars,
I am the killer of men,
Not for a day or an age
But again and again and again.

I am the Common Man.
But masters of mine take heed,
For you have put into my head
Oh! many a wicked deed.

Introduction

Here's freedom to him that wad read!
Here's freedom to him that wad write!
There's nane ever feared that the truth should be heard
But they wham the truth wad indite.

R Burns (1759-1796)

The deeds of the helpers of menfolk to every age and clime,
The deeds of the cursed and the conquered that were wise before their time.

William Morris (1834-1896)

The Scottish people's poet and the English Socialist craftsman would both find proof of their views in the experience of the first eighty years of the Scottish Trades Union Congress.

So could we all. To learn not only from our own experience but from that of others is an enrichment all too few yet have gained: it is not in the school curriculum for children. But for trade union activists no gains are certain without sharing experiences, not least with those who have gone before as with those who are to come after.

A sense of history then can be a most important tool to open the door into the future united society no longer subject to class divisions, with ever greater diversity of opportunity for individuals: that co-operative society is the ultimate aim of the trade union movement. The first key to that door is not to accept mere academic generalisations nor dope served up by the enemy propaganda machines. It is to be aware of the true facts and the movement of events and the achievements and shortcomings of the men and women who unite to act upon them. To be aware of this and of how our predecessors won – and missed – their opportunities is an invaluable tool at the negotiating table; its usefulness goes beyond that of the most comprehensive electronic computer aid.[1]

The Scottish Trades Union Congress took shape in the last decade of a century which had already seen immense economic changes in Britain, its Empire and the world. It had to reach maturity in what the Tory Premier Winston Churchill described as "the terrible twentieth century", when Britain's undisputed world domination was virtually wiped out. Those years were to see further and unimaginable new technological developments which, lacking democratic ownership and control, could put humanity's very survival in jeopardy.

With its roots always in the activists amongst working people in Scotland's shipyards, mines, engineering and textile industries and transport in land, sea and air, the Scottish TUC was finally to become recognised as the one authoritative voice of the country in virtually every sphere. Its founders were the forward-looking Socialist men and women whose vision of social change found unity with the activists in mine, mill and shipyard who were so painfully aware of their urgent need for self-defence. Most were to the fore in Scotland's many trades councils, then almost identical with the small townships, where the mass of working people could find ready expression of their immediate problems. Here were the indispensable grass roots, having a special significance in Scotland's unique circumstances. As we shall see, it was because of the importance of these never broken links that the Scottish TUC first began; and this at a time when in 1895 leaders of the highly skilled craft unions elsewhere in Britain fell a prey to fixed illusions that their ancient methods of defence were adequate. Through these illusions and their doubts about combining economic with political action the old leaders failed to respond to the industrial upsurge in the eighties and nineties against the economic crises in mines, rails, docks, seafaring and engineering.

In the sixty years of Queen Victoria's reign, Scotland had seen tremendous development in shipbuilding, transport by sea and land and all the occupations associated with these round Scotland's coastal regions, from the Highlands and Islands and Aberdeen down to the upper and lower reaches of the Clyde and beyond the border. A veteran Scottish craftsman, holding many activist positions in the movement could look back in 1985 at some of the extraordinary changes experienced in his own family's time. Says former Councillor, Finlay Hart of Clydebank:

> My grandfather sailed out of the Forth on sailing ships; my father was a marine engineer, having learned his trade in the Carron Iron Works. When my parents were wed there were still horse-drawn trams in Glasgow, only converted to electricity about the time the Scottish TUC was formed.

Secretaries to the Parliamentary Committee and General Secretaries of the Scottish Trades Union Congress 1897 to 1977.

1. Margaret H. Irwin, Secretary to Parliamentary Committee, 1898 to 1900.

2. George Carson, Secretary to Parliamentary Committee, 1901 to 1917.

3. Robert Allan, Secretary to Parliamentary Committee, 1918 to 1921.

4. Wm. Elger, Secretary to Parliamentary Committee and General Secretary, 1923 to 1946.

5. Charles Murdoch, General Secretary, 1947 to 1948.

6. George Middleton, General Secretary, 1949 to 1963.

7. James Jack, General Secretary, 1964 to 1975.

8. James Milne, General Secretary, 1976 to 1977.

And great indeed were the changes and problems to be faced even before he himself was apprenticed to a skilled craft at Beardmore's in 1915. He points out that even as late as the First World War apprentices were not accepted as trade union members. Moreover for many years of the great changes the old craft unions had been slow to react to how the position of women had altered, as well as the young. In heavy and light engineering and even in nursing, education and office work, it had become the practice for women to lose their jobs on marriage and find themselves wholly dependent upon the menfolk, except in jute, cotton and linen industries and desperately underpaid home work. James Jarvie, the Secretary of the Blacksmiths' Society, could tell of the changes his mother had experienced. Agnes Neill, from Barra in the Hebrides, had first enjoyed her fully equal share of active participation working in the croft there. That would have been similar to the position of women 100 years previously taking part in cottage industry, before the very idea of "women's pay" was imposed when they were forced into the factories. Finally having to migrate south, Agnes gained an independent living screening coal on the pithead at Valleyfield in Fife. But at the turn of the century that too ended for women.

Many thousands of Scottish families could quote similar family histories. Another veteran notes the effect of the introduction of uncontrolled new technology and its consequent unemployment following the first major war of the twentieth century, as British industrialists became aware of encroaching rivals. Although only an apprentice at the time, Harry McShane vividly remembers his father being arrested at unemployed demonstrations during the TUC's first decade. He remembers too the vast migrations to the Clyde of unemployed Highlanders; and also of Irish coming over, free of fare "on the rigging", seeking harvesting work and never returning to the even more destitute Ireland. He remembers too the Scots craftsmen emigrating to Canada on their benefit society's free passage scheme, a primitive form of "redundancy payment" escape. He notes too the years of the "great unrest" in those four years of industrial upheaval as preparations were made for the First World War against Britain's formidable new rival, Germany. Following that war, he was well prepared to play a leading part in organising the many permanent unemployed who haunted Scotland's empty factories, mines and shipyards until rearmament began fifteen years later.

Clearly there were indeed formidable problems ahead of Scottish working people back in the nineties. Yet they were to be foremost amongst those in the British Empire to take a stand and begin to break out of the crippling limits of their daily lives. What must be remembered is that it is in production that changes begin; here trade unionists can be vitally important given one condition: that they increasingly understand the movement of trends and motives, and are ready to insist and ensure that there is widespread new thinking, so that the social benefits apply to all and the ill effects to none; and so be "wise before their time" and early bring about the long-overdue new society.

References

[1] Those sitting opposite at the negotiating table have become all too aware of our mistakes and ready to profit from them. There is the story of the American directors of a multi-million "business concern" who fed their crisis problems into a computer. When it grunted out "The solution is Socialism!", the Chairman snatched out his revolver to shoot it dead. But that was an old-fashioned weapon, and those were the early days of automation! (Told by R Palme Dutt, Editor of *Labour Monthly*).

1

Why it Came to be Founded

Section 1: **The Independent Small Scots Unions**

As the nineteenth century was ending, there were over a hundred separate and independent Scottish trade unions, apart from those based in England which had penetrated to the north. Indeed, some of the Scottish unions, like the blacksmiths, had explored and developed southwards across the border, while retaining their Scottish headquarters. Some of the Scottish unions had survived and maintained their independence for generations.[1] Many others had survived by amalgamating. For reasons largely of geography and prolonged lack of adequate land communications and transport, many Scottish unions which had emerged, as everywhere, in confrontation with local employers, had been slow to link up organisationally for defence with bodies based in England. This was especially noticeable in such industries as building, textiles and tailoring, printing, mining, quarrying, canal and harbour working, equipment for fishing and agriculture, baking and cooperage. Close with these went the specialised toolmakers supplying them.

In the Clyde valley, although so close to Glasgow, different industries completely dominated towns like Paisley, Springburn and Motherwell; here there could be a very strong sense of independence and self-reliance. This certainly contributed to the fact that there were "thirty small trades" sending delegates to Glasgow Trades Council in 1895. Much the same tendency could be shown in Aberdeen, Dundee and Edinburgh Trades Councils.

Throughout Scotland, therefore, all the trades councils in different localities had a very important part to play in keeping the small unions in touch and aware of events not only affecting their own trade but other workers and their defence bodies. Many problems and changes were already arising in the British Empire. These included industrial and commercial attempts by Germany to challenge British supremacy: there were already signs even of technological challenges on the horizon from those parts of the American continent to which in the past fifty years so many craftsmen had been forced to emigrate, with all their skills, in the frequently recurring periods of depression. It was in London that the Parliamentary Committee of the British Trades Union Congress was centred, far indeed from the Firths of Clyde and Forth, or indeed of Moray, but at least a small union could be represented through its trades council affiliation once a year at the TUC's annual conference. This was held in different cities, including Scotland's, with the local trades council chairman presiding.[2]

When the TUC met in Glasgow in 1892, for example, fifty-one trades council delegates were present, of whom eleven were from Scotland, including Aberdeen, Dundee, Edinburgh, Glasgow, Govan, Greenock and Port Glasgow. In addition, the smaller unions had access to all the British TUC reports and information sheets sent to the affiliated local trades council. They could not, of course, afford to send delegates to Congress independently from the trades council, unless they had already reached some strength, like the Scottish Typographical Association, the United Engine Keepers of Scotland, the United Operative Masons Association of Scotland, or the Scottish National Tailors Operatives Society.

The local employer, however, had far less difficulty in making speedy contact with his rivals in other areas in Scotland, many having connections with the Liberal Party and Scottish Home Rulers, as against the Conservative Party of the great landowners.

Section (ii): **Attempts to Make Closer Links**

Trade unionists in Scotland who had taken that step forward, ever since Chartist days of the first half of the nineteenth century, had been discussing the need for closer contact between the workers in any industry to match the closer links between employers against them. In the first place, this was seen in terms of mutually protective federations of separate unions in the same industry. Influenced by ideas and practices of the old friendly benefit societies and tontines, the central aim was to provide financial support to a similar local union in dispute.

But progress on these lines was slow. When the Clyde Employers Association organised a lockout of all the iron trades workers in Clyde shipyards in the sixties, it was a financial disaster for trades far removed from the battleground. Their funds were also severely hit by constantly returning economic and industrial crises and resulting bank failures, such as the Overend and Gurney Bank in 1866 and the horrific City of Glasgow Bank crash in 1878: it was hard enough for each union to maintain its own, without going to the aid of others in distress in their industry. Doubts about legal rights and status of unions, and attacks on them in the courts, began to be alarming. Already, in 1862, the Assistant Registrar of Friendly Societies had questioned the rules of the Scottish United Operative Smiths' Protective & Friendly Society. He argued that:

> to unite against all encroachments on their interests, and . . . to afford a weekly payment . . . during the time of sickness or being out of employment . . . might be encouraging a strike.

If that was the sort of decision to be expected from a law court, when a small union was dealing with its own members, what indeed might happen when funds were used to support others actually in dispute?

Throughout the sixties and seventies, Scottish courts were indeed preventing unions from action to establish "the closed shop" or to recover arrears of contributions, treating them as illegal bodies in restraint of trade. Throughout Great Britain, there was very strong feeling about the legal rights of unions, embittered struggles for shorter hours, and how these could be won against the encroachment of employers' organisations. The deep grass-roots response was less complicated than amongst the officers of the biggest unions, which had conflicting sectional interests and funds to protect. So it was expressed notably through the trades councils; thus Manchester Trades Council finally took the lead by calling in 1868 what was to prove the founding conference of the Trades Union Congress, to unify action to defend the interests of all trade unions in Britain. This led to their Parliamentary Committee being set up to lobby Parliament for protective law reform.

In Scotland, action had long seemed urgent to trades council delegates in Edinburgh, Glasgow, Dundee and the newly formed Aberdeen Trades Council, and over the years meetings had been held and documents circulated expressing the need for sectional federation of trades. Now, however, it was seen in terms of a General Federation of bodies within all the industries in Scotland. In 1872, after many consultations with others, it was the strongest trades council which took an initiative. Glasgow United Trades Council called on "the Trade Unionists of Scotland" to send representatives to Glasgow on June 11, 1872. The call included "the Branches of the National Associations having their centre in Glasgow".

Section (iii): **A Scottish Grass-roots Call**

It was a call to establish "a Confederation of the various trade organisations throughout Scotland, having a Central Board for direct communication, with the view to strengthening and extending the interests of trade unionism". It was signed by John Lang, Secretary of Glasgow United Trades Council, and dated 5 April, 1872. This Scottish move, though it did not achieve its immediate organisational aim, went far beyond what could only be attempted south of the border in a weaker form nearly thirty years later. As an expression of creative ideas already alive in Scotland which were to remain and grow in strength, it tells us much.

The call opened by noting "some important changes . . . regarding the social and political position of Working Men". These included the extension of the franchise to some of them; and "if so disposed, they can use their municipal and parliamentary influence".

They had even forced the repeal of "a barbarous relic of the old feudal system", under which the "workman could be dragged to prison as a felon" for breach of contract of employment. How were the gains so far made? "Principally by their own exertions"; for the influence of the trade unions was now "felt to be a power in the country; government has at length acknowledged their thorough legitimacy". Yet, it continued, "only a few years ago, the legalising of trade unions would have been treated as absurd".

Clearly bearing in mind recent successful struggles on the hours question in Glasgow, which had preceded, and perhaps inspired many of those engaged south of the border in the 1871 Nine Hours movement centred in the Tyneside shipyards, the call declared it was "a leading novelty of the age" that employers evince a disposition, or at least make the concession, to meet the workmen in conference to adjust disputes. It remarked: "It is then only the ignorance of the toiling masses, combined with the want of faith in each other, that gives capital the Herculean power and the lion's share."

Quoting a big employer telling the recent National Congress for the Promotion of Social Science that "the ratio of profit was just in accordance with the perfection of the organisation" in any particular trade, it added: "It would be well if every working man pondered over that statement." With employers "not confining their bonds of unity to any particular locality", concentrating their own forces "should be warmly taken up": for, in future, "the trade societies that simply protected local interests will be found to be inadequate to meet the demands".

With the employers' moves and "the concentration of capital, coupled with the application of machinery to be confronted, a general organisation of skilled labour becomes absolutely requisite". The immediate aim then was for the proposed Central Board of the

Confederation "to levy a small sum on each trade to supplement what those with a protective fund could pay out, and in generally assisting those in the throes of a lockout, or a strike that could not be averted without loss or degradation".

The characteristic note of grass-roots feeling in Scotland comes through in every line. It was the note repeated again and again, sometimes in the very same terms, in the next thirty years at every level and in every crisis. It meant that when the collapse of democracy came at the British Trades Union Congress in the nineties, there was little difficulty in Scotland setting up its own, as Ireland was also forced to do.

In this characteristic Scottish document, we hear not only overtones of memories from Chartist days but also undertones of the coming crofters' land struggles and the Scottish Land Restoration League, and of the Parliamentary exploits of the Irish Home Rulers, which stimulated the later Scottish Home Rule Association. All this is detectable in the strong and varied accents of the Scottish grass roots.

The one essential ingredient in the last quarter of a century of the British Empire's world domination was the demand for reform of all aspects of life of the working people. It had notably a Scottish dimension: for Scotland could not escape, being locked into British capitalism's economic problems. Increasingly, there was massive unemployment interspersed with temporary booms, bringing a drain on friendly society benefits during defensive strikes and systematic lockouts. For employers were building their own offensive organisations to destroy the exclusive self-defensive craft unions before the breakthrough by massive new forces might win the traditionalists in the Labour Movement to united action.

Section (iv): **Democracy in the London-based TUC Collapses**

Formed only four years earlier on the initiative of the Manchester Trades Council, the London-based Trades Union Congress was far from being an all-embracing close federation. It soon found itself at the centre of a hurly-burly of plans and counterplans, of conflicting ideas as to direction and methods of reform. Some saw this as nothing but political action to win modest reform item by item, solely by means of effective Parliamentary lobbying of the two existing parties: that, indeed, was why their central representative body was called the Parliamentary Committee. Hence, some leaders with personal records – perhaps only recently established – for carrying on "responsible negotiations" with employers who were their fellow members in the

Liberal Party, strongly favoured getting individual working men accepted as Liberal candidates.

But more and more trade unionists and others began to believe that no reform was adequate or lasting without a major change in society. This was where the emergence of Marxist theory and the Socialists, not least in Scotland, began to have major impact, despite their small numbers, in the last quarter of the century. Even amongst them, there were differences on method and immediate aims. There were those who dismissed any form of Parliamentary political action. Others argued that first emphasis must be on vast efforts of education and explanation to ordinary people. Some concentrated on analysis and skilful exploitation of the haphazard techniques of administration, to equip activists to use them effectively for the movement's benefit. Others, on the contrary, denounced all existing trade unions as an essential part of a totally unacceptable system, and called for nothing but spontaneous industrial action at the place of work.[3]

Rejecting these extremes in Scotland, on the initiative of the man from the Lanarkshire miners' family, Keir Hardie, supported by trades council members later to become active in the Scottish TUC, there was formed the first Labour Party in 1888, then called the Scottish Parliamentary Labour Party. Its object was: "to educate the people politically and secure the return to Parliament and all local bodies of members pledged to its programme". This included abolition of the House of Lords and hereditary office; nationalisation of land and minerals; State acquisition of railways and waterways; State banking; and free education. Though it did not then make any progress, it had the effect of stimulating many trades council delegate conferences on particular subjects in Scotland, thus providing Socialists with many a useful forum.

But the workers' party could not quickly win support without a programme of action on immediate issues uniting trade unionists. A key issue with a long history, including successes on the Clyde and Tyne shipyards and already an international question, was to gain shorter working hours. A great six weeks' strike in 1890-1891 by Scottish railwaymen led to a Select Committee on their hours being set up. When its findings were published about the unbelievable scandal of long hours of the railwaymen and the danger to the public, it really hit home. The Socialists of all viewpoints took it up and brought strong support to the long battle for a miners' eight-hour day to be imposed by law. This, and the campaign for a general eight-hour day, now occupied the time of the TUC Conference, year after year, to the exclusion of all else. The debates were bitter indeed. Deceitful and totally contradictory arguments were used by those who, in fact, prevented progress for a campaign, because methods for achieving it were anathema to them. This infuriated the Socialists and gave rise to embittered personal relations. Finally, after prominent trade union activists in 1893 had joined in forming the Independent Labour Party, which aimed at working-class political action independent of the Liberal and Conservative Parties, there was every prospect of joint action on the conference floor by the ILP with the grass-roots delegates from the trades councils, who wanted speedy action.

It came to a head in 1894, when delegates became impatient because important issues were being pushed aside while wrangling between key spokesmen left the conference a shambles. The Committee was, therefore, instructed to look at changes in the Standing Orders. Then came the final disasterous setback to democracy. For the Committee came up with new Standing Orders, which, in effect, aimed at excluding not only the leading Socialists but also all the trades councils. Not only this, but the block vote was to be used which gave one or two of the largest English unions total power of decision. Finally – and to some Scots who were certainly not Socialists it seemed the last straw – it was decided to operate the new Standing Orders immediately,before they could be considered by the 1895 Congress, and so make it impossible to defeat the fatal change.

Section (v): **The Scots Begin to Fight Back**

Before Congress opened at Cardiff on 2 September, 1895, there was a protest meeting of twenty-six people, including delegates from eighteen trades councils, under the chairmanship of the Secretary of the London Trades Council. Amongst the delegates assembled at Cardiff were twenty from Scottish organisations of varying political viewpoints, and many were to be prominent in the early days of the Scottish TUC. Playing a particularly outstanding part in the subsequent protest in Scotland was John Brown, iron-moulder and Secretary of the Glasgow Trades Council. At Cardiff the protesters passed a unanimous resolution, which J Havelock Wilson, MP, leader of the Seamen and Firemen, agreed to bring before Congress the following day. But when he did it was "defeated on the new card vote by 307,000 to 604,000", as the *Aberdeen Journal* reported. For the rest of the week there was considerable ill-feeling. "Some of the meetings at Cardiff were more like a pandemonium than those of a body of men met to discuss serious business," Alexander Catto, Scottish Bakers, told the Aberdeen Trades Council the following week.[4]

The London Trades Council Secretary made a suggestion that his body might call a conference of all trades councils to protest; in the event this was not to happen. But in Scotland protests began at once.

Immediate reaction came the next week at Aberdeen Trades Council's fortnightly meeting. Here the TUC's action was described as "unconstitutional and despotic".[5] Reporting the events at Cardiff, Alexander Catto, Scottish Bakers, pointed out that hitherto "trades councils had been the medium between trade unions and the Congress", and thus, they were "representing vast bodies of workmen". They should call on all Scottish trades councils to meet to discuss what action to take to get the decision reversed. In seconding, the Aberdeen Secretary, Councillor William Johnston, said that not to be receiving the TUC's information documents "in itself would do a great deal of harm". He added that a few societies at the Congress would boss the show, as they had voting power, and that small unions ought to have a chance of giving their opinion. He added that not only they "but the Congress itself was bound to suffer in future". There was opposition from those who wanted trades councils to go ahead nationally without the unions. Aberdeen's resolution was only carried on the chairman's casting vote against a proposal by a young Social Democratic Federation member, William Cooper, supported by Alexander Robertson of the Masons and Granite Cutters, for an annual meeting of the delegates of trades councils throughout the country, instead of having representation at the TUC.

Answering Aberdeen's call, eleven delegates from Glasgow, Edinburgh, Dundee, Aberdeen, Govan and Paisley met two months later at Mathers Hotel, Dundee. They dealt at length, and from different points of view, with a protest resolution and a recommendation for action. The protest motion emphasised that hitherto the trades councils co-operating "with the Parliamentary Committee have been instrumental in obtaining from Parliament many measures for the betterment of the labouring classes".

In acknowledging the political efforts of Lib-Lab MPs,[6] these terms aimed at being acceptable to the most traditionalist of craft union leaders; so Alexander Catto, of Aberdeen Bakers, dwelt on the fact that at Cardiff, the decision was not made "in a constitutional and fair way". He stressed that:

> The Parliamentary Committee had no mandate to alter the constitution . . . to exclude trades councils from their deliberative proceedings . . . However, by the casting vote of the chairman it was effected. In Aberdeen they felt aggrieved that it had gone from the Parliamentary Committee into the hands of an inexperienced chairman.

From Glasgow's Secretary, John Brown, in seconding came the call that:

> This question ought to be agitated for all that it is worth . . . the councils were the backbone of Congress, building up as they did the organisations which constituted it.

Then he described how important the councils were to the small trades, who could not possibly send a separate delegate to TUC conferences:

> The representatives of the trades councils were, therefore, the mouthpieces of these small organisations. . . Had the vote in Congress not been taken in such a mean, contemptible manner, the trades represented on the Congress would never have been a party to the exclusion.

P Brannigan of Dundee, who had represented the Scottish Bakers at Cardiff, considered that while, in his opinion, the Parliamentary Committee did have full powers to put the new standing orders into effect at Cardiff, he did believe that the policy was wrong: trades councils had been the mainstay and backbone of the Congress and without their co-operation the Congress would in future suffer.

Then came tough opposition from different angles. Aberdeen's SDF member, William Cooper, wanted no request for readmission. Said he, "they should let Congress be allowed to go its own way to perdition, as it would certainly do if left alone". In the past years, there had been variance not only as to the work to be done, but also as to how it was done. Therefore, the result had been that, like Parliament, they had been able to do nothing.

This had been because there had been "two classes of representatives", delegates from the old trade unions and those from "iron trades councils, who represented the new trade unions". Then he expressed the extreme opinion that the time had come when all must recognise that trade unionism was played out – was dead. He thought trades councils "should now have annual meetings of their own. They would never get the old-fashioned trade unionists to come into line". This argument for setting up throughout Britain a Congress to rival the TUC was not supported by the ILP, and leading trade union Socialists, such as Tom Mann, Ben Tillett and Keir Hardie, argued in the *Labour Leader* of 14 September, 1895, that "with two Congresses in the field, one would always be played against the other".

Cooper's view did find support from the Govan delegate, Modden who said that with Congress "as now constituted, the whole of its work was now in the hands of about six trades. (Hear, hear). Six individuals could, in future, rule the whole of the business transacted. . . a clique which could do as it liked".

One senior delegate, David Blackburn, of the Edinburgh Flint Glass Makers, said there was "only semi-labour representation at Congress", complaining of highly paid full-time officials there. He added that judging from his experience of them, "extending over half a century", they were not "labour-representative; they had been representing their own interests. Their representatives ought to be men direct from the bench or the anvil".

He regarded the choice of Edinburgh as the next venue for the TUC as "nothing but a political dodge. . . political wire-pulling". Later he said he would do everything in his power "to make it a failure". His fellow delegate, John Mallinson, of the Cordwainers, who, as Edinburgh Trades Council leader, was in fact to preside over the 1896 TUC, had a different approach. While agreeing with those who believed that "if trades councils were excluded, trades unionism would undoubtedly suffer", he was not antagonistic to the TUC as such. He disagreed with Cooper, and believed that the TUC "would do as much good work in the future as in the past".

He believed they should seek readmission, and answer the excuse given for the exclusion, which had been that trades councils involved dual representation; this, he thought, could be avoided. This was followed up by delegates from Dundee and Paisley, with the chairman, James Mann, President of Dundee Trades Council, making the point that there could be a new basis, with trades councils only sending as delegates to the TUC members of the small unrepresented unions. With this type of argument in their minds, the meeting then decided to recommend Scottish Trades Councils "to bring their influence to bear on trade unions to support the readmission by the next Congress".

It was opposed by Blackburn, who, once again, referred to the bringing of the 1896 TUC to Edinburgh "as the biggest fraud ever perpetuated". The meeting then closed with the two Aberdeen delegates sucessfully urging that the proposed protest conference, to be called by the London Trades Council, should be supported.

But it soon emerged that the mere protest stage was coming to an end. The London Trades Council issued a circular quoted at Falkirk's fortnightly meeting:

> The proposal to have a National Conference of Trades Councils had met with very little support, and it had been agreed to abandon the proposal.[7]

Their distinctly cautious Secretary, far away south, in London, where almost all the full-time officers of the large trade unions were congregated, supplemented this with a mild phrase about possibly extending "the scope of the present Trades Congress" to admit of some trades council representatives being present.

References

[1] Some of the longest lived, still battling as late as 1906, were the following: City of Glasgow Operative Boot & Shoe Makers, founded 1815; Edinburgh Operative Cordwainers, 1822; Associated Iron Moulders of Scotland, 1833; Scottish Tinplate and Sheet Metal Workers, 1833; Twisters & Drawers of Glasgow & Vicinity, 1833; Machine, Engine & Iron Grinders, 1846; East of Scotland Brass Founders, 1848; Glasgow Glass Bottle Makers, 1848; Tobacco Pipe Makers of Scotland & Ireland, 1849; Glasgow & West of Scotland Power Loom Tenters, 1850; Glasgow Coopers, 1851; Scottish Black Printers, 1851; Scottish Typographical Association, 1852; Glasgow & West of Scotland Yarn Dressers, 1853; Glasgow Gilder, 1854; Glasgow Power-Loom Beamers, 1855; Scottish Woodcutting Machinemen, 1858

[2] It had been held in Glasgow in 1875, John Battersby (Printer) presiding; in Edinburgh in 1879, with D Gibson (Brown Saddler); in Aberdeen in 1884, with J C Thompson (Ironmoulder); and in Dundee in 1889, with D B Ritchie.

[3] Broadly, these were the Social Democratic Federation, the Independent Labour Party, the Fabian Society and the Anarchists. The first two provided most of the individuals who founded the Scottish Trades Union Congress.

[4] *Aberdeen Journal*, 12 September, 1895.

[5] *Aberdeen Journal*, 12 September, 1895.

[6] As the loose grouping of Labour and Liberal MPs was called.

[7] *Falkirk Herald*, 25 April, 1896.

2

The Founding

In Scotland, trade union activists clearly shrugged their shoulders and looked for other ways. One form this took was in much revived discussion of federation schemes, in the wake of the current industrial disputes and need for unifying protection. There were the many strikes, not only in textiles, iron works and transport, but in mining, district by district and county by county. Mutual protection both within trades and within whole industries was felt to be widely needed, now that the employers themselves were federating and provoking lockouts. It was not possible for any Scottish trades council to be unaffected; and there had been notable progress in one difficult sphere of which the Glasgow Trades Council was fully aware.

Section (i): **Trades Councillors Meet at Falkirk**

When, therefore, the next spring, Falkirk Trades Council put out a new call, invitations went to some other specialist organisations. Hence, amongst the score of delegates attending Falkirk's Oddfellows Hall on 25 April, 1896, there were new faces, including two people who were to have the most important influence in getting the Scottish TUC formed. These were Margaret Irwin of the Glasgow Council for Women's Trades and Andrew Ballantyne, a factory inspector, delegate of the National Federal Council of Scotland for Women's Trades. They were accompanied by Miss Paterson and Miss Kelly of the Women's Protective and Provident League. Trades Councils sending delegates included Aberdeen, Dundee, Edinburgh, Falkirk, Glasgow, Govan, Greenock, Motherwell and Paisley; while Arbroath, Hawick, Inverness and Kirkcaldy sent goodwill messages.

Falkirk's Chairman, William Marshall (Range and Stove Fitters) opened by saying that:

> The employers had ceased to make war upon the unions individually. They had now formed a federation which was not merely local, but embraced the whole of Scotland. . . . The masters could now dictate to the workmen whether they should work at all, and where they should work,

> and all this tended to show that the workmen must federate to keep pace with the employers.[1]

What was required was union amongst the men, yet leaders of different trades had disagreed, he said, instancing the miners' strike and the same in other industries where the men had, therefore, to accept the masters' terms. "These employers were not the men to fight with gloves on, whilst the leaders of the men had great desire to be on friendly terms with them."

Then he went on to indicate his "collectivist" principles, as socialist theory was then often described:

> Hitherto the masses had had history made for them; henceforth they would make it for themselves; and by federating the organised trades they . . . stood a better chance of getting a more equitable share of the fruits of toil and better opportunities in the race of life.

William Strang, Central Ironmoulders, described how in 1894 Falkirk had tried to get a local federation of all trades represented in the council. It had failed because different sections in several local strikes "were battling against each other". After seeking the advice of Glasgow Trades Council they therefore called trades councils to this conference to seek to bind all trades together in a bond which "might become stronger by and by, and which would be difficult to break". He spoke of experience with the federated ironmasters of Falkirk and concluded "it would be difficult indeed for any trade union, however strong, to do battle against the masters' association".

John Brown of Glasgow said they saw the great difficulty as due to "petty jealousies. The greatest opponent in the way of federation had been the strong and robust financial trades unions, who considered they could do well enough by themselves." His view was that it was linking through trades councils which was of prime importance and once the trades councils were organised and worked in perfect harmony, the work would be easy. Until they reached "that line of action – to organise the trades councils, and the councils to organise the trades unions – there could be nothing done to effect a gigantic federation".

John Mallinson from Edinburgh Trades Council thought some trades were "already showing themselves disposed to federate. In Scotland, at least, a good deal could be done to quicken the trades union movement and . . . they would at the same time quicken the federation movement". Then he developed the question of the British Trades Union Congress, saying of the meetings he had attended, he had "always left with the feeling that, where the Saxon predominated, Scotland had very little chance . . . Ireland had begun to strike out a line for itself . . . Scotland should have a meeting of its own". Although they should still try to regain their place in the British Trades Union Congress, he thought that: "it would do much to quicken the trades union movement if they had a federation meeting in Scotland every year".

John Keir, Aberdeen's President, drew on their experience of a local federation of building trades which was on the right lines but "from being a purely local federation its usefulness was considerably crippled". It was matched by an equally powerful federation of employers. But it would be different if they had a national federation of all the trades; he was applauded when he said one only of kindred trades could not be satisfactory. It would also be "an effective preventative of strikes"; and he won more applause when he added: "strikes which had in the past lasted many months would not have lasted many days if the employers had found that the whole of the workers in the country were prepared to come out in support of their fellow workmen".

Joseph Carr described the brief trades federation they had had in Dundee, where in a year they had increased wages, cut hours and done away with many grievances, and each trade was in better condition, and they had had only one strike for a single day. But he believed a great federation of all trades and industries would be much more successful than sectional linking.

Support for federating trades councils came from Motherwell and Greenock; with Govan's shipwright delegate, Peter Ross, thinking that an early conference of the unions and trades councils of Scotland towards federation would be "an incentive to the National Trades Congress to push forward and not to neglect matters of Scottish interest". But he feared a general federation of all workers throughout the country would do little good: "the conference should be worked by and through the trades councils".

Then came the turning point when Miss Margaret Irwin spoke of the experience of the Glasgow Council for Women's Trades and the new force in it of legislation which "would quicken the pace and progress" as never before. After referring to the splendid work done by starting the Glasgow Federal Council with regard to women workers, she stressed how helpful trades councils were to the unions:

> In many places they formed the only centre for information regarding labour affairs. There were many parts where the trades council was a really important body, and the benefits of many trades unions would be considerably curtailed had they not these centres of information.

She wanted a provisional committee to work out a scheme for a body which would not be antagonistic to the TUC but simply to consider Scottish labour questions, so that action could be taken on Scottish affairs. Her line was developed by Andrew Ballantyne, a factory inspector, representing the National Federal Council of Scotland for Women's Trades. The men's unions, he said, "should take the cue from the women's unions and go in solid for federation". He instanced many trades in Scotland with conditions unknown in England

> with questions which would not be of any interest to Englishmen or Irishmen. There was no reason why in Scotland they should not strike a line for themselves.

He added that they had "dragged England behind them for a long time" and should do so no longer.

Mallinson and Keir moved the resolution to set up a provisional committee for a workable scheme on federation, while Mrs Paterson of the Scottish Council for Women's Trades added the point, seconded by the Govan shipwright Ross, that the recommendation should favour:

> a Trades Union Conference for Scotland, to include the trades unions and trades councils of Scotland, which shall arrange for united action on Scottish labour questions.

These were unanimously adopted and a Provisional Committee set up which included Margaret Irwin as secretary, Mallinson, Keir and Strang and some delegates from Glasgow, Paisley, Dundee and Greenock.

Their main decision was somewhat grudgingly approved by the *Falkirk Herald* on the grounds that it might tend to prevent strikes because "it is the smaller and poorer societies with little or nothing to lose, whose members are, as a rule, often in conflict with their employers". But the journal was horrified at a decision the meeting took before breaking up, which would "be detrimental to its ultimate success at the very outset". For Keir had asked them to send best wishes in a by-election in North Aberdeen, where Tom Mann, the Socialist candidate for the Engineers' General Secretaryship, "had come north to try his strength against capital and so-called Liberalism". The *Falkirk Herald's* attitude to the new Independent Labour Party was made clear when it deplored the intended association

> with an extreme political party with which there is no reason whatever for believing the great bulk of the working classes are in sympathy.

However, the meeting's vote had been unanimous.

Section (ii): **They Get Down to Work**

The Provisional Committee got down to work, and six months later when a well-attended meeting was called when the British Trades Union Congress met at Edinburgh, it was clear that most of their effort had been spent on trying to push on federation; a Scottish TUC was seen by them then only as a side issue. This was because their discussions at Falkirk had been against the background of the engineering employers having just set up their own federation. As the *Falkirk Herald* put it, "the chief cause of the vote to set up a Scottish Federation of Trade Unions was the recent consolidation of employers' associations".[2] Since then, the Provisional Committee had had a difficult time in sorting out the differences between one industry and another; those who wanted membership confined to Scottish unions; those who wanted branches included as well as trades councils. But that something drastic was needed became clear enough when they met to report back in Edinburgh after the British TUC concluded, over which Councillor John Mallinson, Cordwainer, had presided "with conspicuous fairness", combining "tact and firmness".[3] For the Scottish delegates had been complaining there of Government Blue Books being typeset in Edinburgh by cheap labour; of scandalous Government shipbuilding contracts being given to non-union firms, which had led to a twenty-week strike on the Clyde when a subcontractor had sacked all union members; and of blacklegging during a Dundee tailoring dispute. There were also bitter disagreements about young "half-timers" in textile factories; fierce arguments between the miners about the 8-hour day were still raging; and Alexander Catto of Edinburgh yet once again pleading for support for the Scottish Bakers' shorter hours as a special case.

When the Provisional Committee put forward the draft federation scheme as the British TUC delegates dispersed on 11 September, 1896, the mildly worded plan was to "assist societies financially and otherwise" if called upon, although the aim was "to prevent strikes and lockouts". The object was to "promote harmony", and an amicable end to inter-union disputes. Unions based south of the border could join to cover their Scottish members; and there could be district committees with "fullest local autonomy" to avoid "needless friction". In moving it, John Keir of Aberdeen admitted that "if a fault was in the scheme it lay in its moderation".[4] The Chairman, John Brown of Glasgow, said that the Committee found it had proved:

> necessary to continue the scheme to the narrowest limits before anything like unanimity could be arrived at.

Finally, after "considerable discussion", it was agreed to recommend it to the various trades and consider it again at another Conference the following spring.

Then they moved on to what was to prove the real achievement for the future: "to consider the advisability of holding a Scottish Trades Union Congress annually". Moved by John Cronin, the Glasgow Steel & Iron Worker, it was finally carried 22 to 6 against an amendment by two other Glasgow delegates that it be "delayed" until federation was working. Again, arrangements were left to the organising Provisional Committee, with power to add to their number.

They got down to work, mostly in Renfrew Street in Glasgow, the offices of the Women's Protective and Provident League, of which Margaret Harding Irwin had become full-time secretary. As she then was secretary of the Scottish Council for Women's Trades, where her excellent work was already well known to them, there was firm help from the Glasgow Trades Council officers in her position as Provisional Committee Secretary. Other Provisional Committee members who worked hard on it included Andrew Ballantyne, a civil servant who was a sub-inspector of factories in Scotland; and Ronald Burrows, tutor in Classics at Glasgow University, founder of the Fabian Society in Aberdeen and Edinburgh. He did much Fabian Society activity in Dundee, close to Margaret Irwin's birthplace in Broughty Ferry where her father was a ship's captain. She had been appointed a sub-commissioner by the Royal Commission on Labour to get evidence on the conditions of Scottish women workers. This had brought her into close contact with many trades council officials.[5] Using to the full her wide connections and experience of the labour movement organisations, she set to work. Standing Orders were drafted, resolutions were prepared and were sought when notifications were sent out for the meeting in the spring. The federation scheme was also redrafted.

There were problems; some of the machinery and rules of big unions did not allow for sending delegates to such a gathering; others had to await annual conferences before they could do so. When they met, therefore, for the first and founding annual Scottish Trades Union Congress in the Berkeley Hall in Glasgow, from 25 – 27 March, 1897, they were scarcely more than 70 strong. But, as the Arrangements Committee's Chairman, John Brown, said, it was "a fairly representative gathering", adding:

> even the British Congress was some years in existence before it could number the amount of delegates or societies represented.[6]

Of some 56 organisations represented, 38 were purely Scottish, not from branches or districts of English unions. While in shipbuilding and engineering quite a number of the unions were British-based, many of the craft unions were purely Scottish and remained so for many years. These included granite cutters and building trades, textiles, printers, tailors, several metal industries, bakers, coopers and the like. One of the most powerful British unions in the early years, the Associated Society of Engineers was only represented by one delegate, from Govan No. 3 branch, and he was the last from the union for many years. The four big trades councils of Glasgow, Edinburgh, Aberdeen and Perth were there, together with those of Falkirk, Govan and Greenock.

Fraternal delegates were present from the Scottish Section of the Co-operative Union, and also from the Irish Trades Union Congress, for which James McCarron of Londonderry made what *The Clarion* described as "a naïvely enthusiastic little Socialist speech".[7] Keir Hardie, being also invited to speak, said they knew that the fairly good trade would not last so they should make their organisation as effective as possible whilst it did. He added:

> but trades unionism, co-operation and labour representation were only good so far as they led to Socialism.

Amongst the platform visitors were Glasgow veteran trade unionists (both former British TUC Parliamentary Committee members) Baillies Battersby and Jack; the newly elected Councillor Shaw Maxwell; and two keen supporters of working women's rights, Lady Mary Murray and Professor Adam Smith. After the civic welcome speech and election of conference officers, John Brown handed over the Presidential chair to Duncan McPherson, Tinplate Workers. In his first Presidential Address, McPherson stressed that the Congress

> is not (as some imagine) got up in opposition to the "British Trades Union Congress" but because we believe that if we want anything well done we have got to do it ourselves, and while doing our own work we are, in some degrees, lightening the work of the "British Congress"... there are many questions which affect Scotland particularly to which our English fellow trade unionsts cannot be expected to devote the necessary amount of time and attention they deserve.

After this tactful opening, with its first public use of the adjective "British" for the London-centred body, he adroitly quoted at length the Lib-Lab Northumberland miners' MP Thomas Burt's criticism of the British Trades Union Congress. Only then did McPherson argue about "disenfranchising the smaller trades" by excluding trades councils and the new block voting, which on "almost all questions" gave decisive power to a few large trades like the textile and mining industries. Hence there was "ample scope and a real necessity" for the Scottish Trades Union Congress. With industry "now at least five times as productive as it was sixty years ago" working-class families should have corresponding increases in good housing and all comforts instead of "intensified want by the side of exaggerated and injurious abundance". He added:

> these are the two extremes of human life and the problem is – "How to adjust human affairs so that life for all will be worth living?" The replies given and the remedies offered are numerous and conflicting.

His own was "collectivism", and meanwhile to "teach the principles of morality which will prevail under a reformed condition of society". After recommending temperance he contrasted the lack of workers' representation in Parliament with the absurdity of nine University seats being reserved for an electorate of 35,000 people, whilst

> the millions of artisans and workmen in this country obtain scarcely any direct representation.

Then Congress got down to its resolutions, starting with those on special Scottish questions. It was right that it should be a miners' representative, Robert Smillie, to move improvements to the Fatal Accidents Inquiry Act, which aimed to put an inquiry on the same basis as a coroner's inquest, with the onus on the jury to report at once whether blame should rest on an employer and his servants. In Scotland, Sheriffs were ruling that out of order, and there were long delays before inquiries were held at all. Again, the miners took the lead when John Wilson of West Lothian demanded improvements in the Employers' Liability Act in several respects, especially to prevent them being able to shift responsibility for compensation to penniless subcontractors; in Scotland they had suffered from many inadequacies in pursuing claims.

Other special Scottish problems in industry were felt to be capable of being tackled only by the Board of Trade setting up a Scottish branch of their Labour Department. Councillor John Cronin, Steel & Iron Workers, supported by John Brown, Ironmoulders, pointed out the need for inquiring into declining industries and how they were carried on elsewhere, and how to replace them, and about the role of Arbitration Boards. The Labour Department Branch should be in Scotland; for while confined to London, with interest scattered over various State Departments, they "could not expect much good would be done". Cronin gave an example of how his union had had to send to

Belgium and Germany to find out the fact that iron and steel workers enjoyed much better conditions. Scottish law on tenure of houses needed action in two respects. Firstly, they wanted to change the law by supporting the Smaller Dwellings (Scotland) Bill which aimed to prevent tenants being forced to give an incredible year's notice to quit when they had to move. Secondly, both the Lanarkshire Miners and the Broughty Ferry Bleachfield Workers won support for a proposed Bill protecting workers in tied houses; this was widespread in mining areas, and in the north-east among textile and other workers.

A score of other resolutions, nearly all meeting with little or no controversy, shaped at their first Congress the line of work ahead for some years to come. These included: the right of non-householders to serve on juries; payment of salaries and expenses to MPs; a second ballot where an absolute majority had not been won at an election; a Central office to be set up for Factory Inspectors; protection for women witnesses giving information to Factory Inspectors; reform of miners' checkweighing laws; restricting age and hours of labour by children and half-timers; Factory Acts to be simplified and consolidated; Scottish law to be amended to ensure enforcement of shop and workshop sanitary arrangements; earlier closing of shops; support for the Miners' Eight-Hours Bill; seats for shop assistants; increase in wages paid by the Admiralty; extending to all trades information on piecework prices; and the amendment of the Conspiracy Law which put unionists at risk when in dispute, including when peacefully picketing.

There were two big debates in which there was disagreement and it took a long time before a decision could be reached. First came the question of limiting hours. The Arrangements Committee had found great opposition to the plan for legal limitation to an eight-hour day; "many trades objected. . . because it might compel them to work eight hours on Saturday". After Robert Smillie had tried unsuccessfully to get agreement for an eight-hour day and a five-day week (or 40 hours), and Aberdeen delegates had argued for an eight-hour day in a 45-hour week, a cautious resolution for 48 hours with a nine-hour day limitation and some escape clauses was carried by a very narrow margin. Clearly it was a topic which they recognised would have to be fought out in each industry, and by each union; and the most the new body could hope for was to win agreement for the general principle of the working day to be legally limited. Indeed, it was to be 21 years later, after two wars, that the Scots led Britain in a tremendous battle for shorter hours.

Similarly, there was difficulty over what had been the major question of federation. William Strang, the Falkirk Ironmoulder, proposed the general principle as agreed the previous year in Edinburgh, with the Parliamentary Committee to take the trades' vote on it. The Dundee delegates favoured the Independent Labour Party's scheme publicised by *The Clarion*. James Reilly, of Glasgow's National Union of Labourers – often in dispute with the British Dock Labourers Union – thought they should make the different societies in any industry federate at once. Finally, it was agreed that the incoming PC should draft a scheme to be sent to all trades unions in Scotland to consider at next Congress. Long before that day came, however, they were to witness the devastation caused by the national lockout of engineers. On their own plate there was already the long and bitter rivalry between the National Scottish Tailors and the Amalgamated Society of Tailors, who were recruiting – and some said black-legging – from south of the border.

But two historically important topics followed which had an enthusiastic reception. For the miners, John Wilson moved that

> the workers cannot obtain the full value of their labour and strikes be avoided, until the land, mines, railways, machinery and industrial capital are owned and controlled by the State for the people.

Taking first the land, he gave telling figures of the vast quantity owned by the 545 members of the House of Lords, and the 220 million pounds paid annually on land rent alone. There could be no reasonable argument why the people should pay this "to non-producers for leave to live and work on the land". Then he pointed to the fact that on the Continent, minerals were nationalised, quoting figures of mineral royalties in France and Germany. He pointed out also the enormous advantages of Glasgow having recently municipalised water, gas and tramways; and also the national ownership of the post and telegraph. The Musicians' Union delegate spoke against such public ownership as being "neither feasible nor practicable". But when the vote was taken only three out of all the delegates voted against it. In fact, it was to be nearly 50 years before two of these concerns were nationalised.

On the last day of this first Congress, the centrepiece was a speech by Margaret Irwin, who had just been elected top of the poll for the PC with 60 votes, with Robert Smillie next with 56. She moved that women should be allowed

> a direct voice in the making of the laws which so seriously affect them, by extending the parliamentary franchise to women on the same footing as to men.

She said that while she had always believed in women's suffrage, until she

> came to be associated with the labour movement, it was more a pious opinion . . . than a living faith.

Now it seemed to her "the first thing women had to work for". Trades unionism, good as it was, had its limits. They needed legislation to remedy women's grievances, since it was so very difficult to get women to organise. She would

> rather organise ten men's unions than one women's union. It was not the fault of the women – it was the fault of their conditions.

It was a labour question,

> because so much of the legislation of today dealt with industrial and social questions in which women had as great a stake as men. The pressure of the time was driving more and more women into the labour market.

She thought women should work at anything that was suitable; she only

> objected to their taking men's work at 50% of their wages.

She won warm support from the delegates.

The Parliamentary Committee started their first year with Robert Smillie as Chairman, Andrew Ballantyne as Secretary, five others from Glasgow, one from Govan, two from Edinburgh and one each from Aberdeen and Arbroath.

Section (iii): **How They Were Received**

Nearly half the delegates had previously attended the British TUC conferences either from their union or from the larger Scottish trades councils. Now in Glasgow the mood throughout was far closer to the policies of the Socialist parties than at the British TUC, where overwhelming approval for a resolution for public ownership would have been impossible. This was not lost on the newspaper editors; and the editorial comments showed what the new Parliamentary Committee had to expect both from Tory and Liberal and Socialist quarters. *The Scotsman*[8] started from its position of contempt for any proceedings of Congresses of trade unionists, describing them as "little more than pieces of machinery for passing certain formal resolutions, like barrel organs that always play the same tunes". These would stress "that Collectivism is the only cure for social ills", and after[9] "a glimpse of a distant Utopia" would pass "stereotyped resolutions". These would be on limiting hours, employers' liability and State ownership which "presents a strange contrast to the practical character of their other demands".

It selected points for some degree of approval as being "more moderate and business-like than is wont to be at such gatherings". But then it remarked that "it did not get the inspiration from its President", and concluded with a stinging attack on Duncan McPherson for seeing the ultimate solution in "collectivism", in an address which was

> an inconsequential jumble, a hash-up of many mis-statements and vague theories.

By the following year, *The Scotsman's* "worst fears" were fulfilled; the editor found the Aberdeen Congress "permeated with collectivism". For the "organisers and orators" were not "the industrious, shrewd, well-informed and prudent class of workmen". They represented

> the comparatively few workmen of extreme opinions, whose heads were filled with class prejudices and political delusions, and who imagine that the interests of other classes of the community are hostile to the interests of working men.

The *Glasgow Herald's* editorial of 26 March, 1897, predictably adopted a more moderate tone, saying that the Congress "cannot but be regarded as an interesting incident in the labour movement". Though there were criticisms to make,

> one can welcome the Scottish Congress as an offshoot from the incoherent and inconsistent body that has done so much to bring ridicule on trade unionism.

McPherson had "made out an excellent case for the independent deliberations of the Scottish unions", whose special interests

> are lost sight of in the deluge of resolutions and speeches that reduce the business of the English Congresses to a farce.

Here at least "a more practical and business-like spirit prevails". But that ended any note of praise. In particular the journal deplored "collectivism" for aiming to make man "a mere automaton in the State machine". But, above all, it opposed "the right of trade unionism to be directly represented in Parliament"; for that would be a serious threat to Liberal and Lib-Lab MPs, to whom all political questions should be left. Working men were "always welcomed" in Parliament and local government, "but in their political and municipal, not in their trade capacity".

In contrast *The Clarion*, as organ of the Independent Labour Party, hailed it as "thoroughly representative of Scottish trade unionism" and an acknowledged success, despite the fact that "previously there had been some anxiety". For Socialists its three days' sittings "were full of the best kind of encouragement" – trades councils fully represented and no block vote. The writer, Katherine Bruce Glasier, was delighted that "not only did the Socialist resolution pass by an overwhelming majority, but in almost every speech on other questions there was a general and generous recognition of the evil of the system", while "personal abuse of the individual capitalist was conspicuous by its absence".

She made special reference to six people – Keir Hardie sitting on the platform with his wife; the Fabian, Ronald Burrows, speaking on the Conspiracy Laws; Margaret Irwin's election at the top of the poll when, "on any narrow sectarian basis, she might easily have been blackballed by the fatal adjective middle-class"; Robert Smillie as "one of the trustiest and bravest champions of Socialism in Scotland"; and noted with interest that, although he was a factory inspector, Andrew Ballantyne had been regarded as reliable enough in active work for trades unionism to be elected as secretary. But for her the most important point was the question of federation schemes to be recommended to all trades unions. As a result, they might hope within the year

> to see in Scotland at least some real and practical endeavour towards an active recognition of the solidarity of the workers which will hasten the day of the co-operative commonwealth by many decades.

There was no official welcome from the British TUC. Nor was the first year to be plain sailing. Within two months their Secretary, Andrew Ballantyne, the factory inspector, was forced to resign. Clearly, the Tory Government at least had not failed to notice the existence of the Scottish TUC nor underestimate its potential.

Ballantyne had been one of the delegates of the National Federal Council of Scotland for Women's Trades and had assisted his co-delegate Margaret Irwin when she had taken the lead in the preparatory Arrangements Committee. He was elected by a three to one majority over a miner's delegate for Secretary; and might well have had Margaret Irwin as his Chairman had she not declined nomination for that post. At the first meeting of the Parliamentary Committee, she said:

> considering all the circumstances and that feeling was not quite ripe enough for a woman to occupy such a position she thought it better to withdraw her name and allow Mr Smillie to be elected.[10]

At the second meeting, the Committee instructed Ballantyne to ask Scottish MPs to receive them at Whitsuntide in Edinburgh, and also "try to meet Lord Balfour and the Lord Advocate on the forenoon of the same day".[11] He wrote to the two Scottish Whips who both suggested the time was unsuitable. He, therefore, went to see them when on a visit to London.

But the next Committee meeting was to end with a letter from Ballantyne to Smillie notifying him of his resignation, "owing to objections raised at the Home Office".

> I accepted the position in perfect good faith and from a strong desire to help in a movement that so much deserves to be successful . . . There is nothing in the regulations supplied to me from the Home Office that would lead me to suppose objection could be made to my holding such a post.[12]

They determined to try to get the Home Office's threat reversed; Smillie proposed that appointing a permanent Secretary should be delayed, and that meanwhile Margaret Irwin would be interim Secretary. Having no success by their next meeting, Smillie asked Ballantyne at least to remain a member of the Committee, while the Govan Shipwright, Peter Ross, and the Edinburgh Flint Glass Maker, David Blackburn (who exactly a year before had been an ILP delegate to the Workers International in London), moved that Margaret Irwin be permanent Secretary. She, however, would only agree to remain interim Secretary, saying that she

> feared that at this early stage of the Congress work, it might be somewhat prejudicial to its interests were the post to be filled by a woman.[13]

In the event the Home Office could not be forced to relent and all that Ballantyne could do was occasionally attend the Parliamentary Committee as a visitor; he was never mentioned again as having any public connection with the Scottish TUC, except for one appearance as a delegate some years later. It was unfortunate that Margaret Irwin took this view and maintained it to the point when some years later, once she believed it to be consolidated, she finally declined nomination and ceased to stand for the Committee. For her successor as General Secretary in 1901, was Robert Carson. Despite his first-hand industrial experience in the small Tinplate and Sheet Metal Workers' Association, he could not match her wide outlook and considerable knowledge gained from close study of conditions and work in many industries. It may be that, advanced as the Scots proved themselves compared with the BTUC involving women as delegates in the leadership,[14] Margaret Irwin may well have judged correctly the low level of understanding in some of the craftsmen's societies even there at this time. Nevertheless her dedication and organising ability took them through the essential formative years, despite the very difficult problems on agreeing priorities which also resulted in personal antagonisms. There were certainly those who recognised her contributions; for example, a remarkable tribute was paid to her at the end of their first working year. At Aberdeen, in closing their second Congress, their President John Keir said of "their esteemed Secretary" that all knew of her "great ability and earnestness of purpose, and of the enthusiasm which she displayed on all questions affecting the welfare of the working classes". Not only had Keir sat on the Committee with her during the first difficult year, but he had followed her efforts through all the preliminary stages during the previous three years. The fact that he was a co-founder gave special emphasis when he said that

> it was not too much to say that to Miss Irwin, more than any man or woman in the country, was due the position of the Scottish Trades Unionists assembled there as a Congress.

It had been Margaret Irwin, who had prepared the Report of their first year.

References

[1] *Falkirk Herald*, 2 May, 1896.

[2] *Falkirk Herald*, 2 May, 1896.

[3] *Dundee Advertiser*, 12 September, 1896.

[4] *Glasgow Herald*, 12 September, 1896.

[5] A useful brief account of her career appears in "Women in the Leadership of the Scottish Trades Union Congress 1897-1970" by S Lewenhak, "Scottish Labour History Journal", No. 7, July 1973.

[6] Report of the First Annual Scottish Trades Union Congress. In fact in its fourth year, the Scottish TUC had 114 delegates whilst the British TUC in its fourth year could only point to 77.

[7] *The Clarion*, 2 April, 1897.

[8] *The Scotsman*, 26 March, 1897.

[9] *The Scotsman*, 29 April, 1898.

[10] *STUC Parliamentary Commitee Minutes*, 27 March, 1897.

[11] Ibid, 24 April, 1897.

[12]. Ibid, 22 May, 1897.

[13] Ibid, 10 July, 1897.

[14] The point is forcibly made in "Women in the Leadership of the STUC 1897-1970' by S Lewenhak in the "Scottish Labour History Journal" No. 7, July, 1973.

3

The First Years

This second Annual Congress in the spring of 1898 took place in Aberdeen Trades Council's own "Trades Hall"; Robert Smillie as the Parliamentary Committee's Chairman congratulating the Aberdonians on its being "solid Aberdeen granite masonry" in which they could "meet under their own vine and fig trees without any fear of eviction", added

> No other town or city in Great Britain had such a place as this for trades unionists to meet in, a hall which they could call their own.[1]

That year there were 114 delegates representing nearly 100,000 from over sixty societies and branches, the vast majority being purely Scottish based, together with eight trades councils. There were several impressive outside demonstrations and recruiting meetings, and among the visitors were some notable Scottish Socialists. Margaret Irwin had prepared an able report; it included a verbatim account of how the PC deputation had been received by the Secretary of State for Scotland and the Lord Advocate on subjects of "purely Scottish business", of which "there seemed to be a reasonable hope of immediately promoting".[2] They also succeeded in meeting a few of the Scottish MPs from time to time; and they had been represented at a large conference in London on Home Work, called by the Women's Industrial Council, to which the PC's representative had contributed with good results. But when it came to describing how they had tried to progress the first Congress decisions with Central Government it was another matter.

But before describing the setbacks and indeed insults they had encountered from Government circles, the Report stressed that most important of all was

> the work of forming a national labour policy and opinion . . . making possible concerted national action . . . consolidating Scottish labour interests and gathering them round one common centre.

The Committee felt this was "the necessary first step towards that international labour unity to which we all look forward". The first reply regarding questions they hoped to raise with the Home Secretary was that he doubted "that any useful purpose would be served by his receiving a separate deputation from persons resident in Scotland". Congress's reaction was to pass a unanimous resolution protesting that "the discourteous refusal" was "a deliberate affront . . . to the organised trades of Scotland". It was moved by John Elric, Masons and Granite Cutters, and John Wilson, Scottish Amalgamated Miners.

When this protest was later notified to the British Trades Union Congress, along with their other decisions, Margaret Irwin discovered some disagreeable facts, which she disclosed at a PC meeting two months later. It appears that when the British TUC went on its own deputation to the Government it had failed to raise certain key Scottish resolutions, "while on other matters there was an important divergence of opinion between the Scottish and the English deputations". Margaret Irwin was then instructed to tell this to the Scottish MPs who had received them in Edinburgh; and

> to say further that the Home Secretary was under a misapprehension in concluding that the views of the Scottish trade unionists were adequately represented at the British Congress.[3]

Indeed, to have their deputations received as of right by any Central Government was to be a continuing battle for many years; nor was any serious support for it forthcoming from the British TUC.

Section (i): **Employers Take Revenge**

Nevertheless, delegates at Aberdeen met in what should have been a mood to congratulate themselves on a highly promising start of their project. But throughout their spirits were overcast; for, less than two months before, a savage seven months lockout begun by the newly federated engineering employers had shaken the movement throughout Britain to the core. When workers in some London factories went on strike demanding an eight-hour day, the recently federated engineering employers ordered a country-wide lockout; they intended to break the power of the many unions concerned in engineering before unified action could develop. In the minds of activists it caused considerable bitterness and raised deep misgivings amongst those in other industries affected by it; doubts even about the effectiveness of any industrailisation; and a turn towards seeking much needed change by reliance on Parliamentary action alone. At the same time it added powerful point to the arguments of the Socialists that nothing but total change in the capitalist system of society was acceptable, despite conflicting views of how this could be brought about. These were sometimes explicit, and it was noticeable also both in heated debates and muted contributions on such topics as federation, collectivism, the school-leaving age and employment of half-timers, the hours question, the import of immigrant workers and even on women's suffrage.

The tone was set and the problems suggested by the Aberdeen Basketmaker, John Keir, in his Presidential Address. After outlining the steps taken to found the STUC, in which he had taken a strong part, he described the enthusiasm and "quantity of work overtaken" as encouraging in the extreme. He stressed how energetically they had worked; and once more that they were "in no sense antagonistic to the British TUC", but were "proving a helpful ally in bringing about much and urgently needed labour legislation". But while recognising the encouraging reforms won by trades unionism during the year, they could not forget

> the prolonged and severe struggle which took place in the engineering industry.

In his opinion probably never

> has such a fierce battle been fought between capital and labour, and probably never was such a determined and organised attempt made to deal a death blow to trade unionism by stamping out one of our oldest and most influential societies.

Then he made the point which would certainly be echoed by many of the veteran leaders of the other smaller societies.

> While expressing admiration at the way in which the engineers conducted the fight, I do not wish to be understood as approving of strikes as being a satisfactory method of settling labour disputes . . . a strike should only be resorted to after every other means of adjustment has failed, and I am confident that this opinion is largely shared by the trades unionists of the present day, whom, I believe, regard strikes as a misspent force of trades unionism.

But then the question would naturally arise "what do we propose as a substitute in order to secure for the workers anything like a reasonable return for their labour?" In his view to meet "the ever-increasing combinations of the employers in all and every branch of industry", they must wake up immediately to the need "of meeting federation with federation". For far too long individual and isolated unions had tried unsuccessfully to combat employers' combined forces; too often "employers have proved more loyal to each other than have the trades unions". Moreover

> the workers seem to rest satisfied as long as their own trade was organised, regardless of the lot of the less fortunate and so-called unskilled section of their fellow workers. But I am glad to say this feeling is rapidly disappearing.

A federation solely amongst kindred trades could never hope to deal with a federation of employers, despite the obviously valuable services rendered in the past. After quoting "our eminent fellow-countryman Thomas Carlyle" that "organisation of labour is the universal vital problem of the world", he added that it was essential to get all working men and women into unions, "thus paving the way for a federation of those unions".

Then he took his concept further. Contributions to put a general federation on a sound financial basis – not to waste it "in fighting the employers by means of strikes" – could then lead to industrial co-operative production. That remedy, first mooted even in the seventeenth century and popular in the declining years of Chartism, was being adopted by Socialist sects in the United States at the time. Keir Hardie now saw it as "a natural sequence to trades federation". At least a beginning could be made and it would

> be a much more profitable investment for the workers to engage in one or other of our industries than to exhaust their means on an extended period of industrial warfare.

He added:

> co-operative production is no Utopian idea . . . many productive societies on the co-operative principle already exist.

Saying that "the views held by the workers throughout Scotland on social and labour questions are very advanced indeed", he turned to another which was to be discussed: legislation to gain the eight-hour day. He thought that the belief of those who held that it could be best won by the trades unions themselves was false. This was

> painfully demonstrated to us by the struggle in the engineering trade . . . when one of our most powerful, wealthy and influential unions failed in the attempt, how utterly hopeless it would be for the vast

> majority of the smaller societies to expect to secure this reform through the medium of their trade organisations.

Those who feared legal enactment would reduce earnings, should realise how large was the number of unemployed "whom one can almost pardon for being prepared to accept low wages rather than starve". But with legal enactment he believed absorption of surplus labour would inevitably follow, "and the question of wages would very soon adjust itself". His last point was that they should use the franchise to support only those Parliamentary candidates pledged to make labour's interests the first on their programme.

Delegates' first reaction was to decide to hear two Welsh miners on the effect of the current lockout in South Wales, Brothers Reiss and Gardiner. Saying they represented 100,000 miners and half a million women and children suffering from the consequences of lockout in allied industries, Reiss made a strong appeal for the men who got less than £1 a week. Saying that he "never spoke English except when out of Wales, and that was not very often", he got a warm reception. A resolution of sympathy followed and instructions to the Parliamentary Committee to issue a statement and appeal to trades councils and unions; later over £50 was sent with strong support from the print industry. For in Glasgow the book-binders had just come through a lockout during which two of them were gaoled for two months, and Congress sent them messages of sympathy. Nor were they alone. For the Glasgow Branch of the Cabinetmakers' Alliance, John Burgess described how the employers had tried to impose a document forcing them to work with non-unionists. The employers were aiming to bring in the new Truck Act and to reduce the overtime rate. Not only did Congress agree to call for loans to help them, but it also passed a resolution demanding a Bill

> to extend the abolition of the truck system to farm servants in Scotland and that the old feudal system of hiring fairs and six-monthly payments be abolished and that it be held illegal for an employer to retain the wages . . . for longer than fourteen days.

Nor were these the only instances of the employers attacking in various ways.

In a resolution for law amendment to stop intimidation when factory inspectors were visiting, and that they should not be accompanied by the employers, examples were given. Miss Elizabeth King, delegate from the Women's Protective and Provident League, said she

> knew from experience that while inspectors were going round the factories the foremen watched whom they spoke to, and if the masters were put to any inconvenience the girl generally was dismissed.

Other examples of low tricks were quoted in a debate during which the miners finally succeeded in getting withdrawn an Aberdeen Trades Council resolution to prohibit "the importation of foreign destitute persons" and "the landing of aliens who have no visible means of subsistence". A Tailors Amalgamated Society delegate, John McBain, described how they had been handicapped; "whenever a strike took place alien labour was imported to defeat the men". Robert Smillie, however, won the argument; hoping "the time was not far distant when the word alien would not be used in their Congress", he made this point:

> if they were hunted out of their own country the chief duty as trade unionists was to get them into the trades unions and have them working under the same conditions as their fellow-workmen.

In the next half dozen years the pogroms against Jews and labour activists in the Russian Empire even increased and Smillie was himself obliged to bring to Congress the problems caused by the mine-owners importing immigrant Poles into the pits.

There was some controversy too on how to handle other problems employers were trying to exploit, when it came to debates on the pernicious half-timers' system and the related question of raising the permitted school-leaving age; should this be fixed by law at 14? or 15? or even 16? Some were very conscious that low wages in the whole family could not be ignored. When the Glasgow Brassfinisher, William Greer, retorted that some men would be willing enough "to pay 2s. 6d. for a seat in the grandstand at a football match, or 1s. 2d. for half a mutchkin of whisky", and be indifferent to their children's welfare, "something approaching disorder ensued". Finally resolutions were passed for the school-leaving age to be 15, free meals to be compulsory and the half-timer system to be abolished. This enraged *The Scotsman*, which described it as "the Socialist principle that the children are the property of the State"; adding that there was "no self-respect in the men who formed" the resolution.[4] There was no disagreement when it came to the housing question, the rules on tenure of houses applicable only to Scotland and how the bleachfield workers and the miners in tied houses could be coerced "into accepting most objectionable conditions of labour". Resolutions on safety at work, especially relating to railwaymen and those using harbour gangways were readily accepted. When it came to the eight-hours question the objection of those opposed to the strongly worded general resolution from the Typographical Society was only expressed in mild terms by the masons, it having been argued strongly as important to lessen unemployment.

Then came what should be the big debate, that of federation, taking place just a month after the British TUC had held a special conference on General Federation which aimed to provide a mutual fund to ease the burden of paying out strike benefit. In presenting the scheme which the Parliamentary Committee had been instructed to produce, Robert Smillie admitted that it was "weak because it was local and weak in its frame"; they had had to make one "to deal with trades unions as they were at present". No delegate was even ready to second a motion that it be adopted. After a prolonged discussion it was rejected in favour of the scheme by Philip King, which had long been pushed by the Independent Labour Party and was known as "*The Clarion* Scheme". A motion came from Peter Grieve of the Scottish Typographers recommending it, and saying

> no scheme of federation is of any use . . . which does not provide a benefit equivalent to the weekly wage of those affected by a strike, and combining equal payments, equal benefits and equal representation.

He stressed that it had to be "for the three nations". Seconding, Robert Handyside of Glasgow's Spindle and Flymakers, said the PC's scheme would be bankrupt in a month and remarked that "the great labour leaders – the men with over £300 and £400 a year – did not want federation". A successful amendment merely wanted the reference to strike benefit equal to a weekly wage ruled out. Alex Robertson and George Younie for the Aberdeen Masons and Granite Cutters said it would not be practical. Thomas Anderson of the Carpenters showed how it must fail by illustrations from the cost of paying the locked-out furniture men. But Robert Allan, Edinburgh Typographer, disagreed with his colleague on any scheme of trades federation at all: "the logical conclusion of trades federation was a general strike". They could not meet the employers on equal terms; federation was not the solution to the labour problem; they had better "strengthen their present organisation". When the amended resolution supporting federation in general and *The Clarion* scheme in particular, was carried, a further resolution instructed the PC to press it on delegates to the British TUC. In the final analysis, although the Scottish TUC sent members to conference after conference concerned with general federation, the Federal Labour Parliament and the like, it never took off. One reason perhaps is because "the great labour leaders" of the big unions had their own views. So the practice continued decade after decade of amalgamation from weakness and federation in kindred trades at best.

Section (ii): **Seeking New Ways of Resistance**

Meanwhile there was a growing trend after all these industrial dangers and setbacks to look more at political solutions. In this the Scots were amongst the first; six months after this 1898 Congress they were responding to the development by the Independent Labour Party of Keir Hardie's initiative in 1888 for a Labour Party to win workers' representation in Parliament. But at Aberdeen there were already signs in debates on "collectivism" and allied subjects.

One indication came from Alexander Robertson, Aberdeen Masons and Granite Workers, when he moved a resolution demanding the referendum principle. This was that "all questions on which great diversity of opinion exists" should be submitted to the people before becoming law; and that

> should any considerable section of the community believe that a certain social or political reform is necessary they should have the power to compel Parliament to take a direct vote of the people on the question.

Answering doubters who thought they should stick strictly to social questions "and refuse to touch the rather corrupt matter of politics", he stressed that "the House of Commons was not really a reflex of the views of the country".

The different attitudes of the various sections of socialists and Lib-Labs emerged clearly in the debate on twin resolutions and an addendum under the heading "Collectivism". The Amalgamated Section of the Scottish Miners (the Oil and Shale workers) declared:

> the workers cannot obtain the full value of their labour, and strikes be avoided, until the land, mines, railways, machinery and industrial capital are owned and used by the State for the people.

The next part, originating from the Edinburgh Typographical Society and seconded by their representative, Robert Allan, was in considerably tougher terms: that only when these are

> held as common property will the working class be free from the domination and tyranny of Capitalism and Landlordism.

It added that "the easiest and most effective method to secure the emancipation" was to use "the power they already possess to capture the political machinery". To that end, the unions should "morally and financially support the working-class Socialist parties already in existence". Allan said if they acted on this they would "secure a new lease of life for trades unionism", and he deplored pious resolutions being accepted year after year in "humbugging fashion", and nothing being done to realise them. He put forward the ILP's policy for independent representation:

> Let them constitute a party distinct from the two great political parties, because neither Liberal nor Tory would accept many of their proposals.

The Aberdeen Baker, Alexander Catto, moving an amendment that the Parliamentary Committee should merely do all in its power to secure nationalisation of land, the means of production and exchange, said that the second part of the motion amounted to demanding that Congress "should delegate its powers to a socialist party" to do its work. While he gave credit to the socialists "for forcing the pace", he argued that if they delegated their "powers to outside parties, the rank and file of the unions would say these were not their unions". Margaret Irwin in effect supported the amendment by asking were the funds "to go for Parliamentary election purposes or for general socialistic propaganda?" However, the Dunfermline railwayman, T Ross, said Parliament "was one of the biggest fads in this country": the members were merely "elected as representatives of Conservatism and Liberalism and not as representatives of Labour". The amendment was finally defeated 25-50, and the Scottish Tinplate and Sheet Metal Workers delegate, Robert Chambers, succeeded in including an addendum that the trade unions be asked what they would actually subscribe annually to support the aim. He remarked:

> As much money was spent on the engineers' strike as would have contested 400 seats in Parliament.

Throughout none of the miners' county unions joined in. That night, however, at a trades and labour demonstration, Robert Smillie supported a resolution moved by Catto that "the claim of labour in Parliament had been neglected" and urged support for those candidates who would "place labour questions first, irrespective of the convenience of any political party". Smillie argued that "something more than trades unionism was necessary if workers were to get fair treatment". That could only be got

> by direct legislative representation and by the nationalisation of the land and of the means of production and exchange.

It was on these lines that five months later the PC under his chairmanship took the first steps in persuading the Scottish trade unions to create a working men's party, established before a similar move amongst the British TUC.

On the last day of Congress, however, while not an opponent of women's suffrage, Smillie did not agree with the tactics to achieve it in the resolution moved by Miss Elizabeth King of the Women's Protective and Provident League. This repeated the same resolution "in view of the important legislative measures relating to the social and industrial conditions of women which are at present before the country", it was important that women should be allowed

> a direct voice in the making of the laws which so seriously affect them, by extending the parliamentary franchise to women on the same footing as to men.

At that time of course men who were not householders had no vote. An amendment was defeated in which James Murdoch, from the Bellshill Colliery, stressing that he was a bachelor, urged they should make "no endeavour to get women's suffrage until manhood suffrage is secured". However, the Edinburgh Typographer, Robert Allan, moved an amendment in favour of adult suffrage at all elections. One delegate retorted that Allan had no more chance of getting a Bill on those lines "within the next five years than he had of marrying one of the Queen's daughters". Margaret Irwin explained the "motives of expediency" with which the motion had been framed. While all favoured a large extension of the franchise

> they did not think the best way of bringing that about was to introduce the thick end of the wedge first. As practical politicians they could not expect to get more for women than men had got. If they once secured recognition of the political existence of women they would afterwards get much added to that and all the extensions that men had . . . She had come to feel what a vital question this one was for their having some say in the industrial laws which affected every hour of their lives. Until they got that power for women they could do very little to improve their economic and social conditions.

Smillie was afraid the law the motion demanded would be "used against the emancipation of working women", few indeed of whom would be householders. Finally, the Allan amendment for adult suffrage was carried by 57 to 18.

The previous evening Margaret Irwin had been the main speaker at an important meeting of women from the Factory Workers' Union. She described how women "were being constantly made use of to undersell men in the industries open to both sexes". Among some of the horrific facts she quoted was that "in some districts of England whole families were now working for the wage formerly earned by one male member". Amongst the facts emerging from her Inquiry into women's work in Scotland for the Royal Commission on Labour she had found even in trades which were under the Factory Acts that "illegal overtime was frequently worked", and Glasgow women in tailoring got only 4s. a week. Amongst several other speakers Councillor Johnston said Aberdeen had the credit for forming the first female workers' union in Scotland in 1884; that the Aberdeen Jute Workers women had "greatly improved their conditions" by joining a union; and that there were some 10,000 women workers in and around the city, and great scope for organising amongst them.

As the Aberdeen Congress closed, Robert Smillie and the incoming Parliamentary Committee had a harassing year before the next gathering at Dundee in the spring of 1899. The pressure of unemployment was growing. Nor was it temporary; the total decline of some industries, such as textiles and sugar-refining, had increased since they were reported to the previous Congress. This year they would have to repeat with added emphasis their demand to the Board of Trade, for

> enquiries into the causes of declining industries, and . . . if not remediable, what facilities might be granted for starting others.

They felt too the urgent need for national and local relief works, "for persons willing but unable to find employment", stressing that it must not be on conditions which would render them as paupers not entitled to the vote. The engineering strike was still overshadowing them, and Steel and Iron delegates from the Clyde looked anxiously for further efforts to establish a National Conciliation Board "as a means of averting those industrial disputes which have such disastrous effects on the whole community". They were meeting in one of the areas worst hit by declining trade, the City of Dundee, only a few months before the Boer War broke out. Speaking at an evening meeting of Mill and Factory Workers there, Thomas McBurney, the Chairman of Dundee Trades Council, said there were 40,000 textile operatives in the neighbourhood, of whom only 7,000 were organised. At a reception later in the week he described changes since the BTUC had met there in 1890:

> Within the past ten years the feeling of the working class had materially changed. Then they were inclined to rely solely on their unions; now they were disposed to look to our legislators to bring about the desired changes.

With Smillie and Margaret Irwin at last received by the Home

Secretary in London, lobbying MPs and writing to the Board of Trade on the many decisions taken which needed legislation, there was also a growing feeling that this was both expensive and not the best way for the Scottish TUC's aims to be realised. Some felt it could lead to neglect of industrial work which they should be forwarding.

An important factor was that the PC found itself obliged to lay the basis for what should be the attitude towards inter-union disputes. This was because of prolonged and bitter differences between the Scottish Operative Tailors and the Amalgamated Society of Tailors of London. It was claimed that the English Society had "invaded", setting up branches in towns where the Scottish Tailors had long been organised. The English Society, claiming that their rivals had "by forcible means" compelled their recruits to give up their membership, asked for a "definite pronouncement" that in such a case a union should be excluded from the TUC. The PC replied that, put as an abstract principle the answer must be in the affirmative, but that such a decision "must be greatly modified by special circumstances of such cases as might be submitted to them". Congress approved a recommendation that a working agreement should be arranged between the two unions. But that led to no settlement, and there was to come a stage when, after an exhaustive examination of it all, the PC recommended that the two Societies should "confine themselves to the well-defined boundaries of Scotland and England", with members visiting either country to pay dues meanwhile to the union of the territory. A happier arrangement was reached with the Co-operative Societies agreeing to set up a Joint Committee of Arbitration in any dispute with their employees.

Through the years that was to work satisfactorily; but problems like the tailors' were to reappear all too often. This particular year was especially embarrassing because the President of the 1899 Congress was himself a member of the English Society, and so Thomas McBurney had to vacate the chair whenever it was under discussion.

Section (iii): They Re-form a Scottish Labour Party

The feeling that trade unionists could not progress without some basic demands being won by independent political action in Parliament, however this might be organised, had grown fast. After this bitter inter-union debate, it was not surprising that Duncan McPherson put it strongly in his presidential address:

> What Parliament could do for them should not be done by trades union effort. The engineers' strike for an eight-hour day was still fresh in their

> memories, and should act as a finger post . . . Surely no other industry would try to get the eight-hour day through the stomachs of their wives and children, together with the loss of their own union funds, when at a tithe of the cost an Eight-Hours Bill could be got for the organised and unorganised alike by the workers sinking their political differences and making an unbroken demand.

One of the most important decisions at Dundee was to call a special congress on Labour representation in Parliament and Scottish policy at the next General Election, due in a year's time. How this historic decision was finally achieved, with the differing views which were expressed in the guise of tactics, emerges in the PC's minute book, carefully written by Margaret Irwin. The first move had been six months earlier, when she called a special executive meeting on 8 October, 1898, with Smillie, Peter Ross and John Mallinson, in order to meet Keir Hardie and Bruce Glasier from the ILP. They came "to lay certain proposals for promoting Labour representation". They were asked to put in a written statement for the next Parliamentary Committee. But what was to prove the starting point of considerable delay began there when it was decided that "a communication received from the ILP be held over", while circulated to committee members "to be held as confidential". When it was discussed on 19 November, the enthusiasts, Joseph Carr, the Dundee painter, and Peter Ross, the Govan shipwright, moved

> that we either co-operate or take the initiative in getting together a joint committee to arrange for the proposed conference.

Finally, Margaret Irwin was to write to the Scottish Co-operative Society, the Social Democratic Federation in Edinburgh and the ILP to send representatives to "a preliminary meeting". For the Co-operative Society's General Council, James Deans replied that they could take no action whilst it was still to be considered by all the members. There was strong Lib-Lab influence amongst co-operators, and the failure to send representatives was to provide the core of the case of those who opposed setting up any new political party. Month after month it was left over until on 11 February, 1899, the line-up became clear. When George Carson, Tinplate and Sheetmetal, and the railwayman, James Innes, urged that they should meet the two Socialist societies without the co-operators "to settle whether we are to have a conference or not", Councillor Mallinson agreed to withdraw his opposition to proceeding without the co-operators, provided that the joint meeting with the others should merely discuss and report back to the PC without indicating any decision. Yet another month passed before nine men met jointly representing the three bodies, with Margaret Irwin taking the notes, on 4 March, 1899.

There were sharply divergent views, the whole argument turning on whether to press ahead with the Conference in time for their spring Congress, or to postpone action until the co-operative movement should – or might – give official support.

Arguing strongly against delay were George Carson, Keir Hardie, Bruce Glasier and the SDF representatives, with Mallinson in the lead for postponement. A significant contribution came from Margaret Irwin herself, there ex-officio, but with permission to give her views, which she minuted as follows:

> No precipitate action should be entered upon which was likely to weaken the chances, or to in any way imperil, the great object they all had in view . . . What had prevented the Labour Party from winning parliamentary elections in the past was that they had not been able to move the great general body of working class voters. This force, she believed, the co-operators would be largely able to influence. In some constituencies it was said the co-operators' vote could practically carry the election. It was worth waiting for. And if a year hence was soon enough for the co-operators, it was soon feared they would gain nothing, while they stood to lose a great deal.

At the key moment, the Chairman, Smillie, tactfully suggested as an alternative to a conference being held at their coming Congress, that the PC be recommended to put to it a resolution asking for approval to call a conference later that year. This was agreed and Mallinson drafted the recommended resolution, which George Carson successfully moved at their April 1899 Congress, with Robert Allan, the Edinburgh compositor, strongly seconding. That was a portent; and both these men were to be prominent in both bodies. Robert Allan became Secretary of the Scottish Workers Parliamentary Elections Committee, as it was called for its first three years, while George Carson in 1901 took over the secretaryship from Margaret Irwin of the Scottish TUC, with Allan following him there eighteen years later. Indeed, the differences over this question seem to have sown the seeds for removing Margaret Irwin as Secretary, for Mallinson was nominated against her. On that occasion he withdrew his name, although urged by several PC members to continue; amongst them was Margaret Irwin herself. She said: "it was not desirable to give the impression that her appointment as Secretary was a permanent one. She had not accepted the office on that understanding".[5] Finally she remained the only nomination; "on his again declining it was agreed that the present arrangement should be continued in the meantime".

That was to prove her last year as Secretary and there were other changes following the 1899 Congress. There was no further progress on organising the Workers Representation Conference until the fourth PC meeting after Congress. Then on 17 June, 1899, "in view of the large increase of work" two subcommittees were set up; one composed of Carson, Allan, John Keir and Peter Ross was given the job of organising the political conference whilst the second arranged a conference for trades councils on the eight-hours day. These, however, were not called until October 1899, exactly a year after Keir Hardie and Bruce Glasier first approached the Scottish TUC officers. When, however, both gatherings met at Edinburgh on the first weekend of January 1900, it was an admitted success, for which George Carson gained the credit.

There were 226 delegates, nearly 100 more than the British TUC could muster at their similar gathering seven weeks later. What is more, unlike the British TUC's gathering in London, there was a number of co-operator delegates, including those from four co-operative conferences and no less than 14 individual co-operative societies. In addition, there were more trade unions, ILP and SDF branches. The door was also open to trades councils, 16 sending 29 delegates. Conference then elected a Joint Committee of four co-operators from Lanark, Glasgow, Kilwinning and Paisley; two each from the ILP and SDF branches in Edinburgh and Glasgow; and four trade unionists, headed by Robert Allan, with George Galloway, Alex Robertson and Hugh Stewart from Glasgow, Aberdeen and Edinburgh Trades Councils. Once again in advance of the British gathering, they indicated the programme topics[6] which the new body should press on candidates for the coming General Election, which proved to be only nine months ahead. There were those amongst them for whom, like Keir Hardie himself, it must have been a great moment to see this – the first ever Labour Party – reformed a dozen years later on a solid base amongst trade unionists.

Section (iv): **The New Century's First War**

The Scottish trade unionists started a new century with a new political party, with economic crisis and deep divergencies throughout the movement about whether the war in South Africa was just or unjust, necessary or an avoidable disaster. Meeting in Edinburgh, Congress received no civic welcome from the Conservative Town Council, who regarded the Scottish TUC as "a political organisation". There was also bitter disagreement over the Edinburgh Trades Council's

"Stop-the-War' policy between those who were described as either pro-war or pro-Boer: a Carpenters and Joiners Branch argued that "political questions should not be introduced", as "their whole time ought to be devoted to trade matters". One result was that the trades council's chief officer did not preside over Congress; instead colleagues proposed the Edinburgh Bakers' Secretary, Thomas Wilson.

In his presidential speech Wilson said "the busy trade has passed its zenith", and they were compelled to face "the problem of these ever-recurring cycles of depression . . . The irony of it! People starving because our warehouses and stores contain more of the necessities of life than can find an outlet on the market". After denouncing the chaotic system of industry being carried on "for the personal profit of the few individuals who monopolise the means of life" instead of what should be their goal of "wealth production for use", he turned to the war.

> Without a doubt, depression of trade is being hastened by the war [illegible] from any standpoint we have to admit that it is a national calamity . . . history will give it a place on our lengthy list of unjust wars.

He deplored that the press and the politicians

> at the dictation of a gang of unscrupulous financiers by distortion of facts and wholesale falsehood can so readily gull the people into believing the war to be a righteous one.

Then he moved on to an issue arising from it on which the movement was to concentrate:

> Not only will the continuance of the policy of Imperial expansion create a demand for increased armaments, with . . . increased taxation, but it will bring us face to face with military conscription.

Voluntary enlistment was "severely strained" and would be useless if in conflict "with one or more of the great European Powers. Are the workers prepared to pay this price for their jingoism?" He spoke bitterly about the cost of the war being quoted as preventing the introduction of a non-contributory old age pension, and then stressed the need for political action and "the stupendous task of rousing the worker from his lethargy". Then he said there must be a change of methods; for the future usefulness of trades unionism would

> be determined by the weapons chosen. The principal weapon of the past – the strike – is becoming less and less powerful. It has done good

> service, but it is two-edged and often cuts deep into the flesh of its user . . . If the ballot-box is to be the weapon of the future, our battalions must be trained to its use, the same unanimity of action as has taken place during strikes must be acquired.

On the third day of Congress Wilson vacated the chair to move Edinburgh Trades Council's motion on Imperialism, carefully avoiding any direct reference to the war. It argued that the "Imperial expansion" of successive governments brought Britain "within a short distance of conscription", that voluntary enlistment was enough for home defence; and that therefore every effort must be made "to check the popularising or glorifying of war" and oppose any non-voluntary recruitment system. Fourteen years later this was to be the centre of the labour movement's response to the First World War, not least in Scotland. An amendment was narrowly defeated, which demanded "a national citizen force to cope with any national emergency", which was supported by the Glasgow Joiners, Tailors and Miners. The only speaker against the general principle was Margaret Irwin who said that though she was "almost a peace-at-any-price woman", she believed there was no need to raise it, as there was no immediate likelihood of conscription, and the best preventative of war was to be prepared for it.

Whilst this discussion on the war and support for setting up the Scottish Workers Parliamentary Elections Committee, as their political party was still called, were the main points at the 1900 Congress, there were difficult industrial problems to handle. The PC report included a special section on the collapse of the Dundee Textile Workers Union. This followed a major strike and lockout after a group of non-union workers, described as "principally young people in other mills", had struck even before a claim for a 5% increase had been presented to Dundee employers. Finally, it became general and the Dundee Textile Workers Union applied to the Scottish Mill, Factory and Bleachfield Workers' Federal Union for help to meet the strike benefit it was paying out. The burden of this would have fallen largely on two richer branches which refused to pay because of the failure to comply strictly with the Federal rules, which required two-thirds support from its dozen branches.

Hard as life was already becoming for textile workers in the East of Scotland, things could be harder still for the young in the West, who were tramping to Dundee for work. Four months later when the Independent Labour Party's *Clarion* van was on tour towards Dundee from Stirling there was an encounter up in the hills. Enid Stacy, the famous Socialist speaker was in charge of the van. She described it in her diary[7] of 22 August, 1900:

> We caught up with eight lads and girls who were tramping from Glasgow to Dundee. Poor things! none of them could have been over 16 and they had walked through the soaking rain of Tuesday. The girls' shawls were still wet; they had had scarcely any supper and no breakfast.

They piled them into the van, gave them food and drink and good company. Then they took them on to the village of Blackford, where they held an open-air meeting.

"At Blackford we parted with them – I think they were sorry to leave us", she commented, having been given by them "vast stores of information concerning jute mills. They were only earning 5s. a week in Glasgow and hoped to 'better themselves' in Dundee."[8]

Nor was it only in textiles that there were new and pressing problems but also in the mines, ironworks and bakeries. This came out when miners described how dangerous it was to have large numbers of foreigners who could not understand English working underground and without any proper supervision. Robert Smillie described how there were between 3,000 and 4,000 foreign miners in Lanarkshire. It had come about some years back when

> a strike took place in the ironworks in Ayrshire and in order to undersell British labour, Poles were imported. Gradually, they found their way to the mines, and when they saved sufficient money they sent home for more of their countrymen.

Councillor John Cronin of the Glasgow Steel & Ironworkers said the Poles "were employed at half the rates paid to British workmen, and it was difficult to make them understand that they were doing anything unfair. The whole of the importation of foreigners was done for pure personal profit by men who were continually preaching about patriotism, and were the first to advocate war with foreign countries." W G Hunter of the Glasgow Bakers said that ten Russian Poles had been brought into the municipally owned gas works.

Other difficulties continued in the seasonal trades, about which Margaret Irwin demanded an enquiry, for the work might "with a little knowledge and forethought, have been spread more evenly". For example, in the clothing trades "it was slavery in summer and starvation in winter". The Edinburgh Trades Council Secretary, H W Stewart, described how they had induced the Town Council to have the police clothing made in the slack season and the painting of the public library in winter. They should move on it themselves already and not await an inquiry which could take four or five years.

A leading co-operator, ex-Baillie Murphy of Lanark, got a good reception as a fraternal delegate from the new Scottish Workers Parliamentary Elections Committee, giving a lively picture of earlier days, and how the working-men "stalwarts" on the Corporation of Glasgow had pushed through "every step of progress", and how they had prevented important questions being "quietly shelved" between elections. Yet they had no voice in the House of Commons which "has become the rich men's club, where an endless stream of talk flows on, signifying little or nothing so far as the needs, the thoughts, and the aspirations of the people are concerned". He added:

> The past history of both political parties is a record of broken promises, which makes it hopeless to look to either party for remedial measures.

Other recollections came from Councillor Cronin during a debate demanding that employers and management should be brought equally within the Conspiracy and Protection of Property Act. He said he himself was

> once charged with breaking the Act under six different clauses, for each of which he was liable to 3 months imprisonment or a fine of £20. They let him off cheaply with 60 days, which he had the pleasure of doing in Calton Jail.

It was to be only a short time before this issue of trade union rights would take central place in the concern of the whole Labour movement.

That year all the officers were new. Margaret Irwin when being thanked as retiring Secretary, said she had declined nomination due "entirely to the increasing claims of other work". But she was elected to the PC with a vote second only to the incoming chairman, John Keir, who was replacing Robert Smillie. George Carson started on his 18 years' service as Hon. Secretary.

When they met the next spring in Paisley there were three main topics on their minds: the war in South Africa was showing the European powers that British troops could be defeated; the Government had rushed through the "Khaki Election' to ensure that they stayed in power; and the Taff Vale case against the railwaymen's unions was beginning to bring it home to the movement that a major attack was gradually being mounted by the employers yet again. Now there were not only doubts as to whether industrial action extending to strikes was helpful, but also disappointment at the slow progress in the Parliamentary spheres; no gains in Scotland had been won in the General Election when there was response to their manifesto and questionnaire[9] from only a few Scottish candidates.

They had a pointed rebuff from the British TUC's PC. When Carson wrote suggesting a joint deputation on key issues to the Home Secretary and Board of Trade not only had Sam Woods MP replied by a refusal, but he pointed out that

> his Committee regretted the existence of sectional conferences which . . . divided the forces of labour, weakened their influence and made them an easy prey to the Capitalistic classes, and the time had come when they should cease to exist and they suggested that a joint meeting should be held at a convenient time and place to have this much to be desired result brought about.[10]

When they went ahead with seeking to send their deputation to London, the Home Secretary tried to evade them by suggesting they should join the British TUC's deputation. Carson replied that they had

> on several occasions made overtures to the committee of the English Congress with a view to having a joint deputation but had never met with any response.[11]

Finally a deputation of Margaret Irwin, Baillie James Jack of the Ironmoulders and John Wilson of the miners was received, but only after the General Election.

It was a year "anything but favourable to the promoting of any kind of reform, whether industrial social or political", as the PC's Report began. This was due, it continued, to the Government having, "with scrupulous disregard for all other consideration except their own burning desire to renew their lease of power, forced upon the country a General Election . . . when they knew their war policy would ensure them a successful result". In his Presidential Address, Councillor John Kent of the Scottish Typographical Association, spoke of the war still continuing "its weary, sanguinary and profitable course" after 18 months. Differences about the war continued. Once again there was a call for "the abolition of Standing Armies", to be replaced by a "Citizen Army", with the further proviso that the people should "decide on the question of Peace or War". Moved for Dundee Trades Council by William Morris and seconded by Robert Allan as delegate for the Edinburgh Typographers, it was opposed by Glasgow Bakers and Railwaymen, with the Glasgow Trades Council delegate contending that

> the effect of their proposed agitation would be to strengthen the hands of those who were seeking to drive the people into the toils of conscription.

Finally, it was carried with more than half the delegates abstaining.

The same main antagonists lined up on a demand that the South African war could only finally be settled if it did

> guarantee to the people of these territories the right of Self Government.

Otherwise, argued Robert Allan, "50,000 soldiers would always have to be locked up in South Africa". He considered that the British people "had been fooled and landed in a terrible mess". Once again R G Muir, the Glasgow Railway Servant, sharply differed, but to no avail. At that stage, delegates had no idea of the severe unemployment that would follow the end of the war, as one of its worst features.

Section (v): **Many Disputes and the Taff Vale Threat**

In his 1900 Presidential Address, John Kent looked back, since "a new century had dawned upon the world", at the changes in the past hundred years and especially during the long reign of the Queen who had just died. He noted that even the skilled workers then had a 72-hour week of 12 hours a day with no half holiday. Wages in Edinburgh's building trades were between 12s. to 18s. There was now a reduction in the hours of 25% to 54 hours, the skilled male rate had risen, although women workers, agricultural and labourers' wages had not kept pace. "These results have not been achieved without many a hard and bitter struggle and protracted strike"; and he described the vicious attacks on the early unions and trade societiers and how the power-loom had caused weaving, "the staple trade of our town", to collapse, and "brought it to the verge of ruin". He stressed the "centralisation" in so many industries by the formation of rings, syndicates or trusts; the closing of public works putting people "more than ever at the mercy of the wealthy capitalist"; then "over all there is the shadow of the awful and costly war". He thought it was time,

> at the opening of the twentieth century of the Christian era, that other methods should be found for the settlement of both international and industrial disputes than wars, strikes and lockouts.

The search for "other methods" in the "altered circumstances of labour" were frequently referred to during Congress "to meet the speedily growing combinations of capital".

The fraternal delegate from the Scottish Workers Parliamentary Elections Committee, once again ex-Baillie Murphy, called on them to use their "political power for all that it is worth, not in the narrow groove of your own particular trade, but in the broader channel of improving the condition of all the working population"; they must build up a Labour Party organisation in every town and village.

Another fraternal delegate was Alex Gossip, urging them to get their unions affiliated to the general Federation; he found that moral support of General Federation had

> considerable weight, and employers did not hastily rush into conflict with trades who were closely banded together; the tendency was to settle disputes by parties meeting and conferring together.

Later that day, for the Scottish Cabinet and Chairmakers Association, he moved their resolution that "compulsory arbitration in all Labour disputes be established by law". Whilst not a solution "it was at least better than the present method of strikes", which were never final; for concessions "wrung from unscrupulous employers in a moment of weakness were generally taken back when opportunity afforded". On this, however, there were sharp differences. It was opposed by the Aberdonian Mason, John Elric, and the Glasgow Baker, F Payne, as establishing "a dangerous principle in trades unionism", whilst others were against compulsion; but it was finally passed.

The stress on the need for effective political action was already beginning to be stimulated by the shock of the Taff Vale case, when the railway company successfully claimed damages against the union on the grounds that individual workmen, when picketing began, had been induced to break their master-and-servant contract. With the Railway Servants taking it to appeal, a manifesto had gone to affiliated societies with a plea for funds against this "vicious and dangerous principle". The Associated Ironmoulders had contributed nearly half of the fund received already as Congress met. They themselves were in dispute, having supplied J & G Weir's foundry at Cathcart with men to do the work of Brassmoulders on strike. In the spring of 1902, it led to the famous Association of Ironmoulders of Scotland being expelled and their General Secretary, Baillie Jack, MP, so long prominent in the British TUC and its PC, losing his position as Scottish TUC Chairman, to which he had just been elected.

There were a number of strikes and lockouts being considered in 1901 at the Paisley Congress: it received a deputation from the Shipwrights' Society about a strike at Fairfield, while Smillie referred to the foreign blacklegs imported to the Glenboig pit by the employer-backed "Free Labour Association". Congress expressed support for the women underclothing workers on strike at Wishaw as reported by Mrs Galloway of the Womens' Provident and Protective League.[12]

The Paisley operative bakers were also in dispute with the masters, and their delegate asked trade unionists to "be careful where they ate" in the town. The Scottish system of house-letting by the year which in hard times was "a positive hardship", was described in his demand for weekly tenancies as in England by Alex Gossip, the Cabinet Maker:

> A man might today be working in Glasgow, and immediately after re-taking his house for another year he might be compelled to tramp across the country, possibly to Aberdeen. He had his house then left on his hands, and in many cases he had considerable difficulty in getting it sub-let.

Others favoured a monthly let, believing that with a vindictive landlord there could be trouble when there was illness. Finally the miners, with their experience of company houses, got it carried for three-monthly lets. This was still an issue ten years later. When they came to Falkirk in the spring of 1902, they were nearing the end of the war but deep in many problems. Most painful were continuing disputes amongst unions in three important industries, both on charges of scabbing and strike-breaking, and also the constant friction in the building trade owing to lack of any demarcation agreement between masons and bricklayers. This was especially untimely when the wholesale legal attack on all trades unions' legal rights and funds through the Taff Vale case called for maximum unity and urgent action, without which it could become every employer's field day. The tone was set by the address of the President, William Muirhead, of the Central Iron Moulders Association, who opened Congress with a plea for unity:

> Absolute unity is the lost chord of our endeavour and, having struck it once in the morning of our movement, we seem never to be able to strike that great chord again.

With the experience of his own union's bitter experiences at Weir's fresh in mind, he continued:

> When the trade union idea was first put into practice it promised to work our industrial salvation, but after all these years of effort it has not yet been given anything like a fair trial. Why? Because working men have failed to co-operate unanimously; failed to arm themselves to the teeth; failed to see that their emancipation depended upon their absolute unity.

He added that in the House of Commons each vote gained counted two in a division; but "every workman who acts in opposition to the interests of workmen counts infinitely more in the struggle between capital and labour". Referring to the war bringing no food to the hungry or comfort to the poor, and adding that "the froth of empire" was expensive, he complained:

> We are patriots first, working men afterwards; jingoes of Greater Britain first, citizens of our own country afterwards. What a paradox! . . . We tumble over ourselves in our haste to support a government which has already spent £200,000,000 in fighting the Boers.

If 2,000,000 trade unionists were to unite upon a definite political policy, "there would be no need for Labour candidates, for both of the great political parties would go down on their knees to serve them". Yet before the first day was out, the biggest delegation, the nine delegates of the Scottish Miners Federation, including Robert Smillie, withdrew from the gathering, leaving only the two delegates of the County Union of West Lothian and their Secretary, John Wilson. This was in connection with the expulsion of that union from the Federation, when under Wilson's leadership they had decided to continue to work, he having sided with the owner, Nimmo, when there was a strike against the dirt scale operating at Polkemmet Colliery.

Six months earlier there had been a by-election in north-east Lanarkshire and when Robert Smillie decided to contest as a Miners' Candidate, the PC decided to intervene in an unprecedented way. They did it because they recognised

> that if trade unions are to continue to exist and maintain their usefulness . . . it can only be accomplished by sending men to Parliament whose past record would be a guarantee for their future action.

This was in light of the Taff Vale case.[13] As well as appealing to all "trade union electors" to support him, the PC decided to send their three officials, Robert Girvan of the Glasgow Tailors who had taken over as Chairman from the excluded Ironmoulder James Jack; James Reilly, from the Glasgow Docks; and the Edinburgh Baker, Thomas Wilson. They campaigned for Smillie for three weeks, based for the most part in Bellshill; they had been told "no meetings could be held there owing to the rowdyism pervading".[14]

Smillie got a reasonable vote but was not elected. But this and the results of "the Khaki Election" and the anxiety about the Taff Vale threat and need for legislation to correct it was reflected in the note of disillusionment on which the PC closed its report to the Falkirk Congress in 1902. It showed less faith in political action quickly influencing any unreformed House of Commons. They complained that in current political action "the rate of progress is so slow, compared to the time, energy and money spent to achieve" the few concessions they could claim. They stated that

> the House of Commons as it presently exists is a place well-fitted and indeed, in our opinion, meant to prevent the passing of any legislation of a democratic or progressive kind . . . so long as the present class of members are sent by the workmen to represent them it need never be expected that any increase in the rate of progress can take place.

Trade unionists' duty was to see to it "that they are represented in the House of Commons by men of their own class". The first step on the road to progress would have been taken "when a fair number of Labour members of the right kind are sent to Parliament". Until then the PC's work would be "much more difficult than it otherwise would be", the Report concluded.

Much time had been taken up over Taff Vale, with many consultations, discussions with solicitors and taking counsel's advice on possible devices which were being put forward aimed at putting union funds under protection pending legislation. But by the special meeting of the PC on 30 November, 1901

> it was made quite clear . . . that it did not matter where or how the Protective Funds of Trade Unions were invested, if this could be traced and located they could be impounded for any damages that might be laid against the Union.

A written statement was to follow answering the many queries unions had submitted through the PC.

At the Falkirk Congress, therefore, they held a special closed session addressed by their Solicitor, Mr Wallace of Robertson & Wallace of Edinburgh. He answered questions and explained recommendations – which were to be withheld from the Press – and to be put later to a special conference of trades councils. One proposal that was circulating was that trades councils might organise voluntary picketing groups, to be paid out of trades council funds; it was thought employers would not sue, since there was virtually no money to be got out of trades councils. That idea was behind the proposal from the Glasgow Enginemen and Cranemen's Society calling for a committee to be set up to "put into practical effect" the benefit to be derived from "the moral support of one union to another during times of dispute". This was heavily defeated (57 to 7). They were still at the beginning of major legal attacks on trade union rights which were to be repeated in 1927, 1972 and the 1980s with the aim of destroying the unions.

That year no miner nor woman stood for election to the PC nor were any of the founding members on it. The most notable absentees were John Keir, who was a sick man, Smillie and Margaret Irwin. She remained a delegate in 1903 and 1904, but by their sixth Congress the formative years to which she had made such a marked contribution had ended; she did not return as a delegate except briefly in 1909 and 1910.

References

[1] STUC Second Annual Report.

[2] On the Fatal Accidents Inquiry (Scotland) Act; Tenure of Workmen's Houses and Smaller Dwellings Bills; a Scottish Department of Labour; Seats for Assistants in Shops and sanitation there.

[3] STUC Executive Committee Minutes, 22 June, 1898.

[4] *The Scotsman*, 30 April, 1898.

[5] PC Minutes, 13 March, 1899.

[6] "A Legal Eight Hour Day; Old Age pensions and Ample Provision for those Disabled; Accumulative Taxation of Land Values and all other forms of Unearned Income, save on Investments made under the Industrial and Provident Societies Acts, the Organisation by Imperial and Local Authorities of Self-Supporting Industries by which right to work would be secured to every one, especially in times of trade depression; the Fixing of a Minimum Wage by Law, particularly in the Sweated Trades, as has already been done in the Colony of Victoria". (Report of the First Conference of the Scottish Workers Parliamentary Elections Committee).

[7] In the possession of the author, Enid Stacy's niece.

[8] *The Clarion*, 1 September, 1900.

[9] On amendments of Factory & Workshop Acts; amendments to the Workmen's Compensation Act following recent legal decisions; Legal Limitation of Hours; Non-contributory old age pensions; and the Scottish Workmen's Dwellings Bill, to prevent employers being able to make living in tied houses a condition of employment, and power to evict during strikes and lockouts.

[10] Scottish TUC Parliamentary Committee Minutes, 11 August, 1900.

[11] Ibid. 19 January, 1901.

[12] Her husband, of the Scottish Plumbers, was also present as a delegate from Glasgow Trades Council; they had both been delegates to the founding Congress.

[13] Parliamentary Committee Minutes, 17 September, 1901.

[14] Ibid. 5 October, 1901.

4

Doubts and Difficulties

For the next half dozen years the Scottish Trades Union Congress faced many doubts and difficulties after their brave start. Some of these they shared with the trade union movement elsewhere, notably the Irish Trades Union Congress with whom they had close relations from the first, but for some years they were unable to exchange fraternal delegates. There were all the major difficulties of tyrannical employers taking advantage of the Taff Vale judgment; the crash of the trade boom and resulting mass unemployment with loss of funds following the Boer War; and problems arising from new technology and increased rivalries from overseas. The Scots also shared the doubts and disappointments about the slow results of political action at Parliamentary level, with continuing queries about whether the new Labour Party was a quick way to progress.

Section (i): **The STUC's Special Disadvantages**

But some of the difficulties especially affected the Scottish trades unionists in particular. Chief amongst these was the refusal of Central Government to recognise the STUC and to receive its deputations, even on uniquely Scottish problems, with the British Trades Union Congress leaders apparently totally unconcerned, to put it mildly; it took many a year to finally overcome this.

The Labour Party (then known as The British Labour Representation Committee) was also at odds with the Scottish Workers Parliamentary Elections Committee, aiming to drive it into being a regional grouping without powers. All this led even to moves at Congress to stop serious activity at all, under the guise of "reorganisation" and to concentrate on political action directed only to local government. Demarcation disputes and problems about organising the employees of the Co-operative Societies were a continuing factor.

In a number of respects, therefore, STUC activity fell away. It was significant that Margaret Irwin's successor, George Carson, became so engrossed with Glasgow housing affairs that he became Secretary of Glasgow Trades Council for a dozen years in addition to his duties to the STUC. The follow-up of Congress decisions in the main was left aside for many months; sometimes the Parliamentary Committee became deeply concerned with the single issue of the dangers and accidents caused by unsafe scaffolding in the building trade as in Glasgow. Several Parliamentary Committee meetings were devoted solely to joint consultations with building trade union officials; there was prolonged correspondence between Carson and the Glasgow Town Clerk and Master of Works, and also with the Home Secretary and Secretary for Scotland, who recommended to them to approach all town councils in Scotland with proposals of how to check contractors' failings. His concern about it was apparent for several years.

Section (ii): **The Employers' Onslaught**

Even in its least effective years, however, the STUC's annual Congress provided an opportunity for the voice of Scotland's grass roots trade unionists to be expressed. In the spring of 1903, they met at Ayr for the first time, after months when the PC had been short of funds; "a large portion of their time had been taken up in trying to settle differences" between trade unions and Co-operative Societies, involving tailors, bakers, furniture and boot and shoe workers, as well as the long-drawn-out difficulties between the miners' county unions. During their four days of meeting there were further indications of the onslaught of employers, big and small. The Glasgow Calico Engravers complained of "the gross abuse" of the right to combine, for employers were preventing workmen leaving one shop to enter another without the permission of their first employer. Mary Macarthur told of the long hours of shop assistants. Edinburgh tailors had been forced to go on strike, with 1,200 out, the masters having "taken the initial step towards breaking the union". During Congress itself the Clyde engineers were confronted with a wage cut "not at all justified by the state of trade". Congress also passed unanimously a resolution denouncing "the tyrannical action" by the owners of the Ballachulish Quarries, after hearing the quarrymen describe how they only got paid once in six weeks, were heavily charged for tools and equipment they used and prevented from employing a doctor of their own choice. Nor were they the only quarrymen in difficulties; there was the famous case at the Bethesda Quarries in North Wales, where their owner Lord Penrhyn had sacked the lot for taking their traditional May Day holiday.

In his presidential speech Robert Smillie described that "terrible struggle", in the course of which "one man was defying not only trade unionists, but practically public opinion throughout the length and breadth of the world". That was all part and parcel of the consequences of the Taff Vale case, as an immediate result of which owners had successfully claimed no less than £125,000 damages against the Yorkshire Miners' Association because of a dispute at the Denaby Main Colliery, as well as another claim for £75,000 against the Welsh Miners.

Smillie commented:

> There had appeared what seemed to be almost a disguised effort on the part of the capitalist classes to crush out trade unionism by different methods from those which were previously employed.

The aim was to leave unions without their backbone, the "funds for the protection of members", he added. Deputations "had perambulated the lobby of the House during the year seeking for small scraps of legislation", but "without the slightest attempt being made by the House of Commons to introduce or carry forward any important Labour representation". But there had been progress towards direct Labour representation; and "men who for the past ten years had fought inch by inch against Labour being independently represented, were being brought by sad experience to adopt the views they had up to this been fighting". If workers now began to use their votes wisely soon

> they would not require to beg at the door of the House of Commons year by year for little scraps of legislation.

In fact, during the past year the STUC's four officers had gone to London to hold a Conference with Scottish and Labour Representation Committee MPs (of whom 30 did not attend) on 21 July, 1902, to raise all the points decided on at previous Congress apart from the Taff Vale decision. On that point they had issued a whip to all Scottish members to support a motion to amend the "judge-made law" and later another to make peaceful picketing legal. They gave the names of the Scots and how they voted. Only 25% of the Scottish MPs were in favour.[1]

The most urgent question was whether there was any immediate way of protecting funds until a change in law had been forced through. The PC held a conference attended by 36 delegates from 13 trades councils on the legal advice given them as how to get the rules amended, after much disagreement had been expressed. The follow-up was not to prove at all simple. Three months later the PC decided to press trades councils to report what they had done about the scheme; it had not been put either to the British TUC's Committee nor to the Shipbuilding and Engineering Federation. In the debate on the general question of the need for legislation, there were different ideas about how this could be got. The Glasgow docker, James Reilly, thought those who had abstained or voted against should be pursued, but also that "the day of lobbying was almost past"; he agreed with the Govan Brassfinisher that it should be made "a test question" for every Parliamentary candidate. Mary Macarthur, Shop Assistants, thought this too pious; the only safeguard was direct Labour representation; but a Glasgow House and Ship Painter said it was no use waiting for that, with a Springburn railwayman adding that "it would be foolish to stand still" meanwhile. A Lanarkshire miner thought that as yet not "half the members of the unions knew the gravity of the situation"; delegates should go back and point it out. The PC member B H Shaw, of the Glasgow Shop Assistants, said even the lawyers did not know exactly what the present situation was, but in his view "Judges were sensitive to opinion"; and the Edinburgh Trades Council delegate said that at least it would be good policy to bring every pressure to bear, and if they could not alter the MPs' opinions, at least to "alter the opinions of their supporters in the constituencies". But as the months dragged on the Scottish TUC had little to contribute to that central and all-important question; so in a number of respects activity and high hopes tended to fall away.

George Murdoch's presidential address at Perth in 1904 mentioned the horrifying 5,591 railwaymen killed in accidents at work that year; and he stressed the low pay and poor state of organisation of the 275,000 working women in Scotland now entering the labour market in large numbers, while giving credit to the Scottish Council for Women's Trades "for their noble and painstaking work". In fact their delegate, Margaret Irwin, was the only woman present at the Perth Congress in 1904. While there were no differences on principle during the four days' debates, there were some unfortunate exchanges. These began when one delegate in somewhat unmeasured terms denounced the proposal to organise recognition of the work of Keir Hardie, who was at that time ill, as a "humbug". There were some sharp exchanges when he refused to withdraw and was ordered out. The incident gave rise to references to drunken behaviour at Congresses; this gave opportunity, seized upon by the local press, for headings about "Wild Scenes at Trades Union Congress: Strange Charges: A Desire for Sobriety on the Part of the Delegates". But it was not this which impressed the two fraternal delegates from Ireland in their strong speeches. What appalled Councillor James McCarron of Londonderry was that the PC had had to report how few Scottish and Labour MPs were ready to meet them in the House of Commons. He said: "As Irishmen they would not tolerate such conduct." Both he and Councillor P T Daly of Dublin spoke warmly of the resolution passed by Congress unanimously against Chinese labour being forced like slaves into South Africa "at the behest of millionaire syndicates to supplant white and native labour . . . . apparently in order to avoid democratic political development".

It had been a bad year for the STUC, and the months leading up to their Eastertide gathering in 1905 at Hawick showed little improvement. Whilst one reason was that a new Treasurer, Charles Jackson the Glasgow print worker, had to take over and months were spent trying to recover a substantial debt owing by the ex-Treasurer, it was not the only cause for the STUC falling away in influence. George Carson more frequently was wearing his hat as Glasgow Trades Council's Secretary: early in January a conference was convened by Glasgow Corporation on the growing problem of unemployment at the instance of the Trades Council rather than that of the STUC on an all-Scotland basis. Yet again, there was no follow-up of the regular Congress demands until November, seven months after. It is perhaps not surprising that a call came from Edinburgh delegates for the "reconstruction of the PC". They moved:

> that it is desirable to have the PC national in character and representative of the various districts, therefore, instructs the PC to draft a scheme whereby all the centres of Scotland would secure representaton.

With the Glasgow Councillor who had just been defeated for the PC speaking against, the motion was only rejected by 44 to 34 of the 114 delegates attending. Of the eleven members of the outgoing PC only two were not from Clydeside. Clearly, while in contrast with the British TUC the Scottish organisation gained very greatly from the trades councils' participation, there could be regional imbalance and, therefore, weaknesses from that direction. When they came to hold their 1905 Congress this was strongly brought out not only by Keir Hardie, MP, as a visitor, and Robert Smillie once more acting as President in the absence of a powerful local trades council, but also by the veteran John Mallinson, the Edinburgh Baillie, himself a native of Hawick, where they were meeting.

In this border town conditions were very difficult indeed and organisation was in a bad way. At the demonstration during the week, Robert Smillie asked how much of the border land belonged to them? If their brave forefathers had known, they would not have been so ready to die for it.

> This was not their country. Scotland belonged to a few hundred landlords who did exactly as they liked with it. Not long ago they had in Hawick a flourishing branch of the Textile Workers' Union, but it was now non-existent.

He called for organisation again, and especially asked the women to join. Indeed, at Congress itself there was a falling away seen in the fact that delegates had dropped to 114 and there was no single woman delegate, nor even representatives from the Scottish Council for Women's Trades. Yet when attending the Irish Trades Union Congress, Smillie and his fellow delegate Charles Jackson, the Glasgow printworker, had noted women's trades were well represented there.

In his presidential address Smillie concentrated on what their positive role should be; it was not to "exist as a rival to any other similar body", it was

> an attempt to concentrate the energies of the workers of Scotland . . . dealing with some of the many grievances and injustices which affect them locally, which would not be touched by the British Congress, while . . . joining with the British and Irish Congresses in advancing by every means . . . any movement which has for its object the improvement of the condition of the workers of the country as a whole.

The "industrial horizon seems to be blackening again", with wage disputes amongst patternmakers and joiners and serious trouble threatening in engineering. Now there was considerable agitation over unemployment and strong feeling for the Education Bill to provide for State maintenance and feeding of underfed children in State-aided schools, which only a short time previously "was only heard from the mouths of so-called 'Socialist agitators' ".

But still the essential task was to alter the law to give trade unions protection, he said, outlining the recent Law Lords' final decision against the Yorkshire miners. A startling case, with an all too familiar ring eighty years on, which he described in detail. It began when a colliery came out on strike for higher wages without giving a fortnight's notice; the Union officials would not recognise or support the miners unless they went back, which they did. But meanwhile the coalowner posted new rules, and none were to be allowed to resume work without accepting them. On their Union's advice, the miners attended for work every day for a fortnight and then a strike was declared official. Six months later the employers induced one miner to bring an action against the union for continuing to pay out strike money, on the ground that it was illegal use of funds, since notice had not been worked. This employers' tool won his case, whereupon the coalowners brought a successful action for £150,000 damages against the union. The Trades Disputes Bill was before the Grand Committee where, said Smillie, "it is being fought line by line and clause by clause by the representatives of Capital in Parliament". Eight months later it was to be the key question at the General Election which was to set the Labour Party on its seventeen years' attempt to replace the Liberal Party as His Majesty's Opposition to the Tory Party in the British two-party system of government.

Few of the other speeches at the 1905 Congress, however, expressed the sense of tremendous build-up; although on unemployment the Aberdeen Trades Council resolution demanded a Department of Labour to ensure public works being available and extended to Scotland. There were the usual features or resolutions once again repeated, mostly involving Parliamentary action, virtually without debate. Where differences were expressed these seemed to be largely because of misgivings on what progress the STUC was making; except for a Parliamentary whip once again on the Education Bill, the PC had yet again not begun to process the previous decisions for six months. Apart from the attempt to have the PC itself reconstructed, it emerged in various suggested amendments to Standing Orders. True, the PC's proposal to "rearrange delegates' fees . . . more in keeping with the needs of the PC" was rejected by 39 to 18; but others were carried. These included that there should be a roll call at Congress every day; that Congress should not be adjourned for an afternoon's junketing; and that Congress president should always be the PC's past chairman, rather than a leading officer of the trades council in the town being visited.

There were only two topics on which there was any lively expression of differences. In a debate on temperance the abolitionists from Dundee Trades Councils were defeated 34-40 and again by 8-66 when they opposed a demand for the municipal ownership of the liquor traffic, doubting whether it would control drunkenness. Not surprisingly there was an unsuccessful attempt (34-45) to prevent a resolution in favour of secular education in all State-aided schools. It was to be a constant debate, and usually bitter. The newly elected PC member John Howden, the Glasgow joiner, argued that the difficulties could only be solved by getting rid of religious teaching altogether. Opposing it, however, John Kent, the Paisley printer, whilst being against sectarian teaching, thought there was no desire to abolish Bible teaching. It would be hard enough to get the Education (Scotland) Bill through at all without raising the religious difficulty. Point to his argument was given by the remaining two speakers. James McManus,

Glasgow Coachmakers, opposing banishing religious education, said they would have "a larger percentage of blackguards and criminals than at present. France was a typical example to warn them. It was difficult enough at the present time to bring up their children decently." From the opposite standpoint, George Garden, Aberdeen Mason and Granite Cutter, said religious education was being advocated on purely sectarian and religious grounds and not on the grounds of public benefit at all; he praised the United States, "a greater country than France, where there had never been religious education in the schools at all". The evening before at the public demonstration Councillor William Walker, the Irish fraternal delegate from Belfast had said:

> the old barriers of nationalities and different religions were being removed under the growth of the idea that after all, no matter to what country we belonged, or at what shrine we worshipped, our aims were the same, our circumstances were similar; and it was only by the adoption of methods general to all peoples and by unity of purpose that the true goal of trade unionism would be reached – in the elimination of poverty and the affording of equal opportunities to all the sons and daughters of men.

Within three years, however, the subject was debated again in a somewhat different spirit, as we shall see. Although the sectarian viewpoint was still apparent, the efforts of Socialist propagandists like Michael Devitt, John MacLean and the Catholic John Wheatley were already beginning to have a marked influence on Scottish trade union activists.

Perhaps the only completely cheerful occasion at the 1905 Congress was when Robert Smillie, "delighted to think he had been a humble follower under the flag unfurled twenty years ago" by Keir Hardie, the man who had formed the first Labour Party, made their presentation of a purse of £150 to the man than whom no-one "had been more vilified by the capitalist press and his enemies". When Hardie rose to reply:

> delegates rose to their feet, cheering lustily, and concluded by singing, "He's a Jolly Good Fellow".

He had in fact ten more years of life before him, perhaps none busier than the coming year: 1906.

Section (iii): **How They Judged the New Government's Record**

When in 1906 they met at Greenock it was in a better atmosphere. The General Election had decisively rejected the Conservatives and put in a

Liberal Government with a record-breaking majority of 356. While it had no clear-cut policy on the necessary reforms, there were now 30 Labour men elected at last, pledged to work as an independent working-class party to press for changes put forward by the trades union movement, and co-operating with some 20 Lib-Lab members. The STUC had backed their own candidates in ten Scottish constituencies, five of them miners: two seats were won each by trade union General Secretaries; George Barnes of the Engineers in Blackfriars, Glasgow, and Alexander Wilkie, of the Shipwrights, in Dundee. South of the border many of the seats were won by associating with a Liberal in two-member constituencies; in Scotland only Wilkie's was a two-seater.

The Parliamentary Committee had worked hard to achieve these results. They issued a questionnaire on nine key issues[2] to 154 candidates in Scotland and received 35 replies, published in their Report to Congress; they also issued a manifesto summarising the issues for Scottish trade unionists: one of their own number, Robert Smillie, was contesting Paisley. In other respects the incoming PC had improved its work considerably during the year, having active subcommittees and early processing decisions. A Finance Subcommittee kept a watchful eye on funds, and now an office room was taken in the Bakers Union premises at 156 George Street, Glasgow, at a yearly rental of £6, accommodation which the Scottish Workers' Representation Committee and the Glasgow Trades Council also shared; it must have been particularly convenient for George Carson.

They had also sent out circulars before and since the General Election on free maintenance for needy children and free equipment in schools; on the need for the Co-operative Movement to see that employees were members of trade unions; and Carson's special interest: to get proper scaffolding bye-laws in Glasgow. There were two major questions for which they had been pressing for strong action. One was regarding what proved to be a toothless Unemployed Workmen's Act; the other, not unconnected with that, was about the Royal Commission of Inquiry into the Poor Law and causes of unemployment. It was characteristically set up by the Conservative Government to head off ever-growing demands for reform; now if the incoming Liberal Government were not also to shelter behind it for inaction during the new battle for priorities and high expectation, there needed to be good appointments to it. On the suggestion of Glasgow Trades Council, the PC had submitted the name of Robert Smillie. This was refused, and because of such an "affront to Scottish Labour", the PC called a widely based conference to elect a deputation to go to the new Liberal Prime Minister, Campbell Bannerman. It was some time before he could be got to reply, when "for some reason he marked the letter 'PRIVATE' ", declared the Report, adding that it "was altogether unsatisfactory and extremely vague". The PC were to receive another "private" letter from the Prime Minister finally declaring it "impracticable" to include Smillie. The newly elected Scottish Labour MP, Wilkie, raised it openly in the House of Commons. This drew an insulting reply from the President of the Local Government Board[3] saying there were too many on the Commission already; chaffing Wilkie on the many distinguished men Scotland had sent to Parliament over the years and even "the disproportionately large number of men it had given to the Cabinet". Finally, he concluded that anyhow the Commission had a member from the British TUC; if Scotland still felt aggrieved when the Commission reported, hopefully in two years time, they could complain then.

It was such responses that already began to raise doubts and anxieties in Scotland, even at this early stage which, during the next half dozen years of unemployment, industrial and social problems known as "the great unrest", led up to the First World War and distrust on Clydeside of those in command. The doubts were expressed in differing attitudes. To some it seemed the opportunity for the new Labour Party, now with an expatriate Scottish leader in the House, James Ramsay MacDonald; and therefore a case for speedily adding to their numbers. Some saw it more as the new Labour Party's testing ground; and that if they failed to get results, it was proof that no Parliamentary "independent workers' representation" could be effective. Some began to see extra-Parliamentary action by the trade unions as all-important; others regarded the trades unions as too weak, and called for them to become stronger by concentrating only on industrial action, along the lines of syndicalism, with anarchist overtones, which was already emerging in the United States.

Throughout the Greenock Congress discussions, such viewpoints began to emerge. The Glaswegian, John Howden, of the Amalgamated Carpenters, felt they should make their "voice felt with no uncertain sound" to the new Government for refusing them representation on the Poor Law Inquiry, and his motion protested at "the affront offered to Scottish labour". Later, speaking on a resolution expressing indignation at "the further affront" when the Liberal Government also refused them a seat on the Inquiry into Truck, Robert Smillie said:

> the treatment which the organised workers of Scotland had received at the hands of the Government was little short of a scandal.

Andrew Ballantyne, the factory inspector, returning to Congress as a delegate for the Scottish Council for Women's Trades, was "inclined to describe the action of the Government in much stronger terms". He went on to warn Congress:

> that this treatment would continue just so long as they were willing to take these insults "lying down" . . . It may be from the political point of view that they deserved the treatment meted out to them, but let them see to it that, if it were repeated, they took such steps as would once and for all assert their position.

There was a similar warning given by David Gilmour, of the Lanarkshire Miners, when demanding that the Scottish Federation of Miners must be represented on the Royal Commission which it had just been announced was to inquire into Accidents in Mines. He reminded them that "last year there were over 1,100 fatal accidents in this country and between 40,000 and 50,000 persons injured", and pointed out how much more effective it could be to have "a nominee from their own ranks on the Commission". The PC's Vice-Chairman, Councillor James Gavin, of Glasgow Steel and Iron Workers, asked "whether these Ministers were serious in their reply to the deputation" which had asked for a State pension for the incapacitated and for all at 60; they had been told it could not be seen where the money was to come from. Moving a resolution that full protection of the Factory and Workshops Act should be extended to the linen and jute trades, John Hendry of the Brechin Mill & Factory Operatives Union, had sharp criticism of candidates for inspectorship, who might know much of English literature, history, French or German but absolutely nothing on "whether machinery was properly fenced". He hoped

> that when this Government of all the graces, which was to lead them into a land flowing with milk and honey, came into power something would be done.

But when questioned, the Home Secretary had insisted nothing should yet be done to make any alterations. Therefore the workers should demand of this Government that inspectors "responsible for the life and limb of the workers should have a practical knowledge of machinery".

From the same industry, Baillie William Johnston JP of Aberdeen and the Mill, Factory and Bleachfield Federal Union, in his Presidential Address was comparatively restrained in the way he gave expression to the undercurrent of anxiety. While the big increase of Labour members "pledged to independent political action should give us hope, strength and courage for the future", he noted that in Scotland:

> ancient traditions, political and other prejudices, are still the greatest obstacles, with which we have to contend. We must therefore go on agitating, educating and organising.

Against the unfair and unjust distribution of wealth, he pointed out, any legislation in their favour "has only touched the fringe"; and despite the growing influence of the Acts trades unionism had achieved, "not one of them, from a workman's point of view, but requires amendment". While some people might "minimise the importance of the Labour Party in the new Parliament", at least they should expect that Congress resolutions henceforth would "receive more attention than hitherto". After sharply criticising the exclusion of a Scottish unionist from the Poor Law Inquiry, he reminded them of how little faith they had had in the personnel on the 1903 Royal Commission on Trade Unions. That report, issued after three long years, now had had to be disregarded in drafting the present Trades Unions and Trades Dispute Bill, to restore trade unions' rights to before the Taff Vale judgment, just past its second reading though "not yet out of the wood". After detailed criticisms of the Workmen's Compensation Act, he spoke bitterly of the behaviour of the Distress Committees under the Unemployed Workmen's Act, incapable of dealing with "the eternal competition of labour-saving machinery". Here he gave recent instances from his own sphere:

> In the mill, factory and agriculture – and in every branch of industry – the production of machinery has displaced from 20 to 30 per cent, and in some cases as high as 50 per cent, of human labour.

At home and abroad, everywhere "capital is combining into huge trusts and syndicates, with the object of securing control and a monopoly of industries with increased profits". With the stability of employment "every year becoming more precarious, social legislation of a drastic character is required to put an end to this canker". Therefore it rested

> with the new Labour Party in the House of Commons, backed up by the organised workers in the country, to formulate such demands as the Government will be compelled to organise the industries in the country in such a manner as will obviate the necessity of providing work for the unemployed.

Another subject on which he spoke with disappointment was that since the engineering lockout the campaign for the legal eight-hours day had been allowed "practically to lie in abeyance"; and while it was regularly on Congress agenda was not pushed as it always was a dozen years before. He thought it "futile" to use the strike weapon; but urged delegates not merely to pass a resolution, but to press it. However, during Congress there was only a brief debate, with the usual amendment for a 48-hour week being defeated 16 to 69 to Aberdeen's routine motion.

Johnston's bitterest remarks came in a long passage about the £250 million wasted "on this wretched business" of the South African War, now used to excuse no old age pensions being provided and leaving "the workmen of this country not one whit better off". He stressed that it was worse in Scotland; men and women were sent

> in their old age to the workhouse in England and it leaves them to starve in Scotland.

He contrasted this with the position in Denmark, New Zealand, Australia and Newfoundland. He concluded by reminding delegates that the Labour MPs were still "a small minority". It was the unions' duty to strengthen organisation and increase their number. By unity and using power in municipal and imperial politics trade unionists must "lead on the social revolution of the age", which was "distinctly tending towards collectivism". He concluded:

> Political action must be made an integral part of our methods in the work of industrial emancipation.

During the four days of debate, however, it could be frequently seen how much stronger the trade unions themselves needed to become.

Not only were inter-union disputes reported, as with the Scottish Plumbers. The biggest group of all, the miners, had been unable to stop a mining manager from using a water hose and fire hydrant to prevent the Shale Miners' Association taking a ballot to appoint a checkweigher. Congress suspended Standing Orders to allow an emergency resolution on it. The weakness of organisation amongst women in the Scottish clothing trade, not least amongst the pieceworkers, was stressed and conditions were said to be "almost barbaric". A grim picture emerged too of non-recognition of the unions, the long hours of work and lack of safety inspection on the railways. Within Congress there continued to be subjects on which there were basic differences. A long sectarian debate was repeated on secular education, which was finally supported by 61 to 11; nearly half the delegates stayed away from this. They were eager however to take sides once again on the temperance question, on which much time was spent before agreement was finally reached (82-24) on the municipalisation and local option policy, with the opposition coming mostly from the total abolitionists. At least there was no division on a Scottish grievance about housing reform. The main obstacle to such schemes for local government action, Charles Stuart of the Dundee Bleachfield Workers pointed out, was

> that the repayment of loans in Scotland for such purposes have to be met in 30 years, whereas in England such loans can be repaid up to 80 years.

Nor was there division on the demand that to meet unemployment there should be State establishment of "self-supporting workshops". There was only difference on tactics when John Lawson for Falkirk Trades Council successfully moved for complete adult suffrage, and equal voting rights for all men and women. The Shale Miners' Secretary, John Wilson, and a railwayman wanted it restricted to "all householders and lodgers above 25". Smillie yet again pointed out that to extend it on a property qualification would only enfranchise a small number of women "and leave outside the vast majority of working-class women".

Their only fraternal delegate that year was an Englishman, Will Crooks MP for Woolwich; the Irish TUC could not afford to send a delegate. The British TUC as was their custom did not communicate, but Ramsay MacDonald sent a telegram. The Scottish political labour group, now re-named The Scottish Workers Representation Committee, however, were not represented. They were at the time in controversy with MacDonald on the question of allocating share of fees and whether they were entitled to have applications from Scottish organisations addressed to them instead of having to be addressed to the Labour Party in London.

Section (iv): **Criticisms Grow Sharper**

Throughout 1906 they processed the decisions with one or two new methods. In the deputation to London where they met the Secretary of State for Scotland and the Lord Advocate, and also two small groups of Labour MPs, with Smillie as usual taking a leading part for them, they raised the new subject of loading by harbour workers. It had been reported from Aberdeen, where men were being grossly cheated on tonnage rates. They also had complaints to handle about textile workers' strikes; there had been an amazing case of a mill girl's whole family being sacked because she was on strike. A new type of action by the PC was to circulate a score of Scottish town councils about whether they welcomed raising the time for repaying housing reform loans to 80 years, as in England; they could then prove the majority were favourable. Much of their work might be thought to overlap with what the Scottish Workers Representation Committee should be doing, on which both Carson and Smillie were also Committee members. But this party seemed to confine their activity to working for municipal and Parliamentary by-elections. There was no fraternal delegate from the SWRC at the Aberdeen 1907 Congress, although a number of their committee members, including their secretary, Robert Allan, were present and spoke as delegates from their unions.

But when Congress debates began in Greenock Town Hall the general attitude was increasingly one of disillusionment. While there had been some success, with the Trade Disputes Act at last being passed, some of the "many defects" of amendments to other Acts were regarded as the result of having "a Government of shams", said David Gilmour, Lanarkshire miner. Speaking on the lack of a non-contributory pension scheme, he said

> They had got absolutely nothing out of them except what they had been able to do by compulsion.

He quoted other Bills where "they had exactly the same experience". Other miners, masons, steel workers, and printers had similar sharp criticisms throughout Congress, which had been opened by similar complaints in the presidential address of the Carpenter and Joiner, H T Howden from Glasgow. He was particularly bitter about the Education debate and "the utter waste of time, energy and temper which characterised the passage of the English Bill through the Commons". He added:

> Thirty-three days were spent on the measure, mainly squabbling over which sect was to show the children the way to heaven, and then the Lords declined to pass it because they did not agree with the pilots selected.

In his view it was "better to leave the matter to priest and parson, and insist on secular education, and that alone, being taught in our day schools". He believed the Labour Party had justified its existence, but added:

> until they as a party realise the impossibility of permanently benefiting our class by merely tinkering with palliative proposals, and set their faces resolutely towards the abolition of the present system of production

> for use, the complete emancipation of the workers must still be a long way off.

In their "whole-hearted support" for political action, an impression had developed "that with a strong Labour Party in the House of Commons, the necessity for trade unionism will be gone". Contrasting what should be seen as "different phases of the same movement", people often asked what had trade union effort won in the past and said that it was "played out", and that "the power of the strike was gone".

That showed "a befogged understanding of the whole trend of our movement". It would be "a bold prophet" to foretell when and how Labour's emancipation would be brought about, whether "by purely political methods", or backed up "by the active assistance of the economic force behind organised Labour"; but he believed "both will play no unimportant part in the revolution". Meanwhile, it was essential to strengthen trade unionism, and cure the defects of different crafts organisation, demarcation disputes and the like. So he welcomed the proposed federation and coming into line of iron trades, the miners' county unions and the woodworking trades. But, with an eye to syndicalism on the horizon, he said they should "look upon with suspicion" any attempt "to create another organisation, however broad its principles, which leaves out of its reckoning the working-class movement as it stands today".

It was notable that during Congress successful meetings were held by various trades: including the Tailors, Electricians, Coachmakers, House & Ship Painters, Shop Assistants, Warehousemen and Clerks. Amongst the industrial issues Congress took up was the important claim by Brechin Mill and Factory Workers that a maintenance allowance should be paid for three months after childbirth to "mothers during their enforced idleness without the necessity of any application of the Poor Law authorities". The Central Ironmoulders from Falkirk wanted all women prohibited from working after childbirth, unless they were widows. Although once again there was no woman delegate present to speak against this amendment, the resolution was carried by 68 to 26. New and faint portents to grave developments to come, were two references to international affairs. The Lanarkshire miner, John Robertson, supported by Robert Allan, the Edinburgh typographer, moved "fraternal greetings to the Russian people, who are fighting for political and social emancipation". The miners had already sent a donation to be forwarded; and a receipt for this "handsome demonstration of International solidarity" was read to Congress.[4] In his Presidential address Howden had referred to the Hague Conference, with 46 countries expected to be present at the second Conference that summer. What hindered universal peace in his view was "the interests of financiers and international gamblers". He quoted a Glasgow paper's view that the defeat of the German Social Democrats in the German Reichstag meant that the German Government had a free hand "not only in its colonial schemes, but in its schemes of aggrandisement, by building up the German navy". It was on that note that he closed his address on 24 April, 1907.

Section (v): **Effects of Short Time and Unemployment**

The picture became even more gloomy as depression, short time and unemployment mounted. Employers demanded wage cuts: 6,000 were affected on the Clyde by a shipbuilding lockout. Another industry to suffer intensely was textiles: strikes about low pay at the Newburgh Lino and Floorcloth Printing works and also away over in the Dundee Bleachfield were both defeated after a long struggle. The Bleachfield workers lived in tied houses and their employers took proceedings to evict them. Such conditions added to the force of the arguments and evidence given by John Howden, Carpenters, who at last, through the STUC's efforts, had been accepted on the House-Letting Inquiry Committee. It was also a factor in the startling evidence given by Robert Smillie and others to the Truck Inquiry Committee, as applying not only to miners but also railwaymen and iron workers. The crying need especially in Scotland for good cheap housing in which working families could be independent was being shouted loud and clear to the Liberal Government and the Labour Party group in the House.[5] The unemployment also caused renewed concern about the need for an early non-contributory pension scheme and for shorter hours. Delegates from Aberdeen and Glasgow wanted 55 years as retirement age, which was carried 89 to 4, the Glasgow Shop Assistant, B H Shaw arguing that:

> It was notorious that the speeding up of industry in most trades during recent years had been such that men were too old at 45.

On the legislation for the long-delayed eight-hour day for miners, the PC sent out circulars for pressure and a questionnaire to which only 16 Scottish MPs replied favourably.

A further unhappy consequence of the depression was the increasing number of disputes within the movement. The trouble between the Patternmakers and the Joiners in the Fairfield Shipyard continued despite the PC subcommittee efforts under Smillie. The Boot & Shoe

Union was in dispute with St Cuthbert's Co-operative Society about the excessive number of boys to men employed.

At the Edinburgh Congress in 1908, a fraternal delegate made a first appearance from Canada, but the Irish TUC could still not afford to send a delegate. However, an Irishman's voice was heard: this was a remarkable contribution in the debate on secular education in all state-aided schools. For and against having been moved by the usual parties, there came a speech reported virtually verbatim – which in itself was unique – and at very considerable length from a Glasgow delegate of a newly affiliated union, the Postmen's Federation. John Gillespie was clearly a member of John Wheatley's newly formed Catholic Socialist Society. He made a devastating attack on clericalism that was rampant, which was his reason for supporting secular education. He quoted Michael Davitt, "whose fervent Catholicism and robust Nationalism have never been questioned" as being

> a most strenuous supporter of the Secular solution of our educational difficulties.

Those opposing the motion because they were Catholics were in his opinion "fighting for the retention of clerical control and nothing else. Religion is not at stake at all. Religion is here but a shield used to divert blows of an advancing democracy from one of the last bulwarks of Toryism and reaction." After he had given a number of examples of how clericalism worked, the vote was taken, resulting in secular education being carried by 85 to 13, a record vote.

Less than three weeks after Congress, Winston Churchill won a seat in Dundee for the Liberal Party, which he was to hold for fourteen years, although he changed parties yet again; against him Congress had sent good wishes to the Labour candidate, who was third, a Prohibitionist with a substantial vote behind him in that hard-drinking city. From further north there came a clear indication of dissatisfaction and doubt of STUC progress. David Palmer, who had just been elected to the PC, was spokesman for a motion from Aberdeen Trades Council, virtually calling for the dissolution of the STUC. He believed only "a central organisation, giving local autonomy and powers to each particular district could be effective". The motion itself declared that for Congress merely to deputise Ministers and lobby MPs was "not only expensive, but is obsolete and should be abolished"; it had become "an effete institution". This corresponded exactly to the kind of treatment they had been getting from the Liberal Home Secretary, Herbert Gladstone; they were also about to be told by Labour's General Secretary, Ramsay MacDonald, that it "would not be convenient" to meet them. Palmer's motion was opposed by Joseph Williamson of the Musicians' Union and the Shop Assistant, B H Shaw of Glasgow Trades Council. There was a confused vote, one of 52-51 in favour, being increased on a recount to 58 to 50. It was a portent, and they were moving into what was to be described as a state of bad trade and unemployment "unparalleled in fifty years", with industry in "a deplorable condition". That was the report of the PC in the spring of 1909 to Congress at Dunfermline. While the PC's Report explained that they had decided to do nothing on the demand for total reorganisation, it was clear that all delegates were very conscious that the STUC was being treated with contempt south of the border, not only by Ministries, but also by the Labour Party, British TUC and leaders of the big imperial unions. How to deal with that position was unclear to many; but it was not perhaps surprising that an extreme view concentrating on criticism of the STUC itself came from the under-represented north-east. Year after year Glasgow and the west of Scotland had more representatives on the PC than the rest of the country put together. Indeed, during the key period not only was George Carson Secretary but John Howden joined him as Chairman on both bodies. There were also the PC and the Glasgow Trades Council; often three or four other prominent trades councilmen on the PC with them; Edinburgh, Aberdeen and Dundee would normally only have one representative each. It was not until 1914 that George Carson ceased to be Secretary of both organisations. The Glasgow Trades Council was also especially concerned with City politics, where there were more than a dozen Labour members, while George Carson himself was to win the Maryhill seat in 1910.

With growing unemployment the central issue, Glasgow Trades Council had been organising many mass meetings and also urging support for those of the Right to Work Committees. In all of them, Carson, Alex Turner, James Walker and Emanuel Shinwell from the Trades Council had been in the lead. It was they who manned deputations on behalf of the Trades Council to the Corporation when unemployed meetings had been broken up. In December 1908 when the PC decided to be represented at a massive two-day conference in London by the Right to Work National Council, it was by Carson and Gavin, both fresh from their Trades Council activities, who were instructed to attend on behalf of the STUC. The conference included 320 people from 188 organisations of all kinds and from all parts. Throughout Scotland elsewhere the effect of unemployment had had other consequences. At Congress fewer delegates in 1909 represented fewer members; demarcation disputes continued; and there was a noticeable increase in emigration. This was referred to in the fraternal address from W A Trotter of the Trades and Labour Congress of Canada. "Emigration was no solution," he said, and protested at "the emigration operations of the Salvation Army".

In the past half dozen years, the number of miners at Congress had increased very greatly and now far outnumbered all other delegations in 1909, accounting for nearly a third of the total; Smillie was no longer their representative on the PC being replaced by William Adamson of Fife. An indication of major action ahead was already in the air when they moved a resolution that the present time was "opportune" for the Government immediately to nationalise all mines and minerals. With 5,000 accidents a year and 1,400 men "annually carried out of the mines dead or dying", said William Gallacher of the Lanarkshire County Union,

> the conditions under which the miners laboured, after years of legislation, were still a disgrace to the State.

The average wage was only 25s. The Hamilton seconder described conditions in Fifeshire, where the Wemyss Coal Company possessed

> everything above and below the ground there, and had therefore complete control of the men body and soul.

Others demanded the right to post notices and to hold meetings at the pitbank; a third demanded legislation to prevent employers from evicting workmen and their families during trade disputes. A watchful eye was also being kept on the railway companies' practice of "engaging to run special trains to certain sidings adjacent to their system, well knowing that a trade dispute is existing in the locality". Clearly some were already aware that the coming unrest meant major action ahead, which the other side were already preparing for.

References

[1] The first motion was defeated: for 174 against 203 absent 288; of the Scottish MPs – 19 were for; 22 against and 31 absent.

[2] (1) Trade Unions and Trades Disputes Bill; (2) Mines Regulation Act; (3) Miners' Eight-Hours Day Bill; (4) Employers' Liability Act; (5) Education Act; (6) Fatal Accidents Inquiry (Scotland) Act; (7) Factory & Workshops Act; (8) Old Age Pensions; (9) Workmen's Compensation Act. It set out detailed amendments to the existing inadequate laws, and basic argument about proposed Bills.

[3] 28 February, 1906, John Burns, originally leader of the new trade unionism and member of the SDF, was now an official Liberal, and regarded by many as a renegade.

[4] The receipt came from Theodore Rothstein, 51 Thistlewait Road, Clapton, London, and was addressed to Robert Small, Lanarkshire – "Dear Comrade, Thanks very much for your letter, and the sum of £4.9s.6d. collected among the members of the

STUC. It is a handsome demonstration of International solidarity which will, no doubt, be highly appreciated by our fellow-workers of Russia. . . . I will transmit the money to St Petersburg, and you will no doubt, either directly or through me, receive an official acknowledgement from the Party. Fraternally Yours."

[5] The percentage of population living more than four to a room was quoted by a Glasgow TC delegate during a debate on state maintenance of children: Pollokshaws and Clydebank 18%; Johnstone and Hamilton 20%; Motherwell 21%; Airdrie 22%; Coatbridge 24%; and Wishaw 27%.

5

Industrial Warfare Breaks Out

In its first years the Scottish Trades Union Congress had provided encouragement and a rallying point to grass-roots activists, resistance and demand for fundamental changes in the life and conditions of Scottish working people. It had ignored neither the hard-pressed skilled crafts nor the shifting masses of labouring men and women. It had attempted to respond to the problems both of the craftsmen being driven to plan to emigrate and also of workers lacking modern skills who were forced to migrate into industrial centres of Scotland from areas even harder hit by the economic troubles and technological changes. It had done much to resist disunity and deception when Great Britain's imperial forces had come so close to defeat in a colonial war that conscription unbelievably was on the cards: this in itself provided a basis for the immense Clydeside movement which came so early in World War I. Year in and year out, the STUC had continually tried to get specifically Scottish problems adequately dealt with at Whitehall and Westminster, regardless of whether it might not suit the current tactics of the young British Labour Party in efforts to negotiate priorities with the ruling Liberal Party. But as the first decade of the twentieth century ended with Britain's economy under severe attack, the STUC was in for a long period when its direct innovating role and independent activity was much weakened. Yet it would be wrong to regard it as having quite fallen away. Even in the most difficult times the STUC remained an open forum and important sounding board at least once a year for voices from the factory floor activists to know what was moving in the rest of Scotland. Here they could judge whether desperately needed changes were more likely to be brought about by industrial methods, by political action through Parliamentary and local government or expressed in extra-Parliamentary means. Even if that sounding board were only to be in full use once a year, nevertheless it was there. To hear its own voice is of first importance if class consciousness is to grow and be maintained. Lacking that, to be distant can mean to be separated in the face of ever more menacing and centralised forces. In Scotland's wide open and unevenly developed spaces regionalism could be a dangerous fetter on the growth of trade unionists' grasp of what was happening to them and their response to it.

Section (i): **The Whole Economy Under Challenge**

For the essential objective factor in these times, long incredible to many older hands, was that the economy of the whole of Great Britain was now under serious challenges: "the workshop of the world" and the monopoly of trade and raw materials which its worldwide empire had won was now under pressure from vast forces from without. Smaller employers, of whom there were so many in Scotland, were ruined or forced to merge: one effect was what Professor W H Marwick describes as a "virtual economic unification of England and Scotland".[1] Thenceforth for a number of years, therefore, we tend to get from the STUC's Annual Congress frank expression of what was general to Great Britain, often expressed more bluntly than was usual in the south. This Scottish view of the general picture is therefore useful before we look for the particular new consequences for Scotland's people. Soon the signs began to build up of what lay ahead. James Gavin of the Iron and Steel Workers told the Edinburgh Congress as early as 1908 that "the trade boom has collapsed". In shipbuilding "it looks as if there is a crisis ahead", which would affect 6,000 on the Clyde. The consequences of unemployment were "increasing daily". He concluded:

> If the number of the unemployed got beyond a certain limit, and that through cold, hunger and destitution men are goaded to take action on their own behalf, the Government may then wake up to find that society is in imminent danger.

He stressed that "the wage earners are in no way responsible for the revolution in the method of production and distribution", nor for the consequences of "the competitive world of commerce". He was especially aware of the need for a minimum wage in the sweated trades. It was "a point very often overlooked by the larger and wealthier societies, and by a great many trades unionists (so-called)". He warned against them accepting with complacency "at one end of the industrial ladder the wealthy and strong trade union and at the other end – chaos".

> The Parliamentary Committee's Report to the Congress stated: The Wealthy and employing classes are getting thoroughly alarmed and their strongest opposition is now being offered to every proposal calculated to promote the interest of our class.

It was added too that:

> a certain section of politicians are endeavouring in a most insidious manner to side-track our movement on questions of no real importance to the workers, their purpose being to destroy our solidarity.

This was, in part, a reaction to the long campaign by the Walthamstow railway porter, W V Osborne, to prevent union funds being used to finance political action. With highly dubious financial support this employee of the most reactionary employers of all, the railway companies which barred trade union recognition, was able to get his own way after seven years. It took another three years before the movement succeeded at the height of the "great unrest" in forcing the Liberal Government to bring in legislation to reverse it, by providing the right for the indivdual merely to "contract out" of paying the levy to Labour Party funds, instead of a total ban. It was one of many similar ploys which reactionary governments yearned for in after years.

Nothing had improved by the 1909 Congress at Dunfermline, to which the Parliamentary Committee reported that the year's depression had been without a parallel "during the past 50 years. Trade in every department has been in the most deplorable condition." All employees began to be subjected to unprecedented clamp-down; the trade unions were under much pressure, their membership and funds already hit by unemployment which soared together with prices. The "economic unification" called for country-wide responses. These included acceptance centrally of the Right to Work Movement organising the unemployed, originally the creation of the trades councils, especially in Scotland. Another country-wide concern was the Food Supply Conference held in London about the growing dependence on imported foods. Whilst far from giving a hearing to Socialists of varying viewpoints, which had been a matter of course at the STUC since its foundation, they were becoming clear that something fundamental had to be done. Whatever the individual political opinions of the English-based trade union leaders, the immense unrest forced action upon even them to urge the Parliamentary Labour Party to put great pressure on the Liberal Government for specific reforms. This obliged the Liberal Government to introduce some degree of change in many directions.

Lloyd George brought in a Budget which roused the fury of the upper classes to such a pitch that the House of Lords intervened to throw it out; this led to two General Elections within a year – one to meet their veto and the other to introduce questions of reforming the House of Lords and its powers. The comment by J C Hendry of the Scottish Mill and Factory Workers to the Kilmarnock Scottish TUC in 1910 was that it was

> almost necessary to go back to the time when the "Divine Martyr" lost his head in front of Whitehall for attempting to arrogate powers not one whit more extravagant than those sought by certain gentlemen, whose only ground of claim, as in Charles's case, is that they are their fathers' sons.

Their use of the veto was part of a "melancholy record of opposition, mutilation and maltreatment of measures demanded by the Democracy". The Scottish University Students cheekily added a new verse to the folk song entitled "When Joan's Ale Was New":

> The next to come in was a dyer,
> As proud as any squire.
> He said the House of Lords he'd disgrace,
> And the Crown should have bottom place,
> And the top for the dirtiest hands and face . . .

The need was becoming desperate for pensions and what in later years became known as social security benefits to deal with poverty and the effects of unemployment with which even the richer unions' funds could no longer cope. Not least important was this in Scotland. The Scottish Operative Masons in the past, for example, had provided considerable grants for funeral allowances, tramping and strike relief, sick, accident, superannuation and idle benefit, as well as for assistance to emigrate. Legislative measures at this time therefore were brought in, following Poor Law Reports, to provide a 5s. old age pension, contributory sickness and unemployed benefit; and Labour Exchanges introduced for the first time. Such legislation as the National Insurance Act, 1911, was seen as inevitable, however ill-thought-out and toothless its administration proved. Under it the trade unions were to pay out sickness benefit, for example, and for this they were reimbursed; it helped to pay salaries for branch officials. For some of the unions the changes

Parliamentary Committee of the STUC elected 1912.

R. Allan *(3rd back row)*, W. Allan *(1st front row)*, R. Climie *(6th front row)*, G. Carson *(2nd front row)*, P. Gilmour, J. Hendry, Kate McLean *(2nd back row)*, H. Murdoch, J. O'Connor Kessack, D. Palmer and A. Turner.

involved complicated rules revision, which kept their officials busy for a long time; this brought special problems for the smaller unions, and added to the trend for amalgamation. In Scotland throughout this period there was confusion over the relative roles of the STUC and the Scottish Labour Party (as the Scottish Workers Parliamentary (Elections) Committee was now called) in responding to the flood of legislation. It had been constantly in difficulty with the British Labour Party, to which Ramsay MacDonald, although an emigré Scot, sought to insist that Scottish trade unions should affiliate rather than to its Scottish equivalent. However, this Scottish Labour Party actually disbanded shortly before the 1910 General Election which had resulted in 42 Labour MPs at Westminster; from Scotland only the miner Willie Adamson was added to the two moderate trade union leaders, Alexander Wilkie of the Shipwrights and George Barnes of the Engineers. The PC had been active, however, by putting comprehensive questionnaires to all Scottish candidates. Until the Scottish Advisory Council of the British LP was finally set up in 1913 it left political questions involving Scottish industry and social questions to be taken up at Westminister only by the already weakened and disregarded STUC. Winston Churchill, then the Liberal Home Secretary, seized on such an opportunity to refuse to see deputations from the STUC on the ground that he had all he needed from the British TUC and Labour Party nationally.

Section (ii): **Clashing with Winston Churchill**

At the Dundee Congress, in 1911, there was particularly strong feeling against Churchill, who only a short time before had moved troops to be ready to assist the Cambrian Combine in its lockout of Welsh miners; two of them died in the clashes at Tonypandy with the Home Secretary refusing a public enquiry into the police batoning. A delegation of Welsh miners was welcomed and supported at Congress, and in his presidential address, James Brown of the Ayrshire miners referred with bitterness to the Government attitude in what he described as a "tragic and saddening year". There had been, he continued,

> horrible railway accidents and appalling mine accidents. There have been fierce and bitter strikes, an unjustifiable lockout, backed by the brutal force of the power of the purse and of class influence which a few years ago were undreamt of.

He was afraid that they had long acquiesced in the theory "that in trade disputes the workers have no rights, but that the power of capital should be paramount; that our police force and military force exist exclusively for the capitalist and landowning classes". He thought it said much for

> the restraint of the British working class that they are not roused to fury by the treatment they receive from the authorities during almost every labour dispute.

Delegates had a number of local Scottish struggles in mind. Among them were the long-standing dispute of the lead miners in Weardale Valley; the 600 miners in Kilwinning who were refused arbitration after three months; the long dispute of the Edinburgh typographers when sweated female labour was introduced for skilled work; and the lockout following the boilermakers' dispute at Partick. Delegates were meeting after many local actions taken by the carters for a "restricted darg", and in particular for special payment for Sunday working or day off in lieu. These were particularly remarkable amongst the "railway carters" employed by the special contractors to the railway companies. This linked with a similar demand from railway clerks on the North British Railway, which had refused even to discuss a memorandum from them for several years.

The Great North of Scotland Railway Company had forbidden its employees to take part in any form of "public speaking, heckling or canvassing". Eviction from company-owned houses during disputes was still continuing, and the threat of it had just ended a strike in Dundee. There were also cases of legal action under the Conspiracy Act against picketers, notably against the Edinburgh Coopers in their long strike.

It was not surprising, therefore, that when Churchill refused to receive an STUC deputation on the grounds that "all the principal unions comprising the Scottish Congress" were affiliated to the British TUC, which represented "the whole of the United Kingdom, not merely England and Wales", there was considerable feeling. A resolution was fully discussed which "strongly resented" Churchill's attitude, and emphasised that

> the STUC is the body empowered to act on behalf of the trades union movement in Scotland.

It was carried with one dissentient, the Miners' delegates thinking it unnecessary after the British TUC had been received. The remaining speakers came equally from Scottish unions and English-based unions. All were very much aware that Churchill represented a Scottish constituency as a Liberal, and it was not surprising that delegates should speak strongly from the Jute and Flax Union, the Mill and Factory Workers and the Calender Workers' Union, all with many members in Churchill's own patch. Delegates from the English-based unions, like the Shop Assistants, Municipal Employees and the Clerks were not far behind. But it took a Gasworkers and General Labourers' officer from Sunderland at Congress to make a point which might perhaps be wryly remembered by Churchill in later years, when for the second time he changed his political party allegiance. Councillor William Sherwood said:

> Mr Churchill had no right to represent the working classes. He was as much a Tory today as he was when he was Tory Member for Oldham.

In closing his presidential address, that spring, James Brown noted that "the desirability of federation and amalgamation is beginning to be discussed among the workers. Seeing kindred industries drawing more closely together, with workers realising that the interests of one were the interests of all, makes what looked hopeless yesterday the desire and expectations of today." Within a very short time of that Congress the Sailors and Firemen and those around the docks, uniting in the National Transport Workers Federation, an amalgamation on industrial lines proposed by Tom Mann, were in full action. The ports of Glasgow and Dundee were strike-bound as throughout the whole of Britain; the key blows were being struck in Liverpool, with Churchill's Government sending warships to attempt to cow the dockers on Merseyside, as they were to do three years later in Leith.

Section (iii): **Retreating Ends**

No retreat was possible any longer. Looking back during the spring of 1912, the President of the Congress at Glasgow, David Palmer of Aberdeen Trades Council, described the year as "momentous". It had "been marked by industrial warfare – warfare which has demonstrated with outstanding clearness a splendid spirit of solidarity amongst the workers. The spirit of revolt amongst the so-called unskilled workers against degrading and brutalising conditions indicate great possibilities of future progress, if the opportunities are wisely and cautiously used". The delegates read in the PC's Annual Report details of "the great unrest". Nearly all sections had taken part in what

> practically amounted to a revolt against conditions under which they have had to live and labour in the past.

After the Sailors and Firemen's action

> the Railway Servants were the advance guard . . . . The Sailors, Firemen, Stewards, Cooks etc have also taken their share in the work; so also have the Dock Labourers . . . . The miners of the country have just ended what has been the greatest strike that has ever taken place in the country for the establishment of a minimum wage.

Palmer described the miners' as "one of the greatest industrial struggles that the world has witnessed". He concluded that "the structure of modern society is tottering; it has reached the stage of decadence. It has played its part in social evolution and must perish, as all social systems have done when found economically unfit to survive."

Section (iv): **The Drive From Below**

There were two features of this formative period which are often overlooked. They are indeed significant and although general were perhaps nowhere more important than in Scotland. Firstly, the drive into action surged up from below; secondly, and related to it, there was very considerable spontaneous support whenever other industries took action, officially or unofficially. Over and over again there was a purely local and sporadic movement in trade after trade. With the centralised leadership in the far south so close to the corridors of power slow and often reluctant to act, many locally despaired of waiting and started on their own, sometimes even dropping into temporary breakaways, just when the widely recognised needs for amalgamations were being put slowly into effect, with ponderous organisational consultations. In Scotland this was soon particularly noticeable amongst the transport workers. The seamen and dockers were indeed busy and gained successes locally in Aberdeen, Dundee, Leith and Glasgow, while everywhere the carters – with the motormen already beginning to appear – were raising the key issue of their restricted darg, payment for Sunday work or time off in lieu. The local small contractors were unable to hold out for long when the carters began to take their own time in leaving and returning to stables. Moreover, they could not but be in close contact with the dockers, whose mood they shared. Above all, when the carters used the same methods against the two all-powerful road contractors to the railways in Scotland, the railway grades also became closely affected. Moreover, the miners could not fail to understand the carters' case; for they had their own demand for a restricted darg; this was for shorter hours and a minimum wage, as colliery owners refused to pay when the men's output and earnings were reduced by having to work in abnormal places. That was to provoke finally the long delayed miners' unprecedented strike.

The spontaneous and finally official movement in all forms of transport was to make that inevitable. But, meanwhile, as the railwaymen's historian, Philip Bagwell, points out:

> That the pot boiled over on the railways in August, 1911, was largely due to the fact that it had first boiled over on the docks . . . . the railwaymen, particularly those serving in port areas, were inevitably drawn into these struggles.

He stresses that "in an ever-increasing number of centres the men were taking the law into their own hands and coming out on strike without waiting for authorisation from union executives". Certainly in Scotland the railwaymen were already and quickly moving against the North British Railway without awaiting London's call. While the dockers and seamen helped the railwaymen in some places the miners did so too, by refusing to allow coal to be shifted where there was local action, so when the miners were in movement the transport workers also gave spontaneous help to them. The carters, although only a small union, was local and reachable. Moreover, their General Secretary, Hugh Lyon, who had been on the STUC's PC when it all began in 1910, had introduced the shrewd method of house collection of the dues of these itinerant workers, and when it came to paying out strike benefit it was paid at the home, direct to the wives. Not only did this restrict weakness from lack of understanding in the family, it must have been one of the special factors in Scotland influencing the attitudes in other working families where the breadwinners decided on local acts of defiance.

Another factor might well have been the long-standing demand that both the established Church of Scotland and the United Free Church should adopt a fair wage clause in their building contracts. It was not possible for this not to have become known to and influence the thinking of the women folk and families for years before the industrial warfare actually broke out. It was, in fact, an extension of the fair wages clause, to be inserted in any contract put out by local councils or for Government Departments' subcontracting. The Churches had called for "an active crusade against social evils". In the spring of 1908, Walter Bell from the Edinburgh Trades Council got a resolution carried unanimously for the PC to approach the General Assembly of such bodies. This was repeated over and over again, with the Assemblies refusing any deputation from the PC on the ground that it was solely a matter for the local congregations. Two years later the STUC circularised all trades councils in Scotland urging them to bring pressure to bear on the local church bodies. The effect of this on the congregations and finally on the employers in building and consumption trades must have been marked. It certainly squared too with actions against long hours, Sunday and sweated trading. Speaking less than three months before the Executives of the Railway Unions in London found themselves bound to intervene if their authority was not to be undermined, James Brown in Dundee was telling the delegates of 44 unions and six trades councils:

> I wonder if it were possible to cover not only our pulpits, but the walls of our churches and chapels with the shirts made at from 9d. to 1/3d a dozen, whether such devilish tapestry would waken us all to a sense of responsibility. And if in these same garments we could see the tears, and heartbreak, and misery, and degradation that went to the making of them, I am sure that everyone of us would swear by all we hold sacred and dear that sweating would cease.

How was sweating to be abolished, evictions to be prevented, better housing conditions got, "our children insured against hunger and nakedness?" He answered very much in the spirit moving the Scottish grass roots:

> When we have ceased to trust to the promises of any political party and have learned to trust one another . . . . when we go to the ballot box in the same way as we go into a trade dispute. When we have learned to go hand in hand, regardless of racial differences, regardless of religious differences, regardless of political differences.

Trade unionism was becoming a great political power; far from being obsolete, its day had only begun. Its leaders, he said,

> have raised their voices almost without exception, against increased armaments, against war, against oppression wherever found. They realise that not only is this feverish preparation for war an intolerable burden, but that it is a crime – against our fellow beings of whatever nationality, and a crime against ourselves.

This was far indeed from the uncertainty and doubts which were so widely expressed in Congress only a few years earlier.

Section (v): Re organisation: Causes and Problems

There were many of such self-help activities; spontaneous and reciprocal expressions of support; sympathy and financial aid going to the Dublin transport workers in their struggle with owners and police. All this emphasised the interdependence of the railways, the mines and road and sea transport. It was the solid ground base from which the great Triple Alliance could grow and was finally consummated at top level early in 1913. In the same climate there was a considerable drive towards amalgamations, mergers and industry-wide federations, seeking the greater strength which was now seen as both necessary and possible. This affected quite a number of Scottish unions; but it also had some opposite results and unforeseen effects on the role of the STUC. Whilst the trend to amalgamate could provide ways of healing demarcation disputes for which the new technology was largely responsible, it could also give rise to resistance from smaller bodies, especially amongst the older crafts, until they were forced to amalgamate through weakness. The stress on centralised administration also led to angry complaints by those far distant from the head offices that their local interests were misunderstood or neglected. That became clear over the Irish transport workers' troubles; it was also true in Scotland. There were further difficulties where general unions were recruiting in a number of occupations as against sectional unions. In Scotland not only was there the long-drawn-out dispute between the Boot and Shoe Operatives and the old Cordwainers; there was constant need for the STUC's Joint Arbitration Council with the Co-operative Wholesale Society to handle difficulties involving Co-operative Societies and unions, especially with the emergence of the Shop Assistants, the Municipal Employees' Association and the Amalgamated Union of Co-operative Employees. Some of the prominent new STUC activists were members of such unions; but they often would attend Congress rather as a delegate from a trades council; the Glasgow Municipal Employee, Councillor Alex Turner, was an outstanding example of this trend.

Indeed, activists from the new unions and amalgamations had strong motives for concentrating their strength at trades council level rather than taking it to the STUC. It was on trades councils that members of the English-based unions which had recently formed Scottish District Committees or Councils, could be represented. It was there that the expression of union policy might be modified, and their officers sometimes obstructed. That indeed became clear when the war brought the Clydeside Workers' Committee into life. Many of the great unions, such as the Amalgamated Society of Engineers, were strictly controlled by rule about local affiliations and had limited district negotiation rights. Frequently as many as four out of eleven members of the PC were elected as trades council delegates, and not as representing their union as such. In time of stress this led to fierce hostility from official quarters towards trades councils, and efforts to cut down their powers, as we shall see. On the other hand, rank and file opinion might find a quick response there easier to win than at the district or regional level of their union. In Scotland this was of practical importance because of trades councils' prominence in the STUC. It could and did sometimes mean that activists came to consider certrain trades councils as of more importance than the STUC itself.

Consequences of the groundswell and "industrial warfare" during the early years of the second decade were far-reaching and varied. On the union side it meant great pressure for and acceptance of the need for wider and more permanent organisation. Amongst the miners in pursuit of shorter hours and fairer pay in their dangerous occupation, the basis was strengthened for opposition to the coal owners' exploitation of differences between coalfields insisting on district control and district negotiations. Again, on an industrial basis, it led to the formation of an all-grades body, the National Union of Railwaymen, and the long-term co-operation with the two major craft unions in the industry. In the other forms of transport it linked dockers, seamen, road transport workers with non-craftsmen into a general union which was in time to become the biggest of all. Between these three groups was now forged the all-important Triple Alliance for defence when any should be under attack, which was to be so severely tested in the first post-war recession. However, in the centre of the all-important technological change, shipbuilding and engineering, a restless search had to continue for methods of effective consultation and co-operation; in Scotland there was some progress here amongst the small and long-standing craft unions of the iron and steel trades, reacting against premium bonus and group contracting methods. In occupations too where local employment had tended to be the rule, as with textiles and clothing, building and carting, and even to some extent in the printing industry, there were moves to organise or reorganise.

Another consequence was that there were far more frequent demands for nationalisation, public ownership and control, not least in the accident-prone industries. Each year between 1912 and 1914 resolutions were carried for public ownership of mines, railways and canals and the infirmaries and hospitals, with the mercantile marine being added in 1914. On no less than seven of these occasions the mover or seconder spoke as a Glasgow Trades Council delegate; usually it was Councillor A R Turner, Municipal Employees or Manny Shinwell, Officer of the Sailors and Firemen in Glasgow. Where legislative reform had already been forced upon the Government there was much discussion over its effects, shortcomings and improvement, together with demands for Government action in other respects. The Government's reaction in its difficulties over Irish Home Rule and the threatened mutiny of the officers of the Curragh was seen as closely linked with the use of police and military in the industrial disputes throughout the United Kingdom.

All this was reflected at the pre-war Congresses of the STUC, with the PC sometimes taking the initiative, sometimes responding to pressure at Congress to heal differences. At the Dumfries Congress in 1913, John Wallace, Carson's fellow delegate from the Tinplate and Sheet Metal Workers in Glasgow, moved a resolution calling on the PC to consider how to encourage federations and "secure the complete unity and concerted action required for protection and progressive purposes". He was supported by Falkirk Trades Council and won unanimous agreement. This plunged the PC into activity laying bare demarcation difficulties similar to that which they had had to tackle year after year.

By the time the PC made its report to the Kirkcaldy Congress in 1914, they had spent a great deal of time on the subject. They had heard cases between the Scottish Horse and Motormen and the Northern Horse Motormen; the Plumbers of Great Britain and Ireland against the Scottish Plumbers, who refused to meet the PC; the National Union of Dock Labourers against the Scottish union of the same workers. They felt obliged to abandon consideration of the differences between the Co-operative Employees and the Shop Assistants, because the British TUC was in the process of handling it, as they informed the Scottish trades councils. After inquiring from the miners they refused affiliation from the Firemen and Shot Firers' Association.

Over one dispute they had reason to criticise Glasgow Trades Council which must have caused some embarrassment to the five Glasgow members on the PC. In this case the Amalgamated Musicians Union complained that Glasgow Trades Council had admitted affiliation from the breakaway National Federation of Professional Musicians. After meeting the PC, Glasgow Trades Council insisted that the whole question should first be submitted to Congress itself. As it happened, the breakaway dissolved before Congress met; but O'Connor Kessack of the National Union of Dock Labourers moved a resolution critical of Glasgow Trades Council:

> that the PC shall be empowered to cancel the credentials of any affiliated body which flagrantly and deliberately violates the decision of this Congress with respect to breakaways and new Unions.

His fellow PC member, Councillor A R Turner, tried unsuccessfully to modify the criticism, urging there should always be due enquiry to hear the reasons for any breakaway. There were unions, he said,

> whose administration had been carried on in a careless and indifferent manner, and it was because of that careless administration that it would have a salutory effect on the organisation in which the breakaway had taken place.

The same year George Carson at last ceased to be General Secretary of the Glasgow Trades Council in addition to the STUC. Up to 1912 he had been receiving a salary from the STUC of £52; but that year it was decided to grant him an honorarium of £25 "in view of the extra work involved in the position of Secretary", and to consider "making the position such that the Secretary shall devote the whole of his time to it", with "suitable remuneration". The PC reported that the income was insufficient to allow him to be paid "for devoting his whole time", but increased his pay to £80 a year; it remained at that figure until his final retirement in 1917. While remaining delegate from the Glasgow Tinplate Workers, he then handed over to his old running mate, Robert Allan.

Section (vi): **The Scots Take Action on Sweated Trades**

There was however one organising attempt for which the STUC

worked persistently over several years and in which the PC finally intiated action. It became clear that it was important for Scotland, and not least for the Dundee area, to keep together the unions in textiles, trades which affected so many women workers. The questions of sweating and outwork conditions were, therefore, bound to be linked. From earliest days Margaret Irwin had tirelessly impressed this on delegates, quoting evidence in Scotland which she had prepared on behalf of the Scottish Council for Women's Trades; their delegates, such as the Reverend A Laughlin, kept the issue moving at Congress in the years when she was not there. In 1906 at Greenock the Scottish Operative Tailors and Tailoresses demanded a minimum wage in all clothing trades, and "that sweating be made a punishable offence". The revelations by the Council for Women's Trades of "scandalous hours worked" in laundries, of 16 and 17 hours a day and an 80-hour week, were frequently raised by the Lanarkshire Miners, themselves concerned about female labour still worked about the mines. Back for a couple of years as a delegate, Margaret Irwin supported the tailors in 1909 at Dunfermline with further details, while organising deputations to Government Departments to press for standard rates to be paid for clothing in public contracts. At that same Congress the Jute and Flax Workers sent their first woman delegate, Mary Rae, to speak on a resolution deploring "the evils existing in Indian Textile Factories", which were having such serious effects on their work in and around Dundee. The movement as a whole was also warned by a clothing trades delegate of "the growing tendency of employers in all trades to substitute underpaid women labour for men's labour". Calling for equal pay for equal work a resolution urged all women workers to organise, to put a stop to a competition unfair to "men and women alike". Indeed, within a matter of months the Edinburgh print trade found to their cost the prestigious quarters of the typographers themselves were invaded and a strike provoked.

At length the PC, on which there were serving J C Hendry of the Brechin Mill and Factory Workers and Charles Stuart of the Bleachfield Workers, both from the Dundee area, decided to call all the unions in textiles together, except the Tailors. The representatives of 14 unions therefore met on 25 February, 1911, at the STUC offices. Some of these were amongst the oldest workers' defence groups in Scotland. They were:

> Scottish Textile Federation, Glasgow; Handmill and Horizontal Workers, Glasgow; Female Weavers, Glasgow; Power-Loom Tenders, Glasgow; Power-Loom Beamers, Glasgow; Lace Workers; Dunfermline Yarn

Dressers; Dunfermline Textile Workers; Fifeshire Cloth Lappers, Dunfermline; Kirkcaldy Textile Workers; Dundee Jute Workers; Brechin Mill and Factory Workers; Aberdeen Mill and Factory Workers; Scottish Mill and Factory Workers Federation.

Amongst the absentees were the Calender Workers' Union and also the Dyers, Bleachers, Finishers. The PC's Chairman, James Brown of the Ayrshire Miners, presided. Stressing the need for textile workers to federate their many separate organisations all over Scotland, he pointed out the important advantages the miners had enjoyed since federating. The discussion showed that in textiles much levelling up of wages and conditions was needed. They finally adopted unanimously a resolution that federation was essential and fixed a further conference three months ahead at which a provisional committee could be appointed to draft a scheme.

Before this could take place, however, Congress met at Dundee, when it became apparent what expectations this had aroused in several quarters. There were no less than six women amongst the 132 delegates. They included Jeannie Spence and Rachel Devine of the Jute and Flax Workers' Union of Dundee, and for the first time four representatives from the National Federation of Women Workers, including their national leader, Mary Macarthur.

With her were Mrs Lamont of Edinburgh, Agnes Brown of Glasgow and also Kate McLean; she moved a resolution calling for the Truck Act to be amended to make all fines and deductions from wages illegal. She was also elected near the top of the list to the PC, remaining an active delegate until she married a Dunfermline miner. At that 1911 Congress, delegates from the sectional textiles bodies spoke no less than sixteen times on eleven resolutions of various kinds. A month later on 25 May, 1911, they met again and set up a provisional committee to draft a scheme, which was accepted by most of the sections; and they set up the Scottish National Textiles Federation. The Jute and Flax Workers, and the Calender and Dye Workers of Dundee remained aloof, nor did the Scots mesh in with the Amalgamated Society of Dyers, Bleachers and Kindred Trades.

At least some considerable progress had been made; and thenceforward the STUC was never without women delegates; the occupation of the majority of women remained for a long time in textiles. Although it took the Textile Federation a long time to grow and gain confidence, it was clear that the women on the factory floor were much encouraged. In the spring of 1913 the net weavers in Kilbirnie stood up to all the firms there demanding better prices. Kate MacLean spoke for them at the Dumfries Congress, where delegates promised "to do all in their power, financially and morally" to support them. Later the new Textiles Federation tried to negotiate terms unsuccessfully with the many local net weaver employers, and finally asked the PC to intervene. They succeeded in getting a breakthrough with one firm first, and finally the several hundred women won a victory with an average increase of no less than 1s. 6d. a week. The report to the 1914 Congress states their victory

> was largely due to the splendid financial support they received from the trades unionists all over the country.

It was indeed an achievement.

The rights of women when at work had always taken precedence at the STUC over equality in other respects. No separate issue was raised about women's suffrage, because "the extension of the franchise to all adults, male and female" was the first in a seven-point programme for electoral reform repeated year after year. But the number of women holding positions in the trades unions themselves remained abysmally low; it was not until after the 1914-18 war that a woman first appeared even as a delegate for a trades council. Yet the need for due representation of women on other bodies was often stressed when the Government or Secretary of State for Scotland set up committees and inquiries. It had been regarded as remarkable when in the early days Margaret Irwin had always been a prominent member of deputations to Whitehall and Westminster.

Section (vii): **Acting on the Reforms Won**

The PC began resuming deputations especially in connection with the legislative reforms the Government had been obliged to take to stem "the industrial warfare" in 1911 and 1912. Foremost was the National Insurance Act, one of the "surprising legislative enactments", the PC reported to the 1912 Congress, which the Government had introduced "without any particular demand on the part of the trades unions of the country" for it. Soon they issued circulars to all trades councils and trades unions in Scotland, with their explanation and doubts, and also to the Scottish MPs and the Labour Party. After it had become law they called a conference in Glasgow, attended by 300 delegates from 102 bodies, on 6 January,

1912, at which Scotland's three Labour Party MPs spoke and answered questions. They explained objections both on the unemployment section and the sick benefits, of what they described as "the germs of a national medical service". Whilst they were far from totally rejecting it they stressed heavily the problems it raised for unions becoming approved societies. A month later the PC met in Edinburgh on 12 February, 1912, with members of the National Health Commission; and in view of the many questions that were raised one of these Commissioners before the year was out had to attend to answer questions from another national conference. This was Miss Mary Paterson who dealt with a section on workmen's compensation as being "of enormous importance to the workers". She said that during 1911 in Scotland there had been 50,000 accidents at work reported. There had been 9,000 registered settlements, mostly with the help of trade unions; but in the less well-organised trades which employed women and casual workers there were occasions when:

> there was simply a little pressure brought to bear on the workers to take something down, and very often this had worked out very badly.

When the meeting went on to discuss the Health Section, there were delegates who bitterly attacked the doctors, some referring to them as "despotic" and displaying "extraordinary greed" for objecting to low fees for attending panel patients. Robert Smillie,who had just been appointed chairman of the British Miners' Federation, defended the doctors in their "first attempt at trade unionism" for the profession; but he said delegates' aims should be to establish a non-contributory State Medical Service

> under which any person, poor or rich, could claim medical attention when he required it.

This was not the only special conference called by the PC at this period.

The state of housing in Scotland which for so long had caused very considerable anxiety led to determination to see that the Royal Commission on Housing should be well informed. The PC, therefore, called a conference on 27 September, 1913, to consider what evidence ought to be submitted. This brought representatives from two miners county unions; Natsopa; the Ironmoulders; and the Aberdeen, Edinburgh, Glasgow, Rutherglen, Motherwell, Stirling and Wishaw Trades Councils. It was presided over by Baillie Robert

Climie, himself from Ayrshire. The one point on which they were totally agreed was that no future housing should be on the tenement basis. They returned for further discussion on 11 October, 1913, and decided on some minimum requirements. The PC itself submitted detailed claims, with supporting facts. These included the point that in all the major Scottish cities "over 50 per cent of the occupied dwelling houses are houses of one and two rooms". To the Kirkcaldy Congress in the spring of 1914 there was a full report of a deputation to the Secretary of State for Scotland at the House of Commons on 17 February, 1914, on the House Letting and Rating (Scotland) Act. The facts given about how property owners in Glasgow had used the compounding of rates and rents under it to impose big increases, provoking big indignation meetings, was fair warning of what was soon to come when the housewives got going. The same day the Scottish TUC's four officers sought a meeting with the Scottish MPs in Westminster to complain that once again the Home Secretary, now Reginald McKenna, had refused to receive them on the usual ground that in his view they were fully represented when he received the British TUC; but the twenty Scottish MPs who listened to them then arranged for McKenna to receive them. Amongst the points raised with him by both the Scottish Dock Labourers' spokesman, Joe Houghton, and his opposite number, O'Connor Kessack of the Dock Labourers and Riverside Workers, was about the appalling dangers for the 16,000 Scottish dockers. He was also told of the workmen's compensation problems of the trawling fishermen, as well as the need for compulsory weighing in the iron and steel trades, first raised with his predecessor as long ago as 1889. The next day John Burns at the Board of Trade had to listen to the dangers seamen faced through bad loading and sanitation, told in graphic detail by O'Connor Kessack and Peter Cairns of the Ship's Stewards, Cooks, Butchers and Bakers. Both were to speak at Congress two months later, with Kessack insisting on the need for escape openings in all ships' bunkers for the coal trimmers. Four months afterwards when the war broke out, these dangers and the regulations they condemned for altering the level of the Plimsoll Line, were to mean life and death.

Section (viii): **The Government Resorts to Force**

It had not been only what they felt to be Whitehall's neglect or indifference to their many harassing problems which angered Scottish trade unionists. It was the experience there as elsewhere of the oppressive use of police and military measures against the movement. More than seventy years before miners throughout Britain in the nationalised coal industry were to learn what they would face from Tory Government forces there were scandalous cases of interference with pickets at Scottish mines. The PC raised sharp protests in deputation after deputation. At a strike at Dumfries in 1912 four miners on picket duty were arrested and sentenced to thirty days; during the trial the constable when cross-examined said he had "been instructed to prevent picketing". Smillie also told the Kirkcaldy Congress how Kirkconnel miners while only on their way to the collieries for picket duty "were attacked by an organised mass of armed and drilled men and unmercifully beaten". They too were imprisoned. John Robertson of the Glasgow Typographers, warned delegates against "the enrolment of Special Constables for service during trade disputes", which he said was tending

> to cause riot and bloodshed rather than prevent it, at the same time prejudicing the cause of the workers.

Robert Stirton, JP, got unanimous support after telling Congress that employers around Dundee were "using the weapon of eviction during trade disputes against their workmen and their families". Every kind of excuse was given by him when it was raised with the Lord Advocate by the deputation from the PC as to why the Scots law allowing this to happen could not be changed immediately.

Some months earlier an "open letter" had been written by a Liverpool building worker and published in *The Irish Worker* calling on British soldiers not to fire on their working brothers. In the aftermath of the railway strike, a footplateman from the London & North Western Railway had reproduced it as a leaflet, travelled to Aldershot and distributed it to soldiers in the camp there. He was sent to prison; and when it was reprinted in *The Syndicalist* the editor and printers were also gaoled. In protest against this when the miners' strike began a month later and troops were drafted into mining areas, the engineers' leader, Tom Mann, read it out at meetings. It was not long before he was given a prison sentence of six months, which brought the whole issue well into the open.

The STUC sent two past presidents, James Brown of the Ayrshire Miners and Councillor Alex Turner as fraternal delegates to Cork in 1913; and next Congress received a deputation from Dublin Trades Council who described the hardship caused by the lockout of Dublin transport workers and their vicious treatment. As a result an appeal circular was sent out and an amazingly large sum was collected.[2]

The feelings delegates expressed in May 1914 were strong indeed. Two resolutions which were both unanimously adopted were in fact moved on the first of May 1914. O'Connor Kessack called for strong condemnation of

> the importation of vast numbers of police and the armed forces of the nation into strike areas, believing their presence to be a menace to the peace, and also unwarrantable and unjustifiable use of national forces in the interests of the monied classes of the community.

He described how two cruisers had been stationed in the Firth of Forth to intimidate the workers recently on strike at Leith. After referring to the attitude of the army officers in Ireland, he went on to remind them how during the railwaymen's strike

> Mr Churchill, the autocrat, was organising a huge army for the purpose of conducting railway business and intimidating, crushing and shooting down railwaymen.

If national forces were to be used in that way, the only alternative was "to organise forces to meet the forces opposed to them". Baillie Tom McKerrell of the miners, noting that the trend of the times was "settling Labour disputes by legislation on Government's intervention", said that political action was needed to supplement industrial action; for if left "under the control of the men whom they were fighting against, all the forces of Government would be used on behalf of that class". The only remedy was for working people

> to secure control of the Government, the Army and the police, and that could only be done by using political action as well as trade union action.

This indeed had been a major theme of the hard-hitting Presidential Address by Baillie Robert Climie, of Ayrshire Trades Council. Noting the recent announcement foreshadowing the Triple Alliance, he welcomed "with the greatest delight" the tendency to "come together in larger unions, making common cause against their common enemy". They were making gradually towards the goal of "demanding the full product of their labour". His twenty years' experience in the Labour Movement had taught him that

> the creation of a strong Miners' Federation and a strong Railwaymen's Union has done more for the miners and the railway

> workers in the United Kingdom in the way of bettering their conditions of labour than all the promises of party politicians for the past 65 years.

But he recognised that trade union effort alone made no attempt to solve all questions. They had just recently had "a most salutary lesson" about the need to combine both political and trade union effort from South Africa. He was referring to the deportation thence of trade unionists by a South African Government, acting "for the financiers of the Rand" aiming to smash the Federation of Trades. STUC made their protest in defence of the nine deportees, and indeed within a couple of years were to have their own Scottish deportees from Clydeside.

Climie closed his Presidential Address, thirteen weeks before World War I was to break out, with a section entitled "Army Versus the People", with what he saw as "the absolute necessity of strengthening our direct labour forces" at Westminster. He pointed first to what was to be learnt from the situation in Ireland.

> The officers of the Dragoons and Lancers in the Curragh gave an object lesson of class bias and privilege. If these gentlemen had been called upon to move during an industrial dispute can we doubt but that they would have instantly obeyed the order.

He could not forget past experience that the armed forces of the Crown did "not object to shoot and murder on the slightest provocation". Delegates knew there was

> no hesitation on the part of the officers to range themselves alongside the employers and shoot, if necessary, men who are only seeking to secure a somewhat better share of the wealth they help to create.

He quoted the gunboats used at Leith. He could have sympathy with a soldier objecting to being "used by the Government to shoot down his own kith and kin". But when soldiers did not hesitate to shoot in an industrial dispute, "it is time the workers of the country were reconsidering their position". He declared, "in the name of the organised workers in Scotland", that they claimed equality before the law. Then he said, referring again to the Irish army officers:

> if one section of the community can be allowed to arm and drill themselves with the avowed intention of resisting the deliberate opinion of the majority in the House of Commons, then objection

> cannot be taken if another section of the community seek to gain their ends by drilling and arming themselves with a veiw of being in a position to meet an armed force sent out to break up their ranks and force them to capitulate to employers.

The safest and surest method, however, was "to capture control of the armed forces of the Crown and to capture the control of the House of Commons". While they remained content to allow "employers, army officers, and retired naval officers to represent us in Parliament", for just so long they would "have to contend against the brutality of the police and the bullets of our soldiers in our industrial disputes". He had no doubt "that the propertied class will fight to the last ditch". To him "the determination of the privileged class to continue their domination of the workers" was proved by

> their action in the last big railway strike when they sent an army of men to intimidate the strikers; in Dublin, when they used the police to batter out the lives of men, women and children and where they have 1,500 walking the streets at the present moment unemployed; in Leith, where they sent gunboats down to coerce the strikers, and their latest move in the Curragh, when the army officers sought to lay down terms to the Government . . . .

He ended by saying "we are fighting for justice, fighting for that time

> When the war drums beat no longer,
> And the battle flag is furled,
> In the Parliament of Man,
> The Federation of the World".

Scotland was drawn into the Great War only four months later, some 150 years after the ruler of an immense empire had said:

> The only way to save our empires from the encroachment of the people is to engage in war, and thus substitute national passions for social aspirations.

But the domain of the speaker, The Empress Catherine of Russia (1729-1796) was to be in her people's hands before the First World War ended.

What part did the Scottish TUC play in the different stages of the first major war of the twentieth century?

References

[1] A Short History of Labour in Scotland. Chapter V.

[2] Although at a time when prices were soaring between October 1913 and April 1914, the appeal produced £867.18s.10d., including contributions from many small Scottish bodies which were not affiliated; such as the Floorcloth & Linoleum Union, the Gilders Union, the Glaziers Union and the Settmakers Union.

6

World War I: The First Stage

The bitterness of the industrial warfare which had already lasted some five years had led to the Socialists of all groups gaining in Scotland a respectful hearing from the shop floor, in study circles and public meetings. Not only did they listen to outstanding speakers like Tom Mann, busy in Glasgow for the Sailors and Firemen, and the economic study courses of the legendary John MacLean; there was also a ready sale for their papers, *Forward* and *Vanguard*. That the trade conflict between emerging foreign competitors had motivated their employers' oppression and could now threaten even war between nations was well to the fore in the Socialists' teaching, although their remedies might vary.

Section (i): **Might it Really be Going to Happen?**

Attitudes to the general question of war between the nations were emerging already, with hints of the confusion to come, at the previous Congress in 1913. The President, Councillor Alex Turner, of the Municipal Employees, had his eyes fixed on world-wide class struggle. "The greatest cause in human history" was for him at the time "international world-wide Brotherhood based upon economic freedom". In that cause they should be ready to fall,

> that the oppressor may be overthrown and that the people may be free.

On "militarism" he said that "war is an enemy of the workers" and referred to the "recent disclosures in Germany of how wars are created and fostered and the despicable tactics adopted by certain capitalists to bring about war". The average working man had "no illusions on the subject of militarism. He knows quite well what foreign working men think of conscription". In his view

> the working man does not believe that the German bogey is founded on reality and, before he is convinced of that, it will require better argument than is supplied by the Yellow Press

When it came, at first he was to be in deep disagreement with the majority of his colleagues in the Parliamentary Committee.

During the 1913 debate on the war danger, views were expressed which appeared to turn on tactical differences. A resolution was moved for the Scottish Miners Federation, which strongly condemned

> any action likely to lead to war between nations, and pledges itself to use every endeavour, by co-operating and fraternising with Continental workers to make war impossible.

This was moved by Robert Smillie, whose personal opinion, like Keir Hardie's, was opposed to participation in the war; it was seconded by John Robertson, who later supported taking part in the war: but in fact the miners agreed that individuals might differ, provided the majority decisions of the union were adhered to. To this resolution an addition was moved by James O'Connor Kessack, of the Dock Labourers, arguing that it was "no use passing pious resolutions which meant little or nothing. To talk piously about the iniquity of war was useless, and the time had arrived to get something done to stop war". Seconded by A W French of the Sailors and Firemen, he moved that the PC be instructed

> to confer with the PC of the British TUC, the National Transport Workers Federation, also the British Miners Federation, with a view to opening up negotiations with foreign trades unions for the purpose of making agreements and treaties as to common international action in the event of war.

Smillie opposed Kessack's addition because "he thought the time had not come for the step proposed", and did not think they would be able to carry it out. He did not believe to go to war was caused "by a primary desire of the common people". But, he added,

> war was brought about largely by the capitalist manufacturers of war material and dreadnoughts, and also by the Yellow Press

and thought there was "a close connection between these two". Congress decided not to include Kessack's addition by a small majority, 53 votes to 43, with a third of the delegates not voting at all.

In the STUC Congress at Easter 1914, the question of war between the nations had not been raised directly; as we have seen, they were far more deeply concerned with "industrial warfare" and the use of the armed forces within the British Isles. How, then, would they react, many of the leading figures being so well known for activity amongst the various Socialist parties, when war was declared? Through the early summer the PC had been concerned merely with minor moves to avoid problems about various amalgamations, with no meeting in the crucial month of July. Then by the irony of fate, the whole committee was due to attend on various Government departments with their usual annual "processing" of Congress decisions on 4th August itself, the actual declaration date. The day before the Chairman, David Gilmour of the Miners, instructed Carson to wire all members cancelling the deputation "as nothing would emerge in present circumstances".

Section (ii): **The Immediate Problems in Scotland**

The outbreak of the first twentieth century world war, and on a scale never before imagined, brought acute problems of many kinds to the British working people and labour movement. More than any the Scots were deeply affected because the Clydeside heavy industry and other areas of shipbuilding and engineering were to be supremely important for munitions work. But also the sudden change from peacetime production in textiles, building and local government projects meant that much current work was delayed or abandoned forthwith. Not only was there suddenly massive unemployment but also a shortage of workers in sweated industries when workers left to find jobs in the new wartime expansion or to join the forces.

As well as in mining this was happening in textiles, as a deputation to the PC from the Dyers and Bleachers reported, much worried about their funds. For within three months

> in Scotland they were losing 1,000 members owing to the war. This being due to the very small wages earned.[1]

The Dyers' trouble was part of another difficulty; the recent legislation of social security measures, forced upon the Government during the "great unrest", meant changes for the unions to become approved societies which were far from complete. Now an explosion of demands on union funds of the small unions required massive Governmental support. Then there was an enormous rise in the cost of living in Scotland especially; the landlords' factors immediately pushed up rents beyond all reason. Food supplies and their prices were disrupted by hoarding and by home and overseas transport problems. The sudden and startling drop in the standard of living gave considerable urgency to the already pending engineers' demand for 2d an hour, for the miners' claims and, in some industries, negotiations on the shorter working day and limited darg.

On Clydeside, engineering employers' provocations, including importing American workers at much higher rates, and derisory and divisive counter-offers, led to massive unrest, overtime bans and threatened a general strike. With the District Committee of the Amalgamated Society of Engineers, on London head office instructions failing to oppose the employers' moves, the shop stewards won support for forming the historic Clyde Workers' Committee.[2] Later leading members amongst the shop stewards were deported from Clydeside under the wartime legislation, and so carried Scotland's viewpoint south of the border, together with the lessons of some of the successes which had been achieved. This was no sporadic outburst; it was a grass-roots reaction to the totally unacceptable and uncontrolled rise in the cost of living. Early on, the housewives went into action on the streets and soon began to organise street rent-withholding committees in the absence of any control of profiteering landlords. In Govan, for example, the women had an organising committee in every street as 5,000 tenants went on rent strike, refusing to pay higher rents. The men in industry became involved when some score of rent strikers had eviction notices served on them. This was taken up by the Clyde Shop Stewards Committee. When the householders were due to be sentenced, they organised a stoppage of work and a march, joined by an army of women, to the Sheriff Court in Glasgow. The protest was fully supported in the shipyards and workshops. The rent issue became merged with the industrial struggles; and the Government had no alternative but to rush through the Rents Restriction Act.

All these movements started at local level and came quickly to the trades councils on the Clyde, not least the Glasgow Trades Council, where so many members of the STUC's PC and regular delegates were based. But at this level another problem factor entered; this was the political question of what was, and what should be, the movement's attitude to the war itself? Here there was division and complex attitudes, including amongst the various Socialist Parties. These changed as time wore on, and were reflected in the Glasgow Trades Council itself and also in what the STUC did and refrained from doing for many months. Without realising how these differences affected action, the role of the STUC during the war could be misunderstood.

Section (iii): **Attitudes to the War**

One view held from the first was that the British trades unions and Labour Party should abide by the recent decision of the International Conferences, which the STUC had tacitly accepted without sending delegates to represent them. This had provided that in the event of a war threatening, caused by the conflicting interests of the capitalist class in each country, each group of workers nationally should act against their own employers to prevent it. Leaders of the British Labour Party and trades unions almost all now argued that since the German workers had failed to prevent their capitalist class from invading "little Belgium", the British movement was released from this agreement.[3]

Their duty now was, therefore, to support the British and Allied Governments in resisting the Germans in what was to be called "aggression" in later years. Amongst those who immediately and fully supported the war, expressing a typical attitude, was so prominent a PC member as Robert Allan. A Social Democrat, he explained his attitude three years later in his 1917 Presidential Address, when attitudes were changing, and they were "longing to see the finish". He had "never wavered", however; he was

> an Internationalist, because I believe in Nationalism. Therefore, the outrage on Belgium and the invasion of France were to me a violation of International principles.

Sharing his attitude was the ageing Secretary, George Carson, no longer officer of Glasgow Trades Council. At this early stage trade unionists like these, believing it would be a short war speedily won, concentrated on to what degree they should accept wartime legislation, including changes in working practices, etc., if necessary. Some saw this in terms of how strongly they could force trade union and labour movement representation on war emergency committees. Indeed, some saw it as a great opportunity to enhance the trades unions' national status at last. Some believed that the best way to defend conditions would be to argue on such committees that some action or inaction by the Government would, in fact, handicap the war effort – such as failure to control rents or introduce food rationing, limit prices, or control all industry. They soon found themselves in considerable difficulty – and sometimes with the interests of one industry in opposition to another – on such questions as whether industrial conscription was necessary, what safeguards could and should be made if dilution of labour were permitted. The question of military conscription as against voluntary enlistment was also a very difficult issue, together with the individual rights of conscientious objectors.

Those who held the opposite viewpoint also differed on how they should act. Some held themselves bound in their action by what proved to be the majority view decided on by their union; they would within that limit seek to change the pro-war attitude, stressing the need to keep open every international connection possible and seek an early armistice. Others held that they must individually carry their war resistance to the point of refusal to fight or take part. These war resisters were brought close to, but did not identify with, the conscientious objectors on religious or moral grounds, with whom they often found themselves in gaol. Socialists, however, continued to make their points, whatever the immediately prevailing mood: the titles of some of Tom Mann's lectures in October 1914 to the Social Questions Circle are indicative. They included: "The United States of Europe: No More Kaisers: Abolish the War Lords"; "The International Socialist Movement: Its Limitations and Prospects"; "The American and French Revolutions of 1776, 1789 and The Present War".

Section (iv): **What Says the STUC?**

On both sides at an early stage Scottish trade unionists were very much worried by the movement being divided, with so many urgent new problems on their hands. Amongst some there was a strong desire to avoid any public discussion which aired views about the war, which they feared would increase the divisions: as we shall see they were in the majority on the PC of the STUC. Others felt such discussion was essential, and that the urgent problems could not be usefully tackled without it. Two prominent Glasgow Trades Council members, Alex Turner and O'Connor Kessack, at a special PC meeting on 5 September, 1914, tried unsuccessfully to have Standing Orders suspended so that the war could be discussed. Kessack himself, formerly a *Clarion* Scout and ardent ILP speaker, had already joined the cavalry. Both belonged to the ILP which nationally had sent out a circular urging members not to raise questions on the nature of the war. Earlier they had pressed the PC to issue a circular asking affiliates to investigate how their funds were affected by the enormous unemployment already on them, which was agreed "after a lengthy discussion". A fortnight later Turner returned to the subject. There was a bitter discussion when he

> raised the question as to whether the Committee were going to make any pronouncement on the war to the trades unionists of Scotland. After considerable discussion the subject was allowed to drop.[4]

Amongst those absent on this occasion were the Secretary, George Carson, who was frequently ill at this time, James Gavin of the Steel & Iron Workers, and "Sergeant James O'Connor Kessack". Those taking part included Robert Allan, the typographer, for Edinburgh Trades Council; Neil Beaton, Edinburgh Shop Assistants; the miner, David Gilmour; W G Hunter of the Glasgow Operative Bakers; and Councillor Wm Muirhead of Central Ironmoulders, Falkirk. Turner regarded himself as insulted during the long debate and wrote resigning; but he was unanimously invited to withdraw his resignation when at the next meeting Hunter regretted if remarks made seemed as "meant to reflect upon him". The same anxiety was present when on 26 December, 1914, Gavin and Muirhead successfully carried a decision not to hold the regular Congress in the spring of 1915, although opposed by Allan and Beaton and despite protests from Glasgow Trades Council and the Sheet Iron Workers.

But the problems continued and would not solve themselves, not least on Clydeside, with engineering workers on strike and banning overtime until the War Emergency Committee was forced to call a mass meeting in Glasgow. This demanded cuts in fuel, food prices and rents, with many urging Arthur Henderson, as the Labour Party's national representative to come off the Government's main recruiting council unless action was taken by Whitehall. The PC itself had refused to call such a meeting as Glasgow Trades Council had asked. Instead it tended to send some member of the PC to represent them when mass conferences were called in the spring of 1915; at the same time issuing informative circulars on cost of living, supplementary grants and protection of union funds to its affiliates. The PC tried to arrange deputations to London to Ministries, the Prime Minister and the Lord Advocate and to seek representation on War Enmergency Committees. These fell through, except that the National War Emergency Committee agreed to accept as their representative David Gilmour when in London for the Miners Union. But with the Scottish Advisory Committee for the Prince of Wales National Relief Fund they got nowhere: after several letters and a deputation the Committee insisted on choosing its own members and refused Robert Allan as the STUC's representative. Finally, after rejecting a request from Edinburgh Trades Council "to hold a Congress as usual to discuss serious questions", on 29 May, 1915, a compromise decision proved unavoidable.

> After a statement from the Chairman (David Gilmour) on this question, Councillor Muirhead seconded by Mr Palmer moved that we convene a one day conference to consider certain questions relating to present conditions.

At this meeting the only PC members absent were O'Connor Kessack, Gavin and Turner, who himself had now joined the forces.

Section (v): **"The Cost of Living Conference"**

When it opened on 3 July, 1915, at the Christian Institute in Glasgow, it was on Congress scale, with no less than 200 delegates, despite the strictly limited agenda of subject. President David Gilmour referred to doubts whether the Conference even so should be called. He explained:

> There was a fear expressed that there might be some people who might raise very dangerous topics regarding the war. The PC, however, decided they would only discuss questions on which Scottish trade unionists could unite upon.

It was conducted throughout on these lines.

With some twenty delegates being heard, in later days it was always referred to as "the Cost of Living Conference", because this was the topic with which delegates were most concerned. The other topics were how war relief benefits and pensions should be organised and "After-war Problems", which concentrated particularly on what would happen to demobilised apprentices. Viewing with alarm "the indifference of responsible statesmen", the main resolution told the PC to press Government and Labour Party for urgent action about

> the serious grievances the masses of the people are suffering under by reason of the enormous and unjustifiable increase in the cost of living.

The only differences of opinion were on whether the Government should choose to fix maximum prices or take full control of food and subsidise pre-war prices for it. In any event the people must be prevented "from being systematically robbed as they are at present". Already, in less than a year, the cost of living had increased by 35 per cent, as David Gilmour pointed out in his presidential address. He went on to make a brief reference to the important struggle by the Clydeside engineers for a 2d. an hour increase. He described it as "a most moderate and reasonable claim"; and "it would not have given them the same standard of living as they had before the war, had they won it". As for his fellow miners,

> it was only when the country was face to face with a stoppage of the whole collieries that through Government intervention the owners in Scotland conceded 9d. per day.

Yet the cost of coal to the householder "had been almost doubled, and this had hit very hardly and very unfairly the very poorest classes of the community". The effect of low wages had resulted in 20,000 of Scotland's 120,000 miners joining the army as soon as the war broke out. One of his remarks was received with applause from the 200 delegates from all parts of Scotland. This was when he said, fresh from attending the National War Emergency Committee meeting in London, that they "hoped the Government would deal with profits in a strong fashion and not allow anybody to make profits out of the sacrifices of the people in this war".

The all-important cost of living resolution referred to "the serious grievances" which were being suffered "by reason of the enormous and unjustifiable increase". Alarmed by "the indifference of responsible Statesmen" and the continued rise, the PC was instructed to stress to the Government and the Labour Party the urgent need to revise prices of all commodities

> either by fixing maximum prices or taking full control of supplies into their own hands, in the interests of the people, and thus prevent them from being systematically robbed as they are at present.

In moving this for the PC, David Palmer of Aberdeen Trades Council "hoped nothing would be said or done calculated to embarrass the Government in conducting this war to a successful and speedy termination". While trade unionists recognised the Government's responsibility in the conduct of "this disastrous war", it was imperative that the working classes should give their opinion on controlling cost of living, and their present conference was "absolutely justifiable in order to give a clear lead to working-class opinion". Those remarks were indeed mild after a year of strikes, demonstrations and rent strikes, resistance in the Scottish shipyards, factories and streets. Joseph Sullivan of the Lanarkshire Miners, who was on the Standing Orders Committee, seconded in a similar tone, defending reasonable demands, and adding:

> If they were claiming to make excessive wages as the result of extra prices charged by somebody else, they would be just as bad as the

> Capitalist class, who were trying to make enormous profits for the same reason.

A different stress came from another Lanarkshire miner.[5] John Robertson said that similar resolutions had "been frequently passed of late, and what was needed now was the active putting into practice of their terms". He believed they were "in for another object lesson from our superiors, in the proposed National Thrift Campaign engineered by aristocrats to show the workers how to live on less while they themselves continued to live in the good old fashioned way".

Criticism came from Alex Richmond, delegate from the Glasgow Sheet Iron Workers, who were deeply affected by the Clydeside industrial action. He had "a decided objection" to letting the Government fix prices, probably at "a maximum to which no private trader aspired". Instead they should insist on the Government taking full control of foods and supply them at pre-war prices: "they were subsidising the employers right and left". Ben Smith of the National Amalgamated Union of Labour pointed out that many trades unions and trades councils were already in action on these lines; but the Dunfermline Trades Council speaker wanted the circular sent out to all in terms of the resolution to encourage joint action in the localities. General support was expressed by speakers from the Scottish Painters, the Musicians and the National Federation of Women Workers, for whom Mrs Lamond stressed the plight of the old and of widows with large families.

The second resolution was on War Relief, including pensions and employment of disabled service men, their widows and dependants; all these should be "under one authority, responsible to Parliament and democratically appointed and controlled". In moving Baillie Robert Climie of Kilmarnock Trades Council complained that any relief was still administered by middle-class people on the County and Burgh Committees. It was increasingly necessary for workers to be strongly represented on them. When seconding, J F Armour, the strong Socialist delegate from the Glasgow Operative Masons, stressed "the destitution which was being systematically engendered" by Government agencies telling employers to "delay as much work as possible". John Robertson of the miners came in again, urging trades councils to set about the local Relief Committees to get them controlled "by the people whose sons were doing the fighting". J C Hendry of Brechin Trades Council, supported by the Locomotive Engineers, wanted all relief to be met by the Government and not to depend in part on workers' contributions. Other speakers included Hugh Lyon, General Secretary of the Scottish Horse & Motormen.

The third resolution, "After-war Problems", was moved by Robert Allan, who recalled how "the ranks of the unemployed in Edinburgh were crowded with ex-soldiers and ex-militia men" who had fought in the South African War, and on their return "had to fight for a living. Having for war purposes assumed control of railways, ships and factories, docks and mines, the Government should if necessary keep control for peace purposes". The resolution called on the PC to start considering all "Labour problems created by mobilisation", and especially safeguarding the interests of broken-time apprentices "on their return to civil life". In seconding, William Shaw spoke on the Glasgow Trades Council's accepted addition that the Right to Work and Eight Hours Bills would be "the most practical methods of dealing with after-war problems". Two delegates spoke against, James Brown, the Glasgow Typographer, and Hugh Lyon, General Secretary of the Scottish Horse and Motormen. They felt that other problems, like "female labour", needed more consideration than the general principle of hours limitation, long since approved by trade unionists. Of the 200, only 74 voted on it, eight being against the full resolution.

Before the one-day conference broke up, after arguments on the Standing Orders Committee a new resolution came up demanding nationalisation of arms manufacture. It demanded this "in view of the unsatisfactory production of munitions of war in the privately owned armament factories". This was to eliminate "the element of private profit" and ensure that those on munitions would be "working solely in the interests of the State". Not unnaturally it came from the troubled Clydeside engineers, moved by Councillor James Walker, of the Steel Smelters Society, who twenty years later was to be President of the Iron and Steel Confederation in London, and Chairman of the Labour Party. He told the Cost of Living Conference that

> private enterprise was utterly impossible as a means of carrying on a successful war against an enemy.

Before it ended the Conference authorised the PC to endorse an appeal for the textile workers at the Clyde Spinning Company in Glasgow, after hearing Miss Bella Reilly describing the dispute.

In practice they did little to follow up these July decisions except by reissuing circulars on the cost of living whenever they received them from the National War Emergency Committee. They had not begun to process them until a deputation saw the Scottish Secretary in Edinburgh on 8 October, 1915, by which time they had become deeply involved in differences over questions of military and industrial conscription.

Section (vi): **Industrial and Military Conscription**

Although the timing and reaction to the problems which arose differed, industrial and military conscription inevitably became linked in actual practice. First the Munitions of War Acts one after another throughout the war imposed many restrictions in the factories, some were obviously inevitable given wartime needs, others were regarded as unnecessary and as unjustifiably favouring employers. The problems deeply and immediately concerned those on the factory floor, their shop stewards and trade union officials who had to negotiate on immediate issues without awaiting support from remote head offices. Involved was a massive sacrifice of long-established workshop and craft practices; new technology and processes; and the introduction of ever-increasing numbers of unskilled labour, including unprecedented numbers of women doing work never before open to them. Not only were many "new starts" in the munitions factories unfamiliar with trade union practices; but traditional methods of resistance, like strikes, overtime bans and "ca' canny" actions rendered those taking part liable to prosecution. There were deep-rooted fears that the wartime restrictions would become permanent in the post-war period. Finally, there was loss of freedom for those on war work to leave without formal permission in writing, while the employer was free to sack whom he chose. This in itself was bound to link industrial to military conscription.

Introduced by a succession of Military Service Acts, conscription into the armed forces had been strenuously opposed by the whole Labour movement when it became a possibility during the setbacks in the Boer War; the response then by the Socialists had been to demand a voluntary Citizens Army. But in 1914 this was no small colonial war, but something new for the British Empire and those forced to enlist by hard times and unemployment. In the first days of August, therefore, the lead given by the Labour Party, the British TUC and the General Federation was to preserve the voluntary system by encouraging and campaigning for recruitment. As the 1925 official history[6] of the Labour Party put it:

> As they became more and more impressed with the national danger, they conducted a special recruiting effort on Labour platforms throughout the Labour movement in the autumn of 1915. This was done at the special invitation of the Prime Minister, Mr Asquith, and the Minister for War, Lord Kitchener.

But there were problems of many kinds, including the strong reaction to the uncontrolled price and rent rises which were rousing such deep anger on Clydeside. The Government, therefore, sent Lord Derby campaigning round the country to get single men to "attest" that they were willing to join when called upon, to spare the married men who would not be asked to "attest". But when the Derby scheme was said to have failed with 600,000 men refusing to attest, the Government brought in a Bill forcing first the single men to attest and later with full-scale conscription. Thus the policy of voluntary enlistment campaigning by the LP, the British TUC and the General Federation finally was seen to have failed to prevent all-out conscription.

This was the background to the immediate aftermath of the Scottish TUC's "Cost of Living Conference" in July 1915. As early as 8 October, 1915, the PC decided to ask the British TUC what enlisting propaganda conferences were to be held in Scotland, while reminding Lloyd George as Minister of Munitions and Lord Kitchener of the War Office that the STUC should be consulted. This they followed up after a special PC meeting by promising their help to the Joint Recruiting Committee if it were to continue despite Lord Derby's scheme. To this only Neil Beaton objected. When a week later the British TUC replied, saying they were "willing to hand over the work of recruiting in Scotland", the PC evaded direct participation "owing to the lack of sufficient finance and other help", for it would be "more than we could properly overtake". They would, however, give "all possible help".

But with the industrial unrest on the Clydeside, the arrest of Fairfield shipwrights, the intervention by Govan Trades Council to win their release, legal action against the Socialist speaker and teacher John MacLean, the mood expressed through the shop stewards of the Clyde Workers Committee was growing against any form of conscription. Two organisations throughout Britain were already making protest at conscription their sole concern. The Manifesto of the Non-Conscription Fellowship, issued in September 1915, was signed by an impressive group of intellectuals, including Clifford Allen and Fenner Brockway as Chairman and Secretary. They were "bound by deep conscientious conviction". Believing in "the value and sacredness of human personality", they declared themselves

> prepared to sacrifice as much in the cause of the world's peace as our fellows are sacrificing in the cause of the nation's war

With the same object but with a very different tone, the early Manifesto of the Anti-Conscription League declared themselves "totally opposed to conscription in any shape or form, whether military or industrial"; and their attitude was based on recognising

> the urgent need that has arisen for offering immediate and whole-hearted opposition to the threatened further enslavement of individuals through legislation.

In a leaflet entitled *British Worker! Are You Pro-Prussian?* it expressed strong class attitude. It declared that "Prussian militarism" was a system by which an army of "compulsorily enlisted workers is used by the military class for the holding of the mass of the people in subjection, and for the conquest of foreign territory". It was not confined to Germany, the manifesto concluded, urging the reader not to be made a tool in the hands of the Anglo-Prussians. That meant

> taking part in the quarrels of Governments arising out of their rivalry for the capture of world markets.

If such leaflets did not find general acceptance in the first bewildering months elsewhere in Britain, on the Clydeside their industrial difficulties gave such views some credibility. This was increasingly expressed through delegates to trades councils along the Clyde.

Although there were divided opinions on the Glasgow Trades Council, the majority felt strongly that there should be a conference on conscription and wrote to the PC asking that the STUC organise it. The PC held another special meeting when they decided to refuse; there "was no need to convene" a conference, because they agreed with the British TUC that a voluntary recruitment with the Derby scheme "provided all the men required". Beaton dissented; the PC decided to circularise affiliates on it. But within four weeks the situation in Scotland was in different case. There had been the arrests of munitions workers for withholding rents, massive demonstrations in support of them and against John MacLean's gaol sentence, the suppression of his *Vanguard* and the Glasgow *Forward* owing to their comments. Activists of Glasgow and Govan Trades Councils, following the industrial protests of Harland & Wolff, Fairfields, Beardmore's Naval Construction Works, and Dalmuir Shipyards, set up a Free Speech Committee. On 4 December, 1915, B H Shaw, JP, and two town Councillors came to plead once more for the STUC to hold "a conference to discuss the question of conscription". But Robert Allan and David Palmer of Aberdeen Trades Council successfully carried a resolution "that the present time was not suitable to hold a Conference". Only Neil Beaton and Bailie Climie of Ayrshire Trades Council favoured it.

But it was impossible for the PC to remain wholly inactive. Within a month not only had the Clyde Workers Committee taken over and silenced Lloyd George at the meeting in Glasgow where he had come to make his case; the next step, his Military Service Bill, had been introduced; and his further move towards conscription shook even the higher ranks of Trade Union leaders. The PC was forced to send representatives to give a joint lead in a two-day conference on housing and rents convened by the Scottish Advisory Committee of the Labour Party. The 750 delegates set up a Scottish National Labour Housing Association. The following day, 6 January, 1916, the Labour MPs held a conference in which they decided they could not accept the new move towards full conscription. This may well have changed the attitude of the PC majority. For two days later they held a special PC about the new Bill which was attended once more by Ben Shaw and James Walker from the Scottish LP Advisory Committee; they agreed to a joint conference between the two committees on conscription. This was held on 15 January, 1916, and illustrated some differences in view amongst the thirty Scottish leaders present. Robert Smillie and Neil Beaton moved a resolution of

> emphatic condemnation of the Government's Military Service (No. 2) Bill and demands that even at this late hour it should be withdrawn.

It included a warning to the Government "against any attempt to bring about industrial compulsion in this country". It was finally carried after two amendments had been defeated. The first move by delegates of the Glasgow & District Glass Bottlemakers Trade Protection Friendly Society and the Boot & Shoe Operatives declared that free institutions and liberties depended "entirely on Great Britain and her Allies winning this war"; and though opposed to military conscription in any form in ordinary circumstances, they could not "recommend any action that would weaken or injure our country in the present crisis". Therefore, the Bill should be accepted, together with the Prime Minister's promised safeguards. It ended with a pledge to do everything possible "to bring the war to a speedy and victorious end". Only four voted for this amendment. The second amendment, moved by Palmer and Allan, recommended "a ballot vote of the affiliated organisations" on the questions of "National Military Service for the duration". This amendment received six votes. The Conference passed unanimously a resolution condemning the suppression of *Forward*.

A month later, however, when the Sheet Iron Workers and Light Platers Society's Executive called on the PC for a further Conference on the Military Service Act it was decided to take no action. By this time, George Carson was frequently ill and Robert Allan was virtually in charge. With massive unrest, the arrest, sentencing and deportation of leading Clydeside shop stewards quickly followed. This failure by the PC to call another conference after the Act had passed was sharply criticised when Congress opened on 27 April, 1916. Emanuel Shinwell and William Shaw, the Glasgow Trades Council delegates, moved a resolution of protest which was defeated only by 58 votes to 47. This, the 19th Congress, and the first regular Congress with normal agenda in wartime, was held at the Scottish Co-operative Wholesale Society's Hall in Glasgow; the Falkirk Hall they had aimed for was in use by the military.

There were some 140 delegates, including six women, one of whom was Eleanor Stewart of the Workers' Union, who was to be a delegate for many years, and two from the Textile Federation. Present amongst the Sailors & Firemen was Tom Mann, who made several important interventions. Serious accidents in Lanarkshire pits delayed the arrival of David Gilmour; he then made a strongly pro-war speech. Because of differences on the PC he had previously submitted his address to them "to suggest such alteration as they thought desirable"; but it was decided that "would be a departure from all previous practice", and the address was an expression of the president's personal opinions.

He started by recalling the first Congress when he himself had been Minute Secretary and then the "terrible changes" in the two years since they had met at Kirkcaldy, "the nightmare of the greatest war" in the world's history. After speaking about the outbreak of and conduct of the war hitherto, he added that "the perpetrators of these atrocities will be punished before terms of peace are settled". Then he spoke directly to those who differed from his view of the origin of the war and how it should be ended:

> To those who insist the negotiations for peace should be entered upon immediately, I would say that such cannot be thought of so long as a single German or Austrian soldier remains in the countries that have been devastated, the villages and towns of which are now in ruins.

Although the Easter Rising in Ireland had just taken place and Gilmour was speaking just before the Irish TUC's Secretary was to be arrested, their records confiscated and their Congress postponed, this was never mentioned directly. But it was not perhaps wholly accidental that Glasgow Trades Council put forward once again the resolution on the principle of Scottish Home Rule which had been unanimously accepted in May 1914. Seconded by M McColl of the

Glasgow Shop Assistants, it was finally adopted only after "a negative was moved and seconded", although the minutes gave no detail of the discussion.

Section (vii): **Anxieties About Industrial Problems**

Whatever their attitude to the nature of the war, how soon and in what way it could be ended, in April 1916, with the turmoil outside the hall in the streets and factories, the delegates concentrated on the industrial problems the war had created and increased. On these facts there was no disagreement, though there could be differences on methods of tackling them. Despite the vast discussion and actions at trades council, branch and factory committee level, this was the first time in the twenty-one months of the war, which few would have believed could last so long, that a full gathering of STUC delegates could face up to the problems and solutions. Now they were concerned with profiteering; failure to nationalise fully; Scotland's ghastly housing conditions; the invasion of civil rights by the Munitions Acts consequences; the post-war problems in restoring trade union practices and normal employment; and defending and advancing the status of the STUC and its right to representation on the proliferating committees.

Total opposition was moved on military conscription by William Shaw for Glasgow Trades Council as "a violation of British civil liberty", and that Continental experiences proved it "the chief weapon used by the employing classes in times of industrial dispute". The resolution called for its repeal; after a lengthy discussion, an amendment declaring that it was necessary to win the war, but must not continue afterwards was defeated by 66 to 46 votes. A long resolution moved by him detailing "the gross interference with the rights of the workers" by the Munitions Acts in so many respects was carried unanimously. Tom Mann also had total support in the protest against trade unionists and munitions workers deported from Glasgow, together with "the vindictive sentence passed on Mr John MacLean MA". William Shaw and Robert Allan for Glasgow and Edinburgh Trades Councils joined in denouncing the Government's action in banning working-class papers and withdrawing "the right of freedom of speech"; for this they got full support.

After dealing with niggardly pensions and loss of benefits by soldiers' wives delegates ran into differences on how they were threatened by dilution in the factories. This was largely because the Bakers concentrated their fire on restricting female labour, and said that it must only be for the war period. When Shaw for Glasgow Trades Council stressed an addition for "rates or wages operating in the trade" to apply, the resolution was carried. On the general question of unemployment after demobilisation, there were two approaches. Some delegates, including Glasgow and Edinburgh Trades Councils, looked to the Parliamentary LP at once to bring in a Bill pledging the Government to provide post-war "right to work" at standard wages and full unemployment payment pending getting work. Tom Mann had no reliance on that: he urged the PC to get co-operation of both the British and the Irish Trades Union Congresses to set up "a trade union clearing house"

> to collect information respecting Surplusage of Labour at the close of the war and to secure united action on the part of organised labour to adjust the working hours that there shall be no surplus labour.

At first he moved this as an amendment but later after heated discussion he withdrew it and presented it as a separate resolution. In the event both resolutions were carried. Tom Mann's, however, was only carried by 65 to 43, after both the leading Trades Councils' delegates had opposed, Shinwell speaking for Glasgow.

There was extremely strong feeling about housing, with many delegates disappointed at the slowness of the Provisional Committee of the Scottish National Labour Housing Association to get moving, after the enthusiastic support for it when the Glasgow Labour Party had taken the initiative for the enormous two-day conference, nearly four months earlier. This led the STUC miners' delegation, of 30 strong (by far the biggest), to demand that they set up "a special Housing Committee". This sign of criticism of the PC was dropped after private guarantees of quick action, and Congress passed unanimously two resolutions which established the Scottish basic standpoint. The central one moved by William Shaw for Glasgow Trades Council and seconded by a Glasgow Councillor, George Kerr of the Workers' Union, demanded Treasury grants to enable local authorities to provide suitable houses "built and let free from the burden of interest", private enterprise having failed, in view of "the present house famine". The "interest-free" capital was the key principle. Meanwhile Edinburgh Trades Council sponsored an equally successful demand for early publication of the report of the Scottish Housing Commission and an Act to include four basic measures for improved housing.

Although the Government Commission report was still to be long delayed, action on the miners' criticism was not to wait until Congress resolutions were processed the following October. At its first meeting after Congress the PC had to agree to a letter from the Scottish Advisory Committee of the Labour Party to call the various committees together within a week to a joint discussion on Housing. On May 20, therefore, the Executive Committees of the Scottish LP and the Scottish Labour Housing Association met the full PC at their offices; the Miners had also been invited but refused. However, the miner, Bailie Tom McKerrell, being newly elected to the PC and its Vice-Chairman, was there in that capacity as well as Robert Smillie, representing the Scottish LP. This body was prevented by the British LP's rulings from affiliating directly, because of fear of Parliamentary and local candidates being set up independent of the LP. Nevertheless, branches of the Association had been formed in Dundee, Dunfermline, Falkirk and elsewhere, although considerable differences emerged during the discussion both on the constitution and several policy points. For example, when McKerrell asked whether the LP in London had endorsed the all-important non-interest principle, Bailie James Stewart of Glasgow replied "No; the Labour Party were not advanced enough". There was, however, general agreement that the Association must be an all-embracing body which dealt only with the question of housing and rents; it was not for the Scottish LP nor the STUC to take up housing "as a small part of their work". Finally, it was agreed to re-draft the constitution and meet again. When finally the PC sent its deputation to London, McKerrell provided the Scottish Secretary with horrifying details of "a house famine such as this country had never seen before", with "no possible solution" without building with interest-free loans. It was to be yet another war year before the next Secretary for Scotland was admitting to them that when the Scottish Housing Commission's report was finally complete, it proved one of the most "appalling State documents" ever published.

Section (viii): **Sympathy With Ireland**

Hardly had the 1916 Congress packed up than the PC received a letter from Thomas Johnston, President-elect of the Irish TUC, with the news that their Secretary P T Daly and others had been arrested and all their records seized. The PC therefore decided that

> we render such help as was possible and ask Mr Johnston to advise on the matter; also to advise him that if Congress be held we would send delegates.[7]

Letters followed and on 7-9 August, Robert Allan and Hugh Lyon went as their delegates to Sligo to what had then become the Irish Trades Union Congress and Labour Party. They reported that "it proved a most successful and inspiring gathering" of nearly 100 delegates. They "passed upstanding" a resolution of sympathy with those bereaved in "the tragic events of Easter week". The PC's report noted that "well-known names will be missed" from their report, and continued:

> without for a moment pausing to consider the rightfulness or otherwise of recent events in our land, this we can say, that in the deaths of James Connolly and Richard O'Carroll, staunch trade unionists and champions of the rights of the common people, this country suffers deep and irreparable loss.

By the Scottish TUC's 1917 Congress the Irish Secretary P T Daly had been released and came to Scotland to convey "the fraternal greetings of the Irish trade unionists in an eloquent address". He was given an especially warm welcome and presentation.

References

[1] PC Minutes, 14 November, 1914.

[2] Originally called the Clyde Labour-Withholding Committee, to avoid using the word strike which was made illegal under wartime legislation.

[3] When the author as an eight-year-old girl in Bristol during the August 1914 holidays asked her Christian Socialist grandfather when would the war stop? he replied: "When the German working class do their duty, and overthrow their bosses". When with childish logic she asked: "When will the British people do that?" he was heard to mutter: "Out of the mouths of babes and sucklings . . . !"

[4] PC Minutes, 18 September, 1914.

[5] It should be noted that the miners' official, William Small, was responsible for the official report of the conference.

[6] "The Book of the Labour Party", Vol. I, p. 207. Edited by Herbert Tracey.

[7] PC Minutes 13 May, 1916.

7

World War I: The Second Stage

Since the 1915 summer "Cost-of-Living Conference" the move had begun into ever darker, tenser days which were already felt before, during and after the spring Congress of 1916. It was proving to be no short and easily won war. There had been the heavy defeat of the pointless Gallipoli expedition advocated by Winston Churchill at the Admiralty; the ghastly and long-drawn-out slaughter on the Somme; and the murderous Battle of Mons.

Section (i): **Mounting Losses**

Well before they met at Falkirk in the spring of 1917 there had begun a marked change of mood in what might be described as the second stage of the war. For by then there was developing deep preoccupation with when the war could be ended, and how the labour movement in Britain could influence what was to follow. The first important factor was that there was no relief from the effects of the war, food shortages and high cost of living. Indeed, these had worsened; and for Scotland perhaps the worst feature, which was to give rise to immense activity less than two years later, was the cumulative effect of the long hours. This was seriously felt not least by the new element in the workforce – the masses of women sent into munitions factories, sometimes far from Scotland. In factories throughout Britain there were also the technical changes accompanied by dilution of labour, leading to shelving of trade union practices. Whilst employers were making their huge profits, skilled men on day work reacted against widespread piecework and premium bonus and rate fixers cutting base rates. Employers victimised individual skilled men by refusing to grant trade cards exempting them from the Forces. By the winter of 1916 strikes began to break out in engineering led by the fast-growing national movement of shop stewards committees, which had to deal with so many problems on the spot.[1] The Labour Party was now deeply involved in the Government under the new Prime Minister, Lloyd George. Meeting in their Annual Conference in January, 1917, three months before the

STUC, the Labour Party delegates at Manchester found "the engineering shops seething with unrest".[2]

In addition to the effect of these problems on the home front there was considerable reaction to the mounting losses in the army, navy, the merchant navy and the new air force during the massive offensives following Lloyd George's encouragement to the generals who wanted a "knockout blow". All too often there seemed no gains and little apparent purpose; and by the autumn of 1917 there were many mutinies amongst the Allied Forces. Not least was the mutiny at the Étaples training camp, with its appalling conditions, on the eve of yet another planned "knock-out blow" in September, 1917. Here there were many Scots, including the Gordon Highlanders. While there was total official silence for many years, the wounded, the men on leave and the Aberdonian nurses in Étaples Field Hospital would scarcely remain silent.[3]

Such experiences at home and abroad were increasingly prompting the question of whether all this was avoidable, and how it could be stopped, when a far-away event in March 1917, "came like a thunder clap". From the effects flowing from it "a new alignment of forces developed within the Labour Party", out of which "there was to come a new conception both of organisation and policy".[4]

Women textile workers in Petrograd had called for a one-day strike against the war; many thousands joined them "shouting for bread and peace"; the Tsar was forced to abdicate and the first proletarian revolution had begun, with the setting up of a Workers and Soldiers Soviet (Council) in Petrograd alongside a Provisional Government.

Throughout the British working-class movement, this called out an immediate welcoming yet divided response; it may be usefully illustrated by the first messages of the British leadership in London and of the delegates to the Scottish TUC Congress. The message from the leaders of the British TUC, the Labour Party, the General Federation and the Labour Party Members of the Government, after expressing "deepest sympathy" with the Russian people's efforts "to deliver themselves from the power of reactionary elements which are impeding their advance to victory", urged the leaders of the Russian Labour Party to

> impress on your followers that any remission of effort means disaster to comrades in the trenches.

Their main emphasis therefore was to hope for greater efforts to win the war.

Section (ii): **STUC and Revolution in Russia**

As their first business on the opening day of Congress the STUC on the other hand accepted "by acclamation" a resolution moved by Tom McKerrell, the miner, on behalf of the PC, sending "its fraternal greeting to the free peoples of Russia, congratulating them on the successful termination of their long struggle with an irresponsible autocracy". But then it went on to hope that their freedom "will be maintained and extended, and that their example will be followed by the peoples of all lands". Moreover, they decided it should be sent not only to the Provisional Government but also to "the Council of the Soldiers and Workers Delegates". When a fortnight later the Provisional Government had announced its intention of continuing the war against Germany, the Petrograd Workers and Soldiers Council urged the Socialist International to call a Conference in Stockholm to find ways of ending the war. This was warmly welcomed by a remarkable convention in Leeds on 3 June of over 1,000 delegates with Robert Smillie in the chair, which also called for setting up Workers and Soldiers Councils all over Britain. One was formed in Glasgow, but received no support from the PC, who were well aware that the London-based majority of the leadership of the labour movement tended to fear that the Stockholm project might strengthen the demand for a separate peace in Russia. Under the leadership of Havelock Wilson, the Sailors and Firemen's Union went so far as to refuse to allow Arthur Henderson and Ramsay MacDonald to set sail from Aberdeen for Stockholm, although they held passports from the Government to do so. The PC did react to this at its meeting on 29 June; William Shaw of Glasgow Trades Council and Joe O'Hagan of the Steel & Iron Workers moved that the Union be informed "that we do not approve of their action".

When after the second revolution in November the Russians' declaration of policy included a call on all countries for immediate peace, followed by the sensational publication of all the secret treaties the Tsarist Government had made, there was immense stimulus to the demand for Allied War Aims to be declared and for immediate preparatory action to be taken at once to face up to the problems to follow. The American President Woodrow Wilson's Fourteen Points for peace and a League of Nations to prevent wars in future, which followed shortly afterwards, were widely seen as a first instalment.

Section (iii): **How Could it All be Ended?**

First moods towards such a trend had already begun to emerge when some 170 STUC delegates met when their 20th Congress opened at Falkirk in April 1917, although it was not much reflected in the actions of the PC in the past or the following year. There were several factors contributing to this. All but two of the PC were from desperately busy Clydeside, deep in long hours and problems of war industry. One was the General Secretary of a union and four others were officials, often with a tendency to be fully aware of attitudes in the corridors of power in London. This did not make them less active in pressing for greater Scottish representation on all official committees, commissions and inquiries to be accepted as a matter of principle and operated in custom and practice. Yet there were different possible responses to the frequent retort that "there are already many Scotsmen down here on delegations from their unions nationally, as British TUC nominations and as MPs".

Another factor was that several were on in years while still holding other positions of responsibility. Amongst the ancients was George Carson, frequently ill and unable to carry out his secretarial duties whilst reluctant to resign. There was a growing practice for the STUC to avoid organising meetings and consultation with the rank and file, many of whom turned to finding expression through shop stewards committees and trades councils instead.

The PC would usually merely send representatives to events organised in Scotland by other bodies. Not that they were unaware of the problems, for they had to spend much time in the end results, often reflected in inter-union disputes, sometimes arising from dissatisfied breakaways, or unions competing to enrol the unorganised.

Indeed, Allan as chairman and virtually acting secretary finally himself became considerably involved over the issue of the shop stewards deported from Glasgow and on trial under the Defence of the Realm Act. At almost every PC meeting throughout 1916 and 1917 the question had been on the agenda. It included correspondence and deputations to MPs and Ministries as well as journeys to visit the men in Edinburgh. In the Annual Report to the 1917 Congress it was stated that

> there was nothing in their conduct or actions to warrant the Government in taking the action they did.

The deportees had only been "fulfilling the duty of shop stewards". There were many moves, counter-moves and devices by the

Government to find means of checking the strong unrest they represented and the instinctive sympathy felt for them. After one of these attempts Allan and Beaton went from the PC to interview the military authorities and the men in Edinburgh. The PC then adopted a motion

> that as these men, it is alleged, were removed from Glasgow because they did not conform to the discipline of their Trade Unions and we are informed that they are prepared now to give an undertaking that they will, if returned, conform to the discipline of their union, we therefore request that such undertaking be accepted and that the men be allowed to return.[5]

But months later there was still no change and in November 1916 Allan went again to Edinburgh to ask one of their prominent members, David Kirkwood, whether he would "be willing to give an undertaking that if allowed to return he would submit all questions of dispute to his trade union?" His blunt response was to hand Allan a letter dated 24 November, 1916, saying: "When I get back to Glasgow it must be as a *free man*. I will sign nothing. Thanking you for all you have done for me." As late as March, 1917, the PC decided that Allan and Carson should submit evidence about it to the National Labour Inquiry Committee; at Congress Glasgow Trades Council's delegates, Shaw and Shinwell, demanded their return and that the sentence on John MacLean should be remitted.

At the 1917 and 1918 Congresses increasingly the new grass-roots mood, despite the differences, was reflected from the floor. When they met at Falkirk they were upstanding in respect for all who had been bereaved during the war, when it was announced that one of their PC members, James O'Connor Kessack, had been killed. Much of Allan's Presidential Address in 1917 was devoted to setting out his personal opinions and changing attitude to "the terrible conflict which is raging". But what he feared now was "a danger of the Labour movement being dragged into a quagmire of Pacifist Impossiblism". But on the central question of the continuing war the delegates accepted unanimously a resolution sponsored by Glasgow Trades Council and the Miners, moved and seconded by two with long-held Socialist convictions, John F. Armour and Robert Smillie. It regretted that "peace negotiations did not ensue" following President Woodrow Wilson's note to all the belligerents, and then called for the STUC

> to join its efforts to that of the International Working-Class Movement to oppose in all countries policies that tend to embitter nation against nation and delay the achievement of a just and lasting peace.

After this Glasgow Trades Council added "its strongest opposition to Compulsory Military Service", as "a violation of Civil Liberty and a menace to working-class interests". The same delegates moved a protest against "compulsory mobilisation of labour so long as profiteering is tolerated", holding that it was "a form of slavery", being done "for private profit under the guise of National Service"; and that the Government should first "pass an Act for the Conscription of Wealth". The feeling was so strong that a motion was even moved on behalf of the PC itself by Joe Houghton declaring against "any form of Industrial Conscription".

Section (iv): Fears of Demobilisation Problems

Then Robert Allan concentrated upon a question he knew would win response from all delegates even as early as 1917. This was about post-war problems and the vast confusion and unemployment he feared would follow demobilisation, whenever it might come. He saw the need in terms of the wartime State control of industries being continued and carried over into State ownership with workers directly represented on the controlling boards of railways and mines. Exactly the same demands had to be repeated almost in the same words some thirty years later after a second world war. He believed also that apart from establishing the right to work, there would be "little real social reform" in Scotland until the housing question was "drastically dealt with". He concluded:

> What has been accomplished by the workers in Russia is an example of what can be done by labour united. We too have a revolution to accomplish. Our revolution is an industrial and social revolution.

He felt sure that the close of the war would see them united again "in spite of differences existing at present".

After closing on this optimistic note Allan asked whether Congress would be willing to give a hearing to a Mr Neville Chamberlain, the Director of National Service, whom the Government had actually sent to address these turbulent Scots. In fact the purpose was to head off antagonism to plans for further dilution, following planned call-up of more to support the coming offensive. Delegates only agreed to hear him by 77 to 32, and he was closely questioned.

In the same mood resolutions were passed calling for immediate action to enable local councils to provide houses at reasonable rents, and action on health, pensions and factory inspection. There was also a fierce attack on the "raids carried out by the military and police on trade union meetings", which they regarded as "needles and provocative acts". Several on working women's pay and conditions were effectively moved, particularly by Eleanor Stewart of the Workers' Union and Bella Reilly, Textile Workers, and many details of the Workmen's Compensation Act were criticised sharply.

When it came to facing up to what they feared after demobilisation for which they stressed there should be an immediate plan prepared, they saw the need of better and closer organisation in the movement, welcoming moves towards closer working with the Scottish Sections of the Labour Party and of the Co-operative bodies. On the political side they urged the newly appointed Speakers' Committee which was to discuss electoral reform to insist on complete adult suffrage, cutting out the business and University dual vote; and made a strong plea for a Scots' Parliament, regretting that "at this juncture the Scottish people should not be represented on the Imperial War Council".

Their fears about the problems of demobilisation were expressed in two resolutions, both moved by Glasgow Trades Council delegates, the first by the PC member William Shaw. This demanded "a deliberate plan of national organisation" to cope with the expected unemployment, for which the Ministry of Labour must set up machinery in advance. The second moved by Shinwell was blunt about the abuse of the powers to suppress freedom of speech and writing; that the Munitions Acts had been used for "industrial conscription and subjection". Therefore the STUC was pledged

> to work for the full restoration of civil and industrial liberties of the workers, including the restoration of all the rules, conditions and customs that prevailed in the workshops before the war.

All this implied the need for stronger trade union organisation and on how to achieve this there is always room for dispute. On this occasion the Scottish Oil Workers' delegate, Michael O'Hagan from West Lothian, supported by Motherwell Trades Council called on the PC, "or some other body appointed by Congress", to be responsible "for the efficient organisation of the semi-skilled and unskilled workers", with affiliated unions agreeing to a levy and appointing National Organisers. Not surprisingly an amendment was forthcoming, once again from the Glasgow Trades Council. They called instead for such a body to investigate "those districts when organisation is inefficient or non-existent" and to "assist the work of industrial organisation" in conjunction with the trades councils. This was to set a pattern which, with many ups and downs, after many years was to be accepted as a typical Scottish practice.

But one of the major immediate post-war problems, which in Scotland was to mean a bitter struggle indeed and was to put the STUC into major disarray, was their oldest problem of all; the form of the battle for a shorter working day. At the Falkirk Congress, however, there was no sign of the trouble ahead when Aberdeen and Edinburgh Trades Council delegates moved eight hours a day with a maximum 44-hour week for all trades in the UK by Act of Parliament. They regarded it as

> one of the most important preliminary steps towards the emancipation of the working class, and will tend to lessen the number of unemployed, increase their health, strength and intelligence.

Yet all through 1917 up to and after the next Congress the PC's day-to-day work was no easier. It was in fact weakened; there was no miner on it, Tom McKerrell having taken a Government post, being replaced by David Palmer of Aberdeen Trades Council; and Allan was now responsible for all Carson's work, with a busy General Secretary of a fast growing trade union, Hugh Lyon, as Chairman.

Section (v): **Disputes and Confusion**

Particularly unhelpful were the many disputes between unions, not least with the general unions moving into areas which others wanted to organise on an industrial basis; so the PC were indeed far from carrying out instructions to improve trade union organisation. More and more it was left to the initiative of the new "Triple Alliance" set up of the Scottish Sections of the Labour Party, the Co-operative Union and the Co-operative Wholesale Society and the STUC. It was this "Triple Alliance" which handled and called conferences on such subjects as the Education (Scotland) Bill; the setting up of Labour Exchange Committees and representation on them; about approving candidates for future General Elections; and above all on Scottish housing. While the PC all agreed there was now urgent need for closer working between organisations dealing politically with the needs of the Scots as producers and consumers, there was one activity which the PC turned down early on. At its meeting on the third anniversary of the declaration of war, the PC had an invitation from the Workers & Soldiers Council, so enthusiastically formed in Leeds that June, asking the STUC to be represented at a meeting the following week in Glasgow called to form a Scottish Workers' and Soldiers' Committee. According to the Minutes "a long discussion ensued on this matter, all the members taking part". The majority decision was not to be represented, after Climie, Shaw and Beaton had spoken in favour. Those who opposed were Allan, Carson, Hendry, Houghton, Hunter and Palmer. However, Allan was constantly raising the question of STUC representation on all official committees, whether Governmental or of the Labour Movement centrally.

These were proliferating as concentration increased on what was to come and the labour movement's role in it. Often this led Allan into bitterly worded disputes. When it was announced that a War Aims Conference was to be held in London in December 1917, he fell out seriously with the London leaders of the Labour Party like Arthur Henderson, now excluded from the Government. Middleton wired telling him to discuss it with Henderson who was at that moment visiting Scotland. The PC, therefore, decided that Lyon and Allan should at once see Henderson, and that Joe Houghton of the Scottish Dock Labourers and O'Hagan of the Steel and Iron Workers who were to be delegates in any case, should represent the PC. But when they insisted to Henderson on the general principle of the "representation of the STUC PC at all special conferences called by the Labour Party", Henderson was not having it. As the Minutes of the PC on 12 January, 1918 report:

> The interview had been a somewhat lively one. Mr Henderson, while agreeing that the PC can be represented at the War Aims Conference and the Food Conference, not being sympathetic to our claim that we should as a matter of right be represented at all special conferences. It was pointed out in course of discussion that the Labour Party had issued a memorandum advocating Home Rule all round. Resolved to write Party Secretary insisting on the recognition of Scottish PC as an independent unit in the Labour Party.

As they feared this might weaken their case for representation on State Commissions and Inquiries and reception by Ministries, Allan raised the question with the "Triple Alliance" and began writing to the Labour MPs still holding office. They raised with Clynes representation on the newly formed Consumers Council; and with Addison about the reconstruction subcommittee for Scotland. They got refusals from both, with Clynes writing: "It may be some satisfaction to you to note that some of the members of the Council are drawn from Scotland". Allan wrote furiously again to Henderson; and it was decided to urge all Scottish Labour MPs "to use what influence they had to see that the claims of this Committee were not so systematically overlooked in the future, as they had been in the past".[6]

That year the STUC delegates sent to Derry had found a very strong mood at the 23rd Annual Congress of the Irish Trades Union Congress and Labour Party. Over 100 delegates from 51 trade unions heard "an able and fearless" presidential address; then they welcomed the Russian Revolution and the proposed Stockholm Peace Conference; declared against "partition of Ireland in any form, temporary or permanent"; and came out in favour of an International Labour Day, housing reform and minimum wage and a 48-hour week. This must have gone rather too far for Hugh Lyon, the STUC's new chairman who was to prove a restraining influence on the PC. Through shortage of cash they only sent a small delegation to London to process their other decisions. With the general mood and expectations throughout the movement, though not so openly expressed as in Ireland, the Imperial Government was alarmed at what effect the controversy about the proposed Stockholm international gathering might have on their coming offensive in France, not to mention the autumn mutinies; and also the resulting changes the offensive demanded in the munitions factories. On this occasion, therefore, the STUC delegation of Lyon, Climie, William Shaw, Houghton and Allan was received by the Prime Minister, Lloyd George, himself. He gave them a long and crafty answer, largely devoted to reminiscences about his own past interest in Home Rule for Scotland and Wales. In this he set the tone for the evasive replies from the other Ministers they met; the general response was that committees were sitting, and that prospects for early legislation were "appalling", and would need "drastic alteration in Parliamentary procedure". Moreover, six months later the Secretary for Scotland was ready to attend the 1918 Congress at Ayr to give a long address on the Education (Scotland) Bill. A leading member of the Labour Party's National Executive was also sent to make a fraternal address, followed by James Deans, described as "the Grand Old Man of the Scottish Co-operative Movement". Besides these there were also present two Americans, the President of the Washington State Federation of Labour and the Editor of the *International Moulders' Union,* who were on a mission studying methods of war production. But clearly the Ayr Congress in the spring of 1918 listened most closely to the two Irish fraternal delegates, with their Secretary P T Daly reporting on how their strike against conscription had "been a great success, everything having been held up throughout the country, except in Belfast".

The Report to the Ayr Congress had expressed satisfaction at "the large increase in the membership of the trade unions in Scotland", especially noting "the enormously increased influence of the trade union movement in the life of the nation". Among the 206 delegates, five per cent were women – mostly in textiles and print, a notable increase. Congress now learnt for the first time of Carson's retirement. This prompted the Glaswegian Councillor George Kerr, Workers Union, to observe that "as Societies had no knowledge of the Secretary's impending retirement", nominations should be thrown open, with Congress having an opportunity to nominate. There was some discussion before "ultimately it was agreed to receive nominations"; but in fact the Standing Orders Chairman finally "intimated that no additional nominations had been made" other than Allan's by Edinburgh Trades Council. His reign therefore began officially; it was short, with an unfortunate ending, after the PC had to suspend him two years later.

Throughout the 1918 Congress other differences emerged on major issues; meanwhile on most of their usual topics delegates predictably expressed themselves in particularly strong terms. On Scottish representation and Home Rule generally, for example, they insisted that a Scottish Parliament "should be inaugurated at the earliest possible moment", for the "neglect of Scottish interests and the growing congestion of public business in the Imperial Parliament render it imperative". This was linked with a demand that "Scotland as a nation be directly represented at the Peace Conference". On industrial questions "no National Committee can be considered as complete unless Scottish Trade Unionism is officially represented".

A new angle on demobilisation and current problems came when Agnes Adams of the National Federation of Women Workers described the difficulties of the new labour force who had done so much in the war factories. Hers was a strong protest against the Government delaying demobilisation proposals. Already

> thousands of women are being discharged, many of whom have borne the burden of overtime and night work for a long period, and who are faced with unemployment before reconstruction proposals become operative.

There must be a general enquiry of what firms would need women workers when war work stopped; the information should be distributed in advance to employment exchanges; and through trade unions, forms should be issued which war workers and women substitutes could fill in about what future employment they wanted. Government factories should give reasonable notice or wages in lieu; and women who had left their homes to work away be given railway fares home. Where there had been excessive overtime, four weeks' paid leave should be granted to restore their health. Government factories should be used as national production centres; and re-training with maintenance for women who were without work in their own trades to go back to.

Section (vi): **War and Peace Aims**

Other new points came from trades councils when education was being discussed. Glasgow declared the STUC must be "unalterably opposed" to the introduction of military training of any kind in the schools. From Aberdeen, James Balfour urged that there should be compulsory teaching in all schools and colleges "of Industrial History and Economics". Perhaps this last remark was prompted by the same conclusions which led to the increasingly detailed demands that year about nationalisation in mines, land, railways, shipping and the banks; it must provide for "effective control" through industrial organisations "in partnership with the State". Where there was strong division of opinion it was on aspects of war aims and peace aims. There had long been differences about peace aims on the PC. Very soon after the Russian new Soviet Government had dropped the bombshell of publishing the secret treaties, Neil Beaton (Edinburgh Shop Assistants) tried to get the PC to issue a memorandum on war and peace aims. Instead, one of the busy subcommittees was left to draft one; but two months later they decided not to issue one, as they "thought it was not an opportune time to intervene in this discussion".[7]

At the Congress, six weeks later, Hugh Lyon made the attitude of the outgoing majority clear in the course of his Presidential Address. He said that after the Russian revolution, about which they had at first rejoiced, "we have watched with fear and anxiety the fate of a great people tremble in the balance. Those who authorised the demobilisation of Russia were either simple fools or German tools". He went on to complain that "the German workers as a whole have disappointed Social Democracy". He therefore concluded that

> we must continue this war until we have taught Germany that militarism does not pay.

And what of the future?

> We hear a great deal of a League of Nations preventing war in the future. I am not so optimistic. I ha'e me doots.

The International in the past was "only a name because of its want of strength and influence". In his view a "Labour International Board should be set up, composed of men who will have the confidence of the workers". Later he referred critically to "certain Labour Peace Men", and said that "fighting amongst ourselves" should be avoided. Finally he suggested as "a Scots monument to the memory of the thousands of workers who have made the supreme sacrifice in this war", the PC should take up the attempts which had been made for years "to build offices and halls to house the activities of Trade Union and Labour bodies". It was a project that Allan also was extremely keen about, as we shall see – indeed, too much so.

On the League of Nations the Railway Clerks moved a resolution favouring it "to enforce the maintenance of peace on the plan advocated by the President of the United States". But Aberdeen Trades Council and the Mason and Granite Cutters laid the emphasis on

> co-operation with the labour organisations in other countries and to assist in organising a Federation of Nations for the establishment of suitable machinery for the adjustment and settlement of international disputes by conciliation or judicial arbitration.

The resolution was carried, with 21 voting for the amendment. Shinwell for Glasgow Trades Council, seconded by Robert Smillie for the Miners, called on the British Government at once to make "a declaration of War Aims" based on Woodrow Wilson's speech to Congress. They also called on the Government "to cancel all treaties having for their object territorial aggrandisement and economic warfare". The Sailors and Firemen tried to cut out the words "economic warfare"; but the resolution was carried 108 to 35. There was "an animated discussion" when the Sailors and Firemen condemned "the brutal murders and robbery of British and neutral seamen on the high seas by the commanders and crews of German U-boats". They added three other clauses, concluding that "there can be no peace by negotiation with a nation who attempts to justify such abominable crimes". They named leading German trade union members of the Central Council of the International Transport Workers for justifying these actions and called for "no intercourse with the German nation" for five years unless they overthrew Kaiser and Government and made "full reparation". Glasgow and Motherwell Trades Councils' delegates succeeded in getting all but the central protest deleted, but only by 78 to 52. The Sailors and Firemen were also involved in an unsuccessful attempt to prevent conscientious objectors being released from prison, which Glasgow Trades Council had successfully moved. That year with half their delegation coming from English or Welsh ports they were the biggest of any group except the miners.

References

[1] See "Engineering Struggles", Edmund and Ruth Frow, 1982.
[2] Francis Williams describes this in the official history of the Labour Party, written after the Second World War, "Fifty Years March".
[3] Described in "The Monocled Mutineer", William Allison & John Fairley 1978.
[4] 'Fifty Years March", op. cit.
[5] PC Minutes, 3 August, 1916.
[6] PC Minutes, 2 March, 1918.
[7] PC Minutes, 9 March, 1918.

8

World War I: The Third Stage

While Congress delegates, some seven months before the Armistice was signed with Britain's trade rivals the Germans, discussed how the end should come to the fighting on the Continent, and how such wars might be prevented from happening again, the pointer to the future came in a different debate. In this there were the differences over the old and all-important question of the shorter working week; and it was an early warning of the coming battle on the home front. Not only was the conduct of it crucial for the very survival of the STUC; it illustrates the special characteristics of the Scottish trade union movement, with important lessons to be learnt from both its strength and weakness.

Section (i): **The Battle on the Home Front**

It was no accident that there should be a major battle on the home front as soon as the war was over on the Continent; nor that Clydeside, with its shipyards and factories totally concentrated on war production for the biggest offensive, should be in the forefront. Was there to be an immediate return to "normality"? And what, in fact, could that mean, after such immensely changed conditions? From the point of view of the men and women delegates from the war factories, that spring of 1918 was seeing the beginning of the third period of "the Great War" – war continued by other means, with major risings and counter-risings on the Continent and throughout the British Empire. And at home?

Through these months rapidly rising distrust, anxiety and anger were seeping through, as became very clear from the unusually busy Minutes of the PC meetings. They themselves continued constantly concerned to seek recognition on the many Government and Ministry conferences, committees and inquiries which now were proliferating. When unsuccessful at least they now got information about them, for the Government was more than eager to be seen as active about future plans; in addition one of their number might be present in some other capacity. But also a PC meeting now never passed without being called upon to respond to complaints of many kinds. There were appeals about the repression in Ireland and interference with the transport union there; frequent calls for protest about the frame-up in California on a bombing charge of Tom Mooney from the USA Moulders' Defense Committee; against the imprisonment of the Tiree crofters who had seized land on which to grow food. Then Aberdeen Trades Council complained of Chinese labour at low wages being put to build roads; Dundee Trades Council reported on the inadequate pensions for the troops' dependants. Quite a new feature was the number of complaints from trades councils south of the border on which the PC took action in Scotland. They followed up Brighton's demand for homes and better benefits for war orphans; the protest about the Socialist Labour Press being dismantled from Halifax Trades Council; from Bradford Trades Council that "all raw materials" should be controlled "on the declaration of Peace". From Merthyr Trades Council came a very strongly worded demand, very close in spirit to what was being said on the Clyde. It referred to

> the unmistakable signs that the Government contemplates the immediate rehabilitation of private ownership by handing back to their original owners the Mines, Railways, Shipping and Industrial Factories.

It went on to demand that National Executives should prevent this, and special national conferences should be called

> to authorise the Parliamentary Committee of the Trades Union Congress and the Labour Party Executive to sit in continuous session to prevent it.

This the PC endorsed. They also, but after "considerable discussion", adopted by five to three a resolution from Bristol Trades Council protesting at "the military expedition of the Allies in Russia and Siberia", describing the intervention as

> being carried out under the orders of the various representatives of capitalistic nations, whose fear of the overthrow of their accursed system will drive them to adopt any and every cruel and subtle method to stave off the inevitable.

When, therefore, the outright clash came on the question of hours it was no mere incident, but the culmination of many bitter grievances and deep distrust of the Government.

When that year he reported to his own Scottish Carters' Association,

Hugh Lyon said that the education gained from the war had opened their eyes:

> They have gained more in the last four and a half years than their forefathers learned in fifty years.

He himself had been the STUC chairman throughout 1918, and had indeed much to learn himself. Throughout the war the long hours worked had been incredible. For the older men, now tending to be among the leading officials at most levels, their minds were full of what had happened after the Boer War and the years of unemployment following that relatively so much smaller war. For the younger activists the keenest memory was "the Great Unrest" years immediately before the outbreak in 1914, and their awareness that they had then been on the point of breakthrough: the Engineering and Shipbuilding Trades had then already been nine months in negotiation for a 48-hour week. It was unthinkable that they could now be forced back to the 53 to 56 hours they had been working. The same held true of the 40 types of craft unions in the railway workshops or those in the general union on the lines. All were aware of the new technology, not least the smithy men and boilermakers; the dilution of labour, premium bonus and piecework problems.

In Scotland for the men and women on the shop floor and their stewards instant action was vital, with the immediate run-down of munitions factories and mass demobilisation to come, threatening immense unemployment. They would not and could not accept delay. Any who argued for "patience" might well be seen as covering up Governmental betrayal of pledges. It was impossible for there not to be a mood that for any section of the labour movement to seem not ready to break out of wartime total collaboration stamped them as "employers' men". It was true that many of the leadership of the British trade unions were indeed in some considerable disarray; they had developed their outlook and methods in coping with problems of what now could seem a very different epoch. During the war emergency they were of course committed to sharing with employers' attitudes on the basic need for maximum war production. Here was indeed a change; as issue after issue came up for urgent treatment, at Westminster or in the factories, quick decisions were needed; yet every trick was resorted to, from time-wasting "enquiries" and "advisories" to sudden apparent concessions hastily introduced. Many of these problems puzzling negotiators in London were irrelevant to the men and women at ground level, especially in the war-dependent industry of Clydeside: they agreed with their shop stewards on the need for immediate action, there and then, together with industrial action and in the streets if there was no movement at the top alone, or it got bogged down. A leadership pleading for time and discipline could seem to them only the familiar voice of the enemy.

Long before, even during the 'Cost of Living Conference" in 1915, an Eight Hours Bill was seen as the key to the "After the War Problems". It was strongly repeated in 1916 and 1917; yet the PC had taken no follow-up action. But that was now changed at this stage of war. So the PC got together with the Scottish Advisory Council of the Labour Party to convene on 14 March, 1918, a conference of trade union officials, prompted by "the growing feeling that a movement for shorter hours and a shorter working week is overdue". There were 80 officials present, who decided to recommend to their head offices that there should be a Bill to take effect on demobilisation for a 40-hour maximum week, with Saturday as a holiday, made up of an eight-hour day with an hour dinner break. They were to return with their union's answer to the 1918 Congress at Ayr a month later. But the angry Clyde shop stewards favoured a more drastic claim. When the PC's recommendation was moved at Congress, there came an amendment from Councillor Emanuel Shinwell for Glasgow Trades Council and G Jackson of the Sailors and Firemen that

> the first act of reconstruction after the war should be a reduction of the hours of labour to six per day.

After what was described as "a full discussion" Congress carried this demand for a 30-hour week by 77 to 51; so that became official STUC policy. This was to illustrate the difficulties throughout the entire British trade union and labour movement and was to present the PC, and finally Congress itself, with a major problem. If the STUC was to prove unable to face up to it and give a sound and creative lead, its days were numbered.

It is never difficult for armchair strategists to fight other peoples' battles at a safe distance in time: but to understand what the STUC did achieve it is necessary to know their circumstances in some detail and what the situation demanded at the turning point of what could have been a new era, which was what so many looked for after all their sacrifices. First, it must be realised that there was no strong Parliamentary Labour Party then capable of immediately taking power to form an alternative Government which could stand up to the employers and take the immediate minimum steps towards the total social change so longed for. Direct industrial power alone was available. This would need to be concentrated on a single central demand. To make it effective the movement needed to confront employers and State with the power of overwhelming action from the ground up, capable of uniting and holding the support of employed, unemployed and the troops impatiently awaiting demobilisation.

A fearless and determined powerful lead was possible; to a considerable degree it was forthcoming in Scotland, notably from the shop stewards movement. They made a mistake, however, perhaps due partly to their long experience of neglect from the centre of the British Empire: they now had little or no regard for potential allies outside their national borders; yet that was where their opponents were concentrated. They disregarded the upper reaches of those unions centred in London, and to some degree misinterpreted any slowness or apparent reluctance to move quickly. This was not unnatural; for they could see the workforce being broken up and knew how soon their own strength could, therefore, be dissipated. But they carried disregard of the capacity of the movement elsewhere to such a degree that the Scottish activists did not even stay in touch with or keep informed the shop stewards' movement in engineering then being formed all over Great Britain.

Section (ii): **Shorter Hours a Key Question**

On the other side for twenty years leading negotiators in the engineering unions had been confronted with different district levels of demand on most subjects: they had not found – and perhaps had not always sought – ways to unify common action. For that to be possible they would need to concentrate on a unified central demand. The shorter working week would certainly be that, in general terms; but when it came to being expressed in detailed claims, the grounds for division were immense. Of this the employers could and did take full advantage.

It was here that the STUC sought to play a unique role, in the spirit of their characteristic closeness between grass-roots and top leadership. Yet the STUC in the principled stand which they did now take also made mistakes: they did not realise soon enough how absolutely essential was speedy action, to demonstrate to all the impatient and suspicious people in the war factories that they recognised that time was of the essence. Yet the central point remains that, in the long run, once action had begun their stand for solidarity prevented the essential links being broken. It meant that confidence in the STUC at least was not lost; the STUC remained a going concern in the years of extreme difficulty ahead, and could preserve an essential base on which the

Scottish Trades Union Congress, Parliamentary Committee, 1918.

Back Row (left to right) – W. G. Hunter, *Vice-chairman* (Operative Bakers' National Federal Union), William Shaw (Glasgow Trades Council), J. O'Hagan (Amalgamated Steel and Ironworkers), N. S. Beaton, *Treasurer* (National Amalgamated Union of Shop Assistants), R. Climie (Ayrshire Trades Council).

Seated (left to right) – J. C. Hendry (Brechin Mill and Factory Workers), R. Allan (Edinburgh Trades Council), H. Lyon, *Chairman* (Scottish Horse and Motormen's Association), George Carson, *Secretary*, and J. Houghton (Scottish Union of Dock Labourers).

future could one day be built, when once the time and opportunity came again.

The difficulties were great indeed, both of aim and of method. The detailed claim varied on at least five levels – and by the enormous margin of 18 hours a week between highest and lowest – in the different industries, trades and unions, some recently or on the point of amalgamation. Production needs varied: with so much dilution and technological change there were differing considerations of piecework, premium bonus, lieu rates, unavoidable overtime and its permitted limits. That alone was enough to lead negotiators to concentrate on problems of method and to give rise to doubt of how legal terms for a Bill of universal application could be drafted effectively. That had been the centre of the controversy that had raged in the British TUC in the 'eighties and 'nineties.

Many claims for 48 hours were already under negotiation. In road transport, with its special features and Saturday working unavoidable, they might get a 44-hour week of an eight-hour day and half day Saturday; it could be won from certain employers. For many in the poorly organised occupations where a 56-hour week was all too common, 40 hours worked in five days would be a triumphant and demonstrative target for vast improvement. The engineering and shipbuilding trades, so important for Clydeside, Belfast and Tyne and Wear, had resumed negotiations over the 48 hour demand which dated back to early 1914. Now in view of the rising feeling, they were cunningly offered an immediate decrease to 47 hours, to start at once, provided they instantly took a binding ballot. This created an immense upheaval, not least amongst the Clydesiders. Their shop stewards had been pressing for the 30-hour week to absorb all the returning men and the unemployed; the Socialist speakers had been advocating it as a first step "towards the emancipation of the working class". But now they were being called on by their unions from London to ballot, not on a choice of hours, but to accept or refuse 47 hours at once – a mere hour better than they had been on the point of winning in 1914. This, which the employers in fact very soon succeeded in evading, was now suddenly pushed on them in the aftermath of a rushed post-war General Election. It was the last straw. Indeed for the Clydesiders "the reduction of hours by seven a week was the most unpopular victory I ever experienced", the former shipyard worker, Finlay Hart, was to say in after years. For when it became operative they found it involved the loss of an important meal break; this saddled the Clyde shipyard workers "with the most agonising, long-drawn-out spell between the new starting time and their only meal break after midday". At the time Finlay Hart was an apprentice in Beardmore's shipyard at Dalmuir.

Many were accustomed to travelling long distances for an all too early start at 6 a.m., with no food before the welcome break at 9.15, when the locals could even get home for a quick cooked breakfast. But although with the 47-hour week they had a later start, which did give them a little extra sleeping time, they had to wait four and a half hours to break their fast at all. Naturally, an unrecognised "custom and practice" arose of making tea on the job and eating a "piece" in the morning. "Whereupon managers and foremen went round kicking over tea cans and fining the men when caught." That was to keep shop stewards busy with complaints for many a long year, Finlay Hart adds.

This was one of the many factors which had a considerable effect on grass-roots attitudes, including the demand put forward by the Clyde Workers Committee and the many supporting shop stewards determined on the 30-hour week. They were also utterly resistant to anything like a delaying tactic, whether by Government, employers, London officials or any apparent hesitancy of the Parliamentary Committee.

The PC of the STUC indeed had a major crisis to face, which was to last many months. All through it there were divisions between them all. Now twelve in number, including the aged Carson as "consultant to the Secretary", only two were members of British unions, the Railway Clerks and the Shop Assistants. Alongside them were a miner and a shale miner, who had their own hours claim; the Scottish Dock Labourers were represented by the Treasurer; there were also the small Steel & Iron Workers and the even smaller Tinplate & Sheet Metal Workers; and two from textile unions where hours had long been a nightmare. William Shaw of Glasgow Trades Council was inevitably in close touch with the Clyde Workers Committee. Of the remaining officers, Secretary Robert Allan was a typographer, and the Chairman Hugh Lyon was the busy General Secretary of the Scottish Carters Association. He was in a particularly difficult personal position; at one time on behalf of the PC he was publicly demanding that all should be on strike in support of the 40-hours claim, while he was concluding negotiations on 44 hours for his own members, who were committed to returning on those terms. Several of the PC members in their youth had been prominent Socialist speakers; some of their former comrades were in jail or on their way there.

They had long been committed to joint action with the Scottish LP Advisory Committee, operating the Joint Committee with them. Just how far could they go on doing so without referring back to the PC again if a change in STUC policy was involved? That got their representatives into real difficulty. When the STUC 1918 Congress had accepted the 30-hour amendment it had been a useful victory for the Clyde Workers Committee and the Socialists in their persistent campaign; for the PC it was an embarrassment. Their representatives on the Joint Committee agreed on a recall of the trade union officials conference on 20 June, 1918, to whom they explained that the STUC's policy was now "to some extent in conflict" with the previous decision; they should therefore "consider the technical aspect of the case". The Joint Committee's statement explained that "quite a number of societies" had put in different claims, including the Associated Ironmoulders' complicated call for a 44-hour week with many breaks in each day. Their statement went on to say that it was obviously necessary to "find some proposition which will secure the substantial support of the mass of the workers". After a long discussion of many possibilities, finally "it narrowed down to a vote between 40 and 30 hours", with the 40 hours being finally carried as the most acceptable by the extremely narrow margin of 40 to 37. It was not until October when Lyon was interviewing the Minister of Labour on another matter and warned him of the intensity of feeling in Scotland on the hours question that it was reported publicly that the STUC's policy was now for 40 hours. Other members of the PC objected strongly that their subcommittee had allowed STUC policy to be changed without referring back to the PC.

Section (iii): **Caught Between Officials and Stewards**

Following the Armistice and the speedy General Election, the situation sharpened, with immense anger amongst the engineering and shipbuilding workers about massive unemployment and their union's hasty ballot. In the words of the STUC's Report to the 1919 Congress:

> Large numbers in favour of a shorter working week than 47 hours were feeling aggrieved at not having been allowed to record that opinion. In addition to this, no provision had been made to compensate pieceworkers and lieu workers for the reduction in their hours of earnings. These factors had produced rampant dissatisfaction in the whole Clyde shipbuilding and engineering industry.

The PC decided to call an STUC special conference on 27 and 28 December, 1918. Here their official policy was regularised, and they put it back to 40 hours, but with the highly significant addition that the PC was to be "empowered to devise such methods of industrial action as will enforce this demand". Lyon was in the chair, and was regarded by those well to the right as responsible for a serious breach of

Standing Orders in allowing that addition for action. A fortnight later the PC decided that because of "the very great dissatisfaction" the 47 hours was causing they "resolved to use every means to unify the forces of Labour to bring about a reduction" to a 40-hour week. For this purpose, they would call a conference of representatives from trade union district committees, the Clyde Federation of Engineering and Shipbuilding Trades, Glasgow Trades Council and others, and would urge that their executive committees should instruct their members to strike on 10 February, 1919.

But they were forestalled by the shop stewards movement. Pushing for the 30 hours and for strike action not to be delayed, stewards from all over Scotland were summoned to a Joint Conference on 18 January, 1919, called jointly by the Glasgow Trades Council and the Ways and Means Committee of the Scottish Shop Stewards. On receiving an invitation the PC decided to send four representatives, hoping to reduce the demand to the 40 hours which they believed was acceptable. This they succeeded in doing; but they were horrified when the meeting went on to speed up the demand for a General Strike to start on 27 January, with no proper consultation with the union executives, whom the PC had hoped gradually to persuade into united action. Most awkward of all, Lyon was invited to serve on the Manifesto subcommittee, which produced "A Call to Arms of the Workers" for the Joint Strike Committee. At this Lyon wished to resign both from the Joint Strike Committee and from the PC, where there was a long and bitter debate about it. Finally, by the casting vote of William Shaw, the PC decided Lyon must stay on, although they now appeared committed unintentionally to a far too early strike. Their Minutes of 22 January, 1919, state:

> The opinion was freely expressed that we had been pushed into precipitate action, but on the whole the members of the Committee felt it was difficult to avoid such a result, as undoubtedly if a movement for 30 hours had once been launched it would seriously have jeopardised the position of the 40 Hours Movement and caused no end of dissension. On the other hand the co-operation of the PC with a non-official movement was seriously questioned by other members.

From then onward, while deploring the haste, the PC felt that once the workers had been brought out "it was felt to be impossible for another course to be taken by the PC than to support the strike". This they stuck to, although "well aware the parties involved were in many cases not only non-official but even anti-official". They then set out to work for recognition of the strike by the executives.

But by the time the PC could put the full case to their own

Scotland-wide Joint Conference on 1 February, there was a new situation. The authorities had gone into action and the police had mounted the ferocious attack on the peaceful demonstration with a deputation to the Lord Provost which appears in some history books as "the George Square Riot". Twelve leaders were arrested, including Councillor Shinwell as chairman of the Joint Strike Committee together with two other future MPs, Willie Gallacher and David Kirkwood. A detachment of troops had also been sent into Glasgow. The fury that this aroused throughout the whole movement tended to turn all eyes to the Clyde: but it must be remembered that there had been considerable activity and support for the strike throughout Scotland, particularly from Edinburgh, Dundee and Aberdeen. All these were strongly represented at the Scotland-wide Conference, which protested in strongest language

> against the authorities and the police in their brutal attack upon the strikers and declare the Lord Provost and the authorities are criminally responsible for that attack upon the defenceless citizens of Glasgow, and demand the release of Messrs Shinwell, Kirkwood, Gallacher and others.

Endorsement of the PC's position was moved by 92 votes to 22; while an addendum aimed to get the strike called off at once "with the object of getting National Executives to take all possible official action to consolidate the movement" was rejected by 74 to 24.

The STUC, while taking an independent line, had stuck to the Joint Strike Committee. They warned the Ministry of Labour to intervene and the Government quickly "to deal with the hours question from a national point of view". When later the Government did finally call an Industrial Conference "to consider the prevailing unrest", the PC regarded it as a direct result of the Scottish movement, the Belfast strikes and the independent moves of miners, railwaymen and transport workers. All these bodies in time, and separately, were cheated. But the STUC had proved to the working people throughout Scotland that they would not allow them to be scabbed upon.

Section (iv): **Attacked and Defended**

At the 1919 Congress, held in Perth for the second time, 225 delegates from half a million Scottish trade unionists heard the PC's actions sharply criticised and warmly defended from different standpoints. Neil Beaton (Shop Assistants) put it all in perspective in an able

Presidential Address, expressing the problems and the mood; he was just about to become the Propagandist Organiser of the Scottish Co-operative Wholesale Society. He took the strong Socialist line that the whole "capitalist system stands condemned. The system was responsible for the war and today is tottering to its fall. The capitalists are moving heaven and earth to save it, and unless we are careful and active it may get a new lease of life." At the end of his speech he moved from the chair an emphatic protest about the imprisonment of the strike leaders, and that "every effort to obtain their release" should be made by the new PC. Two people voted against it, only because they "did not consider the resolution strong enough".

Immoderately worded criticism of the PC came from two officials, the fiercest opponents of the Clydeside shop stewards movement; these were Councillor James Walker of the huge Iron and Steel Trades, who was to follow Beaton as STUC chairman; and from Bailie Whitehead, West of Scotland Brass Finishers, which an angry shop steward described as "the miserable craft organisation". Equally critical of the PC was another official, ex-Captain Bailie Alex Turner (Municipal Employees), once a leading Socialist activist. Speaking strongly on the other side was John Fulton (Scottish Dock Labourers); with him were two of the Joint Strike Committee itself, John Auld (United Patternmakers) and George Buchanan, whose fellow delegate and secretary of the Glasgow Trades Council, William Shaw, spoke to justify the attitude of the PC, of which he was a member. So did his colleague, old Robert Climie of Ayr Trades Council; in a thoughtful speech he said they had indeed "been castigated" at the Special Conference for not taking more definite action; and that they had tried hard to get a general Scottish movement for 40 hours and win the Executives to sanction strike action.

No vote was taken in the debate at the report stage, in which the biggest single delegation took no part: for the Miners had much earlier sent a deputation to the PC for a "principled discussion" and had left "evidently satisfied that the PC had given them the fullest information and explanation possible".[1] Not only had they raised the point about "being stampeded" into co-operating in an unofficial strike; their most important question was on whether Standing Orders permitted the STUC to initiate industrial action. As we shall see, this was part and parcel of the whole matter of reorganisation in the next years, both at the British TUC and the Scottish TUC. The Miners did, however, play a part later in Congress in deciding future policy to further the Shorter Working Week. Bailie James Doonan spoke in support of an Edinburgh Trades Council motion that

> each industry should at once take steps to secure a substantial reduction of hours without loss of earnings and an arrangement of working hours suitable to each industry or occupation.

He said the question of hours was "one for the unions to adjust themselves". He continued that it was a mistake to commit Congress "to a policy which only a Union could carry through". An amendment came from the Glasgow Trades Council for a uniform five-day week with a maximum eight-hour day, overtime being limited to 20 hours a month. William Shaw stressed that there were then 50,000 out of work in Glasgow; and he denied that the policy would increase foreign competition, because French and German workers were demanding the same. But Edinburgh's motion was carried by 81 to 41, with apparently nearly half the delegates abstaining.

There was one other significant motion. On behalf of the majority of the PC, Robert Allan moved to amend Standing Orders by introducing the block vote, and conform "to the practice of the British TUC and National Labour Party". Hugh Lyon seconded it; but Robert Climie was amongst those who opposed it. Charles Robertson, Motherwell Trades Council, also opposed, on the ground that it "would give the public a wrong impression of what Trades Congress thought on important occasions". It was rejected by a two to one vote. Perth had shown that delegates would not permit the STUC to give up its basic principles. But it also saw the end of the STUC's campaigning for a 40-hour week for many a long year.

References

[1] Minutes 1 March, 1919.

9

Facing Up to Change

During the Perth Congress there was a moment when delegates looked back to the past to see how far they had come as they bade goodbye to George Carson with a £500 cheque. They recalled that he had been with Keir Hardie at the founding of the first Scottish Labour Party in 1889, of the Independent Labour Party in 1893, of the Scottish TUC in 1897 and of the Scottish Workers Labour Representation Committee in 1900. In reply Carson referred to his activity "fifty-six years ago" in the Glasgow Trades Council. He added that trades councils

> were then regarded much as a Soviet was now, although he was all for order and constitution in the Trade Union Movement. They could not get on very far without discipline in the ranks.

But despite their look back at Perth there were already portents of things to come.

Section (i): **Reactions to the Broken Promises**

For four years from the spring of 1919 until their Congress met in 1923 at Dundee the Scottish TUC went through turbulent and perplexing times and saw upheavals of many kinds, hampered in their response by internal difficulties. All too soon it was clear that there was no "going back to normal", nor to old ways of negotiation and seeking solutions. First and foremost a lasting peace seemed very far off as well as the long hoped-for radical social change. British troops were still in action; but now against Irish trade unionists and Indian nationalists, and also with the frightening threat of them being committed against the new regime in Russia, Britain's previous ally. Indeed, troops were also being prepared to intervene during industrial struggles in Scotland, England and Wales. For the Government's broken promises brought about major national strikes and lockouts in the key industries of shipbuilding, railways, docks, mining and engineering as control was handed back to private ownership, and special war factory buildings were abandoned in Scotland. Everything was now being done to cripple the unions and union rights. Even the newly formed union for the police force was broken and an Emergency Powers Act introduced ready to suppress any future industrial unrest. Recovering unfettered control of their mines, shipyards, docks, factories and transport the employers sought divisions to weaken and prepare for wage cuts. Divisions were all too easy to create: with Britain's normal export markets on which the Clydeside, Dundee and Leith so heavily depended once demand for major munitions ceased, in chaos, disillusionment must soon set in. For just ahead was mass unemployment which was to be a social fetter on the movement until the next world war threatened, nearly twenty years later.

How were trade unionists to respond to this? Some turned to put their faith rather in purely political action following defeats on the industrial front. Attitudes here, however, varied, as may be seen from the different emphasis in the presidential addresses at the first four post-war Congress years.

In 1920 William Shaw, who was at the time also Secretary of Glasgow Trades Council referred to the "unfulfilled promises and pledges" by the Government, especially on nationalising the mines. He said that "direct action", in his opinion,

> should have been adopted by the whole Trade Union Movement in support of the Miners: instead, however, it has been decided to rely upon political action, and at the next election you may be certain that the wily politicians will have an election cry that will have a counteracting effect and the trade unionists may be tricked again.

Different indeed was Councillor James Walker's view in 1921. Referring to the collapse of the Triple Alliance, he said:

> I have never been in favour of a general strike to enforce demands which have a political solution .... The road of progress lies through organisation and education. The ballot box is the finest weapon the working classes possess, and it is only by an intelligent use of that weapon that they will be able to secure emancipation from the conditions under which they are labouring today.

He himself was to contest Rotherham at the General Election. In 1922, presiding over just half the number of the previous year's delegates, C N Gallie, of the Railway Clerks, regarded it as an "affliction that a proportion see their emancipation only in the form of a political ballot box". A contrasting view came in 1923 from an old miner, who had been present at the first Congress. After "well-nigh 50 years as man

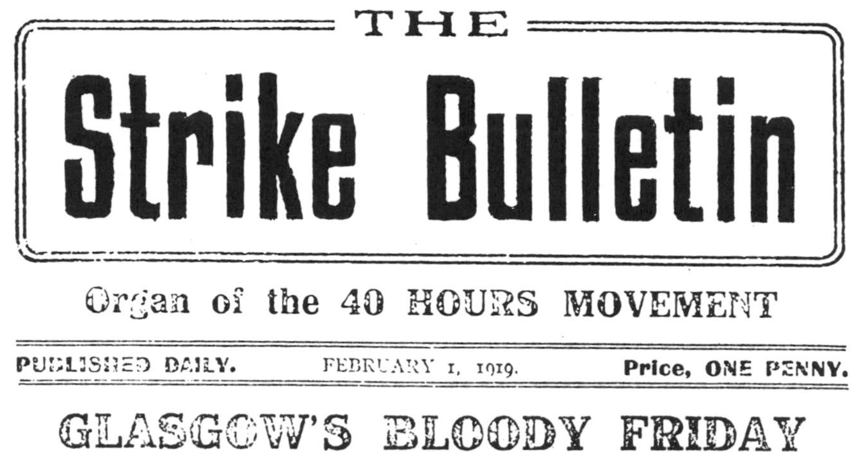

THE
Strike Bulletin

Organ of the 40 HOURS MOVEMENT

PUBLISHED DAILY. FEBRUARY 1, 1919. Price, ONE PENNY.

GLASGOW'S BLOODY FRIDAY

Brutal Attack on Defenceless Strikers

HENCEFORTH January 31, 1919, will be known in Glasgow as Bloody Friday, and, for the crime of attacking defenceless workers, the citizens will hold the authorities responsible. The police have once more been used as hirelings to bludgeon the workers.

The workers will not forget.

The outrage looks like a prearranged affair by the master class. As arranged on Wednesday, a deputation from the Joint Committee, composed of Shinwell, Kirkwood, Neil MacLean, Hopkins, and other delegates, waited on the Lord Provost in the City Chambers to receive the reply from the Prime Minister and the Minister of Labour, in response to his Lordship's *own* appeal for Government intervention. While the deputation were kept waiting for twenty minutes, and, while there, the police were ordered to draw their batons and forcibly disperse the crowd of strikers who were standing in George Square until the deputation returned.

On hearing the sound of conflict, Shinwell and Kirkwood rushed out to help in restoring order; but instead of listening, the police made an attack on them, too, and Kirkwood was felled to the ground. The strikers covered Shinwell successfully, and got him clear away without injury.

Those who appealed for order were also clubbed, as were other strikers who were quietly inclined, as was shown by their defenceless condition.

The bludgeon attack on the strikers in front of the City Chambers was deliberately ordered by the officers, and was unprovoked. The attack was sheer brutality by the police to satisfy the lust of the masters for broken skulls. The masters, afraid to do their own dirty work, employ the police to do it for them.

The meeting in front of the City Chambers was quiet and orderly, and was being addressed by members of the Strike Committee until the deputation returned from the interview with the Lord Provost. Shinwell, before the deputation entered the City Chambers, appealed to the crowd to be of good behaviour, and this appeal was endorsed by the other speakers. The audience, which was turned towards the Gladstone statue, on which the speakers were perched, overflowed into the street fronting the Chambers, and, in this avenue the police allowed two motors to run into the crowd, with the result that two men were knocked down and injured. This annoyed the strikers, who appealed to the police to turn the vehicular traffic by another street—a not unreasonable request.

The reply was: a police attack on the strikers, who stood their ground, and the police withdrew after an appeal from the speakers. The mounted police then arrived, and, in a display of trick riding, two of them allowed their horses to fall, which caused the crowd to chaff the bulky Tod Sloans. This chaff was an awful violation of the sacred

The Strike Bulletin of 1 February, 1919, printed by the Socialist Labour Press

and boy and trade union official", James Murdoch said that while he would "never give up the right to strike", he regarded it at best as

> a cruel and barbarous weapon, especially as often happens in our mining villages, where the strikers are evicted from their homes . . . . We have a weapon which causes no evictions, no starvation, no long weary years of debt to be paid up . . . . Many of present-day problems can only be solved by Municipal and Political action.

Yet since the war the Scots had used a form of "direct action" on one question which was popular and effective.

This was a general issue of prime importance – the question of housing, about which delegates to the 1920 Congress at Dunfermline had been deeply troubled. Not only were the shocking conditions in Scotland not being tackled; far from adequate were such measures of rents control won from the Government by the Scottish housewives' street action and rents strike in 1915, supported by the Clydeside shop stewards. Now the landlords were eagerly finding ways to raise rents. There was a lively debate, with four resolutions. Demanding action to retain and develop the Rents Restriction Act, J Fulton of the Scottish Dock Labourers, said that "to increase house rents by 40 per cent was wicked and pernicious . . . . they would organise a no-rent campaign". On other resolutions about fixing lower rents for the new local government dwellings, some doubted that a rent strike to enforce it would be on. Charles Robertson, the miner, of Motherwell Trades Council, said "not 50 per cent of the workers would support them" if they called a rent strike. James Balfour of Aberdeen Trades Council agreed, because "too many people who were homeless had no alternative". Peter Chambers, a miner from Dalkeith, Edinburgh, however, said:

> What the workers had to do was to get into the houses and fix the rents after . . . If there were wholesale evictions the indignation aroused would give rise to an effective strike policy.

A strong view was also expressed by Catherine Phillips, Shop Assistants: they should "encourage a direct action policy for housing. They should take a lesson from the Irish workers and bring on the construction of houses."

Three months later a special STUC was called on 10 July, 1920, on four burning issues: Ireland, the military action threatened against Russia, the high cost of living and for a rents strike. A resolution was passed calling on the Executive of all trade unions "to render the fullest possible support in the No Rent Campaign". A follow-up Conference three weeks later took the remarkable decision that

> the No Rent Campaign should be inaugurated by a 24 hours stoppage of work.

It was reported to the next Congress that "the call was responded to very loyally by large numbers of workers throughout Scotland, particularly in Glasgow and Edinburgh, a most impressive demonstration being made by the workers".

Whether "direct action" or a Parliamentary pressure were seen as the way to deal with the post-war broken promises, all agreed that unions needed to be strengthened and reorganised to provide an effective unifying factor. It was a preoccupation the Scots shared with the whole movement: but although differing arguments put forward by the British TUC were also heard in STUC circles, the presence here of trades council delegates close to the factory floor led to the emphasis being by no means the same. A background to all controversy was whether unions once in movement on a common policy in any industry could rely on supportive action from all, and how that could be quickly organised. They remembered experiences in an altogether different epoch during the "Great Unrest" following the railway strike in 1913, when the railwaymen, miners and transport workers were brought together into a Triple Alliance to agree on mutual aid. It had aroused immense hopes for the future. Now in the autumn of 1919, with the railwaymen deciding on strike action, what part would their partners in that great Triple Alliance play? But the movement was in for a serious shock: there was no action. When it was found that the railwaymen's leader, J H Thomas[1] had failed even to approach the Triple Alliance and the Parliamentary committee of the British TUC proved unable to move speedily to win support for them, serious doubts arose about the possibility of trade union solidarity being effective. Dismay at ground level became widespread indeed when just before the STUC's 1921 Congress at Aberdeen the London leaders of the Triple Alliance on "Black Friday" at the last minute refused to act in support of the miners in a major lockout.

It was a portent; valuable lessons can be learned from a disaster: four years later the memory and shame of "Black Friday" was to be wiped out by "Red Friday" in 1925, when the other unions in the Triple Alliance imposed a total ban on the movement of coal and stopped a lockout of miners aimed at bringing down wages in all trades. But opponents can also learn from the movement's mistakes, differences and divisions. Some of the same "Black Friday" personalities were involved in calling off, without due consultation with the miners whom it was to defend, the much greater General Strike of 1926 when it was on the point of victory.

From the early 'twenties for more than a dozen years to come throughout Britain, events were dominated by the differing reasons, aims and consequences of "reorganisation" and "co-ordination"; discussions of its limits, whether imposed openly or unadmitted, long continued. It was notably important in Scotland's special circumstances. There were still many small, exclusively Scottish, unions existing alongside those with merely Scottish area or district offices dependent on decisions of the distant Executives. The STUC was frequently unsuccessful in persuading some – notably the Amalgamated Engineering Union – to affiliate on their vigorous Scottish membership. Attempted amalgamations were accompanied by bitter long-standing demarcation and other problems.

In the vital coal industry decontrol had reinforced all the Scottish owners' aims at "district negotiation". This increased the trend towards "county unions" in the Scottish coalfield, and caused ruinous divisions, as in Fife, with rival bodies in the right-wing breakaway and reform unions.

The main solution was usually seen by the PC as in improving relations with the British TUC, which was due to visit Scotland, meeting in Glasgow in the autumn of 1919. It was perhaps partly with this in mind that Allan had tried to get Standing Orders amended to bring in the block vote, so that they should conform to the practice of the British TUC. When that body met in Glasgow five months later, with James Walker a delegate to it, William Shaw, as both Chairman of the STUC and Glasgow Trades Council Secretary, acted as their Minute Secretary. It therefore fell upon the Vice-Chairman, James Cook of the Scottish Miners, to welcome the British TUC at their first conference in Glasgow for 27 years. He spoke of the need for "Home Rule for Scotland, Wales, Ireland and England", remarking that

> the time is not far distant when the question of devolution, industrially as well as politically, will have to be taken up.

The two PCs held joint meetings during the week. The Scots had once more pressed that the British TUC should influence English unions to affiliate on their Scottish membership and pleaded once again that the STUC should be automatically invited to all national and international conferences, as well as STUC delegations being received by Ministries of right. Later there was a counter-proposal that the Scots should merely be invited to join British TUC deputations on suitable issues, and that perhaps the British TUC would treat them merely as their Scottish district. Naturally, little useful came of such proposals. Clearly, however, the PC was already feeling its way to some form of reorganisation which would have fuller recognition.

Section (ii): **"A Workers' Army General Staff"?**

The crunch came in 1919 with the railway strike. A special PC was called when Allan received a letter from Owen Coyle, Secretary of the Steel and Iron Workers (the Glasgow rival of James Walker's union) demanding a Special Conference to "discuss the question of taking action with the railwaymen". After considerable discussion the PC decided to call a conference of trade union officials in Glasgow; but they were only to be "officials representing head offices of unions". It was pointedly "agreed not to invite branch representation or trades councils".[2] They also sent a wire to the Prime Minister saying that "we are assured that the working classes in Scotland support the railwaymen", and urged the Government to get a settlement "so as to avoid a certain general stoppage". The officials conference met in private, when the strike had just been settled. But a significant resolution was carried, moved by Councillor Shinwell and Councillor John Heenan, both of Glasgow Trades Council, urging the PC

> to draw up a scheme by which joint action may be taken in the event of an industrial dispute and to submit such a scheme for the consideration of the STUC.

It would necessarily involve a central body to co-ordinate action – some sort of "Workers' Army General Staff". In fact the PC did not do so; they became involved instead in reorganisation schemes which the British TUC's PC was preparing to put to a Special Congress in London, to which they were invited on 9 and 10 December, 1920. On the eve of it they got a letter from William Shaw asking them to raise there a resolution from Glasgow Trades Council. They were troubled and in disagreement about this and there was "a very considerable discussion" about what to do. The Glasgow Trades Council was calling for

> the proposal for a "Down Tools" policy if the Government refuse to remove the blockade and establish trade relations with Russia, and to this end urges the British TUC to give a strong lead to the Trade Unionists of Britain, feeling confident that if the truth regarding Russia is put to the workers they will respond.

By five to three the PC decided to take no action. Conflicting moods about reorganisation and how far it might involve joint industrial supportive action were already developing in Scotland. The PC, however, was concentrating on the old story of greater recognition, while fitting in with the British TUC's schemes for "reorganisation". Many of the proposals dominated STUC practice later, when circumstances also forced upon them other changes peculiar to Scottish problems. The only thing on which all could and did agree was the urgent need for strengthening the trade union movement. Just how to do so might well be in doubt, but it might be fair to say that the defensive slogan of pioneering days of "defence not defiance" was now being replaced by another pioneering slogan of "Unity is Strength", coming gradually a little nearer to the desperate needs of the day which required unified support in so many spheres of action.

Throughout all the discussion and differences it needs to be remembered yet again what were the formative influences of those speaking: for the older men, it was the disillusionment of the Boer War and what followed, including the dire threat to union defensive funds of the Taff Vale railway case. The younger men remembered the battles won during "the Great Unrest"; the total upheaval of the different stages of the war, with production under State control; the national and revolutionary risings; for them military terms came readily into their way of thought and speech.

No doubt that was why the British TUC key recommendation was for "a General Council" to replace the Parliamentary Committee and co-ordinate the efforts of the unions on general issues of a strictly industrial nature. To the scores of thousands who had so recently been accustomed to listening to the brilliant speakers of the shop stewards' committees and the many Socialist Parties of the day it may well have sounded like a plan for a "Workers' Army General Staff". The majority of the British TUC leaders, however, stressed the point that its main purpose was to act in a political way, by urging legislative reforms in Parliament; but that, they insisted, had become the job of the Labour Party in general and the Parliamentary Labour Party in particular, now larger and freed from the shackles of being in a coalition Government. While fully co-operating with the Labour Party and the Co-operative Movement, the General Council itself was to stick strictly to industrial problems. Discussion of just what its powers could and should be has hardly ever stopped since then.

What in practice actually needed to be done in the post-war situation, whatever the detail of "reorganisation" and "co-ordination"? First, the unorganised needed to be brought in; and, together with the immense number of new recruits during war conditions, to be held and educated in the movement's general principles of solidarity. This must apply whether the existing unions were general, craft-based or industry-based, about which many arguments were being used every which way by competing unions in their anxiety to win greatly needed amalgamations.

In Scotland's special circumstances there was still often a sound basis for the argument that in certain trades and districts smaller local unions could be far more effective and attentive to members' needs than as a section of a remote giant; the potentially unifying factor was an effective trades council. The financial considerations during amalgamation negotiations, both about premises and office holders, continued to be divisive rather than strengthening factors unless and until disaster struck.

Just how was a "General Council" to bring total support to the "advance troops", now that the major employers assisted by the Government appeared to be "declaring industrial war"? What might a "General Council" do which the Triple Alliance seemed hesitant to undertake for the interdependent industries it had been set up to assist? How should it act and in what circumstances? There were strongly differing views, watched closely by their opponents. Some held that no one union should be in a position to insist that others be drawn into supportive action. On the other hand, some held that no union should be dictated to by outsiders, who had not shared in decision-forming and negotiations as to how it should defend itself. A third point of view was that no supportive action ought to be taken without ballots of members of each and every union; others argued that this would take much time and give warning to the enemy. The preoccupation of some, like James Walker and Hugh Lyon, was that there was always the risk of responsible unions finding themselves committed to supporting an "unconstitutional strike". Some in the leadership, of whom J H Thomas of the National Union of Railwaymen and the Triple Alliance was one, held that supportive action was essentially political, and went on to argue that no industrial strike must ever be taken for political ends. Not surprisingly, in addition to the many differing viewpoints in top leadership, there tended to be strong opinions expressed at lower levels that few leaders were ever to be trusted. Such critics were more conscious of their own day-to-day problems than aware of genuine intricacies elsewhere, including the subtle divisive personal propaganda always present. Some argued that national officials should devote themselves full time to their trade union duties and not also act as MPs; others, including the Scottish PC, felt that an important post, such as their own general secretaryship, should be full time at secure salaries, rather than dependent upon satisfying claims for lost time and the like.

Section (iii): **Delegates' Views on "Black Friday"**

Examples of all these points of view were freely expressed by Scottish trade unionists through the STUC, often with more vigour and directness than were always heard in the "corridors of power". Actual quotations may give a vivid picture of what they were feeling and how they were reacting during this uncertain time. Reaction to the hesitancy and later failure of the Triple Alliance mounted to a peak in the next three years, with much discussion continuing on whether the strike or Parliamentary action in support were the more effective. Here are some to speak for themselves, a week after "Black Friday", 1921, at their Aberdeen Congress.

Peter Chambers, Scottish Mineworkers, after explaining the decontrol of the mines as "a deep-laid conspiracy of the Lloyd George Government and the industrial capitalists to beat not only the miners but the railwaymen", insisted that rank and file of both the railway and the transport unions had been in favour of a sympathetic strike:

> The failure was not due to the rank and file; it was the leaders to blame. It was a notorious fact now that there were certain leaders among the railwaymen and the Transport Workers Federation who had all along been moving heaven and earth to get out of the prospective strike. Mr Thomas had said it was the proudest day in his life when he had got out of it.

He went on to claim that the day the Triple Alliance leaders decided to call it off the Miners' Executive had not been told till late afternoon, while "the decision was known on the Exchange in Edinburgh before one o'clock". In his view local councils of the Triple Alliance needed to be formed: then "it would not be so easy for leaders to let them down". That was to be all too close to what J H Thomas and others did in the calling off of the General Strike of 1926.

J Hallsworth, the General Secretary of the Distributive and Allied Workers, visiting the STUC, agreed that he found "no hesitancy" when he attended the Transport Workers' Federation Conference, nor from his members. These were not "normal times". He added they were

> facing a Government which used the pulpit, the press, the law courts and every conceivable means of so-called constitutional action for the purpose of subverting the positon of the workers of the country. Too often so-called constitutional action was cowardice in front of the enemy.

David Marshall, of the Scottish Dock Labourers, agreed that the "feeling was entirely favourable" at that same Conference of Transport Workers; but "they had handed the matter over to their Executive" and they should wait until these had reported.

> In the West of Scotland they were ready and solid for a strike . . . . The Triple Alliance would revive, but its constitution – a curious one – would have to be altered.

James McKelvey, his co-delegate, took this further. He said "the mistake had been in giving the Triple Alliance Executive too much power". They had been mandated to strike only if negotiations were broken off, but the Government had "reopened" negotiations with a temporary agreement offer, which "gave the Executive a chance to call it off". He had had his suspicions at the final delegate conference, when

> a protest was made not to trust these people in giving them full power. They had received an object lesson to put no trust in officials in that capacity. They should leave them no way out at any time.

John Heenan, Textile Workers, however, asked if the Scottish Dockers had wanted to strike, why had they not done so?

> Whether the leaders made a mistake or not the cause of the collapse of the general strike policy was that the rank and file were not ready for it . . . . Some of the speeches led them to believe that the revolution was coming tomorrow but some person stopped it.

J Fraser, of the Dundee Scottish Typographers, said "baiting trade union leaders was a popular pastime, but it cut no ice", adding:

> Hardly a man in the labour or trade union movement had escaped being called a fakir or a traitor. To indulge in that kind of thing would not help the miners.

J M Cuthbertson, of the Railwaymen, thought they "should avoid personalities and suspend judgment till all the facts were revealed". The news had been as much of a surprise to them as to the miners. Then he said that although "there was a feeling . . . that unless they allied themselves with the miners they were going to let the workers in both industries down", he feared that:

> the general feeling among the railway workers was not throughout the length and breadth of the land what it had been said to be in Edinburgh – over 90 per cent in favour of stopping.

Harry Begg, of the General Ironfitters' Association, when later moving a resolution demanding support for the "independent character" of the Scottish Labour College, remarked:

> If there was a properly organised College for Labour there would be no repetition of the Triple Alliance failure. Labour education would make it more difficult for the workers to be misled. They would lead instead of being led.

The 1921 debate on the Triple Alliance brings out the strength of feeling on the need for supportive action of some kind when any industry took action to defend its vital interests, whether on hours, wages or control.

The threat was clear. The Government brought in the vicious Emergency Powers Act, giving "almost absolute power to the Executive Authority practically unchecked by Parliament or Court of Law". A motion describing it as

> the most powerful and successful attack on their organisation since the repeal of the Combination Laws

was moved by *John Fulton* of the Scottish Dock Labourers. All his contributions were affected by their many weeks of struggle to stop blackleg coal being brought into Glasgow Docks during the miners' dispute. He said the Act "would put trade unions in shackles", adding that

> if it was not cancelled the Labour Party should leave Parliament, to conduct a campaign in the country. The Labour Party should remain out of Parliament until the Act was scrapped.

In seconding it for Glasgow Trades Council, *John Queen* said:

> a large number of delegates dreaded revolution, but there was nothing that would bring revolution nearer than an Act such as this.

Neil MacLean MP, Workers' Union, was against withdrawing MPs:

> They could not afford to lose the Parliamentary or any other weapon they possessed. Rather they should send reinforcements there.

He added, that when the Sinn Fein Party had withdrawn from Parliament it "had not brought peace in Ireland".

The most strongly worded and explicit motion at this important 1921 Congress came from Aberdeen, when Councillor *G R McIntosh* said that if they meant "to attempt big industrial movements" they needed a "new type of organisation" to control "food supplies, the press and all other factors essential to success". It had to be

> some scheme of Finance, Commissariat, Communication and Transport . . . from one end of the country to the other.

It was remitted to the PC for report, but Allan took no action upon it. This was exactly the preparation so desperately needed throughout Britain five years later which Scottish trades councils tried to build, coming into conflict with the PC of the STUC for their efforts.

If now in this year when the Government's fear of a general strike and plans to divert or defeat the industrial warfare seemed apparent to some, what was the alternative open to the STUC? In the immediate future, what steps should be taken to strengthen the movement, especially in view of all the difficulties in the way, including the serious unemployment and consequent lack of finance? The old efforts towards amalgamation were stressed, along with the competing merits of industrial or general unions to replace craft organisation. *George Buchanan* for Glasgow Trades Council deplored the continuing existence of "the old vendetta of craftsmen and labourers". With a new twist it came out strongly in a sharp debate over whether the Scottish Foremen's Protective Association should be affiliated as a genuine trade union. *James Whitehead* of the Brass Finishers thought foremen should be in "the Union of their respective trade". He got support from *William Fagan* of the Engineers who considered

> an active union could keep foremen in their place, in or out of the union. They had no right to a special organisation which would encourage snobbery.

But Glasgow Trades Council delegates were in favour of letting them organise on their own, George Buchanan retorting to the Engineers that "there was as much snobbery among the crafts as among the foremen". The differences were strong enough for the PC to circularise a questionnaire to affiliated societies about the current position, industry by industry, asking their opinion. Allan reported the next year that out of 22 replying, 15 opposed the separate foremen's union.

At least the discussion on the whole question seems to have given further stimulus to Scottish Home Rule, which had already been brought to the fore by events in Ireland. When he seconded it, *Bernard Havilon,* the Dock Labourers' delegate from Kelvinhaugh, remarked:

> There would have been no Triple Alliance failure north of the Tweed if the Scottish Workers had been free to act by themselves.

The few opponents argued that they should organise more strongly on industrial lines, with *Mrs Duncan,* Theatrical Employees, thinking it "disgraceful they should be wasting time" over Scottish Home Rule, as it was "of no consequence to the working class". Her remark was apt. For the relation between working-class emancipation, nationalism and internationalism, with varying stresses according to circumstances, became a vital issue, often dominating STUC thinking for years to come. It could not be ignored with the crucial developments for trade unionists in Ireland.

References

[1] An extremely enlightening account is given by Philip Bagwell in Chapters XV and XVII of "The Railwaymen".

[2] Minutes, 3 October, 1919

10

International Anxieties

Although the war with the Kaiser's Germany was over, it had not ended militarism's expeditions elsewhere in the world, both near and far. For the Scots the nearest and dearest of international anxieties was Ireland. For the next half dozen turbulent years Ireland was never off the STUC agenda. Always they exchanged delegates with the Irish Trades Congress and Labour Party, or warm greeting telegrams when physical presence was impossible. There was always a sympathetic hearing both to their reactions about the military occupation and about the parties to the civil war after the establishment of the Irish Free State. The reports of both Scottish and Irish delegates rarely failed to comment on the many problems they shared and the links between them whatever the differences.

Section (i): **Ireland: Attitudes to the Troubles**

While the Scots were deep in the 1919 hours battle in Glasgow similar action in Belfast left the shipyard owners there "aghast at the manifest unity of Catholics and Protestants".[1] That unity was not allowed to last long in the north, while in the south the English army of occupation forced workers to carry military passes everywhere. This provoked a strike in Limerick in April which prevented the visit of the Irish trades unions and Labour Party leader, Tom Johnson, as delegate to Perth. Here the TUC passed an angry protest against "the repeated imposition of military law" and demanded the "immediate withdrawal of the embargo". The President Beaton stressed that the continuation of Conscription was "on the pretext of fighting for the liberties of small nations, when we refuse to grant any freedom to that great people nearest to us".

But by the Dunfermline Congress in the spring of 1920 the situation was indeed worse, involving hunger strikes and Irish dissenters deported to gaol in London. A fortnight before they met, there had been a general strike throughout Ireland, except in Belfast, against 100 being imprisoned without charge, including leading trade unionists.

Thomas Johnson, their delegate, described it as "unique in Labour circles", and he had been active in the 1913 Dublin transport struggle, for which the Scots had collected relief funds, and was still remembered with warmth. Johnson said that the Dublin insurrection of 1916 had proved to be "the prelude of a glorious resurrection for Labour", which had "bounded forward" and come to include over 50% "of the 700,000 organisable workers". Many towns, he continued, were now "organised to the last man, so that if a strike arose it was a town strike". He described how the unions had responded to the Government's proposal to lift control of food prices by threatening to occupy the factories of the price-boosting bacon-curers seeking high profits by exporting. He commented that "the Irish workers were practising for a future Government of their country based on Labour", adding that "the principles of Labour were the new inspiration of Ireland". He went on:

> they had not talked of Revolution, Bolshevism, Syndicalism, or any other social theory; they had simply done the work nearest, and done the obvious and practical thing. The future of Ireland was consciously with Labour.

His co-delegate Thomas Foran, Transport & General, shared the "prolonged cheers" which welcomed Johnson's speech, when he said that Irish Labour was "having a full dress rehearsal for the Social Revolution", and that what they

> were striving to realise was the ideal of the Workers' Republic for which James Connolly had laid down his life. They were working to establish the rule of Labour.

Having also heard the news that there had already been sit-ins at a Limerick creamery and of miners in Leitrim, the 240 Scottish delegates, with one dissent, carried a resolution demanding self-determination and the removal of the army of occupation, strongly moved by C N Gallie, Railway Clerks, for the PC. In his presidential address, William Shaw of Glasgow Trades Council had also spoken strongly; and an emergency resolution was carried without debate about a prison sentence against the editor of the *Catholic Herald* and for the release of hunger strikers. It had been moved by George Kerr, Workers' Union, and James Walker, of the Iron & Steel Confederation.

But there were worse problems still to be faced that year. On 10 July, 1920, the STUC held a special one-day conference in Glasgow. Not only did they protest at the situation "where every demand of the people for freedom is met by military repression"; they called upon

> affiliated organisations to refuse to manufacture, handle and transport munitions; or to transport troops for the purpose of repression in Ireland.

It was from the Scottish Mineworkers that the proposal had come for a Special Congress "to consider the grave position in Ireland, Poland and Russia". When their delegate Manny Shinwell went to Cork for a few days later, he found the town full of military, who had destroyed the premises of the Irish Transport Workers Union. He considered "the presence of the military was a constant menace"; and he himself "was stopped by the military and subjected to a rigorous search". Because of the furious attacks, boycott and dismissals of some 5,000 trade unionists from the Belfast shipyards at that time, he went there to find out what was happening on his way home. On getting his report and receiving delegates from Belfast Labour Party, the PC sent Shinwell, Shaw and Allan to interview officials of Harland and Wolff in Govan, "urging upon the firm the necessity of excluding all religious or political prejudice in regard to employment of workers in the shipyards and other establishments in Belfast". Later in the year the PC issued an appeal to raise funds for the relief of distress for the Irish Labour Party and Trades Union Congress. They took no action however to stop handling transport of munitions.

No Irish delegate could get to the 1921 STUC at Aberdeen. Here Gallie spoke bitterly again on the whole history and "deliberate lies" by Lloyd George on Ireland, and declared that Irish workers would not be free to deal with their own problems "until their country was won or granted self-determination". The resolution called on the British Government at once to summon a constituent assembly of the Irish people" to get a peaceful settlement, and meanwhile to withdraw the army of occupation. It was carried unanimously after a reference back was moved by Stephen Kelly, Life Assurance, and Bella Reilly Holden, Textiles, in order to complain that the PC had taken no effective action to stop transport of munitions. Councillor John Heenan, Textiles, argued that the reason why they "had been able to do so little for Ireland" was

> that trade unionists were only prepared to go a certain length. They had to face the truth, which was that in the Trade Unions there were too many who did not yet understand the justice of the Irish claim for freedom. The way to make them understand was by education.

Although the STUC sent George Kerr, Workers Union, as delegate that August to the Irish Congress, which followed soon after the announcement of a truce with the IRA, his report is missing. Allan was said to have lost it "and other kindred papers".

In the next months came all the moves and countermoves which ended in the establishment of the Irish Free State, which the STUC welcomed at its Edinburgh Congress. But by then the long civil war had started, with the IRA seizing Limerick; here indeed was a new situation for the Irish trade union and labour movement and their Scottish sympathisers. Councillor David Campbell, Secretary of Belfast Trades Council, was their only visiting delegate; as he explained, his Dublin colleague, Cathal O'Shannon, was busily pressing for a 24-hours strike "to enforce peace on the contending factions". Said he: "The real struggle in Ireland was yet to come: the struggle between the owning classes and the producers of wealth." When George Buchanan of Glasgow Trades Council and a miner colleague visited Ireland that summer they greatly admired the efforts of Tom Johnson and Cathal O'Shannon in the chair "to hold Irish Labour strictly independent and aloof from both warring camps". With such men "at the helm, the shop of Irish Labour is in safe hands, even in the tempests that are raging in Ireland just now".

This was the attitude to be continually expressed by visiting delegates from Ireland. At the 1923 STUC L J Duffy said they had "still an army in Ireland". It was used much as any other army, "to protect the interests of property with little regard to the common people". In thanking him and Senator T Farren, his fellow delegate, Robert Smillie

> appealed to the two divided classes in Ireland to forget they were enemies and to remember that they were brothers. He looked to Ireland to establish the Socialist Republic, the real industrial freedom, and probably the first in the history of the British Isles.

Henceforth the Irish delegates from north and south stressed the prime importance of their economic problems, so many of which were shared with the Scots: one of them said that while such problems remained, "the political form mattered very little" in comparison.

Section (ii): **Contact with Indian Workers**

It was through their delegates to rallies of Congress in Ireland that the Scots made contact with the trade unionists of another great people seeking nationhood and also suffering under militarism. In his Presidential Address in 1920 William Shaw had deplored the Amritsar massacre of the previous year, when General Dyer had ordered fire to be opened on an unarmed crowd, killing some 500, about which details were concealed for months. But it was when Councillor George Kerr and the miner, Peter Chambers, met as a co-delegate an Indian leader in Dublin in 1921 that the personal contact was made. This was Dr K S Bhat; he was then invited to the 1922 STUC at Edinburgh as the first fraternal delegate from the All-India Trades Union Congress, through its agency in Britain, the Workers Welfare League of India. He spoke of how hard Scotland was hit "by the competition of low-paid and ill-organised Indian labour". He said:

> Indian workers are today at the throat of the Scottish workers through the manipulation of one set of workmen against another.

For he explained how capital had been transferred from Dundee to India to get the jute raw material "worked by raw human beings" on low wages, and with transport costs a fifth below Britain's. Thus "continent was pitted against continent". The message from India, he said, was:

> Don't fight against yourselves. If you have been made to suffer through your fellow worker, do not retaliate when his turn comes to be hit. . . . We are fighting to organise the Indian workers so as to come absolutely in line with you. . . . We beginners have to contend with people who have had about two centuries' experience of contention with you.

He urged them to send a man and a woman delegate to the All-India TUC, adding: "It is better to go to India than to go to blazes!"

In 1923 and 1924 their fraternal delegate was an Indian who had just won a seat in the House of Commons, where he sat as a Communist. Shapurji Saklatvala MP held the Scottish delegates' rapt attention with his facts and presentation. After noting that there was closer unity between India and Scotland than elsewhere in the United Kingdom, he went on to describe the horrifying conditions, with the all-India TUC treated as illegal. For example, in the pits which were mostly owned by Scots with the foremen members of the Miners Federation, apart from the children there were 50,000 women working underground because they were cheaper than pit ponies. His basic warning was that

> there were enough dividends in India, South Africa and China to make Capitalists independent of British Labour.

He quoted the staggering profits of the 41 British-owned jute mills in Bengal, made out of monthly wages of 14s. in spinning and 38s. in weaving. Their profit was £42,000,000 out of a £6,000,000 investment. The engineers and superintendents were all British; acting as the "slave-drivers for the Imperialist boss, they were only tightening the screws in the coffins of brothers and sisters at home". He summed it all up bluntly when he said:

> It would pay the Dundee Jute workers to say to the Indian workers: "We will send you a postal order for 5s. from our own wages every week and you need not work."

The trade union movement should send their own Commissioners to India and have the "British financial system fought by an International Federation of Workers".

When he spoke at the 1924 Congress at Ayr the next year he gave a detailed historical account of the export of capital to the raw material countries. He set the serious fall before 1914 of jute production in Scotland against the immense increase of jute bags produced in India from 74 mills owned by Scotsmen there. Again, exports of coal to India had fallen from half a million tons to 87,000, while Indian pits were exporting over a million tons to former British markets. And that was from 250 pits of which 200 were British-owned, paying 7d. for a 10-hour day and 5d. for the underground women workers. He concluded by urging the Scottish delegates

> to set aside the little quibbles and arguments amongst themselves, and to understand that International Trade Unionism was not the ultimate development but the first essential.

He was not with them again until 1926, after the Dundee Jute and Flax Workers had sent a delegation to India. At Inverness their report prompted a resolution moved by the delegate of the Dundee Calender and of the Sailors and Firemen, declaring it "necessary to give all assistance possible to the colonial workers under the control of British Imperialism". It declared the General Council should seek the British TUC's co-operation in sending trade union organisers to assist the All-India TUC, and "lay a solid basis" for the movements to work in harmony and together "fight the common enemy, British Imperialism". After Rachel Devine of the Dundee Jute and Flax had said Congress should not be asked to face the bill, but that other unions should themselves do the same as hers, the resolution was carried.

There is however no evidence that any processing was effectively carried out. A factor may have been precisely the attitude that this was a matter for individual unions to pursue. This view came out strongly, for example, when the Iron and Steel Confederation in 1925 resisted Motherwell and Wishaw Trades Council's complaint that the Confederation

> by assisting the Tata Steel Company to recruit white labour in this country is acting contrary to the spirit of the Trade Union Movement and against the best interests of workers in both countries.

The General Council of the STUC, no doubt influenced by the views of their member, Bailie James Walker, who was on the point of being promoted to the Confederation's London Head Office, did not support Motherwell's complaint. The lessons of Dr Bhat and Saklatvala were left for future generations to learn the most painful way.

But one further comment is relevant, arising from the "Meerut Conspiracy Case", when in 1929 virtually the entire Indian leadership together with some visiting British trade union volunteers, were arrested. When this was announced a protest in the name of the Transport and General Scottish Area was put down, but finally withdrawn without debate. But four years later when the case ended, and judgment was at last announced, a powerful protest was passed at the Ayr 1933 STUC, moved by the Boot and Shoe Operatives. It referred to the "brutal and savage sentences", and to the prisoners being held for years pending the trial. In speaking to it for Glasgow Trades Council, Thomas Scollan, the Vice-Chairman, said "the Meerut prisoners were the pioneers of trade unionism in a backward part of the world", and added:

> It made one ashamed of his country to contrast the silence on this subject with the British Government's and the British Press's hypocritical expressions of opinion about the Russian engineers. A tremendous amount of publicity had been given to the Russian trial, but the Press had quietly suppressed any information about the Meerut prisoners.

The motion was carried unanimously. Sentences were finally reduced on appeal, and there were arguments that those acquitted or held beyond their sentence should receive compensation.

Section (iii): **War or Trade with Russia?**

There was a new and important background to the severity of action against the Indian national movement. The Indian sub-continent was seen as having a vulnerable northern border with the new regime of independent republics replacing the old Tsarist Empire. Tsarist generals and ministers had regarded the suggestion that they might "do a Hannibal" across the Himalayas as a lunatic idea, and merely an excuse to keep up a big British army there: that was at least one view shared by their Soviet successors. But now with the first people's revolutionary power controlling the immense frontier stretching from the Near East and Black Sea to the Far East, disturbances and movements for national independence anywhere south of it took on special importance for the rulers of the British Empire. Besides coping with the unruly Indians there was therefore action in Egypt and Mesopotamia, in which British troops were involved, in the early 'twenties, with the STUC protesting on each occasion.

But most dangerous and alarming of all was the continued use of the British army and navy to support intervention by the Tsarist generals against this Union of Soviet Socialist Republics. Thirteen weeks before the Perth Congress in April 1919, the British Miners Federation, with Robert Smillie their Chairman, had been to the fore in calling for organised resistance to Lloyd George's increasing assistance to the rebel generals' invasion, discussing direct action to stop it. In his Presidential Address, Beaton denounced the Government for refusing passports to British delegates intending to join a Commisson of Inquiry by the International. He protested that in the British Press "everything was being done to discredit those in power"; and that

> the British Government along with the Allies is carrying out the policy of crushing the Russian revolution.

For the Glasgow Trades and Labour Council, William Shaw moved a unanimous resolution demanding withdrawal of Allied troops, and that

> the Allies cease to supply Russian army elements with food and material.

Six months later Glasgow Trades Council was calling for a 24-hours general strike and a national "Hands Off Russia" Committee was set up. This followed the successful initiative two months before by the London dockers in refusing to load the *Jolly George* with munitions for the Polish Marshal Pilsudski's invasion against the Soviet Union; as a method of direct action against that war it was being widely discussed throughout the movement.

But before they met at Dunfermline in 1920 the British Government's support of the Tsarist generals' war had "ended in catastrophe". The costly adventure, their Chairman, William Shaw, told Congress, had been undertaken "without the consent of Parliament to the eternal disgrace of Britain", and was "a miserable failure". He demanded that the Government should now "cease directly or indirectly interfering with the internal affairs of Russia, and allow trading and commercial relations to develop". But the Red Army's successful defence had reinforced fears in the West; their powerful backing was available when Marshal Pilsudski of Poland took over the attack. So on 10 July, 1920, once again on the initiative of the miners' delegation, a special STUC Conference met and protested against "Poland's wanton attack on Russia". It demanded that all support be withdrawn and "political and economic relations" should be established with the Soviet Union. The Scots noted that "the rapidly increasing cost of living" was a direct result of the "policy of military aggression". Indeed, they were just on the point of the beginning of the post-war unemployment which was to last for so many years throughout the British Isles, not least in Scotland.

A month later, exactly six years after the tragic outbreak of World War I in 1914, the Labour Party put out a national call for massive demonstrations to be held on 8 August, 1920, against the war. To this there was very considerable response, with arguments for a general protest strike and with local Councils of Action being set up.[2] Strong support came from an Emergency Conference in the House of Commons from the executives of the Labour Party, the British TUC and the Parliamentary Labour Party.[3] This, and the defeat which the Red Army had inflicted on Pilsudski, caused the Lloyd George Government to hold back, and other less direct methods were used. When in 1922 his Government was defeated by a short-lived Conservative administration, there was still no recognition, and total holdup of any trade was threatened. It reached such a pitch that on 11 June, 1923, the General Council of the STUC passed a resolution circulated to all the Scots MPs. It emerged in response to letters received from the Glasgow Vehicle Builders pressing for Councils of Action to be formed everywhere in Scotland; from the Building and Monumental Workers demanding the calling of a conference; and also from the Glasgow Communist party, wanting a wire to be sent to Russia.

In their statement the General Council were concerned at "the British Government's Notes to the Russian Government" and stressed "the necessity for no provocative action" which might "endanger the preservation of peace"; and finally urged MPs not to support "any demand for cancellation or limitation of the Russian Trade Agreement". With yet another General Election, the first Labour Government took office and hopes were raised, not for merely formal recognition, but to get the all-important trade moving fast. As their 1924 Congress opened, first steps had been taken in an Anglo-Russian Conference but the bankers had moved in, trying to dictate terms to compensate Russian industrialists whose property had been nationalised. So Congress passed unanimously two emergency resolutions. The first was moved for the General Council itself, by C N Gallie, being a warm greeting to the Anglo-Russian Conference, stressing that developing trade would bring close understanding between the two peoples. Seconding it, William Quinn, Municipal Employers, described how much pre-war trade there had been with Scotland, and adding that

> if this country were able to supply the demands for agriculture machinery alone our workshops would be fully occupied for twenty years.

It was Jack Strain for Glasgow Trades and Labour Council who put forward the emphatic protest at

> the bankers' recent attempt to interfere in the interests of British finance and compel the Russian people to establish a Government based on the needs of a foreign group, thus constituting a grave violation of the rights of a Sovereign State to conduct its affairs according to the expressed wishes of the people.

Before the year was out, however, the Labour Government had been thrown out in the wake of the notorious forged "Zinoviev letter", purporting to give Russian instructions to British Communists. Later it emerged that there was connivance not unknown to officials in the Foreign Office, which was then to enjoy five years of Conservative Government until the Labour movement as a whole had recovered and formed a second Labour Government in 1929 as the world economic crisis approached.

Over and over again in the next years at the STUC, concentration remained on the vital need for expanding trade with Russia and in general to strengthen international trade union unity. But after the bitterness following what was seen as the betrayal of the 1926 General Strike by the same forces which had allowed "Black Friday" to happen, there were divided attitudes, and sometimes noticeably contradictory speeches by respected Scottish leaders.

Resolutions came frequently from Glasgow Trades and Labour Council and the Clydeside. In 1927 for Glasgow, Aitken Ferguson and Frank Stephenson urged that there should be action by the British TUC to call a conference of the British and Russian trade union movements to lay the foundation of one united world trade union international. This was unanimously carried. But there was opposition the following year when Sinclair Reid for Edinburgh Trades Council called for action to promote one body. The continued existence of two separate Internationals, it argued, was a weakness in

> the world-wide struggle against the lowering of wages, lengthening of hours . . . and the continual menace of war.

Referring to "the development of Fascism in Poland, Spain and Germany" as threatening "the very existence of trade unionism", he added a warning of what in fact lay eleven years ahead:

> It was wrong to call the present time a post-war period – it was a new pre-war period. Imperialism could only be fought by the workers of all countries getting together.

From Glasgow, the seconder, Jack Strain, Woodworkers, said "it was the obvious intention of this country to declare war at the earliest possible moment against the first Workers' Republic of Russia". But it was strongly opposed by C N Gallie, the Railway Clerks' Scottish Council Secretary. He said that "while the curse of Europe today was contained in Fascism, there was a very thin line of demarcation between Fascism, Communism and Conservatism". The All Russian Central Council had rejected the offer to come into the International Federation of Trade Unions in 1925. The resolution was defeated by 22 to 73, with nearly half of the delegates not voting. But the next year, just before the election which brought in the second Labour Government, Gallie expressed a very different attitude.

The disruption of trade had become serious indeed. It followed on a deliberate break-in and burglary from the premises of the official Soviet Trade Delegation's premises, regardless of diplomatic immunity. The Tory Government had been in hope of discovering "something which would serve as another Zinoviev letter", Gallie said in seconding a protest resolution by the National Union of Distributive & Allied Workers delegates. As a cover-up the Government had broken off diplomatic relations, thus forcing British firms to go to Paris to get any deal on Soviet trade approved and necessary licences issued. This was too much for the Railway Clerks delegate. Every time there was an opportunity to develop trade and industry, the Tory Government "took the entirely opposite direction and prejudiced the possibilities"; it was "a heavy handicap to the industry of this country". He added:

> The form of Government in Russia was no concern of ours, as the only question that should interest us was the getting of enormous business orders from Russia that would go a long way to absorb the goods we could produce.

During the debate examples were given on the work Beardmore's could provide; the loss of herring-curing trade to the North of Scotland; the disruption of transport in Leith and on the railways; and some striking figures provided by the Amalgamated Engineering Union delegate, A B Swales, ex-chairman of the British TUC. The motion demanded reopening diplomatic relations and reaching trading agreements as the only hope

> to secure normal conditions in the ports and workshops of this country and so provide employment for masses of the people now walking the streets unemployed.

It was carried unanimously. The international anxieties of the Scots had linked up with their disappointed post-war hopes on the home front with the ghastly domestic tragedy of mass unemployment, which was to bedevil all their extensive plans for reorganisation as their second quarter century began.

References

[1] G B Kenna, in "Facts and Figures on the Belfast Pogroms, 1920-22".

[2] V I Lenin commented upon this in his speech at the Special Conference on Labour and the Russo-Polish War: "The whole of the English bourgeois Press wrote that the Councils of Action were Soviets. And it was right. They were not called Soviets but in actual fact they were such." They had "presented an ultimatum to the Government in the name of the workers".

[3] Detail in *History of the Anglo-Soviet Relations* and also *Armed Intervention in Russia*, by S and P Coates.

11

Mass Unemployment and Reorganisation

The basis for the post-war high hopes had been overturned not only by the employers' counter-attack, international anxieties and continuing militarism. The important factor was the loss of Britain's economic domination: this resulted both from American development and from the handling of the economies of the defeated countries. For example, the victors' policy of demanding reparation in kind became a serious threat to the British coalowners' markets. Moreover, the victors deliberately built up certain areas of German industry, hoping to stem the growing revolutionary demands for workers' control and socialism in Italy and Germany, under the influence of events in the Soviet Union. Again, the ever-increasing unemployment was certainly not checked by monetarist policies, with Winston Churchill at the Treasury enforcing the return of the pound sterling to the gold standard. As in all industrial areas, Scotland was to respond strongly to this and even more sharply, because of the very great concentration of its specialised industries, largely interdependent, which were extremely hard hit.

Section (i): **The Battles of the Unemployed**

The beginning of permanent mass unemployment was a central feature of the first half of the 'twenties, with Britain's economic decline causing political uncertainties: and 1923 was by no means the ideal moment for a first Labour Party administration to take office on a still limited suffrage, with women under thirty without a vote. The failure of Ramsay MacDonald's government to take strong action on the many bitter grievances, instead of being ready to be thrown out with colours flying if necessary, reinforced the views of those who had always doubted the effectiveness of purely Parliamentary politics compared with industrial action. There was also grass-roots anger and impatience with those amongst the trade union leadership who failed to realise the need for basically new methods in a situation indeed different from that in which they had first come to the fore. The leaders were well enough aware of arguments about whether organisation by industry or by general unions was the more effective way of reaching the goal of 100% organisation of the workers in the factories; but what relevance had that to organising the workers on the stones outside? The hard fact was that skilled men displaced by new technology and loss of markets were now joined in a permanent mass army by many youthful ex-service men and women with no experience of trade unionism. Particularly outrageous was the effect of the belated demobilisation on many apprentices who had joined up as much as six years before, and on their return to railshops and elsewhere were expected to work out their apprenticeship or go without work at all. Who was to organise them, now they were outside the factories, and indeed knocking on the gates? True, some of the craft unions had idle benefits which might keep their members automatically in touch, even if inactive; but this could apply only to a minimum. There were plenty of these small craft unions in Scotland, and their officers were never slow in making the point in the debates.[1] There were therefore two sides to the disastrous new problem of mass unemployment. On the one hand there was the need to put forward plans for creating work and pressing successive Governments to carry them out; on the other hand, the unprecedented new problem of organising the huge numbers of those out of work.

Section (ii): **The Unemployed Workers' Committees**

The second task was indeed crucial. In more than one country in Europe the failure of the organisations of those still at work to deal with the problems of the vast armies of unemployed left them to come under the influence of the fascists, and become a serious – indeed, a fatal – menace to the trade unions themselves. In Britain that did not happen, primarily because out-of-work trade union activists organised their fellow unemployed in the dole queue, at the "Labour Buroo" and at the parish councils' office and workhouse to act together, handling their immediate needs in Unemployed Committees. In October 1920 a London Council of Unemployed – many of them young ex-servicemen – was set up when the Poplar Mayor, George Lansbury, who was also editor of the *Daily Herald*, was leading a deputation of 15 other London mayors to the House of Commons to protest against low poor relief. The many unemployed who turned up in support were fiercely beaten up by the police. From then on the London Council of Unemployed, their unpaid organiser being an out-of-work skilled engineer, Wal Hannington, became extremely active in local marches and demonstrations. A trade unionist to his backbone and ex-shop steward,

Hannington[2] not only used every workshop method, including picketing factories both where strikes and lockouts were in progress and also where excessive overtime was imposed; he insisted on proper approaches to the official labour movement at every level, including achieving a meeting with a subcommittee of the British TUC, with the central programme demand of "Work or Full Maintenance". The activity found a ready response throughout Britain, especially in industrial towns. Unemployed Committees sprang up in many places, and early on in Scotland, particularly in Dundee, Clydeside and Edinburgh and Leith, where Unemployed Committees were active by the spring of 1921. At a Manchester Conference in November 1921 they had linked up throughout Britain in what later became famous as the National Unemployed Workers Movement.[3] The moving spirits were frequently out-of-work shop stewards and sections of the Independent Labour Party and the newly formed Communist Party, with good support from many Labour Councillors and Clydeside MPs, and also some trade union leaders in an individual capacity. The town Unemployed Committees were frequently organising protest marches to local burghs and county councils demanding specific relief works, against evictions, and for better treatment from parish councils. At first the Scottish Committee did not link up south of the border, although always co-operating, preferring to remain grouped as the Scottish Unemployed Committees; but they all came fully together when the first of the famous "Hunger Marches" on London began.

The first group to take the road were the Scots; they were on their way for nearly five weeks. Wal Hannington marched with them, and in his autobiograpy, "Never On Our Knees", he writes:

> The combined contingent of picked volunteers, numbering 350, came from Clydeside, Edinburgh, Dundee, Aberdeen, Lanarkshire, Renfrewshire and Fife. With packs on their backs they marched out of Glasgow on 17 October, 1922. A week later the Tyneside marchers set out and then followed, according to the dates arranged, the contingents from the other parts of Britain.

The response of the general public in every place they passed through was terrific. This was despite fantastic press headlines, such as the following: "Great Communist Plot Exposed", "Whitehall Riot Plan", "Notorious Criminals as Leaders", "Revolutionary Attempt" (*Daily Express*); "Downing Street and Red Plot", "Whitehall Riot Scheme" (*Daily Mail*); "Communist Plot in London", "Organised Plan to Provoke a Riot at Dictation of Moscow", "Incitement to Violence" (*Pall Mall Gazette*). The support throughout the labour movement was so strong that the British TUC decided to form a Joint Advisory Council with the National Unemployed Workers Movement after the march, which was set up early in 1924.

The STUC leadership, however, was not to show active response to assist the organisation of the out-of-work themselves, nor of urging agreement for a common programme on the trade unions' own duties in that respect. But the STUC did in fact adopt many of the policy points of the Unemployed Workers' Charter, agreed between the British TUC and the NUWM. During the chairmanship of Bailie James Walker, then the Scottish Divisonal Officer of the Iron & Steel Trades Confederation, there was no action. But there was movement during the term of office of his successor, C N Gallie, of the Railway Clerks. Robert Allan sent out a circular in September 1921 encouraging trades councils to hold meetings and demonstrations "and every possible method of agitation" to put pressure on the Government, stressing that "work or maintenance is the watchword of Labour". A circular and questionnaire followed about delay and unsatisfactory treatment at labour exchanges, on which the NUWM had been in action. The Report to the Edinburgh Congress in 1922 stated that:

> From correspondence in our possession, we believe that the Trade Councils are taking a keen and lively interest in this matter, and in many instances Joint Committees of the Trade Councils and Unemployed are working together in the organisation of meetings, bringing pressure to bear on local authorities to provide work, on parish councils to provide relief, and on Public Health Authorities to provide milk for infants etc.

Robert Allan and the STUC's Treasurer, Robert Climie, also took two officers of the Glasgow and Edinburgh Trades Councils on a deputation to the Scottish Divisional Controller, Ministry of Labour, that November about delays and complaints of wrong treatment at "labour buroos".

At that same Congress Standing Orders were suspended to receive a deputation from the NUWM, who were "received with cheers". Of their three speakers, Allan Hannah of Glasgow asked "the chief organisation of Labour in Scotland" for support in defeating the sweating of relief workers on public schemes. Edward Carr from Springburn proposed that workers who were locked out should receive the same allowance as the unemployed, "who were fighting the battle of trade unionism as well as their own cause". From Edinburgh J H Douglas stressed that unemployed committees should have the same status on trades councils as trade union branches, and should be admitted to affiliation, and that the STUC should recommend that. Later Alexander Caldwell strongly moved an Edinburgh Trades Council motion demanding work or maintenance, and that dealing with unemployment should be a national rather than local responsibility. This was seconded by the Boot & Shoe Operatives, whose union nationally had taken a firm line in support of the NUWM and its policy. Congress also passed a Dundee motion that insurance stamps should be credited to the unemployed, instead of them being treated as being in arrears.

Before they met at Dundee in 1923 there had been a General Election, when a Tory Government replaced Lloyd George's Coalition; two members of the General Council had been candidates, with Manny Shinwell winning at Linlithgowshire and Robert Climie doing well in Kilmarnock. The group of Clydesiders elected also included Kirkwood and Maxton of the Independent Labour Party. In addition there had been the shock of the engineers' lockout. In his Presidential Address, the miner, James Murdoch, vividly described the effect of new technology in the countryside, and the consequences of increasing unemployment, that

> hydra-headed monster, a terror to the workers and a godsend to the evil-disposed employer, who knows that his workers are forced to accept any wages or conditions he may put upon them, so long as there are two men looking for one man's job.

Increasing unemployment, declining trade union membership and some Fascist group activity in Glasgow – all were in the minds of the delegates when they agreed once again to suspend Standing Orders to hear a deputation from the NUWM, which since they last met had led the first great national hunger march out of Glasgow to London.

Section (iii): **The Unemployed Seek Affiliation**

The following points from what their speakers, Harry McShane and Alec Campbell, told delegates indicate the new mood developing in Scotland.

> The organised unemployed had had the sympathy of every other organised body of workers; but they did not want any more sympathy and did not require it.
>
> If the unemployed had not organised themselves under the Unemployed Workers Committee Movement the organised workers would have gone from defeat to defeat . . . in spite of whose sympathy and indifferences they had built an Unemployed Workers Committee.

> They had come to the Congress as an integral part of the working class and they came as a movement that had demonstrated its worth, not in words but in deeds.
>
> They had the right to seek affiliation to Congress and to the local Trades Councils.
>
> While there were 1,250,000 unemployed challenging the employed for their jobs it was necessary for the trade unions to co-operate with the Unemployed Workers Committee.
>
> We have organised the movement in spite of you, and now we have organised we come to you for your support . . . As good as any organisation represented here today, and we have no paid officials.
>
> In 1921 the National Joint Committee had declared itself in favour of full maintenance but proposals to bring about a general strike had been discussed and defeated. Parliamentary action alone was not sufficient. The trade unions had not had the courage to fight.
>
> He asked for the support of Congress for a general strike for full maintenance. Wages were reduced because of the unemployed army, and it was deserved if they would not fight the proper fight.

After the chairman had thanked them "for their very frank addresses", Councillor William Shaw, for Standing Orders, recommended that the question of affiliation should not be discussed until the incoming General Council had considered it. Sharp objection to this remit came from J H Moore, Laundry Workers, C Bleakley, Boot and Shoe Operatives, Bailie George Kerr, and Neil McLean, MP, both of the Workers Union. However, James Whitehead, JP, supported the Standing Orders recommendation, with William Elger, the STUC's new General Secretary, and Bailie Climie arguing that any amendment to permit affiliation would have to have been circulated to affiliates before Congress. The remit was therefore carried by 83 to 36 of the 174 delegates. When a general discussion on unemployment took place later, James Walker took the opportunity of saying that whether they affiliated Unemployed Committees or not would make no difference, while G S Aitken of Coatbridge and Airdrie Trades Council did not agree, and added that any difficulties to affiliation "could be cleared out of the way".

But when it came to the Ayr Congress in 1924, another General Election had taken place and the first Labour Government had been elected. There was no deputation from the NUWM, and it was decided not to read a letter from them about affiliation because an amendment to alter Standing Orders to permit affiliation was ruled out of order, as the Paisley Labour Party and Industrial Committee in whose name it stood were not affiliated to Congress. When the Lanarkshire Miners and the Boot and Shoe Operatives moved that nevertheless the letter from the NUWM be read, they were defeated 74 to 40. That year there was merely a general motion on unemployment, demanding national schemes for public works.

By the Dumfries Congress in 1925 there was positive hostility to the NUWM in some quarters, matched by sharp feeling on the other side, with an ineffective Labour Government defeated and a new Tory Government going into full attack with a declared aim of bringing down wages, starting with the miners'. Although Congress did decide to receive a deputation from the NUWM, the Standing Orders Committee prevented them from speaking until after the debate on affiliation, following the example of the British TUC's similar action. There was a full debate when Aitken Ferguson for Glasgow Trades and Labour Council moved an amendment to Standing Orders to permit affiliation of the NUWM committees both to trades councils and the STUC, provided delegates to Congress were "members of recognised trade unions". In making the case he said:

> Two million workers were likely to be permanently on the street and he asked the Congress to take the logical step of bringing them into the closest possible relationship with the trade union movement.

In seconding, J B Figgins, NUR, warned that "looking before them were big upheavals". He went on:

> The refusal of increase of wages was going to be transformed into an attack on conditions; and if they did not affiliate the unemployed, they would be in danger of losing all they had gained.

Some of those who opposed argued that it would mean dual representation – the reason given thirty years before by the British TUC for excluding trades councils, and so leading to the founding of the STUC. Other opponents said unemployed committees were not necessary, and that their function could and should be performed by the trade unions. J Whitehead, Scottish Brass Turners, said affiliation would "split up the trade union movement", and added:

> The Unemployed Committee was simply trying to sow the seeds of dissension and to undermine the trade union movement.

The General Council argued against the scheme which was finally defeated by 36 to 116 of the 174 delegates. As soon as the vote was taken, the NUWM deputation was received and the Scottish organiser, Fred Douglas, gave details of all the activity they had undertaken, including the close co-operation in the East of Scotland, in Fife, Dundee and in Kirkcaldy, with the Edinburgh Trades Council anxious for affiliation. In Aberdeen a new Labour Party had been formed to accommodate the unemployed. They were soon to be pressing for major relief work schemes, adding about the road bridges over the Forth and Tay that nothing had been done since it was first mooted.

Edinburgh Trades Council moved that unemployed committees should at least be able to affiliate to trades councils, while William Shaw from Glasgow Trades Council recommended enrolling individual unemployed in individual sections of trades and labour councils. Both these modifications were defeated. Then Edinburgh Trades Council through Tom Drummond, who had just been elected on to the incoming General Council, moved that "a permanent Committee be set up with powers to concentrate on, and deal solely with, the question of unemployment". This was finally accepted. But an attempt by Glasgow Trades Council was ruled out of order when they proposed setting up a Joint Committee of the NUWM and the STUC General Council. Councillor H McNeill pointed out that this meant they were not even willing to do the same as the British TUC in that respect. The most that could be achieved was to carry a general motion that there should be a campaign in the labour movement to get the Unemployed Six-Point Campaign adopted.

Three months after this Congress there had been throughout Britain the upsurge of feeling that brought about "Red Friday", when the threat of a general strike forced the Government to produce a temporary subsidy to the coalowners to postpone the showdown. The NUWM had certainly played its part in its many marches and activities in making this mood possible. On the other hand, the hostility of leading figures in the STUC to the NUWM and its demands for supportive direct action on all policy issues caused many at grass-roots level to turn to trades councils and be disillusioned with the STUC.

The causes, scope, consequences and policy differences about the post-war mass unemployment underline the question of reorganisation, with which the trade union and labour movement throughout Britain was deeply preoccupied at this time. In retrospect it may be felt that there was over-concentration on techniques, structure and methods rather than with aims, objects and unity, and how these could be most effectively achieved and defended. But undoubtedly concern for change was felt both from right and left; not only the NUWM but also the development in 1924 of the National Minority Movement within the unions, critical of slowness in response to change in the upper reaches, were characteristic. In Scotland, while all these factors were present, the STUC had a difficult internal problem to cope with.

Section (iv): **Reorganisation and a New Secretary**

Nowhere was there greater need for reorganisation than in Scotland. For the STUC was in a notably difficult position, going through a special crisis involving the virtual collapse of its day-to-day administration and the overdue departure of its General Secretary. A strong and determined character, the abilities of Robert Allan were not those which would enable him to cope with the growing and onerous duties he had taken over when replacing his ageing contemporary, George Carson. Routine administrative duties were not his forte, but neither could he adjust to the new problems requiring new thinking and action; meanwhile no rising generation had been introduced into the administration since the war ended. Before this domestic problem came fully to a head in 1922, there had been much discussion throughout the unions after the defeat of the 1919 railway strike about what form of reorganisation should be adopted and in particular what form would be appropriate to Scotland.

One of the changes the British TUC finally adopted was the trade grouping system of representation. While this system stopped short of going all out to answer the demand for each industry to be organised within one body, it was argued that having what amounted to subcommittees considering common problems in their respective industries would reduce friction, lay the basis for future amalgamation and provide a General Council, on a card vote, of representatives from each group. Supported by such advisories the General Council would then be able to develop research bodies and valuable information. In the British TUC this would not, of course, include the trades councils; the rank and file's voice therefore might be less audible even than before at times of stress, when rapid knowledge of the mood would be essential. It would not therefore be acceptable in Scotland on that basis to go the whole hog, despite the many joint discussions with the British TUC's General Council.

When it came to firm proposals for change, after such frequent discussions with the British TUC, the PC finally called a Special Congress on 15 January, 1921, with a scheme proposed which was very close to the British TUC's main stance. It was recommended that the STUC's new governing body should be a General Council elected from ten trade groups, but it was still to be elected by all delegates at Congress, and not by the financial card vote. Another decision was that a full-time paid Secretary at a salary of £300 should be appointed. This was moved by a delegate attending Congress for the first time; he was a 31-year-old clerk in a paper works firm and had just become President of Edinburgh Trades Council. In a little over a year, William Elger was himself to be short-listed and finally chosen as the STUC's next General Secretary. On him were to rest the changes entailed by reorganisation, and in unusual circumstances.

The reason for this was that as soon as the war was over and while membership was higher than ever before, a proposal had come up on the PC that large premises should be acquired in Glasgow to be run as the "Scottish Labour Institute". Allan was particularly taken with this idea, after seeing at the 1919 Congress the remarkable premises and social organisation of Aberdeen Trades Council. His plans began to assume formidable proportions. With much of the negotiation and enquiries remaining in his hands, hardly a month went by without some new elaboration which he introduced. But finances were falling, as unemployment grew and union membership and affiliations dropped. Numbers represented at Congress had doubled by April 1920 over 1909, with 240 delegates attending representing 550,000: now they fell to 170 representing only 213,500; affiliation fees went down in proportion. The final blow came when it emerged at a PC meeting on 6 March, 1922, that the STUC was under threat of a lawsuit, having been committed by Allan to purchase property on which an option had already been paid over, which there was no possibility of them meeting.

This was within six weeks of the 1922 Congress at Edinburgh; they immediately suspended Allan, which of course meant that he could not be nominated again as Secretary. But in less than a week of his suspension it was reported to the PC that Allan had had an accident at Carlisle railway station and had lost both legs. It was therefore possible at Congress to avoid stressing the dismissal of this foundation member and to express regret at his loss, and a collection was taken up. There was only a brief reference to "the unsatisfactory manner in which the duties of the Secretary were being discharged", and David Marshall, Scottish Dock Labourers and PC member, was made interim Secretary. The facts about the ill-fated "Labour Institute" were explained at a secret session of which no records were kept. It was not until 1925 that the STUC escaped a threatened lawsuit by paying a further £160 and costs. Marshall was on a short list of seven who were interviewed on 3 July, 1922, when the number was reduced to Elger and Edward Hunter, and the final choice made three days later.[4] Elger was then employed on a month's notice. He remained in the post until his sudden death in 1946 at the age of 55. He had the administrative skills which were foreign to Robert Allan; these matched the type of reorganisation finally agreed, largely similar to that of the British TUC, to which body Elger always paid rapt attention.

They had many delegate conferences and special meetings besides consultations between the two PCs before they finally reached sufficient agreement in 1924 and could put new ways fully into operation. An early reason for delay was that some wanted to avoid finalising the scheme until the Britsh TUC had decided upon theirs, in case they should be invited to serve merely as their Scottish District Council. But that proved never to be a starter. Finally, with ten trade groups and the trades councils making it eleven, the "General Council", as the new governing body of 12 was called, was elected from each group, with the Mining and Quarrying large group having two. The block vote and exclusion of trades councils were firmly rejected, although both moves were attempted. These were basic principles on which they differed from the British TUC. In two other respects they also differed; in 1923 for example, in Scotland there were 1,500 affiliated members per General Councillor; in the British TUC it was around 6,225. There was a higher proportion of women delegates attending in Scotland. That year, in all, sixteen delegates attended both Congresses, including the PC members Climie, Gallie, James Walker and Shinwell, now an MP.

The new "General Council" was certainly not to be the fighting General Staff conception of an Army Council which was once in the minds of many shop stewards and activists. As G F Duncan, of the Scottish Union of Farm Workers said introducing it in his Presidential Address at the 1924 Ayr Congress:

> The General Council should be your clearing house for ideas, your source of information, from which anyone interested could get necessary information and assistance.

In a report on "The Functions of Congress", the General Council argued that in future the trade union movement, "irrespective of the political party in power, demands Control in Industry". To work towards that there must be a development of trade unionism and its idea, and therefore the General Council recommended that "each Annual Congress must be made the medium for the discussion of such problems as have to be faced". The report listed eight such problems[5] and proposed that each Congress should ask the General Council to prepare a detailed report on a given subject for discussion the following year.

Duncan then told the 1924 delegates how their General Council had been spending its time already; they had been "dealing with a small part of the problem and at once it got up against the questions of the One Big Union, Industrial Unionism etc". That was indeed bound to happen, having members of industrial, general and craft unions sitting side by side on the General Council. It happened too at the long and interesting debate in Congress. All points of view on the type of organisations came out, with one delegate saying that One Big Union would only be possible under Socialism: Jack Strain for Glasgow Trades Council urging union by industry, said "they wanted an organisation capable for conducting the class struggle now". Several others also got down to stressing the importance of the need to reach the unorganised, not least the unemployed. Particularly enlightening contributions came from the mining delegate and future MP, Alexander Sloan, for South Ayrshire Trades Council and from Glasgow and Aberdeen Trades Councils' delegates. They pointed out that in fact it was the trades councils that did the actual organising, not the unions; and one difficulty was that no one knew the actual position in Scotland as to numbers and problems.

When Duncan replied he said it was "the first time for thirty years the Congress had got down to trade union business and had not taken the line of always running away to the political field". He added that for a whole day they had discussed "problems of the working class, and nobody suggested anything political". Responding to a complaint from a delegate that like other trades councils now Glasgow "was dominated by the political Labour Party", anything outside the constitution "was taboo", and they could not even get a discussion on a recent strike. Duncan took it further. He complained "that in the history of the movement we found a continual swing of the pendulum" about political or industrial action; and he quoted many examples of such swinging, from the Grand National Consolidated Trades Union Movement of 1832 to the Chartist Movement two years later. Then he formally moved:

> That the General Council be instructed to make a survey of the extent and structure of the trade union movement in Scotland and to report.

This was carried after Glasgow Trades Council delegates had tried unsuccessfully to push it a little further to gain a practical outcome, by demanding there should be firm "proposals to affiliated organisations calculated to give effective organisation". While the majority regarded research, reports and discussion of this kind as an indispensable first step towards amalgamation and recruitment, others may have seen it more as an end in itself or even as a means of delaying inevitable amalgamation without exacerbating existing difficulties. In practice the trades councils were to respond unevenly. Some on Clydeside disaffiliated, such as Greenock and Motherwell. Many more affiliated but without sending delegates, or, like Falkirk, stopped attending.

Co-ordinating the results of questionnaires, circulars, information and general research suited the new General Secretary down to the ground. The next few years resulted in a mass of such material. It was very well assembled, although that in itself was no guarantee that it would be put to good use. While this tended to set a new tone to debates in Congress, there were extremely pressing problems that would not wait.

Section (v): **Preparations**

Already moves were on foot when the new Tory Government was returned in November 1924 to let the coalowners drastically attack the miners' position, as a preliminary to the policy of all wages being forced down; this was thought to be all that was necessary to restore Britain's full economic recovery. But in fact there was so strong a reaction, not least at grass roots generally, but reaching the executives of many unions individually, that the Government had to supply the coalowners with a temporary subsidy, to give time to prepare for the major showdown that must come. It finally took place in the unprecedented General Strike of May 1926, nine months later.

What preparations would the two sides make for the inevitable major conflict? The Government and the employing class certainly began making theirs at once. The essential question was what preparations would the trade union and labour movement make, and would such preparations be encouraged and co-ordinated by the British TUC and the STUC? So it now becomes necessary to look closely to see what the STUC's General Council was doing or what they failed to do, before judging the fairness of the severe criticisms later.

Following the Dumfries Congress of 1925, the Minutes of the General Council with the Farm Servants' leader, J F Duncan, the new chairman, reveal no initiatives taken within the first six months. There is, perhaps, an indication of attitudes. This emerges three days after the British TUC's General Council had met the Miners' Executive and pledged full support and thus encouraged the "Red Friday" Conference of Executives, which resulted in the Government's nine months' subsidy. Elger was instructed to write to the British TUC suggesting that "an exchange of circulars issued by the Congresses take place in future".[6] Three months later he reported he had received various circulars, including one about the crisis in the coalmining industry. These were said to have also been sent to trades councils; but Elger adds: "I question if this circular was sent to Scottish trades councils when national negotiations are going on."[7] Whether the British TUC did, or should, circularise Scottish trades councils was the point which remained under discussion for some time. It was decided that Elger should meet the General Council to discuss it "informally".

However, that "informal discussion" was long delayed; because in Scotland one group of miners found their employers had gone beyond mere preparations to put their attack on wages into force. Scottish Oils Limited announced a 10 per cent cut in wages. This case came to the General Council not from their fellow member, O'Hagan, who represented the National Union of Shale Miners and Oil Workers, but from the Edinburgh Trades Council; they sent Elger on 23 September, 1925, a copy of a resolution calling upon the Government

> to devise ways and means to carry on the Shale Mine Industry without further depressing the present low standard of wages paid to the workers employed therein.

At their meeting of 12 October, the General Council merely "noted" this. But on 1 November, 1925, the Union wrote that a ballot was being taken and asking the General Council's help to take it up with the Scottish Labour MPs. The terms recommended were rejected and the strike began on 10 November. From then on for some six weeks Elger for the Emergency Subcommittee was fully involved in negotiations at Bathgate with the Union and the firm's managing director, and in seeking help from MPs and the Ministry of Labour. The Ministry was willing to co-operate in setting up a Committee of Enquiry, but would not make it a term that the *status quo* on wages should prevail meanwhile. Finally the British TUC's Chairman and their Acting Secretary, Pugh and Citrine were brought in; a Committee of Enquiry was to be put in hand on terms negotiated by them jointly with Peter Webster and Elger for the STUC. The Enquiry was to decide whether Scottish Oils Ltd and their associated firms were able to maintain the rates of pay without a subsidy, findings on wages to be binding until 31 March. The Union's Executive finally recommended acceptance and the strike was called off. Even when Congress met in April the Enquiry still had not made its award. The Shale dispute in Scotland might indeed be regarded as a mini dress rehearsal for what was to come nationally – except that there was no general strike to support the shale miners.

When reporting on the Shale dispute on 14 December, 1925, Elger mentioned that because of their long negotiations over that, "the informal conversation" with British TUC officers about circularising Scottish trades councils "had not taken place". However, his agenda for the following meeting referred to British TUC circulars and quotations from their Monthly Report to Trades Councils since received. Two he quoted in detail: that "Councils of Action are totally unnecessary and should not be formed"; and that "affiliations with the National Minority Movement" were not approved of. There was one other Minute that month which might be regarded as having a bearing on preparations for the General Strike. It had been reported to Elger that the Vale of Leven Trades and Labour Council called on the General Council

> to organise at once mass meetings of workers to protest against the arrest of members of the Communist Party.

Following widespread raids, twelve national leaders of the Communist Party had been arrested in October charged with conspiracy "to publish seditious libel and to incite diverse persons to commit breaches of the Incitement to Mutiny Act". They had been sentenced to a year or six months. The Falkirk Trades and Labour Council also wrote asking for a General Council speaker at a mass meeting they had organised on the case. Elger had replied to them that "it was necessary for a longer notice being received with regard to such requests". His reply was approved, but the General Council did agree to send a protest to the Prime Minister, Home Secretary and Secretary for Scotland about the prosecutions: half of the accused were Scots and several were prominent as former Clydeside shop stewards.[8] But finally, at their meeting of 8 February, 1926, the question of preparations was raised, in general terms. The railway clerk veteran, C N Gallie,

> raised the question of consultation with Transport Workers Unions with a view to preparing a scheme for maintenance of essential services in the event of large industrial disputes.

It took "considerable discussion" before Elger was instructed to "communicate with Mr Citrine for the purpose of obtaining information on the attitude of the British TUC General Council to this question". When that organisation finally replied that it was "not in a position to make a declaration of policy on the question at the moment", and when it put out a circular on 26 February about "the Mining Situation", the General Council did not discuss these. Neither did they consider the report of the Samuel Commission, published in March, a month before Congress.

Section (vi): **Facts and Figures**

What, then, was the General Council most deeply concerned with in preparing for and reporting to the Inverness Congress, which ended a week before the General Strike began? This brings us back to the hard facts and figures of reorganisation to which the new General Secretary was so deeply committed. The need for greater strength during the two years when the research in such depth had been in progress was heavily underlined by the painful number of inter-union disputes and problems within the labour movement as a whole. Many indeed of the affiliated unions were in some measure of dispute with Co-operative Societies in Scotland. There was an open breakaway by the formation of the Scottish Electric Workers; renewed complaints by the Scottish Tailors about their powerful rivals from south of the border. There was the very serious split amongst the Fife Miners, which was to have long-lasting and serious political repercussions. The Woodworkers and the Wood-cutting Machinists were in contention, and so were the Scottish Horse & Motormen with both Engineers and the Transport & General Workers. In other spheres there were disputes between the Actors and the Variety Artistes and between Clerks and Shop Assistants. Perhaps the most persistent, with which the General Council had continually to deal, was the complaint of the Printing and Paper Workers when the Scottish Typographers opened an Auxiliary Section to recruit women and unskilled in the industry.

The General Council members could not but be very much aware of and sensitive to the fact that many officials of the Scottish unions and also the Scottish Divisional officers of those based in England were more than usually on guard against intrusion from any source on their independence: no less than eight of the twelve General Council members themselves held such office. Foremost in their minds must be fear that major industrial upheaval in one particular area could increase divisions. At factory level, however, there was basis for an undivided response in resisting the threat to all wages.

The facts and figures about trade union organisation in Scotland produced by Elger in his series of researches provide much very enlightening material, of which some instances are given in Appendix A. Where they could not be completed, it was because of "a certain reluctance" in supplying facts on membership and estimates of who remained unorganised where unions might compete. This was despite promises "to treat confidentially all information". There was therefore a good deal of difficulty and need to revise methods during the first stage of surveying "the extent and structure" of the movement. It emerged that only a little over a third in Scotland were organised.

First General Council – elected 1923.

Back row – J. F. Duncan, C. N. Gallie, J. Walker T. Law, C. Jackson.
Centre row – P. Webster, Wm. Leonard, *Vice-Chairman,* Wm Elger, *Secretary,* T. Wilson, *Chairman,* R. Climie, *Treasurer,* J. Doonan.
Front row – A. Smith, J. Nairn.

There were 227 unions involved, of which 90 were Scottish; and of these more than half had membership of under 500. It was recommended that any plan must be aimed at the different localities "to develop and co-ordinate the organising activities of the Unions". To meet this it was proposed, after a number of conferences, to set up County Trade Union Committees.

Of the 57 trades councils, some 36 attended such conferences; but a number of them appeared to be critical or else were, in the General Council's view, unable or unwilling to give effective replies to paperwork sent them. Later proposals made on the constitution of trades councils were seen by many as to be likely to restrain initiative. There was, however, to be one outcome of the years of research and reports which later was to have lasting importance; this was the setting up of a permanent Conference of Women Workers, which we shall study later.

It was unfortunate that the Congress to discuss the structure and constitution of trades councils was held in the far north in Inverness; only Perth Trades Council could send delegates other than Inverness, Stornaway and the big four. Introducing the scheme to set up new County Trade Union Committees, Elger said:

> They had to bring into being a propaganda army of voluntary workers who would work in the same unceasing manner for Trade Unionism as the political army was working for the Labour Party.

The whole labour movement had "reached the stage when work must be departmentalised". The network would finally "bring every locality, no matter how far from the centre, and every interest, no matter how small, in direct contact with the work of the Congress and its General Council". Delegates did make a number of criticisms of the existing trades councils from various points of view, that they had failed to develop, or were not running so well as in the past, or were too closely tied into the party political control of the National Labour Party. But from both sides there was some doubt or disapproval about setting up any new structure involving increased costs. This was put most sharply from strong districts where separate Industrial Committees had already been set up. R Forrester of the Glasgow Sheet Metal Union said they "had been continually bewailing that there was a clashing of interests because there were too many unions, yet they had the General Council coming forward with a new babe". Peter Kerrigan from Glasgow Trades and Labour Council, where a Council for Action had been set up, said bluntly that the scheme "entirely ignored the machinery already in existence". The veteran Ayrshire former GC member, Robert Climie, said

> The proposal was to introduce a new set of officials – that was all it amounted to.

He added: "What was wanted was to infuse a new spirit into the minds of the workers." The Bathgate Shale Miner, O'Hagan, on the other hand, supported the scheme because he said trades councils "were largely taken up with fighting for seats on local public bodies"; but they needed as well "a propaganda body whose sole object would be the thorough organisation of workers in town and country". The Shop Assistant T Brown said that in Aberdeen they already had an Industrial Committee tackling special problems, and were currently "considering the question of organising juveniles". Dundee also did not want it, D Dundas from Brechin thinking "they should build on the present structure". While the General Council was finally told to continue, by 134 to 57, in fact there were never more than three County Committees, and these did not last long.

References

[1] Scottish Typographers; West of Scotland Brass Finishers; Scottish Dockers; Engine Keepers of Fife & Kinross; Scottish Horse & Motormen; Iron & Steel Trades Confederation, Scottish Division; Scottish Farm Servants. In the crucial years they were strongly represented on the General Council of the STUC.

[2] Just 20 years later, Wal Hannington was elected National Organiser of his union, the AEU.

[3] Its first title was the National Unemployed Workers' Committee Movement.

[4] Elger was proposed and seconded by Thomas Wilson (Shop Assistants) and Alex Smith (Edinburgh Trades Council) and was elected by 9 to 3 over Hunter, proposed and seconded by the Glaswegians, Shinwell (Marine Workers) and W Leonard (Furnishing Trades).

[5] 1. Reorganisation of structure and whether this should proceed on Craft, Industrial or One Big Union lines. 2. Methods towards reorganisation with reference to Federation, Amalgamation and Regional Structure within the Union. 3. The place of Trades Councils within any industrial reorganisation and the improvement of their existing industrial functions. 4. The powers of Congress and its General Council with regard to co-ordination of trade union activities and general policy. 5. Increasing membership and co-ordination of competitive unions. 6. Relationship of the Trade Union and Co-operative Movements. 7. Adult Education Policy. 8. Democratic Control in industry with reference to (i) Public Ownership; and (ii) Private Ownership.

[6] Minutes, 13 July, 1925.

[7] Minutes, 17 September, 1925.

[8] Of the twelve there were seven Scots: Tom Bell, Editor of *Communist Review*; J R Campbell; William Gallacher; Wally Hannington of the NUWM; Arthur McManus; J T Murphy; and Robin Page Arnot.

12

The General Strike in Scotland

It is an ironic fact that within a fortnight of the debate the activists from the trades councils, whether called Councils of Action, Joint Strike Committees or Special Organisation Committees were to conduct the biggest trade union struggle ever, despite special problems peculiar to Scotland.

Section (i): **On the Eve**

At the 1926 Inverness Congress the shadow of coming events and contrasting attitudes can be glimpsed clearly enough. The senior miners' member of the GC, Provost James Doonan from Bathgate, moved an emergency motion "the Mining Situation". Expressing hearty endorsement of the British Miners' fight "to maintain their present conditions", it called for the General Councils of both Congresses "to continue their co-operation with the Miners' Federation and as a result secure such terms as will result in no lowering of the living condition of the working class in this country". After pointing out that the highest the Scottish piece workers in the mines could earn was "47s. to 48s.", he was greeted with applause when he added that it was "impossible to ask the miners to agree to a further reduction in their wages". He ended by saying that

> If the miners were by any chance to go down in this struggle, if the standard of living was to be reduced, it was certain that it would affect every industry and trade in the country.

It was seconded for the NUR by James Kiddie of Springburn, saying the miners were "taking up the first line of defence", and reminding delegates of the effect on both mines and rail if the employers were permitted to resort to district rates. He ended that "as one of the rank and file", he hoped

> workers would profit by the mistakes of the past, and when the struggle was over, there would be no more "Black Fridays" behind them.

It was of course passed unanimously.

Three other resolutions were on the agenda as circulated: on related subjects, such as new powers for the General Council, a Workers Defence Corps and the Capitalist Offensive; but before Congress debated these, they had heard the Presidential Address of a man deeply committed to views about the alleged impartiality of the State. Noting "the instinctive rallying" to the support of the miners and the "mingled astonishment and anger" of the ruling class at the new spirit, the General Secretary of the Scottish Farm Servants, J F Duncan, said the Government had belatedly taken the only possible course by appointing the Coal Commission and paying the subsidy. Faced with a national industrial upheaval, the State must step in to compel the reorganisation of the industry, he believed. As national organisations grew on both sides "the State cannot continue in the nineteenth-century attitude of standing aside and holding the ring while the combatants fight it out". What was to be the lesson for those trying to organise the trade unions' ranks? He dismissed contemptuously "the theorists at work", adding:

> What they lack in clarity of exposition they make up for in wealth of phrases. "The United Front", "Mass Action", "General Staff", "Shock Tactics" and so on are being recommended to us.

The rank and file would "not agree to obey without question the instructions of any general staff". There were so many points of friction amongst the unions and some industries, like his own, where organisation was still so weak. But "however powerful an industrial organisation is, it must in the end submit to authority in a democratic State". What was now to happen? "No Government could stand idle if the transport services of the country, for instance, were threatened with stoppage". He dismissed various "emergency organisations" such as the Government-sponsored Organisation for Maintenance of Supplies, "the National Citizens Union or the British Fascisti" as merely "Falstaffian armies". But he also dismissed the key question of trade union preparations in this passage:

> Suggestions have been made that the Trade Unions should set up their own machinery for carrying on essential services during big disputes. So far, however, no attempt has been made to define what are essential services, and until agreement is reached on that fundamental difficulty, the scheme is not likely to develop beyond the vaguest outline.

In future, he believed, industrial struggles would be tripartite affairs; and whilst in recent years the State, acting as conciliator, "has had to preserve an attitude of neutrality, in the coal dispute it has had to go further". Trade unions should, therefore, keep reviewing their practice, and attempt "realistic thinking on these questions rather than prophesy 'revolution' on the one hand or pray for peace in our time on the other". While he was speaking on 21 April, the State's "conciliatory" attitude had already gone so far as to have in readiness on the Clyde the following warships: *Comus, Furious, Hale, Harmattan, Hood, Trusty* and *Warspite*.

The next day delegates from two small Scottish unions, the Packing Case Makers and the Shale Miners, moved that the General Council should be given

> power to call a stoppage of work by affiliated organisations in order to assist a Union defending a vital Trade Union principle.

However, an amendment reduced it to the power merely to call a conference, moved by another small Scottish union, the General Iron Fitters, on the ground that stoppage "would involve great financial loss" to unions who should be first consulted; this was accepted by the movers. On 23 April, a week before the coal owners were to post final notices on miners who would not accept wage cuts, there was a sharply worded debate on a demand that Congress should endorse "the principle of a workers' Defence Corps", and that the GC should assist in forming and co-ordinating them "throughout Scotland under a unified control".

In moving it for Glasgow Trades and Labour Council Peter Kerrigan described how they had faced "organised hooliganism" by fascists at recent election meetings, and how the law had functioned in a biased way on such occasions. He concluded, therefore, that meetings should be stewarded and speakers protected in an organised way under GC control. Some of the opponents on the motion had argued that "such a motion would inevitably give the employers a reason for employing gunmen, as in America" (Aberdeen Shop Assistants). The Scottish Typographical Association's General Secretary Robert Watson said "if they were going to introduce skull crackers they would have chaos on both sides"; he was speaking for the GC. To this Glasgow councillor H McNeill retorted that if the proposal was not adopted, "what were they prepared to do?"; he added that "bands of British Fascists" had driven to the Labour Committee rooms in Glasgow

> smashing in the windows, chasing women into the cellars and terrorising the people in the district.

Bailie James Walker, who was still on the GC, then poured ridicule on

Labour Party branches which could not run a meeting and "prevent the speakers being mobbed". That motion was lost; and on the next and final day of Congress a last attempt was made to get preparatory action from the GC on a different line. It was moved under the title of "The Capitalist Offensive", once again from Glasgow Trades and Labour Council, by Kerrigan. Noting "the expressed intention of the Capitalists to stabilise their system at the cost of further inroads into the standards of life of the workers", it demanded that "effective preparations" must be made. To that end it called on the GC to give all support to develop the Workers Industrial Alliance; and in particular

> to enter into definite negotiations with the Scottish Co-operative Wholesale Society with a view to drawing the Co-operative and Trade Union Movements more firmly together and to obtain united concerted action from these two Workers' organisations in resisting the Capitalist attack.

It was seconded by another Communist Party member from Glasgow, Jack Strain of the Woodworkers, who pointed out that the attack had started in 1920 on the shipyard workers, then the miners and engineers till they now "found that wages had dropped to a worse standard than in 1914". However, the General Council speakers moved an amendment cutting out the reference to the Scottish Co-operative Wholesale Society, and instead stressing that the GC must "keep in touch with the British TUC in any effort to resist the Capitalist attack", which Kerrigan complained was "merely endeavouring to cloud the issue by suggesting that the movers of the motion were going too fast".

Cutting out the demand for negotiations with the Co-operative movement meant that the disastrous failure of the British TUC to plan a food transport policy with appropriate permits was to hit Scotland particularly hard. It was to have long-lasting repercussions amongst the transport workers, with charges of blacklegging against a major Scottish union. Yet there were tremendous possibilities of support from co-operators. One example was reported, when Scotland at last had its own emergency journal, that Bonnybridge Co-operative Society had "reduced all foodstuffs prices by 15 per cent, since most members are on strike pay".[1]

Elger left Inverness and went straight to the British TUC in London where he was joined by the incoming STUC chairman, Peter Webster, of the Scottish Horse and Motormen, and they both attended the Special Conference of Executives and the meetings of the British TUC

General Council, which finally declared the General Strike as from midnight Monday 3 May. Each union was to call out its own members "as and when required by the GC". Elger and Webster reported back that day to the STUC General Council that "arrangements were made for the STUC applying the general plan of strike action in Scotland". The GC decided to remain in daily session.

Section (ii): **Action Stations**

It must be realised that by the May Day weekend the Government's many months of preparation were by no means confined merely to preparing and equipping an organisation to override democratically elected local government; nor to recruiting bodies of volunteer strike breakers, not least amongst students, assured of special privileges and concessions about examinations.[2] From Edinburgh University "students are blacklegging *en masse*, and are receiving £1 per day as conductors and drivers of tramcars", according to the *Scottish Worker*, 11 May, 1926. On the west coast, where not a single docker was working, there was very special treatment for the volunteers, the *Scottish Worker* reported on 13 May. They had been recruited

> mainly by the enrolment of students and youths from city offices. Some employers practically compelled the youths to enrol, and guaranteed their pay would continue. In addition, the youths are being paid £5 a week for blacklegging.

They lived in the cabins of the liners lying in the docks, "with all the rank of first-class passengers", with free meals "supplied by a city caterer". Meanwhile just across the water the Belfast dockers had ceased work; the Dundee docks were solid, except for "one sugar boat, which was unloaded by men said to be Fascisti, brought direct to the docks from St Andrews".[3] Meanwhile HMS *Comus* was in Govan, with marines patrolling the docks there. Their other resources included sending warships to suitable ports and troops to sensitive quarters; control of the radio; the production of a Government daily paper; and guidance to police and law courts. There were threats to make trade unions illegal, get control of their funds; and to arrest leading national officers. A grapevine was cultivated to make certain such threats would carry conviction in appropriate quarters.

But what were the resources on which the supporters of the locked-out miners were to rely? First and foremost there was the overwhelming conviction that the miners' cause was just, and that all would be next in line for attack. From the very first throughout Britain there was immediate response. The surge of solidarity was to grow into amazing self-confidence as they found themselves having to take charge of their daily life in unprecedented and unfamiliar difficulties.

In Scotland there were some especially difficult features, which really required co-ordination at high level. There were three main problems. Firstly the British TUC's GC had not asked the union National Executives to call out their members in all industries in the first place; they concentrated to begin with on the railways, docks and road transport, printing and the press, with only some sections of iron and steel. This left the overwhelmingly dominant occupations in Clydeside, mostly engineering and shipbuilding, waiting to be called out as the "second wave" a week later. Moreover, with so many different small Scottish metal unions, it is not surprising that there was confusion, with contradictory instructions and differences of interpretation at local level. One delay, for example, was over uncertainty whether it was to be lockout or strike benefit, and, where these differed, which was to be paid. With the British TUC laying such stress on respect for each union's autonomy to the extent of not issuing a co-ordinated strike call centrally, the STUC, as their agent and local co-ordinator, was far from likely to take definitive and prompt decisions. A second problem was that in Scotland there was difficulty in the print trade. *The Scotsman* and the *Edinburgh Evening Dispatch*, both non-union, continued to publish, while in Glasgow all the papers joined forces and succeeded in publishing an *Emergency Press*, with daily propaganda against the strike. This made the publication of an authoritative strike paper an urgent necessity, which the STUC failed to do until the second week. To do without the local bulletins, which Joint Strike Committees put out in many areas would indeed have proved virtually impossible. The great distances in the country between the regions into which strike-bound Scotland was supposed to be divided called for a really effective centralised courier service organised beforehand.

Finally, there was the vital question of what goods might be transported, and in what circumstances. Over this the British TUC kept changing its plans and it led to one Scottish General Secretary issuing permits on his own initiative, leaving his members open to intense hostility from pickets. This was Hugh Lyon, of the Scottish Horse & Motormen, who had been in the STUC's driving seat in 1919 during the tremendous "shorter hours" battle. Now, in this crisis, his Assistant Secretary, Peter Webster, was chairman of the STUC, and heading their Emergency Committee; they were constantly having to handle the resulting problems, but could find no solution. The other GC members who were "remaining in Glasgow and acting with full authority", were: the Vice-Chairman, Councillor John Nairn, General Secretary of the Scottish Textile Workers (Kirkcaldy) Union; J F Duncan, General Secretary of the Scottish Farm Servants; the Treasurer, Thomas Wilson, Scottish Secretary of Shop Assistants; Councillor W Leonard, Scottish Secretary of the Furnishing Trades; and Charles Gallie, Scottish Secretary of the Railway Clerks. Two other Scottish Secretaries of London-based unions, James Walker, Iron and Steel, and George Kerr, Workers Union, were almost always in attendance, as was Robert Watson, the General Secretary of the Scottish Typographical Association. However, James Hunter of the Miners and Tom Drummond of Edinburgh Trades Council were busy all through in their own sphere and unable to attend more than once, while the General Council remained in permanent session.

There were amazing grass-roots initiatives and achievements in conducting the general strike in Scotland, including mass picketing and huge demonstrations; and in some areas, like Methil, Airdrie and Coatbridge, Joint Strike Committees virtually took total charge. In Aberdeen salaried officials who were blacklegging at the electrical station and living inside found that the Aberdeen Bakers decided to stop supplies to them. In Glasgow where the tramways were receiving electricity from the Pinkston Power Station, the blacklegs there were "living 'on the job' in not very enviable conditions": for the iron gate and palings around it "have been electrified and a live wire barrier has been constructed around the enclosure" (*Scottish Worker*, 10 May). The same issue reported that at Shotts, where the "Strike Committee is controlling everything", at a public meeting they "formed a 'Peace Corps', its duty being to prevent disorder or anything of that description". There were very different activities also showing high morale. The miners of Kilsyth Co-operative men's choir walked to Glasgow, won first prize in the Festival there, and before walking the dozen miles home, paused in Berkeley Street to sing to the gathering crowd the "Comrades' Song of Hope". In Govan strikers' wives daily held a matinee "to maintain order and to watch local food prices".

However, we must first confine ourselves to noting how the GC of the STUC responded: the key point is that they regarded themselves merely as agents "applying the general plan" of the British TUC, and did not see it as suitable to take any initiative beyond passing on instructions from London, whom they continually consulted by telephone or wire. GC members who were in continuous session for thirteen days in their new offices at 33 Elmbank Crescent, which they shared with the Distributive and Allied Workers, saw their role as being to ensure that Scotland stuck to the exact letter of London's instructions. It was only on the question of publishing an independent

Scottish Worker near the end that they finally did not conform precisely, as we shall see.

They operated from 3 to 15 May; at their second meeting they began to set up "a chain of communications" by courier, covering five regions and extending to Aberdeen. To get this moving they sent their Treasurer, Tom Wilson, Scottish Secretary of the Shop Assistants, to Carlisle, where it was planned that information was to be picked up regularly from the British TUC Publicity Department and passed on to STUC distributing points at Kilmarnock, Kilsyth, Airdrie, Hamilton and to Glasgow Trades Council for the West Clyde Valley. Though documents received at Carlisle from London were much delayed their contents were to be included later in Bulletins, usually prepared by J F Duncan and Elger. But there was a tremendous need for constant information and also for a lead to counter the stream of hostile propaganda over radio and the Scottish newspapers still available. How divisive this could be is illustrated by the fact that there were different attitudes to the strike by the heads of the two main Christian Churches. While fullest publicity was given to one which declared the strike was "a sin against the obedience which we owe to God", the proposal by the other of terms of settlement to include the withdrawal of the miners' wage cuts was suppressed.[4]

The need for information was the first and most frequent question brought to the STUC leaders as recorded in Elger's precise but brief Minutes of the twenty morning and afternoon sessions when they met.

At their first meeting, they decided to send their Chairman, Peter Webster, to a meeting that night of trade union officials called by the Glasgow Trades Council's Industrial Committee, who were planning a major demonstration in Glasgow City Hall: he was to inform them

> that a Public Demonstration was undesirable and to suggest that the Meeting be of trade union officials (full-time and other) with admission being given only to accredited persons.

As a result the demonstration was cancelled, but a Central Strike Co-ordinating Committee representing the different industrial groups, including the "second wave" unions in shipbuilding and engineering, was set up, with Peter Kerrigan of the Engineers and John McBain of the Foundry Workers the leading officers. At the same time, the GC had to reply to the offer of the Editor of the Independent Labour Party's *Forward* "to include any material for STUC in a Special Strike Bulletin". Aitken Ferguson, Editor of the Minority Movement's *Worker,* went further, offering "to place the paper under the full control of any authorised Strike Committee". Both were turned down

> as the general plan of action included withdrawal of all Printing Trades, and as no exceptions were to be made.

Present at the time was Robert Watson, General Secretary of the Scottish Typographical Association, whose executive had decided not to jeopardise their position with the print employers by striking without first giving a fortnight's notice to do so; the GC asked them to reverse the decision, but problems between them and the other print unions continued. When the four Glasgow newspapers produced their first *Emergency Press* on the first day of the strike, at first the GC decided "to take no action", and not to issue a news Bulletin.

Next morning they had an important meeting with a deputation from the Glasgow Strike Committee, which consisted of McBain and Kerrigan, William Shaw JP, Secretary of the Trades Council (Carpenters), John McKenzie, General & Municipal, James Richmond, The Patternmakers Clyde District Secretary, and Frank Stephenson, Vehicle Builders. They discussed serious problems already arising amongst the shipbuilders and engineers who were not yet called out. The GC thereupon told Elger to wire the British TUC, saying:

> Circumstances have arisen in Scotland which make it exceedingly difficult to keep moulders, engineers and shipbuilders at work. Feeling is so strong that we advise these sections be officially asked to cease work.

But the reply was that they should stay at work, and when the GC put out its first Bulletin next day the problem was not handled. It was not suprising that with these and many other practical problems arising locally news sheets proliferated. More than a dozen Scottish Joint Strike Committees began to issue their own in whatever form they could, in some cases running up to 2,000 copies a day. The most effective was the *Workers Press,* put out to counter the newspaper owners' *Emergency Press* in Glasgow by the editorial committee of the Minority Movement's paper *The Worker*, which the GC had rejected. The GC at once sent for the editor, Aitken Ferguson, who was a Communist Party member. The chairman that afternoon, James Walker,

> intimated that the General Council had decided that it was undesirable for *The Worker* to be published during the General Strike, and they requested that immediate consideration should be given to the publication being stopped.

Ferguson replied that he doubted his committee would agree as indeed

Front Page of First Issue "The Scottish Worker"

THE

Scottish Worker

Official Organ of the Scottish Trades Union Congress

No. 1 GLASGOW, MONDAY, MAY 10, 1926 ONE PENNY

STAND FAST!

The Greatest Response in History.

"The Scottish Worker" is published by the Scottish Trades Union Congress to give to the working class in Scotland, and the public generally, reliable news of the strike.

It is not our function to decide policy or to discuss the general situation. The strike is under the control of the British Trades Union Congress General Council, who are solely responsible for the direction and control of the strike.

Our duty, and the duty of all members of the Trade Unions involved, is to accept loyally and whole-heartedly the decisions of the General Council of the British Trades Union Congress, and to give effect to their instructions to the utmost limit of our powers.

We shall confine ourselves to the work that lies to our hands, and we know that we can rely upon the workers to do so as they have done since the strike started.

We shall give, to the best of our ability, reliable information as to the position of the strike in the different localities. It is necessary we should do so, because many agencies are at work endeavouring to influence our people by spreading information which is designed to influence the opinions of the workers on strike and to undermine the magnificent loyalty they have displayed for the past week.

We trust our people. We know we can rely upon their judgment, as we have trusted to their loyalty. We know they will rely upon our honesty in presenting them with the facts.

We want to take this opportunity of paying our tribute to the manner in which the Scottish workers have conducted themselves since the strike began. The eager way in which they responded to the call is the best evidence that those responsible for the conduct of the strike were acting in full sympathy with the spirit of all the workers of the country.

The difficulty has not been to get the workers to answer the call, but to keep those who were not asked to cease work from throwing in their lot with the strikers. It was a severe test to apply to the discipline of our movement to ask workers to remain at work when all were eager to make common cause with their fellows. We have emerged from the test and maintained the discipline which is the best augury for our success. We shall continue to work in the same spirit of loyalty and unity.

We knew our people and expected unity and confidence, but we did not know the reserves of capacity in the local Trade Union movement in Scotland. We had to improvise a machine and construct an administration to meet the emergency which faced us. We have done so, and the capacity displayed by the Local Strike Committees in creating their machinery and setting it to work has been one of the most remarkable developments in the history of the working class. It has been a soldiers' battle and right well have the rank and file risen to the occasion.

All goes well with us. Our cause is good, and the spirit of our people could not be better. We shall continue as we have begun, and carry on until the end, confident in the justice of our cause, resolute in our purpose, and loyal to each other.

England Aroused and Alert

Enthusiasm Everywhere Prevails

Inspiring News

The British Trades Union Congress in the course of an inspiring statement gives particulars of the magnificent spirit manifested through the length and breadth of England. Never in the history of British Labour has a more righteous cause arisen. Never have British Workers made so splendid an effort to meet so unrighteous an attack In the industrial centres all is at a standstill, and every indication points to a grim determination on the part of the men to maintain this condition. In Liverpool there is a thorough dislocation. In Birkenhead a strike of the Dock Board men has rendered 600 men idle. At Bedford the Power Station men have come out. At Birmingham no trams, trains, or omnibuses are running, and quiet obtains in the city. At Hull, Portsmouth, and Plymouth very small quantities of goods are being removed from the docks by tradesmen. The strikers at Norwich have had their ranks augmented considerably since Thursday. The London reports are thoroughly satisfying, both Regents Park and Victoria Park have been closed to the Public, and are in occupation by the Military Authorities; taxi drivers to the number of between five and six thousand have ceased work on their own account, and street traffic has been reduced to a minimum.

From all quarters, but more especially in the North-East, details are being received of the failure of the O.M.S. to cope adequately with the serious situation the strike has created.

In some centres it has ceased entirely to be a vital unit in the maintenance of communal needs.

Food supplies generally continue to be normal throughout the country.

The survey concludes:

"The tendency in England is for men to come out rather than for any to go back"

Front page of the first issue of The Scottish Worker

they did not. Immediately afterwards two members of the Printing Trades Group of the Glasgow Strike Committee came to ask the GC to publish a printed news-sheet, saying they were sure they could provide *voluntary* labour to produce it. The GC then discussed this proposal and agreed

> on the motion of J F Duncan and M O'Hagan that no News-sheet intended for the general public be printed.

Again on Friday, 7 May, Glasgow Central Strike Committee pressed them unsuccessfully to publish a newspaper. Late that afternoon, however, couriers arrived from London with instructions that newspapers were to be published in various centres. This seemed to them at first to put a different complexion on matters: they at once decided

> to make arrangements for publication of a paper called the *Scottish Worker,* which was to be the official strike bulletin of the STUC General Council and to be under the control of the General Council.

J F Duncan was to be in charge as its editor, to consult with *Forward* and to arrange with the Civic Press to print the first copy three days later on Monday, 10 May. But the GC were to be in dire difficulties about it before then from many directions.

Section (iii): **They Insist on Their "Scottish Worker"**

Firstly, on the Saturday morning, 8 May, Hugh Lyon came in person, to know what would be the position of the print workers concerned? Would they be under licence from their union? This was an urgent and awkward question for the General Secretary of the Carters. Lyon had been under sharp criticism because he himself had been issuing transport permits entitling employers to require his members to work. "Mr Lyon expressed satisfaction" when the GC decided that Elger was to tell the Civic Press Secretary, Ben Shaw, that the print workers would give their services, and by making no claim on the Civic Press, would not be their employees. The General Council also decided that "no printed publications would be authorised in Scotland other than the *Scottish Worker*". This, it was felt, would meet the position of the Scottish Typographical Association whose General Secretary, Robert Watson, was present, and it would ease his relations with the other elements of the Printing and Kindred Trades. However, the Glasgow Typographical Society disapproved and threatened to veto voluntary labour, until the GC succeeded in convincing a deputation from them that afternoon. But this was not the end of the GC's difficulties. Their day-long meeting on Sunday, 9 May, was spent almost entirely in differences with the British TUC's Publicity Department who opposed the publication of their *Scottish Worker*. In charge in London was E L Poulton, General Secretary of the Boot and Shoe Operatives. He wired Elger to say that it was merely proposed to reprint the *British Worker* itself in Glasgow, which the Londoners insisted must have "no cuts or additions and every word maintained". It was proposed that a copy should be brought daily for reprinting from Newcastle. The GC unanimously decided that this "was utterly impracticable", and to tell London that they were "proceeding with the *Scottish Worker*". But when Poulton was told this by Duncan and Elger he replied that they were "definitely forbidden" by the Publicity Department to publish any *Scottish Worker*, and "insisted that the *British Worker* should be reprinted in Glasgow". This was too much for the Scots and they appealed over his head to the British TUC Chairman, Arthur Pugh, of the Iron & Steel Confederation.

This led to Poulton conceding that the *Scottish Worker* already on the machines could proceed; but in future three pages of the *British Worker* would be sent daily to reach Carlisle at 4 a.m. for reprinting in Glasgow; a fourth page could be filled with Scottish news and the result published as "The Scottish Edition of the *British Worker*". But the GC decided to proceed with the *Scottish Worker*, while giving London a guarantee that it

> would not be concerned with policy, but would reprint all statements of policy of the BTUC, either from the *British Worker* or from instructions otherwise issued.

The first number therefore duly appeared on Monday, 10 May. Whilst they duly reproduced the official statements from the British and the Scottish General Secretaries and District Organisers, they made a point of featuring Scottish "Notes From Far and Near" and "Strike Brevities", and some lively cracks and anecdotes. One of these underlined how slow communications with the south could be. Two miners' MPs coming north by car, stopped at Preston, where they found a train was leaving for Glasgow driven by volunteers at 9 a.m. in the morning; they set off an hour and a half later and overtook it forty miles on. But when they themselves left Carlisle at three that afternoon they noted that " 'Puffing Billy' had still to arrive". Amongst their quotations was the remark: "Backbones are Better than Wishbones these days". They capped this with:

> The cutest, wisest little thing a modern wit has said: "A bone in the back is worth two in the head".

In their editorial in the first number they paid a tribute to how "the Scottish workers have conducted themselves since the strike began. The eager way in which they have responded to the call is the best evidence that those responsible for the conduct of the strike were acting in full sympathy with the spirit of all the workers of the country. The difficulty has not been to get the workers to answer the call, but to keep those who were not asked to cease work from throwing in their lot with their fellows". They added: "we did not know the reserve of capacity in the local Trade Union movement in Scotland".

They also felt the need to make a special point about the Scottish women, who "have been splendid". For they found that

> one inspiring and wonderful feature of the great struggle has been the loyalty and courage the women have demonstrated.

While they hated strikes, as their menfolk did too, "they hate still more the alternative – that is, to lie down to every successive attack, and be permanently on destitution level". In this fight the women

> have faced privation and hunger with a smile and put encouragement and heart into the men. They have been comrades who have not failed.

It was a well deserved tribute, but published the day after the strike had been called off.

From the first, the GC's problems in publishing the *Scottish Worker* at long last continued in many forms. In the first issue they had to note that in its previous day's Bulletin the Edinburgh Strike Committee had made the "entirely unauthorised and completely erroneous" statement that the paper had been published under the editorship of Duncan and P J Dollan, the Glasgow civic leader and journalist. Elger also had to report that Wilson had telephoned from Carlisle that the London courier was many hours overdue, and had been extremely late for the two previous days. Tuesday, 11 May, showed still more sharp disagreements. That afternoon the London courier had arrived very late with a circular about the reprinting of what it called the *British Worker* and that claims for expenses in producing it would be paid by London. This circular from Poulton, together with a similar announcement in the Sunday *British Worker* which had only just reached Carlisle, would revive all the problems in Scotland with the print unions. Elger minutes coolly:

> The General Council decided to continue the arrangement already made for the publication of the *Scottish Worker*.

The same difficult Tuesday morning they were informed that the Glasgow Retail Agents Federation would be ready to distribute supplies of the *British Worker* which were lying at the station "if they could be uplifted". The GC decided "no authority could be given for them being moved".

But they also had to receive a deputation from Edinburgh Strike Committee, who pointed out that while the newspaper proprietors' two journals were being printed as usual in Edinburgh, they themselves had problems with duplicating and wanted permission to print their Strike Bulletin in future. When they were told it was impossible to give such permission "as it was contrary to the General Strike plans", they suggested they might reprint the *Scottish Worker*. The General Council decided by 5 to 2 that the paper could not be reprinted in any privately owned printing establishment; and since the deputation said they could not guarantee its printing in Edinburgh "under the control of the trade unions or the Co-operative Societies", no permission could be given.

Then came the fatal telephone call on Tuesday, 12 May, that the British TUC had called off the strike. Elger's Minutes record that he was instructed to send telegrams to all on the Scots' lines of communication in the precise terms of the British TUC message:

> To resume negotiations General Council British Congress have terminated General Strike today. Trade Unionists before acting must wait instructions of own Executive Councils. Circulate information in your area.

The same day they also asked about all arrested and convicted during the strike. That night Duncan had 70,000 copies printed of the *Scottish Worker* for the next day. But he complained bitterly that the *British Worker,* in telephoning its message to Scotland, had "made no reference to the attitude of the miners towards the calling off of the strike, other than the miners' thanks for the support of the trade unions, whereas the *Emergency Press* had the information". The *British Worker* had replied

> that the statement telephoned was the instruction of the General Council of the British TUC.

The GC decided to continue to publish and to approach the unions for strike news. That afternoon both Elger and Duncan reported that they had tried to reach the British TUC Secretary, Citrine, but both had been told he was not in. They decided to wire that they were

> surprised no information from you since Monday. We have no knowledge of situation yesterday and today. Strike Committees and Unions are continually enquiring for position and instructions. Essential we should hear from you immediately. Please phone at once.

Citrine replied that since "some employers were attempting to enforce humiliating terms as conditions of resumption", the STUC should "connect with employers immediately and report result". The GC who had been visited by Shaw and Kerrigan from the Glasgow Central Strike Committee the previous day on all that was happening there, wrote to them that with the strike called off, the Executive Councils of the unions were now in control and responsible for negotiations. It was "therefore not possible to authorise any Joint Committee to take action which may result in instructions being given contrary to the decisions of the Executive Committees". But they stressed that "machinery of co-ordination" could nevertheless be used where unions had sent out similar instructions. The next day, Saturday, 15 May, after deciding to ask Citrine what action the British TUC were taking about convicted strikers and arranging to interview the Secretary for Scotland on that, the General Council went out of continuous session, to meet one month later. That day was the last issue of the *Scottish Worker*. Under the title "Pity the Poor Scots Coalowner!" they printed deadly figures of the increases in profits of the six main Scottish coal companies.

While an unceasing problem was the need and demand for information, let alone advice and a lead, there were other difficulties which Elger had to report at each session. Much of this arose from contradictory instructions from London, which were sometimes completely reversed when trade union executives differed over questions which should have been worked out long before. The worst and most complicated was what should be regarded as staple foods and supplies; which should be transported? and under whose permit? The General Council was in daily consultation with the Joint Transport Committee in Glasgow, comprising the three railway unions and the Transport & General Workers, whose main speakers were J B Figgins (NUR) and John Veitch (T&GWU), at whose Glasgow office they operated as a permits authority for transport. It did not include the Scottish Horse & Motormen. The General Council on the first day of the strike contradicted a press report about Lyon being appointed "permit officer for Scotland" as having been made without authority; and next day told him to withdraw all his permits, as his system was "not regarded as satisfactory" by the Joint Transport Committee. Daily the General Council discussed and consulted with them on the varying instructions received about it from London. These ranged from asserting that local transport committees "must exercise their own discretion"; that goods could be moved "under permit"; that such permits must not allow goods to be moved from railway depots or docks; that nothing of any kind must be transported at all; and finally that the only permitted deliveries should be made "of bread and milk to the houses of members of the Co-operative Societies". It took eight days before this fundamental decision was reached, and the Joint Transport Committee could inform the General Council that all other permits would be withdrawn.

Meanwhile, the harassed General Council were having the results of the ensuing confusion reported to them. The most startling, perhaps, was from the Coatbridge and Airdrie Transport Committee, from whom a deputation told them on 10 May that early that morning there had been a raid by police, who confiscated all permit records, took names and addresses of those present and threatened that "they might be charged with sedition or contravention of the Emergency Powers Act". It was a locality where mass pickets had been highly successful. The General Council asked the Joint Transport Committee to take it up with their unions' headquarters.

There were also difficulties in the building trades, with different attitudes of the Woodworkers, the Scottish Painters and another small Scottish Union, the Ironfitters' Association. On the first morning the General Council, after the Building Trades Federation employers had been in touch, announced that the only work which could be done was on subsidised housing and repair work under permit, if needed "in the interests of sanitation or health". The Scottish Painters who had decided on a total ban were persuaded to agree to those exceptions. A deputation from the Woodworkers questioned whether work at hospitals could be continued. But that led to an enquiry from the Vale of Leven Central Strike Committee because the Woodworkers' instructions required building trade workers on maintenance work in Dye Works to continue working; to this the General Council replied that no permits should be issued for that work. The Ironfitters' Association pointed out the difficulty of their members being required to work on light castings as materials for housing only but not elsewhere. The General Council thereupon decided to tell London that "the situation in Scotland made it advisable for all housing and housing supplies to stop". But that was only the day before the strike was called off. There were also queries resulting from the British TUC's telephoned instructions on the first day of the strike, that

> districts were to differentiate where possible between power for commercial and domestic use. Coal would be supplied under permit.

This was followed by later instructions that local strike committees should approach local power undertakings to offer power for various services. It can be imagined what a strong feeling resulted in the Glasgow area where municipal trams were kept running throughout by blackleg tramwaymen, powered by the Pinkston Power Station. The Glasgow Central Strike Committee sent a deputation to the General Council asking authority for calling out the Pinkston Power workers. To this the STUC agreed, with Elger signing an appeal on their behalf jointly with the Glasgow Central Strike Committee and six trade unions whose members were involved.

In the three days after the strike was called off during which the STUC still held sessions and published the *Scottish Worker*, they were beset by angry and sometimes incredulous enquiries, including William Shaw and Peter Kerrigan from the Glasgow Central Strike Committee, who "placed before the General Council views" on the calling off and what should now be done. There was little reply they could make, as they received only little and late information they could pass on from the British TUC.

It may be noted, however, that the last but one issue of the *Scottish Worker* gives at least a hint of the General Council's shock and anger at the way the strike had ended. Their comment was headed "Peace – With a Big Stick"; and referring to the fact that the miners' oppositon to accepting the Samuel Memorandum (on the strength of which the British TUC had called off the strike) had been suppressed, commented:

> We desire to make it perfectly clear that the message we received from the TUC General Council was published exactly as we received it. In the message supplied to us there was no hint of any kind that the Miners were not a consenting party.

All that there remained for them to do was to ask for details about the arrests and convictions, while acknowledging receipt of letters from a whole number of trades councils demanding a Special Congress where they could hear, according to Motherwell, a "statement given in detail by a delegation from the British TUC". They were in no position to handle all the victimisation cases in the print and transport industries; what they did have to cope with for many months after were inter-union disputes.

Section (iv): **The Aftermath**

It may well be understood that the consequences affected every aspect of the life and activity of the labour movement throughout Britain, both for good and ill, for many years to come, and perhaps for longer than we can yet judge. To the man and woman in the street it was a new revelation of the enormous power of their joint action. There was also bitter anger and disappointment at the result and differing estimates of its cause. There was speculation about seeking new methods, especially by those who cried: "Never again!", and moves to expel those who demanded the replacement of "the leaders who betrayed". There were also those who stressed concentration on policies and action to counter the new problems which threatened repression of the trade union movement as a whole. All this was apparent in Scotland; and negative effects were certainly felt by the STUC. It was to be eleven years before the numbers of delegates and of the affiliated members they represented at Annual Congress could even approach the 1926 level. For five of those years the Scottish Miners who had hitherto always been the biggest delegation, did not affiliate, with bitter division amongst themselves.

Taking up much of the time of the GC for the seven months during which the miners fought on alone and right up to the Galashiels Congress in April 1927, were the inter-union disputes in road transport, print and the building trade, from incidents arising during the "nine days". Involved were the Scottish Horse and Motormen, the Transport & General and the Distributive and Allied Workers, together with the Co-operative Movement's complaints of clashes between pickets and carters who held illegal permits. The Woodcutting Machinists, who banned all work, complained that the Woodworkers had accepted their victimised members. There had also been severe victimisation by newspaper owners and the GC co-operated fully with a joint committee of print unions which organised a boycott of the journals; but it failed to gain effective support. When making arrangements for Congress the GC accepted a proposal by the Typographical Association's representative, Robert Watson, to "follow the usual practice in issuing Conference notices to all the daily papers published in Scotland". This had to be reversed when the other print unions heard of it, and the "blackleg press" was therefore excluded at

Congress, where the GC came in for sharp criticism for its first decision. In the meantime the old dispute against the Scottish Typographical Association for poaching continued with the Printing and Paper Workers, who refused to affiliate that year.

At Galashiels there was of course a lengthy debate on the report on the General Strike by the GC, which had been confined largely to discussing the lines of communication, the *Scottish Worker* and regretting that the Minority Movement's *Workers Press* had continued to appear. Motions raised by the "nine days" also dominated most of the other debates, both at Galashiels and throughout Britain.

But there was one topic special to Scotland; this was the question of relations with the British TUC in the conduct of the strike. A motion from the National Union of Vehicle Builders, whose head office was in Manchester, called for the end of the STUC as such. It regarded "the existence of two Trades Union Congresses in Great Britain" as a danger, when "co-ordination and centralisation" was necessary. It demanded that negotiations should be opened to establish it merely as "an Advisory Council of the British TUC on similar lines to those operating in the National Labour Party of Scotland". It concluded:

> The practicability and necessity of this step was seen during the recent General Strike, when the STUC became the representative of the BTUC in Scotland.

In moving it Charles Milne said it "had done good work in the past, but had outlived its usefulness". His Scottish District Committee had nearly proposed the changes before; and "this year the intervention of the General Strike had convinced them and they had decided unanimously". Describing his impressions on the two occasions when he had had to serve on the Central Strike Co-ordinating Committee in Glasgow, he said

> they sent up repeatedly to the General Council, the superior body, and the reply they always got when their delegate returned was that the GC were sitting like so many Micawbers waiting for something to turn up from the other side of the border. In view of the fact that the STUC proved that it could not act in a time of crisis, it should pack up and make way for a body that could.

Ending that "there was nothing dignified about fading away", he suggested "it was better to go out than to die out". Seconding it for Glasgow Trades Council, the Communist Vehicle Builder, Frank Stephenson, said the STUC's ruling "was a parody of the decisions of the British TUC". With all the large unions and important trade union officials associated with that body, "in no circumstances that could possibly arise at any conceivable time could the Scottish Congress act independently". Then he harked back to the 1919 "hours" struggle. Then the STUC "had declared the strike official, and those who loyally responded then had it declared unofficial by their own National Executives". It showed that these "would only tolerate the Scottish Congress so long as it assisted in their organising work". He blamed it for the continued existence of "the large number of Scottish unions", many of which would otherwise "have been forced to amalgamate with the larger unions".

It was ironic that it was the General Secretary of the third-largest Scottish union, the Farm Servants, who had to reply. J F Duncan moved an amendment which was in effect a direct negative, which not only claimed the STUC was necessary, but welcomed the "improved relationship between the two Congresses". The amendment was seconded for the GC by C N Gallie; and both noted the weak position of the Scottish Advisory Council of the Labour Party, with Gallie saying "it would be a tragedy" if they let the trade union movement be reduced to the same extent. Duncan criticised the Glasgow Trades Council for sending three delegates, who being "about a 60th part of the delegates" were taking up "more than a sixth of the time of Congress". The Minority Movement leader, Aitken Ferguson, retorted that "to get Comrade Duncan to adopt a progressive policy, they would have to send 63 delegates" from Glasgow. He closed by saying that during the strike the STUC "was merely a broadcasting centre, and that all national officials took their instructions from the British Congress". The GC's amendment was of course carried "by a large majority", Elger minutes.

Section (v): **Relations with the British TUC**

There was more behind this debate, which was basically about relations with the British TUC, than emerged at Galashiels. In the ten GC meetings held between the ending of the strike and Congress at no less than eight there were indications that they were not satisfied with their treatment by the British TUC. There were even differences of opinion which frequently required a vote to be taken; but Elger's tactful and inexpressive Minutes merely record decisions without the reasons and argumentation, which always had to be described when delegates' speeches at Congress were reported. At their first post-strike meeting in June the GC differed about representation at the Conference of National Executives at which the British TUC's General

Council was to report on the conduct and calling off of the strike. This was to be on 25 June, though Elger pointedly minutes that he had "not been advised" of it. While the Scottish Typographical Association's General Secretary, Robert Watson, and Thomas Wilson, the Shop Assistants Scottish Secretary, voted that all the GC should attend, C N Gallie, Railway Clerks, and J F Duncan regarded it as merely a recall of the April Conference which declared the strike and authorised the British TUC's GC to conduct it. In their opinion therefore, the same members, Webster and Elger, should attend. But although the GC decided all should attend, they got no reply, for the British TUC cancelled the Conference, their GC being by no means anxious at that stage to have to face the National Executives with a fiercely critical Miners' Federation in attendance. The next event was that, in September, Elger reported to the GC that when in London he

> saw Mr Citrine and, among other matters, had a talk about the relationship of the two Congresses. Mr Citrine then advised me that he could let me have a special invitation to attend the British Congress.

He consulted members and an Emergency Committee met to consider it, taking several votes before deciding by 3 to 2 that he alone should be allowed to attend the British TUC.

The next occasion was when Elger received notice of a Special Conference of Executives belatedly called for 3 November, 1926, to assist the miners by a financial levy. The Emergency Committee decided on this occasion to send no one to represent the STUC. After the miners had at last been forced to give in, London announced that it was at last holding the recalled Conference of Executives in January, 1927. Elger wrote asking that the full STUC GC should attend, but this was refused, with Citrine replying that only the STUC President Webster and Secretary Elger could be invited. There were two votes before it was agreed to accept the invitation, on Webster's casting vote, while asking the British TUC to reconsider it. They explained that

> the attendance of the full GC was desirable in the best interests of Trade Unions operating in Scotland.[5]

But Citrine replied that the British TUC "thought it advisable to extend the same invitation to all unaffiliated organisations which, like the STUC, had co-operated with them". Despite "the great work" the STUC had done, it would be "injudicious to make any exception". In making arrangements for fraternal delegates to the Galashiels STUC Congress Duncan and Hunter, the Scots miner, wanted to invite

Citrine himself, but after a vote it was decided merely to invite the London General Council to send some representatives. Thereupon they decided to send Robert Smillie, but stressed that he was not attending "as a fraternal delegate". When it came to the major struggle to defeat the Government's dire Trades Disputes and Trade Unions Bill, discussion between Elger and Citrine brought a repeat of the arrangements during the General Strike, but with some apparent improvement in status. The national campaign against the anti-union Bill was in Scotland to be "under the control and jurisdiction of the STUC GC", and James Walker was to represent them on the National Defence Committee consisting of the British TUC, the Labour Party nationally and the Parliamentary Labour Party.

There was, however, to be a return to the question of whether the STUC should cease to exist the following year, though with different arguments. At the Perth 1928 Congress, Sinclair Reid for Edinburgh Trades Council moved a resolution noting "the serious situation of British trade unionism" and that one united organisation was needed. The GC should therefore open negotiations for

> definitely establishing the STUC as an integral part of the British TUC.

He quoted the great combinations of capitalist forces rapidly put together, such as the recently formed Mond Combine, which "required a corresponding concentration of working-class forces". He was supported by F Wolstencroft, the General Secretary of the Woodworkers, who claimed his union paid fees on 5,000 to both Congresses. He believed it "was no use preaching one big trade union amalgamation and one international organisation and at the same time insisting on two Congresses". Probably there could be an Advisory Scottish Council such as the Labour Party had. This the GC successfully opposed by a large majority; Duncan saying their "experience of advisory bodies did not make them desire to add to their number". While praising their increasingly "harmonious relations", he believed it was possible at the STUC "to discuss matters with a greater amount of freedom" than in the larger Congress.

While the British TUC had now started sending Scotsmen from England to be their representatives at Congress, it was not for a further five years, in 1932, that they began the practice of sending their Chairman himself each year. Meanwhile both Congresses were to be faced with dire problems, with almost always identical responses in the GC, which laid them open to considerable criticism for inadequate action in face of mounting unemployment, economic crises, and the final collapse of the MacDonald second Labour Government. In

Scotland for some years there was considerable alienation from the trades councils; if they did not fall away or become inactive, they were increasingly looking to the left influences of the Minority Movement, with its stress on workshop committee organisation and action by the unemployed themselves through the independent National Unemployed Workers Movement. While Elger's efforts to build up county and area trades councils, organising activities under strictly approved rules, were to be ineffective, all was not gloom. Some factually useful enquiries were continued, but above all there was one innovation of lasting consequence. For 1926 saw the first setting up of a Women's Advisory and its first annual conference in September 1926. As we shall see later, this never faded out, even during the next difficult period; and it was to be followed by a Youth Advisory, which could also in time become a storage house of valuable new thinking and initiatives.

References

[1] *Scottish Worker*, 12 May, 1926.

[2] Ian MacDougal gives examples relating to Edinburgh University in "1926 General Strike", edited by Jeffrey Skelley.

[3] *Scottish Worker*, 10 May.

[4] These were Cardinal Bourne in High Mass in Westminster Cathedral on 9 May and Archbishop of Canterbury, Dr Randall Davidson. See "The Churches", a study by Stuart Mews in "The General Strike", by Margaret Morris. Five Labour MP's, all Catholics, wrote a letter of protest about Cardinal Bourne's statement that the general strike was "a sin against Almighty God". They pointed out they had "striven for peace" which the Government had "denied us". They therefore held "that our fellow workers are doing what is right". They protested "against a high dignitary of the Holy Church making a statement which neither the morality nor the theology of our faith justifies". The letter was published under the title "Cardinal Rebuked" in the *Scottish Worker*, 14 May.

[5] PC Minutes, 10 January, 1927.

13

Reaction and Recovery

It was eleven years later that a really well-balanced estimate of the painful years in Scotland following the General Strike came from a participant and delegate in the Presidential Address, when Congress returned to Inverness in 1937. It was made by the Farm Servants' delegate, Bella Jobson, who was to be the first of only two women to preside during the Scottish TUC's first eighty years.

Section (i): **The Angry 'Thirties**

Too often they were told that the General Strike had been a failure, she said, "but we are too near the event and too much involved in it to pass final judgment". Even after eleven years, she said, there was "still too much conflict of opinion" about what actually happened "in those two hectic weeks, and too much recrimination". Then she declared the fact

> that it was the first example of working-class solidarity that has ever been shown, is too often forgotten. It was the culmination of a period in which the trade union movement had grown to a strength far beyond anything it had ever reached.

A failure? "It certainly did not fail to frighten the ruling class out of their wits", as they rushed through the Trade Disputes and Trade Unions Act hoping to "curb the Labour Movement industrially and politically". At first it did look as though the movement suffered a serious loss of power. While the unions "were badly shaken by the struggle in 1926 and the sense of failure knocked the spirit out of many", it was not that which weakened them. It was the mounting unemployment.

> That gave many employers the opportunity to lower wages and break down standards of employment. Trade union membership decreased and the workers lost spirit. There was a feeling that it was not worth while to struggle against bad conditions.

Yet they had stood the test better "than in any previous depression"; the cuts imposed at the worst time had been restored through "persistent and effective work", and the past year "has shown a revival of the fighting spirit", which renewed confidence in the movement. Noting that the workers were "apt to get impatient" and found the trade union method "too slow for them", she stressed how important it was "to bring the younger workers into active work in the trade unions", since "a number of factors" worked against this. It was they who would have to find new methods of solving new problems.

The recrimination of which she spoke arose from serious differences about the response to the two lines of attack from the opponents of the trade union movement following the General Strike. The first immediate and open attack was through the Trade Disputes and Trade Unions Act, 1927; the second was the far more subtle divisive ploy of "industrial peace", or Mondism as it became known. The hostile attack through the Trade Disputes and Trade Unions Act was bound to be opposed by every section; for it removed all previous legal protection of trade union rights, making mass picketing illegal during general, sympathy and political strikes as well as interfering with the political levy for the Labour Party. As a minimum, a thorough campaign was needed to arouse political opposition in Parliament. The STUC, therefore, set up a Scottish Trade Union Defence Committee, co-ordinating it with the National Defence Committee through James Walker as representative of the British body. Ten area Conferences were held in May 1927; lists of 300 local speakers were supplied with speakers' notes. It was estimated that some 2,000 meetings were held and two million leaflets distributed in Scotland, with members of Parliament speaking at 129 meetings. There were special demonstrations on 26 June, 1927. But then, with the "industrial peace" ploy in the offing, the public campaign closed; it had cost £400 in Scotland of which the Scottish Co-operative Union contributed more than a third. At the next Congress there were severe criticisms of the campaign from Woodworkers, General Iron Fitters and Willie Allan of the Scottish Mineworkers. He claimed they had been saying "that this dirty attack was to be met in Parliament only, and if they got back into power in 1929 one of their first attempts would be to wipe this rotten Bill off the Statute Book. This was policy calculated to create more and more apathy."

It needed to be fought "on the industrial as well as on the political plane", he concluded. Congress, however, passed the GC's motion merely demanding its repeal. This did, however, set the tone of exchanges on the subject. But once the Bill became law little but "pious resolutions" were passed, with criticism continuing and becoming sharper and more widespread as the second Labour Government failed to repeal it, finally dropping in 1931 their unsatisfactory attempt at an amending Bill. Tory dread of the "political strike" and their aim therefore to hamper close and growing connection between industrial and political action by a united working-class movement was expressed in the Act making it illegal to use trade union funds for political purposes. In Scotland finding an answer to this had a noticeable effect on trades councils. Early in the 'twenties they had tended to become joint organs with the developing local Labour Parties. The joint body would handle some matters in Industrial Committees. When the 1924 Labour Party Conference imposed a ban, and all affiliated political groupings had to be eligible for full membership of the Labour Party, members of such bodies as the National Minority Movement, Unemployed Workers Movement and Communist Party were barred; they therefore could be ruled out as delegates to a joint Trades and Labour Council. This affected trades council representation at Congress itself, when in 1924 Standing Orders were altered:

> Trades Council delegates to Congress shall be appointed only from Trade Union representatives on the Councils.

But following the Trade Disputes and Trade Unions Act many trades councils in Scotland altered their own constitution by setting up separate industrial and political funds: in some the Burgh Labour Party moved out of any joint body. Thus Finlay Hart became a delegate from his trade union branch to the newly formed Clydebank and District Trades Council but was debarred from attending the Clydebank Burgh LP because he was a Communist; a separate delegate had to be elected to that.

Section (ii): "Industrial Peace" – Mondism and Bans

Before the Bill had even become law, however, the development of the employers' other device was beginning already behind the scenes. This was to induce leading trade unionists in the corridors of power to discuss with major employers proposals for permanent "industrial peace" in future. At the 1927 Galashiels Congress where delegates were already arguing bitterly about the conduct of the General Strike and even whether the STUC itself should continue, Minority Movement activists won approval against it. A resolution from the Woodworkers condemned

> the propaganda of Industrial Peace conducted by leading trade union officials, whether individually or in co-operation with leading employers.

It declared that such talk "indulged in by leading trade unionists on the very eve of the Government's attack on the Trade Union Movement can only cause confusion amongst the organised workers". In negotiations with employers, workers must rely on the strengthening of the trade unions, and their problems could "only be solved by the elimination of the Capitalist system". It therefore instructed unions to withdraw from the "National Alliance of Employers and Employed" and like bodies. It was seconded by J B Figgins of the Railwaymen, who said that leaders preaching industrial peace "were undermining the movement financially, numerically, morally and intellectually". It was carried with only one dissentient. This was, indeed, in marked contrast to what emerged that autumn; and later Willie Allan, the Scottish miner, was to ask Elger why the resolution had not been taken up with the British TUC? For at that autumn Congress, with many Scots present, "industrial peace" was very much in the air; the Presidential Address from the Building Trade Workers' Secretary offered to co-operate with employers "in a common endeavour to improve the efficiency of industry". Thereupon, twenty leading industrialists headed by Sir Alfred Mond, founder of Imperial Chemicals Industries, got together with the incoming GC of the British TUC to discuss rationalisation and "industrial reorganisation and industrial relations". Their object, said Mond, was "to increase the competitive power of British industries in the world's markets". They reached agreement and formed a National Industrial Council, whose Joint Standing Committee was to operate compulsory conciliation, the strike weapon meanwhile to be abandoned. They reached agreement in London on 4 July, 1928.

As Allen Hutt puts it in *The Post-war History of the British Working Class, 1918-1937*, it was soon clear "that the policy of industrial peace meant war within the trade unions". The opposition increasingly became centred in the grass-roots activists, and in particular the Minority Movement, the trades councils where they were active, the National Unemployed Workers Movement, the Communist Party and sections of the Independent Labour Party, particularly those on Clydeside. When the Mondists reached agreement one member of the British TUC leaders, the miner, A J Cook, spoke very strongly against it. Four days later on 8 July, together with Maxton, he denounced it at a huge meeting called by the ILP at St Andrews Hall, Glasgow. He regarded the Mond Conference scheme "as largely the foundation for Fascist trade unionism in this country. I do not say it is the whole building, but undoubtedly it is the foundation of Fascism". He noted also that

> at the present moment there is going on in a number of unions discrimination against and expulsion of Communists and Left Wingers. This is in line with the policy of "Industrial Peace"; it is a hindrance to the policy of militant trade unionism.

This speech was published by the Minority Movement as a pamphlet entitled "Mond Moonshine", to which there was a sequel entitled "Mond's Manacles".

By that September the British TUC had endorsed the Mond policy despite the efforts of such activists and of the Engineers Union and shortly afterwards not only did their GC oppose co-operation with an NUWM Hunger March, but Citrine wrote to all trades councils on the route not to give assistance. Even with a massive rise in unemployment beginning, the attitude extended in some degree to the STUC. In September 1928, immediately after the British TUC, which Elger attended, he was instructed on the motion of James Walker and C N Gallie, who had been delegates there themselves, to write to all Scottish Trades Councils refusing recognition to those "affiliated to or connected in any way with the National Minority Movement". This was because their activities were "damaging to the trade unions generally". An unsuccessful attempt to refer back their action was made by two declared members of the Minority Movement, the Vehicle Builders' Frank Stephenson and the Woodworker, Jack Strain. A Dyers' delegate from Cheshire spoke against them, saying they reminded him of Industrial Workers of the World supporters who had opposed him in 1911; and the Aberdeen Trades Council Secretary described the Minority Movement as "the No. 2 Branch of the Communist Party". James Walker, quoting the strife in the Scottish Miners, said the GC's view was that it should be understood "that the Minority Movement was in absolute disagreement with the Majority Movement" and that they were "quite frankly without any connection whatever". But there was not unanimity on the GC; for William Leonard of the Furnishing Trades said his union was affiliated to the Minority Movement, and yet "conformed in every way to the ordinary practices of the trade union movement". Only three weeks earlier another body, supported by the Minority Movement activists but disapproved of by the hierarchy, had organised a major march of the unemployed from Glasgow; this was the NUWM, amongst whom was George Middleton, who years later was to become the General

Secretary of the STUC. The bans and recriminations continued, together with efforts to re-form trades councils or to bring in rival Trade Union Organising Committees, and reintroduce the British TUC's card vote system. Yet even in the least fruitful times Congress always remained a place where the voice from the grass roots could be heard. Where trades councils ended direct connection with such organisations as were disapproved of, the activisits reappeared as delegates from their trade union branch; the trades councils found ways of taking part in the campaigning of which they approved, such as Edinburgh Trades Council's huge demonstrations and co-operation with the members of the NUWM.

Section (iii): **World Economic Crisis and Labour Government Collapse**

Such campaigning was later to become considerable indeed and in Scotland was to get much support from the ILP; but in 1929 a lot of campaigning was aimed at returning the second Labour Government to office in June 1929, as the largest single party, but once again with no overall majority.

From this great things were expected by the STUC, with differences at first largely confined to estimates of how soon results could be achieved. But after only four months in office there occurred in October the disastrous economic crisis of the capitalist world, with its then record unemployment and the world's credit system broken down.

Economies became the order of the day. These included tightening up on parish relief and forcing claimants to prove they were "genuinely seeking work", with unemployment rapidly moving towards the three million it was to reach for the first time. With a long line of unemployed "genuinely seeking work" at the gate, employers could begin to lengthen hours and cut wages, often producing what was virtually compulsory overtime. Widespread in all industrial areas, in Scotland it was felt very hard in textiles, the shipyards, road transport and printing. In each industry there developed long-standing demarcation disputes, about which the STUC GC had to spend a disproportionate amount of time, with all too little success. In each of these cases the clash involved an independent Scottish union and major ones from south of the border.[1]

For close on three years the second Labour Government, some of whom seemed willing to shelter behind the lack of a majority, were thought to have made no serious effort to introduce the expected legislation which had been demanded as hardy annuals for years and regarded as priority. With older trade union leaders appearing to retreat in a similar fashion by failing to campaign politically or industrially, the terms in which they were defended or excused were often contradictory and surprising. Just before the 1931 Elgin Congress the Labour Chancellor Snowdon had announced that "sacrifices by all" must be made and so began the process of a total break. The Irish fraternal delegate, P T Daly, having listened both to the young delegates' complaints and defensive apologists from different quarters, had his own type of comment to make on the last day. He began by saying that when he first attended the STUC twenty-six years before, in 1905, he "rather agreed with some of the young men who suggested that the people on the platform who were then the age he was now, ought either to die or be shot". But the young must realise that all they were now doing was "broadening and improving the road that the old ones had dug and made". Then, talking of shooting, he turned his guns the other way. He told how two armed Irishmen were "lying on different sides of a dark road", waiting to "welcome" their landlord. After waiting ten minutes for him to appear after the train had arrived,

> the first man said: "No sign of him yet?" Shifting his gun, the other replied: "No, God send that nuthin's happened to the poor gentleman!"

Daly concluded that "there would have been no Labour Party and no Socialist movement had there been no trade union movement. They should let those people understand that if the trade union movement had made them, as it had, then as they said in Ireland, 'Begorra, we can unmake them!' " The young people should "carry on the noble traditions of those pioneers who had founded the STUC."

There was a startling increase in all these trends when Ramsay MacDonald, Snowdon and the NUR's J H Thomas, having failed to persuade the remaining Labour Cabinet to include new cuts on unemployment benefit as the financial experts advised, dismissed them and called in Conservatives and Liberals to form a "National Government", in October 1931. Its first action was to impose a ten per cent wage cut on all public servants as well as on unemployment benefit, and to introduce the hated Means Test. An immediate startling result was the first mutiny in the Royal Navy for 134 years. It happened in Scotland. Packed off to faraway Invergordon, men on the lower deck of sixteen ships put out a sailors' manifesto and refused orders. It was evident to them "that this cut is the forerunner of tragedy, misery and immorality amongst the families of the Lower Deck". Unless the cuts were withdrawn, it declared,

> we are resolved to remain as one unit, refusing to sail under the new rate of pay.

The strike lasted four days before they won a concession from the Admiralty. This certainly did not go without effect amongst the many civilian Government shipyard workers in Scotland.

On the political front ILP and Socialist activists in the Labour Party, including some MPs, began to look for a united front. It resulted in the setting up of the Socialist League, and later to the formation of the Left Book Club, whose publications had great effect. There was also increased activity amongst the advocates of Scottish Home Rule measures, not least because much depended upon whether local authorities could or would respond with public relief works. This became an ever more urgent question as the NUWM, far from folding when it was banned, became increasingly active in helping claimants and organising the unemployed themselves in massive demonstrations to get quick local government response. Outstanding were those during 1931 in Dundee, Glasgow, Kirkcaldy and Edinburgh. These often resulted in running battles with the police on just as big a scale as those in the Welsh Valleys, Bristol, Merseyside and Whitehall. If it reminded some of the 1919 "hours battle" in Glasgow, to others it brought back the pre-war "industrial unrest" struggles, the rent strikes of the housewives in Govan and Clydeside shop stewards. Nor was the activity only local: a major feature became the nationwide hunger marches, with participants from Aberdeen and beyond, especially those organised by the NUWM in 1932 and 1934. These were being met in London by 200,000 to greet them: indeed they finally even gained a measure of official recognition and much publicity, long before the "Jarrow March" which coincided with the NUWM's 1936 immense national march.

Section (iv): Unemployment Haunts All Debates

Apart from action by the unemployed themselves through the NUWM and through the Unemployed Associations under trades councils, set up in 1933 to counter its influence, there were few activities of the STUC in the first half of the 'thirties which were not related in some way to the major problem of unemployment. It was this which haunted the whole movement, and in this sense they were united in common concern, regardless of differences of emphasis and tone of the delegates' contributions about what should be done. Elger's fact-finding enquiries had to turn in this direction. An example was the far-reaching and immensely detailed "Enquiry into the Methods of Regulating Wages and Working Conditions" throughout Scotland which began in 1927. After concentrating on the effect of Trade Boards, Joint Industrial Councils, the legally enforced minimum wage and workshop organisation, which resulted each year in long factual debates, the enquiries changed direction. Which unions kept their unemployed members in benefit? If not, should not their rules be altered and fees excused during unemployment? Should employers be encouraged to notify the trade unions of vacancies – as with the Engineers, Dyers, building trades and print workers? Or should it be compulsory for vacancies to be registered at the Labour Exchanges? On this there was marked disagreement, with compulsion finally being rejected by 71 to 43, the divide being between the more and the less strongly organised trades. There were enquiries into the closed shop and "compulsory membership", on which there was also disagreement. Another turn was in the direction of adapting trades councils and industrial committees, and introducing model rules for those not working to be transferred to Unemployed Associations. As demands increased for nationally funded public works, such as the time-honoured Forth and Tay Bridges projects, there was concern over local government schemes, and especially doubts on how these in fact worked. In this connection there was controversy and an enquiry into how the Fair Wages Clause of forty years before was being administered and that it should not be extended. The 1931 Congress accepted the motion of the Perth and Dundee Trades Councils that

> the Clause should apply in all business transactions between public bodies and companies, firms and individual employers.

In Perth they had been trying to help the Clerks Union to get clerical workers in the General Accident Assurance Company signed up. The Dundee Town Council had installed multigraph machines for very cheap printing by non-unionist girls on "extremely poor wages", when the work had formerly been done under trade union conditions.

Employers had quickly begun to lengthen hours and to introduce cheap labour of different kinds and in various ways, while at the same time they brought in new technology: all this was to meet foreign competition, they claimed. This gave rise to the question of import controls but especially to regular and bitter complaints that successive Governments were failing to ratify the International Labour Office's Washington Convention agreement on hours' limitation. In the many debates about hours there were complaints about overtime and defence of it being worked; but on the central question of hours the women delegates had especially valuable contributions to make, often arising out of their own Women's Advisory Committee's far-reaching work.

At the 1931 Congress Eleanor Stewart of the Workers Union described the "definite move in Scotland among textile employers to get back to the 55-hour week". Their argument was that

> the English workers were working longer hours and that if they were to keep their trade the Scottish workers would require to follow suit.

Agnes Gilroy, Shop Assistants, pointed out that there were 220,000 unemployed in distribution – more than were organised in trade unions – while people were working 56 hours. In cigarette-making a new machine needed only three people to work it where 700 had been in the operation before. She accepted rationalisation as inevitable, but moved a resolution that hours too should be rationalised "in proportion to the amount of labour displaced".

Associated with lengthening hours and rationalisation was also the problem of cheaper labour which employers were bringing in. Examples were women bus conductors' wages, women being brought in to service new processes in print, and similar complaints in furnishing and in catering. The need to raise the school-leaving age was seen in the same light, while at the other end of the scale there were strong feelings expressed on work done by pensioners. There was no disagreement when the demand was put forward for the pension entitlement age to be reduced to 60 years, in the hope it would reduce competition for work; but there was opposition to a demand that there should be legislation to stop anyone who received a pension of £2 or more from taking a job. In moving it a Glaswegian, P Ward T&GWU, supported by Edinburgh Trades Council said they must prevent "men drawing pensions and competing in the labour market". He explained he "objected strongly to policemen and other superannuated men taking jobs at a lower rate than the ordinary worker could afford to do". There was disagreement from those who thought £2 was too low a rate for a pension anyway, and who feared it might cut out ex-servicemen on pension. It was, however, carried after a recount. For their part the Tailors successfully pressed a motion that spinsters should be treated as pensioners at the age of 55. There were sharp criticisms about Government Training Centres, especially from the furnishing trades; men were expected to be trained as craftsmen after six months, "which was impossible"; and employers would then use them to undercut wages.

Every year there were debates on the difficulties directly facing the unemployed and often criticism of the General Council for merely "processing" the protests instead of conducting public campaigns on them. The topics included the need for the right to work or full maintenance, the Anomalies Act, the hardship of women being newly disqualified for relief by reason of insufficient stamps, and above all the Means Test. At the 1932 Hawick Congress, Glasgow and Dundee Trades Councils' delegates failed to carry a complaint that the General Council had not organised "meetings of protest against the Means Test and inadequate transitional allowances" but had "allowed other bodies to take charge of the campaign". But Congress then carried "by an overwhelming majority" a protest against the Means Test itself and the proposed relief scales, noting the additional burden on workers who had "lost £25,000,000 in wage cuts during the last year" while high rates of interest paid on war debts continued. It protested emphatically "against the class distinction shown". Thomas Scollan, who was just about to become Vice-Chairman, moved it as delegate for Glasgow Trades Council. He said that when the Unemployment Insurance Act was introduced

> it was regarded by the employing class as a safeguard against revolution. Now that they thought the psychology of the workers had changed, they came along with their Means Test. Congress should make it clear that insurance against revolution was still necessary, because it was only when those people realised that they were meeting determined men and women who declined to be pauperised and degraded that they were prepared to give anything.

Whilst two other General Council members opposed it, amongst the supporters were two women delegates from the Women's Advisory. Rachel Devine, Dundee Jute & Flax, pointed out that many under the Means Test had been cut off from all benefits "and were dependent on their relatives, who were thus penalised". Eleanor Stewart, Workers Union, quoting many cases she knew, said "not to protest against such things was something for which Congress would blush".

Before the next Congress the General Council had organised two Conferences at Edinburgh and Glasgow on unemployment and had operated the British TUC's recommendation of setting up Unemployed Associations with model rules. There was also a resolution which urged Councillors and Labour Party local officers not to take up claimants' cases, but to refer them to the trade unions; yet many unemployed had never been in unions or were no longer members. In most areas it was to the NUWM they turned for help, for trades councils had given a poor response to the Unemployed Association schemes and its model rules.

Section (v): **Unemployed Centres and Fascist Dangers**

There was a remarkable debate at the 1933 Congress at Ayr; the background to it was the seizure of power by the Nazis, although the actual topic was Scotland and the unemployed, not Germany. Three months earlier Adolf Hitler had taken advantage of the lack of unity between the German Socialists and Communists, and had become German Chancellor without resistance from the hierarchy. Exploiting the sense of nationalism following the 1918 defeat, exaction of heavy war reparations and inflation, he had built his Nazi movement on the neglected unemployed, reaching them in "Social Clubs". Financed by big business he was then to destroy not only the political movement but all the trade unions in Germany.

In Scotland the debate turned on questioning attitudes about the Scottish Council for Community Service During Unemployment which had been set up in January, with the STUC represented upon it by Treasurer C N Gallie and Secretary William Elger. It was the first debate of Congress, with the Glasgow Trades Council moving the reference back of the General Council report about it. The report stated that the Scottish Bakers had asked for their "observations upon the scheme of Mutual Service Clubs for the Unemployed", because of "certain activities" of the Falkirk Mutual Service Club. The General Council issued a policy statement opposing any movement where goods were "produced by the unemployed and sold to the public"; but said they would help efforts for measures "for the purpose of occupying the unemployed", including making goods and providing services for their own personal use. They added that there must be no payment nor "organised system of exchange", and they asked trades councils for information about such centres. On hearing that a Scottish Council was to be set up as an advisory body to "guide voluntary effort to provide unemployed men and women with opportunities for useful occupations", they sent a delegation, helped in drafting its constitution and then appointed two representatives to serve on it. The Prince of Wales came to Scotland in January 1933 for its opening. It was to have access to the Scottish Office and Scottish Departments of Ministries; and the General Council stressed that it had "autonomous powers in Scotland".

Moving the reference back Frank Stephenson said Glasgow Trades Council wanted the General Council's delegates withdrawn. They had sent members to a meeting about the Scottish Council's Centres called by Glasgow's Lord Provost; after hearing their report Glasgow Trades

Council had decided not only to withhold representation but to issue a manifesto against the scheme. This they had sent to the General Council. He described the whole atmosphere in the Centres as of

> monarchy, with pictures of royalty and captains of the Territorial Forces, and their chief purpose seemed to be the physical culture of the unemployed. He supposed that was to fit them for a Fascist grouping. The Government seemed to be intending to link up those social service groups with their new Unemployment Insurance proposals, and to make membership a conditon of Unemployment Benefit.

(In this he was indeed to anticipate the Test and Task Forces camps, to which the long-term unemployed were committed by the Public Assistance Committees as a condition of relief, about which the NUWM was obliged later to organise tremendous opposition.) Stephenson added that some £10,000 was subsidising the movement, with a Centre making boots in Clydebank where the Government had refused help "to the Cunarder lying in the stocks there". It was C Murdoch of the Falkirk Bakers who had first raised it, describing what was happening there. He said it could mean "another 100 unemployed bakers in Glasgow"; and concluded that in Germany

> the present apostle of freedom, Adolph Hitler, got over fifty per cent of his support from social service clubs of the type being supported by the General Council here.

T Barron, Woodworkers, described what was happening in similar bodies in England where the British TUC had found craft training going on, and that goods and carpentry work was done at well below normal wage rates. With his own union having 25,000 unemployed, he believed the General Council should have waited for a mandate before committing the STUC. Glasgow Boot & Shoe Operatives thought it one thing for them to mend their own boots but another when they mended their neighbours' at a figure craftsmen could not compete with. Charles Milne, Vehicle Builder from Old Kilpatrick, described how in his village it had forced cobblers and hairdressers to close down. The General Council's two representatives could only be "hostages, or at best figureheads with absolutely no power". And he concluded with a glance at the prestigious English General Secretary, C T Cramp, present for the first time as a delegate to the STUC:

> Even a British TUC would not consider this thing, and the General Council had discredited Scotland in the eyes of the whole movement.

Cramp commented humorously that, newcomer as he was, the speech "made him feel perfectly at home". He continued that some English trades councils believed that experienced trade unionists could "wield enormous influence on these committees". What was the STUC's experience? He would wish to know before voting. However, another English delegate, J Jagger, Distributive Workers, said his Executive "had made up its mind and were fighting these things tooth and nail", and it was deplorable that the General Council had acted without a commitment. He gave an example reported by a Dunfermline member that there a full-time supervisor of a completely fitted workshop forced everyone to make and sell for the benefit of the Centre before he could produce the same article for himself. A fellow Distributive Worker, from Edinburgh, said "when they found the other class rushing to support these committees, they knew it was not to benefit the workers. Such things should be under trades council auspices." However, J R Leslie, the General Secretary of the Shop Assistants, supported the General Council, on the ground that all the feared dangers might happen "unless trades councils and the General Council took an active part in these social clubs". Surprisingly a similar argument came from the Minority Movement Woodworker, Jack Strain, who said "to ignore these clubs was to turn their backs on the unemployed and to leave them to the influence of the capitalist classes, who would continue to run them". He remarked that

> if Hitler had secured his support from such social clubs, it was only because the Labour Movement in Germany took the same blind point of view as the Bakers' representatives were advocating.

There was even stronger support from the right-wing officer of the Iron & Steel Trades, and successor to James Walker, now an MP. For J Brown said "these clubs might be the beginnings of Socialism". The objectors were all concerned with the effect on their own particular crafts; but for the past 30 years the movement had criticised the commercial system for commodities being too dear. After hinting at supporting productives he was sharp in attack on "Stephenson, Jagger and Company", appealing to opponents

> to submerge some of their sectional interest in the interests of the general community and not to be a collection of hypocrites.

William Elger said that the Government had not created the movement, but merely given some administrative assistance, "and not one penny" to any association in Scotland; he added the Scottish Council's object was to keep clear of all controversial matters. C N Gallie for the General Council said that after the experience of public assistance, it was "quite understandable that there would be keen antagonism to anything that savoured of Government support"; but he believed that the participation of the STUC would keep the Centres under control in practice in accordance with their carefully worded Constitution, which was unchallengeably on the right lines. But when it was put to the vote the result was 58 to 58, though nearly a quarter of the delegates did not vote. It was left to James Crawford of the printing union (Natsopa) as President to give his casting vote against the reference back. Little more was heard of the Scottish Council for Community Services, nor indeed of the Unemployed Associations, of which only four were formed – Aberdeen, Bo'ness, Dunfermline and Perth – from the 63 Scottish trades councils.

The debate shows how much needed to be learned by the movement in Scotland and what would be the pressures to encourage or prevent this happening speedily. The following year there were first signs of two trends developing: the fear of fascism and war, and the need to reach the young people who had never known their parents to be assured of work.

References

[1] The Dyers & Bleachers; Amalgamated Society of Woodworkers; the NUR; and Printing Bookbinding, Machine Ruling and Paper Workers.

14

The Dangerous 'Thirties

In the 'thirties, changed conditions and world-wide economic, political and social problems brought the need for basic new thinking, from which Scotland too could not escape. It began; but with very different emphasis amongst the controllers of Britain's economy and amongst the employed and the unemployed. The central questions for all were unemployment and the war danger; how to control or cure the one and to win, or prevent, the other. For already the world economic situation had produced the threat that those in control might find a solution by forcibly taking the markets of others where their own were failing or had been stolen. Alongside this they saw public spending on armaments as the one profitable path to economic revival.

Section (i): New Thinking Begins on Unemployment

The necessary new thinking came hard for men and women in their fifties who had reached maturity in an atmosphere when it would seem unthinkable that Britain's economic world dominance could be successfully challenged, and had their views confirmed by Germany's attempt being totally defeated in war, at whatever expense of some ten million lives in all. Yet it had been a war in which other issues emerged. Might the British Empire and its economic dominance from now on be endangered not only by rivals from without, but also by unrest and aims of national independence from within? For example, it was true that the defunct Tsarist Empire had now ceased what had seemed its sixty-year threat to the frontiers of Britain's India, Middle and Far East; but what of their revolutionary successors? Though entirely taken up with their new planning of economic production which must still have far to go before they could be taken seriously as a power, let alone a super-power, nevertheless the process was inevitably focusing ideas about the experiences of socialist planning, with its total elimination of unemployment. Such a solution to economic and perhaps political problems could prove a threat to imperial interests by unrest within the Empire. Meanwhile Britain's defeated rivals were now in command of a totally opposite kind of new Germany, where trade unions were eliminated, and the unrest of the unemployed solved no longer only by attempts at their division from those in work, but by recruitment into an expanding army. How to handle this double threat became increasingly the obsession of the controlling forces in Britain, with far-reaching disagreement amongst them as to whether the threat from without or within was the more immediate.

For the mass of the working people's families, the unemployed and the young, the problems presented themselves differently. To them the questions were: "How can I get a job and decent living?" "If trade unions are still of use to us, how can we protect them from threats like those in Germany and Italy?" "How can wars be stopped or prevented?" "Who are the warmongers?" Hence the immense support for signatures to the League of Nations Peace Pledge petition; for the way refugees from Nazi Germany were received; the support from sympathisers for demonstrating unemployed workers; for anger at the emergence of fascist Blackshirts, and at legal action and laws supposed to curb the street violence being in fact used to ban or restrict normal public demonstrations. It was also reflected in the much-publicised debate by the prestigious Oxford University Students' Union debating to refuse to take part in any war; and the emergence of many young authors and poets expressing anti-fascist and left-wing views. It grew into a demand for action by a popular united front and campaigning bodies on many issues, which spread beyond the members of the Communist Party and the Independent Labour Party to influential Labour Party leaders by way of the Socialist League, for what in later years would be called an alternative economic strategy. Resistance to such attitudes by the old guard, often centred in leadership of old craft unions and declining industries, took the form of official bans, such as "the Black Circular",[1] on any participation with the new activist bodies.

All these trends and opinions were particularly marked in Scotland, as evidenced by pressure from the nervous hierarchy in London upon both the Scottish Council of the Labour Party and the General Council of the TUC through their Joint Committee. The devastating effect on the heavy industries of shipbuilding and engineering and export trading as well as the shattering results on textiles from slave labour in India and Japan was the background to new thinking from the grass roots sounding loud and clear at every Congress. It was thanks, of course, to the nature of the STUC constitution with trades council representation and unfettered voting, that it was heard there. In addition it was notable that by the early 'thirties the STUC's innovation of setting up the Women's Conference and Committee in 1926 was paying unexpected and perhaps largely unacknowledged dividends. Here they could come into play in areas and industries, some with new technology beginning, where traditional opinions had not hardened into fixed attitudes, and basic organisation produced fresh responses. It was seldom that the Women's Committee came in for the criticism which the GC rarely escaped; indeed, points thrashed out each spring at the Women's Conference often laid the basis for fruitful developments at Congress itself a few weeks later. The British TUC could only follow suit after four years; and in 1933 their visiting English delegate, Nancy Adams,[2] told the Scottish Women's Conference that "being earlier in the field the Scottish efforts were being followed with the greatest possible interest" by the new British Women's Committee.

Criticism of the GC in these years was focused largely on what they failed to do, rather than on their actions. This was really due to how they saw the limitations of their role; on this, however, discussion was avoided, although there were sidelong sharp remarks in specific debates. Members of the GC not infrequently took the opportunity of speaking as their union's delegate, rather than as a GC member. While the officers for the GC often asked the opinions of affiliates on many matters they then tended to refer it all to the British TUC's Commissions and Inquiries, rather than themselves immediately campaigning in Scotland. This came up early on over the 40-hour week and the banning of overtime to aid unemployment; and also in campaigning for the Fair Wages Clause to be extended to all bodies engaged in public works. The motive of some must have been to avoid differences and difficulties between Scottish District Councils of England-based unions. But at grass roots new thinking was demanding action, and this was often bluntly expressed at Congress.

As the 'thirties progressed it was not only the English leaders from the textile trades, Distributive Workers and Fire Brigades Union who began to find it advisable to attend the STUC Congress to note trends and to hear sometimes comparisons with the British TUC. Year after year the National Union of Railwaymen had tried to reintroduce the block vote, with the GC remaining neutral; but in 1933 their General Secretary, C T Cramp, was himself present as a delegate and heard it rejected for the third time by a substantial vote. In the debate Thomas Scollan, himself a frequent Distributive & Allied Workers' delegate to the British TUC, and a member of the STUC's GC but then speaking for the Glasgow Trades Council, said he had

> never yet met anyone but who admitted that taking the numbers represented at the Scottish and British Congresses, that the Scottish Congress was of a very much higher standard. That was because every

> proposal coming before the Scottish Congress must have within it the logic to convince the delegates. The big machine of the block vote trampled on all opinions put forward, and the Scottish method of voting prevented the lobbying of the big unions for a proposal. The NUR proposal was a retrograde movement.

Also to hear the debate was the General Secretary of the Railway Clerks Association, A G Walkden, present as the British TUC's President.

Section (ii): **Thought and Action by the Unemployed**

Scotland by no means lagged behind the rest of Britain in activity by the unemployed themselves, together with an immense army of sympathisers increasingly prepared to come out on the street. It was there they would be seen and heard demonstrating, rather than concentrating on providing "educational and recreational activities", as recommended in the "Model Rules" for the Unemployed Associations which the STUC's GC urged trades councils to set up, following the example of the British TUC. In fact trades council delegates soon came to encourage support for the constant activity of the NUWM. As early as the autumn of 1931 there were events in Glasgow over the Means Test which must have made many shipyard workers then out of work on the empty Clyde remember with bitterness the battle on hours only a dozen years before. Huge demonstrations clashed with the police; the arrest of twelve NUWM leaders led to protest demonstrations attended by 120,000. There were similar attacks on a demonstration of 30,000 in Dundee by hard-hit jute and flax men and women, soon followed by demonstrations by Kirkcaldy's unemployed textile workers and their families. For indeed it was the whole family which was to be hit by the Means Test. It was against this background that the STUC's Women's Conference early in 1932 strongly condemned it, and also how the families of the unemployed were deprived of benefit under the Anomalies Act. This Act disqualified women from unemployment benefit when they married, and was not restored when they worked after marriage until they had acquired a number of stamps. All this set the pace for the Glasgow, Dundee and Edinburgh Trades Councils' delegates to take the lead in protests passed by the 1932 Congress.

That autumn a strong contingent opened a new national hunger march by the NUWM when they left Glasgow to be greeted a month later in London by 150,000 supporting a petition of a million signatures against the Means Test. Nationwide new thinking at grass roots had indeed been started, and developed a sharper tone as the Nazis took power in Germany and Fascist groups emerged in Britain. So when the next hunger march started once more from Glasgow, early in 1934, it was already being conducted under the guidance of a National Congress and March Council. It was led by Harry McShane and his deputy, Finlay Hart, and included John McGovern, MP. It acted as a Joint United Front Committee, consisting of several Members of Parliament, including the Clydeside ILPers, James Maxton and George Buchanan, and several leading trade unionists well-known at STUC Congress. Joined by a women's contingent at Derby, it came immediately after Wal Hannington, the NUWM leader, had won a legal case against Lord Trenchard, the Chief Commissioner of the Metropolitan Police, for police irregularities during the "National" Government's attempts to stop the demonstrations. Now because of fear of further police provocation an "Observation Committee" was set up to watch the treatment of this and other marches. It consisted of prominent figures, including the leader of the Parliamentary Labour Party, Clement Attlee; Professor Harold Laski; the veteran Socialist author H G Wells; and D N Pritt, KC, MP, who was to become internationally famous, both at the Reichstag Fire Trial Enquiry in London and whenever the law courts were used against the leaders of the colonial peoples. This "Observation Committee" was in fact the beginning of the National Council for Civil Liberties, soon to take up the question of the Incitement to Disaffection Act (better known as the "Sedition Bill") which was used grossly to interfere with the rights of free speech and holding public meetings. At this stage the Scots Council of the NUWM developed the confidence to concentrate more on marches within Scotland. From Dundee in the autumn of 1934 there was a march to Forfar with representatives from Arbroath, Blairgowrie, Ferryden and Montrose to protest against the new Unemployment Assistance Board's lower standards of relief and the compulsory labour camps. Early in 1935 there was a massive march to Glasgow from Aberdeen, Dundee, Edinburgh, Fraserburgh, Peterhead and also from the Border counties. When they reached Glasgow Green some 160,000 greeted them, while 80,000 marched with them to the City Chambers. Here the Lord Provost of Glasgow received a deputation introduced by J McGovern MP, which included Hannington and the Scottish NUWM Organiser, Harry McShane, and members from trades councils, such as the engineer Peter Kerrigan of Glasgow, Bob Cooney of Aberdeen, Chalmers of Edinburgh and Stewart of Ayrshire. Their report-back meetings became huge demonstrations in themselves.

The STUC Congress that year was deep in the morass of arguments on "the Black Circular" and denunciation of any type of United Front organisation. It carried by 103 to 34, with over a third of the delegates abstaining, the GC's motion to refuse a Standing Order's recommendation that a NUWM deputation be heard. Delegates were not pleased when, in contrast, the General Secretary of the British TUC, Walter Citrine, who was only present as a visitor and not as a delegate, was allowed to make a long address.

Section (iii): **Unemployed Deputation is Heard**

Later that autumn the General Election took place, with Ramsay MacDonald himself defeated in his Scottish constituency and forced to contest an early by-election in the safe Combined Universities seat. The Labour Party recovered somewhat from the 1931 debacle he had forced on them, yet remained well short of the 1929 level; but the results in Scotland were proportionately very much higher than elsewhere. Two months later the GC received a letter from McShane to say that the Scottish Council of the NUWM was "willing to throw its energies, resources and experience into any campaign conducted by the trade unions, trades councils or by the STUC" that will aim at "uniting the unemployed in Scotland". It ended by asking the GC to receive a deputation "to go more fully into the matter". Clearly the proposal was for active campaigning to be sponsored by the STUC, regardless of the specific arrangements, if any, for out-of-work members of the various unions; their rules and practice differed widely both as to benefits and continuing contributions. The GC refused to receive them for any discussion, for which it was sharply criticised at the 1936 Congress, where they maintained their frequent "Black Circular" statements against any type of United Front organisation. Here they produced an elaborate document "for the guidance of trades councils" against the United Front. It included the special instruction that any motion

> presented to the trades council with the object of committing the council to an alliance for any purpose with an unrecognised body should be declared as incompetent by the Chairman.

Moreover, they should not affiliate trade union branches which had similar activities regarded as "prejudicial", and their Executive should be informed. Further, any delegate regarded as acting "outwith their appointing branch" should be reported.

All this indicated that the majority of the GC – for the decision was not unanimous – had not caught up with the new thinking which had already led to unprecedented mass action, with the full support of the majority of trades councils. The GC's attitude, and their failure to respond by at least meeting the NUWM leaders for discussion, came in for very sharp criticism at the St Andrews Congress during several efforts to move reference back to the report on various points. It is worth noting where the criticism came from. This included the delegates of Glasgow and Edinburgh Trades Councils; Scottish Painters; Scottish Typographical; Sheet Metal Workers; Shop Assistants; Distributive and Administrative Workers; the Clerks were divided. Amongst the points made about the NUWM was that "in the recent municipal and general elections innumerable Labour candidates had acknowledged their indebtedness to the NUWM". A delegate from Edinburgh said that what had happened in the past year "had justified a new view of things", adding it "demanded new tactics". His trades council "would not have been nearly so effective had it not accepted the assistance of so-called unrecognised bodies". Another described how much bigger the NUWM was than the small numbers in the Unemployed Associations, and ready "to throw all its energies and resources" into a campaign under the direction of the GC; concluding that the GC

> was apparently prepared to recognise Sir James Lithgow and Lord Elgin and to go knocking at their doors while refusing to associate with a genuine working-class body, even to the extent of receiving a deputation.

The Sheet Metal delegate described how welders on strike in the Clyde area had been consistently supported by the NUWM, "while the GC had almost given its blessing to the trainees who were engaged in strike-breaking". One of the minority on the GC, Thomas Scollan of the Distributive Workers spoke strongly in favour of receiving the deputation. After attempts to refer back were defeated on technicalities a letter was read by the Standing Orders Chairman from McShane asking for a chance to correct any misunderstanding about phrases in their previous letter. At last it was agreed; so despite refusals year after year, the NUWM was "allowed one speaker ten minutes only". McShane expressed his hope that delegates would support the idea of an all-in conference of every unemployed grouping under the guidance of the British TUC, but with which the NUWM would work wholeheartedly. No discussion was allowed; the President James Young, of the Engineering and Shipbuilding Draughtsmen, thanked him warmly, and said he was sure that there was one thing on which

> they would all agree, and that was that they would all be happy if there were no need for unemployed organisations at all.

But nothing further was forthcoming from the GC, even when the biggest campaign of all took place, with massive participation from Scotland. It began that autumn of 1936. There were two Scottish contingents each of 500, led from Glasgow by the engineer Peter Kerrigan, and from Edinburgh by Harry McShane and the young miner, Alex Moffat – over twenty years later himself to become President of the STUC. It was greeted in London by a demonstration of a quarter of a million. The Jarrow Town Council also sponsored an autumn march, headed by Ellen Wilkinson MP, almost simultaneously but holding aloof from the national hunger march of the NUWM. In view of its great success, Aberdeen Trades Council took up the NUWM's proposal, but Elger went to Aberdeen to dissuade them; and when at next Congress Glasgow Trades Council urged them "to initiate a campaign" and co-operate as the NUWM suggested, the Railway Clerk, C N Gallie for the GC successfully moved next business. But by then in the heavy industries the numbers of unemployed were falling; the heavy industries were reviving as rearmament began.

Section (iv): New Thinking Begins on War Danger

A strong stimulus to new thinking came as the development of hostilities and even major war breaking out began to be seen as possible. Already British arms had been used against action for national freedom in Ireland and India; but a new dimension was appearing, under pressure of the world economic crisis. In 1932 it was impeding new capitalist development in Japan, which thereupon attacked China and seized Manchuria. When the following spring the fascist regime, with the announced intention of national expansion, had taken hold in Germany, it was inevitable that some expression of new thinking had to emerge at the 1933 Ayr Congress on this topic. It was not in fact expressed until the last debate on the fourth day; but once again the initiative and strongest demand for action came from trades councils and the minority on the GC.

The main resolution was from Glasgow Trades Council, moved by its moderate Secretary, William Shaw. Noting "the growing danger of another world war", it pointed to "the menacing sign being the ruthless war for the conquest of China" by Japan, supported by "European Imperialist Nations". It linked this with

> the increase of armaments and the growing danger of war with Russia; it strongly objects to the breaking of the Anglo-Russian Trade Agreement and the continued Government-inspired press campaign against Russia.

It called upon "all workers to expose and condemn the war-making efforts" of the "National" Government and work for the return of a Labour Government. In moving it William Shaw pointed out that Russia had "the smallest army in the world" in relation to the size of its "vast territory" and population, with only 7 per cent of its budget spent on its forces compared with the Tsarist regime's 27 per cent, thus answering "the lying and outrageous statements" in Parliament. He thought there was a danger of America being involved in a war in the Far East and there was also danger in Europe "as a consequence of the economic war now being conducted" and preparations "made by all European countries". It was strongly seconded by Sir Ben Turner, of the Textile Workers, saying every door in the world should be opened for trade, with which "embargoes, limitations and restrictions were interfering". It was supported by Thomas Scollan, pointing out that British officials had just urged China in fact to agree that Japan should remain in control of Manchuria. He added this intervention seemed "to be to give Japan a chance to settle down and deal with Soviet Russia in the North. Their rulers in Britain seemed to have set their hearts on the destruction of Russia and were evidently prepared to make Japan the cat's-paw." From Dundee Trades Council, supported by Edinburgh Shop Assistants and Leith Seamen, came an amendment instructing the GC "to initiate the setting-up of Anti-War Committees throughout Scotland to combat preparation for war". They claimed their duty was

> to make it clear to the Government that the workers would follow the lines of the action in 1926 and disorganise the whole industry of the country in the event of a war.

On this, however, the majority in Congress accepted the GC's view that they had neither staff nor money "to do that job efficiently" and that in any event it "was not within the power of the Scottish Congress to call a general strike". The main resolution, however, was passed unanimously. When the British TUC met six months later there was no discussion on the Manchuria question; but the war danger was discussed primarily as a matter for the International Federation of Labour.

But on the last day of the 1934 Congress at Stirling came a composite motion from Glasgow Trades Council and the Printing and Paper Workers, with two of the three speakers supporting it saying they had been 1914-18 war resisters. It viewed

> with grave disquiet the steady drift of the international situation towards war and the failure of the governments to check developments.

It called for a "vigorous campaign to counter in advance" the tendencies "which pre-dispose larger sections of the population to respond to a war appeal". It stressed five points:

(a) the "growing acuteness of the war danger";
(b) the "appalling nature of modern methods of warfare";
(c) economic crisis and deepening of "imperialist rivalries" as a direct cause;
(d) to announce "steps, including a general strike" to organise opposition to any threat of war, and for the national joint bodies to start approaches to get "international action by the workers" on such lines;
(e) to pledge "itself to take no part whatsoever in war".

C N Gallie successfully asked for it to be referred to the GC to discuss with the British TUC and LP following the international conference in which they had been involved. He said: "It would be fatal to let the people who would start a war know months before what steps the Labour Movement proposed to take to frustrate their intentions." The British TUC then came out in general terms for collective security through the League of Nations "plus such co-operation between the League and non-member States as may be established". It added that the basis for world peace was to get rid of "social injustice", which bred "vested interests" and "the scramble for markets" which directly caused war. But Britain's arms might be needed to support the League in "restraining an aggressor nation". It opposed the concept of a General Strike, because of the "lack of an independent Trade Union Movement" in Germany, Italy and Austria, and its weakness in Japan; and also the refusal to handle munitions. It concluded that "development of collective security" was the only "hope of producing a warless world". The alternative was

> to relapse into international anarchy, a race in armaments and sooner or later war or revolution or both.

Following upon this the GC in November 1934 asked the Scottish trades councils to contact branches of the League of Nations Union to organise the Peace Ballot, to be put to all over 18, which received overwhelming support.[3]

The first business taken was a motion rejecting the GC's report on the threat of war from the Clerks, supported by the Vehicle Builders and Edinburgh Trades Council delegates. They saw the GC's report as "a retreat from the idea of a general strike"; that there was no vigorous campaign carried on by "the workers, including those in the proscribed organisations"; and that the League of Nations was "impotent": without the support of America, Germany and Japan, being merely a grouping of the victors in the last war, with their functions merely to "maintain the status quo". Their resolution demanded "unconditional refusal to assist in the prosecution of war except in defence of a Socialist Republic"; petitions, the forming of an anti-war council; a "General Strike to make war impossible", with any favourable opportunity offered by war to be used "for the overthrow of Capitalism". More than one speaker said it was too late to discuss what policy should be adopted after a war had broken out.

If those speaking for the motion were still seeing events largely in terms of the First World War experiences, those opposing them for the most part were also looking back. The Scottish Typographical delegate said they would never take part in a general strike after being let down in 1926 by the movement's refusal to boycott "the rat press". William Quin, JP, just about to be electd to the GC, gibed at the movers as sympathisers out of step "with the Soviets": for the Soviet Republic was seeking security by trying to enter into pacts with "Britain and France and even Fascist Italy". For the GC, the Railway Clerk, C N Gallie said that if they "once began to argue that war was justified in certain circumstances", there was no escape from "complications and difficulties". He added that Britain was the only country where there "was even the possibility of an effective general strike". The motion was rejected by 103 to 22, with a third of the delegates not voting.

New thinking had still a long way to go on how new wars were to come; how they might have been prevented; who would be new allies in the Second World War; and how this was to end with its technology providing the final danger of total world-wide destruction.

References

[1] Aimed at affecting any member of the Communist Party or the Independent Labour Party.

[2] With it still being so much of a man-made language even in the trade union movement there is as yet no acceptable equivalent to "fraternal" to describe a female "sororal", or sisterly, visiting delegate.

[3] The Ballot put the following questions:

(a) Should Great Britain remain a member of the League of Nations?

(b) Are you in favour of an all-round reduction of armaments by international agreements?

(c) Are you in favour of the all-round abolition of national, military and naval aircraft by international agreement?

(d) Should manufacture and sale of armaments for private profit be prohibited by international agreement?

(e) Should nations compel an attacking nation to stop by (i) economic and non-military measures? (ii) if necessary military measures?

15

The Dangerous 'Thirties : Second Stage

The new thinking on the growing danger of war and its connection with the world economic slump which had hit Scottish industries so hard, grew all too slowly. It could not produce a strong enough united drive to change the British Government at the 1935 General Election. While the majority was cut by more than half, it still kept the title "National", although the Conservative Baldwin became Prime Minister again, himself soon to make way for the arch-appeaser Neville Chamberlain: and surviving former Labour men were already on their way out, J H Thomas through the back door because of the leaking of Budget secrets. At the Foreign Office Sir Samuel Hoare immediately produced together with the French arch-appeaser Laval the Hoare-Laval Pact, which connived at handing over Abyssinia to its Fascist invader, Mussolini, who was to be kept in power lest Italy should turn Communist. This effectively sidestepped the League of Nations' sanctions against the invaders, and shook confidence in it. Hoare had as junior to him at the Foreign Office a younger Tory, Anthony Eden, who was to share with the excluded Winston Churchill the view that the great threat to British imperial interests came at that moment from the old enemy Germany, rather than from any national liberation or united proletarian activists. These they feared less, following the destruction of trade unions in fascist Germany, Italy and Bulgaria and attacks upon them in Austria, where armed militia had been in action against tenants of working-class blocks of flats; the Soviet Union's military potential they dismissed as negligible.

Section (i): **Confusion Over Stopping War**

If this division of opinion amongst Conservative politicians was kept more or less under wraps until disaster finally struck in May 1940 with the fall of France to the invading Nazi armies, it was to some extent paralleled by the serious lack of unity amongst working-class organisations. This was not aided by the expulsion and threat of expulsion of leading members from the Labour Party Executive campaigning together with any other group which favoured a Popular Front Government for social and economic progress in view of the new threats, such as had just been formed in France and in Spain. But the divisions were in a different sphere from those of the ruling circles; while there was no doubt about the danger of war between the powers and its causes, there was much division of opinion on how it might be prevented. Many saw the problem solely in terms of the attempts to prevent or end the First World War, and the efforts successfully employed to prevent its continuing after 1918.

It is enlightening to see in some detail the attitudes and differences of the people who had to come to terms, if enough popular unity was to be achieved either to prevent war, or to wage war successfully when that was still a possibility and mutual destruction was not yet assured, and to build a worldwide movement capable of preventing another. It is well to remember that at this time it was still normal to hold large public meetings where those present joined in and individually played a part; that the local press actually reported what speakers said in some detail; and that the media's public screen was not permanently within the home, but had to be visited in cinemas. The range of differences was extremely wide, with many concentrating on past experience. Proposals included adapting the International's 1908 call for a general strike, and reviving bitterness at its failure; an immediate Socialist revolution; industrial dislocation of war production; denying profits to private manufacturers of arms, replacing that by nationalisation; mass conscientious objection and individual pacifist refusal to take any part; economic sanctions to be applied to aggressors; an international peace force, with or without nationally controlled individual units; collective security to be extended by enlarging the membership of the League of Nations; and finally, as confidence in the League diminished, a system of mutual pacts of non-aggression between individual countries, which was strongly pressed by the Soviet Union.

All these were much in evidence as expressed by the more predominantly grass-roots delegates to the STUC, not least of course from the trades councils to which so many were turning who demanded immediate action and strong campaigning. In the late 'thirties, the presidential addresses at Congress usually expressed the general mood as a background to multiple and sometimes confusing divergences during debates. An effective example came soon after the Mussolini action, at the St Andrews Congress of 1936, from James Young, Scottish Officer of the Engineering & Shipbuilding Draughtsmen, whose father had been a delegate many years before. Starting from the shipbuilding slump, still so disastrous for Scottish industries, which "was a direct effect" of the post-war Versailles Treaty, he went on:

> The war which was to end war has led, in the succeeding years, to ever greater fear of war and to the piling up of huge and costly armaments. Freedom and democracy are crushed in Italy, Germany and elsewhere, whilst the national trade union movements in these countries have been destroyed.

While the Covenant of the League of Nations had been violated "and public decency outraged by Japan and by Italy", Germany had gone on to proclaim "an absurd racial doctrine which inevitably practises persecution". Meanwhile "her huge rearmament inspires the liveliest apprehension in all her neighbours". Speaking at a time when the vast multi-national concerns had yet to extend beyond all national boundaries and what was later to be called the Third World, Young declared there could be "no peace and no security until the vicious doctrines of national security give way to a wider conception of law". That was why, he added, "our own country has pinned its faith to public international law as expressed through the League of Nations". In his opinion "public opinion is still a great power in a democracy. The result of the Peace Ballot undoubtedly affected the policy of our own government." But, he warned,

> our present international difficulties are due to the fact that continuous and wholehearted support of the League of Nations has been given neither by the Government of this country nor by the organs of public opinion as a whole.

For example, there had been "no clear and unmistakable challenge" to the Mussolini action, not the "swift imposition of complete sanctions for which the situation called". But "unfortunately, whilst British statesmen were talking peace they were elaborating proposals for rearmament on a large scale". But did effective action through the League involve rearmament on such a huge scale? To this vexed question he answered:

> Sanctions imposed against an aggressor may involve armed force, but a half-hearted application of sanctions makes the possibility of the use of force much greater. We are told that rearmament is for collective security and to take our proper share of League responsibility. But is

> an over-swollen programme likely to achieve this end? Or another armaments race? The last armaments race did not prevent war and neither will a fresh one. An informed public opinion and a well-developed social conscience are the only safeguards against the impending calamity.

In past years there had been talk of an international convention to control armaments, out of which had come talk of taking the profits out of armaments: "but now statesmen only want the armament makers to have a reasonable profit". Then he turned to stressing that although "unfortunately increased armaments mean work" for the long-unemployed in the hard-hit depressed areas, "working people undoubtedly prefer work of a constructive character", detailing the many needs in Scotland for such work.

There were few debates during the four days of Congress which did not provide examples of some of the problems he had outlined, with differing views sometimes bluntly expressed. Early reaction came in several motions to refer back sections of the GC's Report which showed how industrial troubles could be rising in rearmament work. The first Amalgamated Engineering Union delegation to the STUC ever to be headed by its chief officers, General Secretary F A Smith and President J C Little, expressed concern at the beginning already of dilution which had caused havoc in munitions factories of the First World War. J C Little said how "the so-called shortage of skilled labour" had led to "a ramp" by employers to smuggle in cheap labour of Government short-term trainees. Similar complaints came from a Glasgow Sheet Metal Worker, while a Glasgow Scottish National Operative Plasterers Federal Union delegate spoke of such trainees being used to break a Clyde Welders' strike. Similar contributions came from delegates from both the Vehicle Builders and the Building Trade Workers.

There were also very sharp objections expressed to the continued representation by the STUC Secretary and Treasurer on the Economic Committee under the Scottish National Development Council. It was described by a delegate of the Distributive & Allied Workers, whose General Secretary was also present from south of the border, as being only "intended to mobilise industry for war". He reminded them that its chairman, Sir James Lithgow, was "the individual responsible for scrapping Clyde shipyards". A Scottish Typographer said the GC should act on other matters to defend people's conditions: "It was no foreign invader who introduced the Trade Disputes Act and the Means Test". J Jagger MP also for the Distributive Workers "objected most emphatically" to the GC being empowered "to go and consider questions of dilution". For the GC, their Treasurer, the veteran Railway Clerk C N Gallie, defended taking "their share in the direction and planning of industry", adding:

> Were they to sit quietly by and do nothing until they ushered in Socialism and found themselves the possessors of a bunch of derelict industries?

When it came to the direct debates on the war danger, collective security and rearmament, response was equally sharp.

Section (ii): **Collective Security Through the League**

First came discussion of the GC's statement issued on 13 September, 1935, about Mussolini's attack on Abyssinia. It had declared that "the authority of the League and the obligation of its Covenant should be firmly upheld by the British Government", adding that "any action which would weaken the authority of the League to promote international peace would be a disastrous blow against the Collective Peace System". For the Clerks, Tom Taylor of Glasgow took the line that the League "was a farce, and the collective peace system within capitalist society a dangerous illusion". In his opinion it was "entirely dominated by French and British Imperialism" and he believed "the trade union movement should not pledge itself in any way in defence of such a League". A Hunter, the Glasgow Typographer, however, was all for the collective security system: the trouble was that "the Government had never taken any part in such a system of mutual assistance in Europe". Indeed, it "had actually held up sanctions". It had refused to guarantee that it would apply sanctions in all instances, thus giving aggressive Powers "the OK to go ahead when they liked". The GC should give "sane and convincing leadership" to mobilise public opinion so that sanctions would be enforced, and a Labour Government advocating the full terms of collective security brought in. J Pollock, Distributive Workers from Ayr, said the League "had completely failed to stop war and the great danger of supporting it had to be recognised". But from Glasgow, A Gee, Transport Workers' delegate, thought it "premature" to say the League had failed; they should strengthen, not scrap it. There must be an economic boycott; he believed that if the League actually had to declare war on an aggressor, no nation would be strong enough to defy it. The Glasgow

Plasterer H Livingston thought the National Government was only able to sabotage collective security because of the lack of the movement's driving force, while C Murdoch of the Glasgow Bakers asked, was the movement to take "no action at all until they had a Socialist majority? If the League went, no one knew what could be put in its place."

The GC member T Scollan then came in for Glasgow Trades Council; he said "everybody seemed to think they had only to decide between the League of Nations and nothing else; they accepted the League of Nations as one means of bringing about a collective peace system, but government after government had stated that they had no belief in it". But now the time had come when

> one of the signatories took military action in a place which might threaten the interests of the British Empire and then for the first time they found a British Government supporting the Covenant and the leaders of the working-class movement strongly behind them. Those trade union leaders who were in touch with the Government had not clamoured for the Covenant to be put into operation when Japan raped China and Manchuria. They had simply passed a resolution and left it at that.

Closing the discussion his fellow GC member, W Quin, cautiously remarked on "the contradictory nature of the arguments". He stressed that "the USSR was playing a part in the League and supporting collective security". The League had failed "only because the National Government was not sincere in its advocacy of collective security". He concluded that it was now

> the duty of the organised working-class movement to see that the pressure was applied on the Government and compel it to fall into line, just as the pressure of public opinion had compelled Baldwin to repudiate the Hoare-Laval pact.

With that speech he succeeded in getting the reference back rejected. But the argument did not rest there.

The last debate of that Congress was on an emergency resolution by the Shop Assistants on the same subject, recording that Congress was

> seriously alarmed at the terrible threat to the whole system of collective security as seen in the failure of the League of Nations' powers to put a stop to the frightful devastation and slaughter by Italian Fascism in Abyssinia.

It declared the urgent need

> for the greatest possible organised action of the working class of Britain and elsewhere to stop all war supplies to Italy and to compel their respective Governments to enforce the full measures of the Covenant for the purpose of bringing the war to a speedy conclusion.

In moving it C Thomson from Edinburgh said that British firms had been allowed "to draw profits from the supply of war material and oil going to Abyssinia". Had the oil been stopped, Mussolini's line of defence could have been cut seven months ago. Then he added, in what would have been seen as a reference to the speech of the visiting British TUC Chairman A H H Findlay of the Patternmakers:

> From what they had heard that week there was a dangerous tendency among their own leaders to allow the movement to be trailed behind the chariot of the National Government.

But there was "a distinct line of cleavage between the policies"; and he concluded that "every section of the movement must be mobilised along the lines of what happened in France, where they had forced the Government to sign the Franco-Soviet Pact". The seconder said that he believed all the arguments against the League "had really been against the personnel representing the Powers". He reminded them of how successful in 1920 the "hands off Russia" campaign had been. The motion was carried by a large majority, although T Taylor of the Clerks still stressed that the League must be seen "as it was, and it could not be an instrument for peace".

On the main subject of rearmament a strongly worded composite had viewed "with great alarm" that the Government was spending "the vast sum of £300,000,000 on armed forces, as this is likely to lead to war in the near future", while depriving "the social services of money urgently required". It denounced the Government as "the enemy of peace and the friend of fascism", with its support for German rearmament and the German Naval Treaty. It called on the Government, acting through the League, to convene a conference to secure disarmament. Moving it for the Transport & General, H Murphy of Glasgow said Britain "had committed a great international social crime" by rejecting at the 1932 Disarmament Conference proposals which could have been fruitful. The seconder, P Fraser of the Distributive Workers, referred to the "militarisation of the Metropolitan Police, the Sedition Act, the setting up of camps for the unemployed and the activities of the broadcasting machine"

– none of which had been there in 1914 – which could now be used to prepare the people to accept war. But a second Distributive Worker, J Pollock from Ayr, said the League was "composed of dissatisfied capitalist nations". He asked delegates to "send out a message that they would not make war in the interests of the master class". They should instead have faith in their own power. T Taylor continued his opposition once more, with a new line; if they took part in collective security through the League they would be bound to resort to arms in defence of the collective peace system; it was impossible for them to have that "or disarmament while they had capitalism".

Two other brief debates had a bearing on the war situation. The Transport & General delegate moved a welcome to "the growing friendship between the Russian trades unions and the British trades unions", which should be furthered to speed international trade union unity "as the surest barrier against war and fascism". This was unanimously adopted. So was a Glasgow Trades Council motion calling on the GC to circularise the Scottish trade unions to get a delegation sent to Russia. It was supported by a Scottish Painter R Lennox, who had already visited there and found it a revelation "to see how Socialism was administered through the Russian trade unions". The Sheet Metal Workers were in favour but unable to support since the burden of unemployment meant their union could not afford it. It was a policy agreed year after year, but each GC reported failure to raise enough money. Glasgow Trades Council, however, succeeded in sending a delegation.

Before Congress next met, hostilities had indeed begun in Europe.

Section (iii): **War Begins in Europe**

In July 1936 war in Europe had begun. The recently elected Popular Front Government in Spain faced an uprising by fascist generals, headed by Franco, with their rebel Moorish troops, and in possession of nearly all Spain's military equipment. When the rebellion began it had the full support of the neighbouring Fascist regime in Portugal and the obvious connivance of the other Fascist powers. The Spanish Government had no alternative but to seek to purchase arms elsewhere. The fear of escalation into a war between European nations was felt as an immediate danger generally, and not least by sections of the Popular Front Government in its French northern neighbour. There was therefore immediate pressure by France at the League of Nations for a policy of "non-intervention" by the powers in what was to be classed as a civil war rather than a rebellion. The National Council of Labour supported the League's policy in the hope of peace and expressed sympathy for the Spanish people by opening a Spanish Workers Fund. The "National" Government meanwhile eagerly seized on the "non-intervention policy" to ban sales of arms and supplies to the Spanish Government and also to prevent individual volunteers from Britain, not least the Scottish unemployed, joining an International Brigade of volunteers which began to form. For while from early days Franco was getting modern arms equipment from Germany and whole units of Italian troops fresh from Mussolini's attack on Abyssinia, it was soon clear that the Fascist powers had no intention of "non-intervening".

What to do next, the policy and role of the League and how the issues could be made clear was discussed at length throughout the autumn and winter in the whole movement, while campaigning committees were springing up everywhere to support Spanish democracy. Much was on foot in Scotland. In August 1936 the GC issued a circular recommending support for the National Council of Labour's Spanish Workers Fund, but without taking any initiative of its own on Spain, nor in processing STUC previous decisions on war danger and rearmament. Following an International Peace Congress held in Brussels that autumn the GC received an invitation from the Scottish Peace Congress to support and appoint a representative to help organise a three-day conference in Edinburgh. This was to focus public opinion "on the basis of a four-point programme for united action". These matched the points of the 1936 Congress decisions, but the majority of the GC decided "after lengthy consideration not to be represented". They did, however, agree to receive a deputation from the Scottish Peace Council, which had strong support in Edinburgh Trades Council, on 15 February, 1937. After this they issued a statement that the Scottish Peace Congress "appears to have functions which concern the citizen in his individual capacity". Just a month earlier they had refused to receive a deputation from the Scottish District Committee of the Communist Party: it wished the GC to lead a united campaign in Scotland to aid the Spanish Government to protest against the British Government banning volunteers and arms to Spain, to demand that Italian and German armed forces be withdrawn and to support dependants of the International Brigade's British Battalion, which was soon to receive the support and name of the Labour Leader Attlee. The GC replied with some caution that "such fundamental questions of policy" must be raised by bodies affiliated to Congress: five of the GC members had been amongst the 34 Scottish delegates to the British TUC four months earlier which had heard a fierce denunciation by Sir Walter Citrine of the Communist Party and its policies which he described as being paid for and imposed by the Soviet Union. Early on at the 1937 Inverness Congress there was an unpleasant scene when Bailie William Shaw, for years elected as Chairman of Standing Orders, resigned after making bitter remarks about Communist Party supporters, including his own Glasgow Trades Council delegation, which included Thomas Scollan, one of the GC minority. But this was not the tone of most contributions at Congress; for the delegates found themselves faced with a new escalation, which made new thinking and a different emphasis obligatory.

For a week before Congress opened there had come the terrible shock – the first ever air bombardment of a civilian population; Hitler's airforce had bombed the market town of Guernica in the Basque mountains dividing Spain from France. In general this put into a new setting the debates on war, how the arms which were piling up would be used, and the effect on employment when the rearmament boom ended. Then, as President Bella Jobson warned, a collapse and depression would bring a situation "more difficult to deal with than any we have as yet faced". An emergency motion unanimously adopted, calling on the Government to have the League set up a committee of investigation, viewing

> with abhorrence the dastardly attack from the air on innocent women and children in Guernica.

It was moved by the General Secretary of the Scottish Lace and Textile Workers' Union, making the point that he had spent two years in gaol as a World War resister. But they would all "unite in deploring" the Guernica atrocity: "No one could fail to be moved at the thought of the bodies of innocent children and women lying in the streets and fields where children were wont to play." It was seconded in passionate terms by a Catholic member of the GC, William Quin. He stressed that

> there had been no official declaration from the Catholic Ecclesiastical Authorities in support of Franco, nor was it the case that the opinion of the average Catholic worker was to be taken as favouring his rebellion. Freedom of religious expression was not permitted even to Catholics in Germany and Italy.

He spoke of his "despair and disgust" at the human beings who murdered women and children in the Catholic area of the Basque region "while claiming to be defenders of religion".

For the next two Congresses at Inverness and Girvan in 1937 and 1938 many differing opinions were rife. These centred on disillusionment with the League, the causes for its failure and proposals for strengthening it. There was confusion between those who came to believe the Non-Intervention Committee was a trick from the start while others saw its failure as due to the "National" Government using it as a means of in fact intervening against the Spanish Government. For this did not merely amount to forbidding firms to accept their orders for arms and equipment; but also banning British foodships from supplying the besieged port of Bilbao and forcing volunteers to travel illegally to France for Spain. Perhaps the most extraordinary case of intervention was when the warship *Devonshire* entering Spain's territorial waters, near Valencia, boarded the British S.S. *Stancroft* in May 1938, and forced her to go to Gibraltar and discharge there a cargo of foods belonging to the Spanish Government, which they retained, then arrested the Master of the *Stancroft*.[1] Later, the British Navy refused to permit Spanish Government refugees to travel from coasts where they were being bombed by Franco and forced them into the sea.

Section (iv): **Appeasement and its Meaning**

At the STUC Congresses there were complaints at the slowness of the labour movement's leadership nationally to abandon the "non-intervention" policy as practised and instead campaign for effective action to deter the aggressors. Some delegates urged reliance solely through the International Federation of Trade Unions, from which the Russian trade unions were still excluded. Increasingly there were also moves to strengthen relations with the Soviet Union and extend its proposals for mutual non-aggression pacts, such as the Franco-Soviet Pact. Neville Chamberlain in May 1937 replaced Baldwin as Premier and a year later the STUC Presidential Address declared British policy had given "the necessary impetus to Germany to occupy Austria". Herbert Ellison JP the first National Union of Railwaymen delegate to preside at Congress, stressed that

> had the Government given the fascist countries to understand at the outset that they would not tolerate certain of the events that have taken place, I believe we should not now have been compelled to prepare so speedily for something that the workers trust may never occur.

Differences continued on how to campaign to reverse what was later to be known as the appeasement process, but without examining the reasons for it. With further aggression by Japan in China denounced by the League, the GC took the initiative in October 1937 of conferring with the Scottish Co-operative Union and the Scottish Council of the Labour Party; they jointly issued a draft resolution to be campaigned for locally which called for the "National" Government to ban sales and loans to Japan and imports from there. Yet when the Constructional Engineering Union delegates expressed "enthusiastic support" for Southampton and London dockers refusing to load ships for Japan, and denounced as "despicable" any action by leaders tending "to prevent such militancy", there was opposition. This came from William Quin JP, speaking as a delegate from his union rather than as a GC member; he said "unofficial action" would not help the Chinese. It was defeated. However, the GC had sent delegates to the Conference of The Scottish Council for Peace and Freedom with the USSR, which welcomed the Soviet Union's efforts to strengthen collective security through the League by "pacts of mutual guarantees and assistance open to all countries". This was followed up by the GC minority member, Thomas Scollan JP, speaking for Glasgow Trades Council in successfully moving that the STUC should affiliate to the Scottish Peace Council and work for the Brussels International Peace Conference four-point programme, previously rejected. He hinted at the fear about the influence of the example of the USSR by sections of the ruling political party, when he said:

> In the last year of the previous war there had not been a single statesman who was not afraid of his own people, who were sick and tired of the war and ready for anything to change the existing conditions; and if the people who had the destinies of Europe in their hands were not very careful it might be that all the casualties would not be on the battlefields.

Later he moved a composite which declared that the "National" Government had undermined the League over Abyssinia: over its "betrayal of the Spanish Government by the Non-Intervention Pact"; over Austria; over "the ravishing of China by Japan"; and by not reciprocating the call by the Russians and the American Government of Roosevelt "for all democratic nations to use their united strength to curb dictators in their drive for war". In this he went on to characterise Premier Chamberlain and divisions amongst the Tories. He praised Eden for honouring Baldwin's pledge at the 1935 General Election to stand by the League, and continued:

> Fascist intrigue within Conservative circles had removed Baldwin to the cold store of the House of Lords and brought forward in his place a champion of Fascism.

He then said Chamberlain had acted behind Eden's back at the Foreign Office and had sent an ambassador to France offering £90,000,000 if it would break the Franco-Soviet Pact. Scollan added that it was

> not a pact for ourselves that the Government was after, but an anti-Comintern pact such as existed between Germany, Italy and Japan.

He concluded that the "Government was driving Britain on to war in co-operation with international Fascism against Soviet Russia, and even many Conservatives were alarmed at the road Chamberlain was taking". Once again it was passed by "an overwhelming majority". Virtually the only opposition was expressed once again by Tom Taylor, of the Clerks, because of Scollan's praise of Eden. He said:

> Eden believed that the interests of the British Empire could best be preserved by alliances with certain countries. Chamberlain believed they could best be preserved by alliances with other countries. But Socialists were not concerned with the preservation of the British Empire. Only the power of the working class could enable them to obtain peace and democracy.

To him the Baker, C Murdoch, replied for the GC that they were still waiting to know Taylor's alternative to the League; they would have "to tell their children that there was no hope for the world until they had established world Socialism".

Before they next met, at Rothesay in the spring of 1939, Chamberlain had flown to Munich in September, 1938, and arranged with Hitler what appeared to amount to a "peaceful" military occupation of Czechoslovakia, returning to a House of Commons which, except for a handful of MPs, applauded this appeasement as saving "world peace in our time". What other agreements Chamberlain and Hitler reached were not disclosed; but months of pressure by the movement for an urgent approach to the

Soviet Union met with such delays as to prompt the gibe in 1939 that the British special envoy had been sent thither "by way of the slow boat to China".

In the confusion following this high point of appeasement while rearmament continued, the movement tended to concentrate less on the reasons for it than in questioning certain preparations, of which a central point which alarmed them was conscription to be introduced in peacetime.

References

[1] There exists an extremely interesting "Memorandum by Counsel on the recent Proceedings in Gibraltar", dated July, 1938. The Solicitors were Messrs Elwell & Binford Hole and the leading barrister was D N Pritt KC, MP, with G H C Bing as his Junior, opposed by the Attorney General. It was presided over by the Chief Justice, a frequent visitor to Franco territory. At the close, D N Pritt referred to the fact that the judge had said he had no sympathy with the Spanish Government, "a fact which your Lordship had made most painfully and unjudicially obvious", and protested "against the prejudicial statements against them, which you have made without warrant, evidence or justification". When the judge stopped him, Pritt added: "I should have prostituted an honourable profession if I had said one word less than I did."

16

Organising New Forces

After twenty years of what had passed for peace, the next war was at hand. No war is comparable to the last; this Second World War was not only to be waged in a period of much new technology; it was to depend upon new forces and new thinking. To what extent the trade union movement had shaped up to reaching the new groups of workers could be crucial. What of the new generation, who had grown up to unemployment or surrounded by it? Much was to depend upon them, their aims, adaptation to skills and techniques not only in the front lines, but overwhelmingly by the women working in the rear, which this time was also to be a battle zone. To answer this we must look back to see how and to what extent the Scottish trade union movement had responded to the need to organise the women and the youth.

Section (i): **The Women Workers**

It was the question of the women which first came to the fore. In the First World War there had been a considerable increase in the demand for women workers in the factories. Although many disappeared to join the massive numbers of unemployed afterwards, in some occupations where new technology encouraged employers to prefer them for the lower wages, their numbers actually increased in relation to men. This was especially true amongst clerks. As the Scottish Secretary of the National Union of Clerks told the 1925 Congress: "During the last ten years the number of women clerks increased enormously compared with the men, and it was a serious lesson." There was probably no other organisation present which then cut across so many industries. R E Scouller was speaking on a Report the GC had been instructed to make on the general state of organisation in Scotland. It showed that no less than a third of those gainfully employed in Scotland were women,[1] especially in textiles and clerical work, while women almost equalled the men in print. But while some 37% of the men were in the 227 unions operating in Scotland, which included 137 British-based, less than a fifth of the women were organised. After much discussion the

GC were told to produce a general development and co-ordination plan. But in point of fact the only long-term result of this remit was the development of Britain's first Women's Advisory Committee, which opened a new chapter in efforts to win men, women and juveniles to trade unionism.

It began with the GC, after putting out its usual type of questionnaire, convening a conference of representatives of unions "affected by the organisation of women workers" on 30 January, 1926. It recommended that a Woman's Advisory should be elected from an annual conference with both men and women representatives present, which the 1927 STUC Congress approved. At their second conference over two-thirds of affiliated unions affected were represented. Delegates from 15 of these spoke, especially those from the five unions concerned with textiles and clothing; there were also strong contributions from furnishing trades, distribution and shop assistants who were very largely Co-operative Society employees. Others included the clerical workers which cut across a number of industries, amongst them a woman from the Engineering and Shipbuilding Draughtsmen. For the print industry, so long dominated by old craft unions, their leading officers attended, and Mary Alston, of the Scottish Typographical Association, was elected to the first Women's Advisory Committee. Of the other four members, Bella Jobson (Scottish Farm Servants) and Eleanor Stewart (Workers Union), were both full-time officials who made long-lasting contributions as trade unionists. The textile industry in Dundee and Fifeshire was represented by Rachel Devine for the Jute & Flax Workers and Martha Frew, the full-time secretary of the Dunfermline Textile Workers Union. During the first ten years the Women's Advisory was also to have amongst its representatives a valuable figure in Agnes Gilroy of the Distribution Workers, who had been an ardent activist since she was 19; and the Railway Clerks also provided representatives.

In following their activities and debates over the years what is notable from the first is the almost complete absence of bitterness in their discussions at conference. This remained true when elsewhere controversy was raging; with bitter distrust of leaders and complications following the General Strike; fierce demarcation disputes between many competing unions; disputes on what lines, and using what methods, the trade union movement as a whole should aim to reorganise; and with disillusionment over political action, which previously had been seen as the best hope for improving women's conditions. The reason for this healthy attitude of the Women's Advisory Committee and Conference was that with organisation so low, they had to get down to the basic question of proving the advantages at ground level in the spirit of the early pioneers. Larger theoretical questions of whether this could best be done by industrial or general unionism, whether by One Big Union or maintaining special craft unions, could in practice have no real meaning. It was the nitty gritty question of how an individual woman's conviction could be won which was important for them. This remained true even in the textile industry, where so many organisations, historically growing up in different sectors and areas remote from each other, had proved difficult indeed to amalgamate. Indeed, there had been some strange results. Old Bailie Robert Climie (Workers Union) recalled that textile workers had long been admitted to the Ayrshire Miners' Union because there had been no textile union there; he added they would not leave the Miner's Union because "that connection had been so friendly".

Section (ii): **How the Women's Advisory Committee Began**

After Elger had continued his practice of issuing questionnaires to the respective unions for details on the state of organisation with little result, the Women's Committee got down to planning out work on it and the many new ideas about methods which came up at the annual conference. As well as considering motions submitted by delegations, early on they adopted the practice of having a major discussion on one vexed question each conference for a general expression of personal views, without taking any vote on it. This could bring in a useful free exchange of ideas. They made several new approaches. In Glasgow for example they began to give leaflets advertising neighbouring meetings on trade unionism to the women in the queues at the Labour Exchange. Instead of some top official lecturing trade union branches and stewards in passing on the possibility of recruiting women, they arranged for special "visitations" from a rank and file member of a neighbouring branch – and preferably a woman – to speak of their own experiences and successes at it. Soon they extended such "visitations" to all organisations catering for women, especially the Women's Guilds and the Young Women's Christian Association and other religious organisations. At these they were aiming to enlist the support of parents, and especially of mothers, to influence their working daughters, since the usual formal approach to male trade unionists urging them to win their wives and children was normally disregarded. It was also at the Women's Conference that they first raised the problem of office-seeking politicians taking up grievances and representing claimants before Boards and Courts of Referees instead of referring them to an appropriate trade union; by this they aimed to prevent women dropping out of their union, but it was of course an important question for holding all unemployed workers. When they were met with the usual complaint that the problem basically of organising women was that they would leave to get married or when raising a family and drop their membership, they did not accept this as self-evident and insoluble. In fact it led to interesting debates on two proposals. First there was the suggestion of a Marriage (Retiral) Grant as a special union benefit. There was also a strongly argued case for and against on Family Allowances; some unions fearing it could have a bad effect on wage negotiations, while others thought it would only be a good plan if it kept married women out of industry. It was, however, a first airing of one factor in what was to become "the social wage" approach after the war, fifteen years later. Experiences were exchanged on what effect the Trades Boards were having on trade union recruitment, arising from experiences in the Laundry industry. Whilst Robert Watson, Secretary of the Scottish Typographical Association, described them as "a menace", several of the women said they could be useful in clothing and in distribution, and a safeguard in a falling market; but there remained the general view that Trades Boards could and did lead some to feel that wages were arranged by "the State" and there was therefore no need for a union. While that was put aside for further enquiries they brought forward other proposals to help solve the problem of low pay and unemployment; if union fees could not be reduced, surely they could be adjusted during short-term working. But some of the men delegates saw a danger of this encouraging competing bodies to take advantage.

Among the most positive results of early discussions were the Trade Union Women's Groups of volunteers; and also the local day-schools and weekend schools set up for the purpose of training negotiators on just how they should set about recruiting women, which needed new attitudes and a new approach. Even in the Women's Advisory's early years another most important issue arose out of their discussions and new approach. This was the essential question of recruiting juveniles. Dead-end jobs where any existed were now moving into a different sphere; new machinery and seasonal work were already reaching the point when cheaper juvenile labour could be a threat in what was classed as "women's work". Their reaction was to bring out strongly the need for raising the school-leaving age and for restrictions on any form of "half-timer" activity; at the same time they began to look for opportunities for encouraging trade union recruitment amongst juveniles, or at least youth groups to consider it. Meanwhile Bella Jobson had been sent to represent the STUC on the National Advisory

Council for Juvenile Employment (Scotland). It was a natural development from the characteristic approach of the women.

Their free discussions could be illuminating; in 1931, for example, Bailie William Leonard opened the question of "preference" during unemployment. It had been raised in an all-women branch of his union (Furnishing Trades) as to whether it was fair that single women should be first to leave, with married women kept on. Difference in trade practice as well as outlook emerged from print, laundry workers, dyers, tailors, shop assistants and farm servants. Not all realised at once that so much turned on wages of all kinds being too low, which was basically why most married women sought work. Few realised how the whole concept of "women's work" or "women's wage" had arisen in the first place. Yet in their great grandparents' time all worked together for a joint family income within the home; employers had not yet found it profitable to bring only one representative out to the factory to work. But now print workers were finding that to operate the new machinery was classed as "women's work". When she was in the chair for the ninth Annual Conference, Eleanor Stewart made this and similar points in an interesting historical address on the early days of trade unionism; she deplored the ignorance in school history books of trades unionism, just when the centenary of the Tolpuddle Martyrs was to be commemorated. That was a year when both Agnes Gilroy and Bella Jobson were elected to the STUC's General Council. The Women's Advisory had already made its mark; the British TUC was following the example of the women's groups, and the intensive "organising weeks", such as the house-to-house check they had carried out in Kirkcaldy. A special course had been held for women in Glasgow on Courts of Referees: a Joint Council had been set up with the Scottish Committee of Labour and the Co-operatives; they now had their own Secretary, Elger's assistant, Agnes Richmond, who was to remain with them until her retirement. When they held their eighth Annual Conference in Dunfermline, where their member Bailie Mary Frew (Textiles) was the first magistrate, they received a civic reception from the Provost; and that was henceforth the practice. It was perhaps partly in recognition of the work done by the whole Women's Advisory that their senior activist Bella Jobson became STUC President; and in her 1937 Address to the STUC had this comment to make:

> I do not want Congress to think that I regard the organisation of women as more important than the organisation of men. I suggest, however, that it is of equal importance and that their work in the Movement is of equal value.

She went on to comment on the fact that women were still not "carrying a bigger share" at trade union conferences, and added:

> I do not believe that there is any desire to exclude women; it is because women came later to public life, and still require to be specially encouraged to play their proper part in it.

In her address she also included an important call for attention to be paid to the younger workers. In the last ten years too many of the young "when they would usually have been attracted to the Labour Movement have been turned on to the street. Youth wants action, and the period when the unions were on the defensive was not a period to attract young folk." They had not got the young people they should have; she concluded:

> A time of action is the time to bring them in, and for us to make allowance for the impatience of youth, and to keep them in. They will have to face new problems and will have to find new methods of solving these problems.

She was indeed right: and if senior delegates had shown such understanding and the type of approach shown by the Women's Advisory in their work, the formation of a successful Youth Advisory Council would have been very much quicker in coming.

Section (iii): **The Young Workers**

The Clerks, Shop Assistants and the Distributive Workers were all unions in occupations with very large numbers of the unorganised, whether women, boys or girls.[2] Their delegates had been active in the Women's Advisory from the first and had been especially interested in the women's novel proposal to carry out a grass-roots campaign for trade unionism in general, not sectionally, but in the single area of Kirkcaldy. At the 1935 STUC, Bruce Wallace for the Clerks, supported by the Shop Assistants, took up this general approach for another grouping, the youth. Stressing their increasing exploitation, he urged there should be "a special youth campaign", so that the unions generally should "make a more positive appeal to the young workers". His fellow delegate referred to one already existing in Bristol as a Youth Trades Council.[3] It was passed unanimously; but nothing came of it other than the GC issuing a circular. There were reasons for this from a number of angles.

What troubled leading trade unionists – and virtually all the GC members were full-time officials, including four from Scottish-based unions – was the continuing weakness of the unions generally. Even with rearmament beginning to take up the slack, plenty of former members were not re-joining; there was little growth but fierce competition, not least amongst the smaller unions, with long, drawn-out amalgamation talks running into the ground. Some feared that local drives for unionism in general terms could be dominated by one union scooping the lot, including snatching former members of others. Rearmament was also involving new technology both in the developing aircraft industry and the Admiralty shipyards, which especially affected Scotland. Here there were new openings not only for apprentices but for semi-trained youths loosed from Government training camps on low money and long hours, often while experienced men were left unemployed. At the 1936 Congress, therefore, Bruce Wallace for the Clerks, seconded by the Scottish Brassmoulders, speaking to a complicated composite was on delicate ground in instructing the GC itself to initiate a general "twelve months' campaign for 100% trade unionism". He aimed to gain acceptance for the general approach by stressing that "a special feature should be to win the masses of unorganised youth for Trade Unionism". This was to be done by "placing the main responsibility" on trades councils, which were to establish "Youth Fellowships to attract the working youth catering for their cultural and intellectual needs". Whilst doing this the trades councils should "take steps to eliminate the rivalries existing between certain unions" and bring about "closer understanding with the ultimate aim of amalgamation". It was decided to remit it to the GC "for consideration and report": as their speaker James Crawford JP of Natsopa put it, "resolutions on paper would solve no practical difficulties". The Amalgamated Engineering Union was represented at the STUC by their National President and their General Secretary, J C Little and Fred Shaw, who heard this cautious approach of leaders north of the border; they themselves were very soon to be faced with major struggles there.

At the time the only way the GC could see of overcoming the problems on the main question was for special local committees to be set up of officers of particular unions first to discuss it at length and then report back to the GC in due course, but taking no initiative meanwhile. But long before this slow process could get under way, major industrial struggles had broken out, with strikes at Beardmore's for a penny an hour increase, impatient of the time taken in ballots on wages, and with the Glasgow AEU District Committee authorising shop stewards to ban excessive overtime. As the Scottish Typographer A Hunter said at the next Congress in criticising the GC: "Wave after wave of strikes had taken place and there was no authoritative organ speaking with one voice to the public on the questions raised." He added:

> All that had happened since the motion was carried was that while the Clydeside was on fire the General Council had fiddled with reports.

P H Cook of Bothwell Trades Council blamed the GC for unofficial strikes, which had happened "because of the absence of any proper organising efforts by the trade unions led by the two Congresses". The AEU General Secretary, however, intervened to defend the GC, saying that the job of organising "had to be done in the shops themselves"; and he

> did not want the GC to be doing work which ought to be done by the unions themselves.

But what of the youth, not least the engineering and shipbuilding apprentices?

Section (iv): **The Young in Action**

The STUC delegates were meeting at Inverness in 1937 within days of a tremendous movement by the young people themselves. For early in April 1937 some 1,500 Glasgow shipyard apprentices had gone on strike against their low wages and working conditions. Spreading to Edinburgh, Leith and Aberdeen there were 13,000 apprentices out from 100 firms demanding an apprentices charter. A one-day stoppage of nearly 150,000 adult workers in their support took place on 16 April. The apprentices were out for six weeks. The Engineers National President J C Little was to speak to STUC delegates at the next Congress of their "magnificent organisation" that they had set up on the Clyde, adding that it proved to him

> that young people today could do things on their own and that all they wanted was a little guidance from people who had had experience in the past.

A number of the leading Scottish trade unionists in later years had been in that action as youths.

Yet only three months earlier the GC had followed up the separate question of youth organisation by issuing a complicated questionnaire of no less than twenty points to trades councils which tended to focus attention on whether young people would be interested in youth sections or fellowships unless they included youth sports sections. In fact endless argument developed on what the nature of such fellowships might be; whether any trades council could afford to set up a sports section in competition with those already well financed. Again, what should the age limits be? Was it right that the youth should be separated from normal branch life and would not this tend to do that? And, indeed, would these be general youth sections of trades councils or a grouping of individual union youth sections?

Even after the apprentices' action it dragged on unresolved, until a Special Conference was called on 17 September, 1938, when 84 delegates attended from 29 unions, from which a very preliminary Youth Advisory Council was set up under the GC. The decision was that there should be no general recommendation to trades councils to set up youth sections; but that any which chose to do so should operate strictly under a model constitution. Meanwhile the first Youth Advisory Council was to investigate facts following another questionnaire to the unions and to experiment with a weekend school in May 1939 at Dollarbeg. The first young people elected to serve on it were from the Clerks, Distributive and Allied Workers, Scottish Bankers Association, Engineering & Shipbuilding Draughtsmen and the Railway Clerks.[4] Meanwhile the surplus funds collected by the apprentices' strike committee were passed to the STUC, to be used for trade union education for young people at day and weekend schools, with free scholarships to a number of places reserved for those in engineering and shipbuilding.

Section (v): **Youth Advisory, Long Awaited**

At the 1939 Congress this still very modest beginning came in for criticism, with George Middleton for Glasgow Trades Council saying they looked for campaigns in connection with the Youth Charter, and that the youth movement in Glasgow wanted support in their campaign against the National Service proposals, which amounted to conscription. He was told that the Youth Advisory could not determine policy but could act upon nothing until its annual conferences, which were in fact frequently delayed or held over. Meanwhile there was notable lack of any positive encouragement to any youth sections of the trades councils. The elected Youth Advisory itself year after year seemed to be restricted to non-manual workers' unions. There were none from mining nor from the engineering industry in the crucial formative years other than Engineering Draughtsmen, who every year tried unsuccessfully for improvements. Indeed, there was not even a

National Union of Railwaymen youth on it until the beginning of 1944, while the first AEU young man, Ian Towill, came into the youth leadership late in 1946. The GC continued to keep very close control, appointing its officers: Elger's new Assistant, G F Sedgwick, was its Secretary until 1945. His successor, T F McWhinnie, found himself only able to remain for 18 months, when he left to join the staff of the World Federation of Trades Unions, and Jimmy Jack took over as Elger's new Assistant in the summer of 1946. After Elger's death that autumn for the first time the Youth Advisory was to be presided over by one of its own members, Margaret Cairncross (Tailors and Garment), instead of by an appointed GC representative.

From then on the names of young people who were to become important leaders in the Scottish trade unions begin to emerge, including Andy Barr and the miners, Lawrence Daly and Michael McGahey. At very long last the Youth Advisory could be seen to be developing in character.

References

[1] Gainfully employed: 1,655,656; Males, 1,238,390; Females, 417,266. In textiles, clothing, boot and shoe; Males, 51,683; Females, 135,593. In print: Males, 17,884 Females, 15,764. In agriculture: Males, 94,718; Females, 15,764.

[2] The numbers they then affiliated on were: Clerks, 1,228; Shop Assistants, 12,291; and Distributive & Allied Workers 15,698. The last two did not succeed in amalgamating until after the war.

[3] This was much disapproved of by the Bristol hierarchy as being a creation of the Bristol National Unemployed Workers Movement.

[4] Betty Watt; James Norris; Ian McPherson; William Gillan; and D Mitchell.

17

Consequences of Munich

New thinking by the young people was certainly needed in the taxing years to come. Many STUC delegates in their fifties were looking back to their days as young activitists when "the Kaiser's War" was threatening, from 1910 onward.[1] The 229 delegates were meeting at Rothesay at the end of April 1939 just as the consequences of Chamberlain's policy began to appear. With the Spanish People's Republic finally seized by the Fascist rebel, General Franco, now Hitler had taken Czechoslovakia by force only six weeks before the delegates met. As the Scottish Horse & Cartermen's leader, Robert Taylor, said in his Presidential Address: "Today in Central Europe Fascism is triumphant." He went on to describe "the parade of German troops through Prague, swaggering in the intoxication of conquest". Nor could Chamberlain's Government "escape some responsibility for the ravaging of Albania"; and, above all,

> it must stand indicted for all time for the assistance they rendered to their friends to smash the democratic forces in Spain.

Things were going "from one atrocity to another over a large part of Europe"; and he concluded that if the "tide of Fascism was to be stemmed" the most urgent need was that

> the peace bloc should be formed immediately by all nations prepared to subscribe to such a policy.

This of course could be made possible through countries signing mutual non-aggression pacts, such as the Soviet Union had urged upon France and Great Britain.

Section (i): **Conscription in Peacetime?**

Taylor's address expressed the attitude felt far and wide of deepest distrust of Chamberlain's actions and often his motives. When it came to what action then and there should be taken, some looked to insisting upon immediate change of Government without awaiting the General Election due within the year. Others aimed at forcing immediate change of policy on specific points by various methods. The world was being confronted almost daily with dynamic political happenings; it was almost inevitable for the response of the trade unions to lag behind events and only slowly react to them in line with immediate response in the workplace. Things were moving so fast that many motions sent in for the Congress agenda were already out of date. But on their first morning at Rothesay the press presented them with news to which they all reacted with fury, regardless of differences in views on strategy and tactics. Indeed, as one member of the General Council, Charles Murdoch of the Scottish Bakers, known for his vigorous expression of moderate views said, it "had given them for once in their lifetime an opportunity of having a real united front". The issue was what Taylor described as "the first step" towards conscription in peacetime, with all that implied for Scottish trade unionists in their fifties.

That winter a "scheme for National Service" had been introduced by Chamberlain who had manoeuvred acceptance for it by assurances that there should be no introduction of conscription. Only three months earlier, with Elger on the Central National Service Committee as a British TUC nominee, the GC had made nominations to the local Scottish Committee after circularising affiliated trade unions and trades councils.[2] Now the press disclosed that that afternoon the House of Commons would hear a statement which Taylor described as the "first step" towards conscription in peacetime. He asked Congress to take the unprecedented step of adjourning for an hour while the GC drafted a protest telegram. This and the subsequent debates about its terms and what action to take, brought out the key attitudes of the Scottish movement, illustrating both strength and weaknesses, its independence and attitudes to relations with the British TUC at each of the many stages of the Second World War.

The GC's draft declaring that it "emphatically opposes any form of compulsory military service", which would not increase effective defences but "produce a contrary effect", called for its withdrawal. When delegates thought it "insufficient", it was stressed that it was urgent to send it to the Commons at once and that there should be a full debate the following day. After the Government statement was made, the GC were "in practically continuous session", according to Elger, before they could produce a lengthy Declaration on Conscription. There could be little opposition to the strongly worded sentence that

> the continuance of the "National" Government constitutes a danger both to world peace and to the democratic institutions of our people.

Therefore "every effort" should be used to substitute for it "a Labour Government consistently committed to collective security and to the preservation of democratic ideals and practices". But much of the rest of the Declaration was very carefully worded to avoided direct rejection of the "National Service Committees" which were part and parcel of Government policy and bitterly opposed by the Trades Councils of Glasgow, Edinburgh and Aberdeen in particular. The Government's present action would inevitably create "acute controversy . . . when the country's opposition to the aggressor nations demands a united belief in the efficacy of the voluntary principle in national defence". The GC therefore was to contact the National Council of Labour with a view to "determining the most effective steps to combat the Government's action and preserving the voluntary principle". It was recognised that "a reconsideration" of participation "in Voluntary Service Committees may be involved". The General Council was to get "the considered views of affiliated bodies", either in conjunction with the National Council of Labour or separately, in order to "promote united action by their respective memberships".

Amongst the dozen speakers during the debate, seven of them as fifty-year-olds recalled their memories of debates around the First World War, and P H Cook of Bothwell Trades Council reminded them of the similarity of the speeches at the former Congresses. The criticism began with George Middleton for Glasgow Trades Council, who said "delegates should realise that National Service did not provide in any way for the defence of the country", which was linked up with collective security. He added:

> The people of this country wanted an alliance with Soviet Russia, but they were not having it because Chamberlain's policy did not permit of it.

To bring down the Government would be a much bigger contribution to defence, and they should, therefore, strengthen the Declaration by calling for definite withdrawal from "national voluntary service". Amongst those who supported him was W P Earsman of Edinburgh Trades Council, who objected to the GC holding back to consult with the NCL, whose opinion they had already accepted on the "national volunteer scheme" without consulting the movement in Scotland. Opinion in Scotland should be allowed to decide whether "it agreed with the opinions of the leaders in London or not"; without that freedom "there was very little use in holding a Scottish Congress at all". They should announce at once what "methods they were going to adopt to resist conscription. That would be giving the country a lead". His view was supported by William Peat, Scottish Painters, who thought "they were too prone in the Scottish Congress to shirk their responsibilities and be guided in everything by the British TUC". He suggested that they should set up in Scotland an emergency war council, perhaps by doubling the GC, to deal with all the trade emergencies which would arise during war. He proposed that "because they would not have an opportunity between now and when war came". A W Brady, Secretary of Glasgow Trades Council, had come mandated against any support at all for the "National" Government; at present "the man in the street could not distinguish between the policy of Chamberlain and the policy of National Council of Labour". J McKendrick, Scottish Mineworkers, complained that the Declaration gave no lead at all. The Scottish Typographer A Hunter said Congress should issue instructions to the GC to withdraw STUC representatives from the "National Service Committees": this would not split the movement; it would "transfer unity from the realm of words to the realm of action". J Quinn, Distributive Workers, said the Declaration was "another case of the mountain in labour producing a mouse", adding:

> Chamberlain's delays in fixing up an alliance with Russia showed that he was not anxious to establish a system of collective security and would fix up an alliance with Hitler if he could get the slightest concession from Hitler.

The national President of his union, however, John Jagger, thought there had been an immense advance; and the GC's resolution was the wise course. They might well find they would have to come out finally for no participation in voluntary service. But he doubted whether the STUC branching off on a line before consulting the British TUC, Labour Party and Parliamentary Labour Party was desirable. Thomas Scollan, GC, was also against reference back: were they to tell electors they were opposed both to the compulsory and voluntary system? Mover and seconder of reference back made no constructive suggestion, merely "a complete denial of anything at all". Charles Murdoch, GC, regretted the lack of unity behind the Declaration, while Brannigan of the Scottish Horse & Motormen said the only thing he disagreed with in the Declaration was that if they were "invaded within the next few days", they would all be conscripted, no matter who was in power. In replying to the debate, Elger spent most time in defending relations with the NCL, and the Declaration was finally accepted by a large majority.

On the last day, the Miners moved a resolution on international trade union unity supported by the Distributive Workers and Clerks who had withdrawn their own out-of-date motions. Noting that the Fascist powers' advances had put down the membership and powers of the International Federation of Trade Unions, it recommended "closer collaboration and unity" between unions in non-Fascist states, and particularly "closer unity with trade union organisations in the USSR, which numbered 22,500,000", and had "influence with the workers in colonial and semi-colonial countries". The speakers all regretted that no STUC delegation had been sent, as urged in 1936, and there had been no reference to that in the GC's report. After the President had remarked that not enough funds had been raised to do so, the resolution was adopted unanimously. It was the last business at their last "peacetime" Congress.

Section (ii): **An Emergency Special Congress**

It was, however, only on the conscription question that the GC immediately concentrated its processing of Congress decisions. After Elger and the incoming President William Quin, General & Municipal, attended NCL meetings and a Trade Union Executives Conference in London, the GC immediately decided to promote a national campaign in Scotland and at once issued a petition, before summoning a Special Congress to meet on 21 May, 1939. They called for motions which were to be composited and circulated by the Rothesay Standing Orders Committee, to which George Middleton was added to substitute for one unable to attend. It was, in fact, the first official STUC post ever held by that future General Secretary. Some 42 unions were represented by about 160 delegates and 27 trades councils by no less than 51, a far higher proportion than at a normal Congress. While the wording both of the GC's report and petition and the composited motions illustrated previous viewpoints, there were some surprising decisions. The GC's national campaign was to popularise their petition protesting against conscription which called "for a reversion to the traditional policy of Great Britain in National Defence". This, of course, did not exclude participation in the "national voluntary service" scheme. But although two days earlier the British TUC's Conference of Executives had decided by a nine to one majority not to break with the Voluntary Service Scheme, it was a different matter in Scotland. By a substantial majority the Special Congress instructed the GC "to withdraw its representatives from the Scottish National Service Committee" and asked affiliated organisations also to withdraw from the local committee. Later the GC were to report that the national campaign "was not a success", and they dropped the mildly worded petition because there "were so relatively few signatures" – only 4,000 in all.

There were two other noteworthy debates during the Special Congress. The first was on a point showing all the hallmarks of Scottish experience in the past. Two days earlier in London the Executives Conference had defeated by a ten to one vote a proposal to consider calling a "general strike as a last effort" to oppose military and industrial conscription. But by 118 to 54 the STUC Special Congress declared itself "in favour of industrial action to combat conscription", with the General Council to get affiliated unions' views "upon the possibilities of such action being jointly taken". At the same time the GC was authorised "to express willingness to co-ordinate such action". In fact, when the GC did approach 68 affiliated unions, 25 were against such action, so they "proceeded no further with the matter".

The last motion was for a peace pact which was carried without opposition. Just ten days earlier specific suggestions had come from the Soviet Union for a mutual pact between Britain, France, Poland and themselves. The STUC's resolution condemned

> the delay of the National Government in establishing friendly relationship with the USSR and emphasises that a peace pact between Great Britain, France and the USSR is essential in the interests of democracy.

But endless delays followed over such negotiations as the Chamberlain Government could be brought to discuss, while Czech gold had been handed to Hitler and behind-the-scenes negotiations were going on between the Federation of British Industries and their Nazi opposite numbers. Appeasement policy appeared to continue until the third week of August when with Parliament risen the negotiations for the peace pact were finally deadlocked.[3] On 28 August the USSR signed a mutual non-aggression pact with Hitler, who invaded Poland on 1 September.

Section (iii): "Manifesto on War"

It had not been stopped. The price of disunity and the failure of collective security was indeed to be high in the next six years, with the emergence of ghastly new weaponry. Unlike its silence in 1914 the STUC GC issued at once a Manifesto, on 4 September, 1939. It was not debated until the Aberdeen Congress at the end of April 1940, when it was approved by a three to one majority.

Composed fully five months before the declaration of war brought things to a new stage, and prepared before many months of failure to reach agreement on collective security, the "manifesto on war" concentrated at some length on the history and purpose of the trade union movement. This was summed up as an aim to combine immediate demands with "the more comprehensive purpose of abolishing capitalism". To achieve social and industrial emancipation "immense barriers have had to be surmounted" in the past, now under threat by Fascism in all countries. It stressed that Nazi Germany was not described as an aggressor nation on the ground that "the Hitler regime was against British Imperialism; the unions are also against Imperialism". Nor was it so named because it was against the British "National" Government; for the unions too "have had ample cause to doubt the value of that Government". It was named aggressor because "wherever the swastika flies the free associations of the workers, their trade unions and political organisations have been crushed with a ferocious brutality". It then said that if a war came "all resources would have to be mobilised and not be imperilled by a zeal to protect the individual rights of the owners of wealth"; and the worker must "not be used as an industrial pawn for the benefit of profiteers".

Although well received when it was first issued, it was now being debated when there was already a new situation. For ever since September there had been virtually no action by the armies in France, where the Communist Party had been suppressed and the unions disciplined: no British Army casualties had been reported until late in December, more than three months after the declaration of war. Indeed, the man in the street south of the border, with memories of Flanders in 1914, tended to call it "the phoney war". However, while the merchant navy had some losses, there had been some air attacks on the Royal Navy in the Scottish home ports at Scapa Flow, Rosyth, the Orkneys and Dalkeith as they prepared for a major ill-timed expedition to Scandinavia. Delegates who spoke against the Manifesto at Aberdeen, some of whom described it as "an antiquated document", were clearly expressing the continued deep distrust of the Chamberlain Government. Hardly had they left the northern city when the blitzkrieg began in Flanders, with a total collapse of France. Two resolutions were withdrawn which had earlier been sent in on the Soviet Union's action in Finland. At one time there had been division and anxiety on that question before the USSR's reason for the action was understood, which even resulted in fisticuffs at Beardmore's. With France occupied by the Nazis, at last there was the long overdue change of government, with Chamberlain and some associates thrown out by Winston Churchill, who rapidly brought in Labour Ministers.

Total retreat and evacuation from Dunkirk happened exactly a month after the 1940 STUC closed. The battle of Britain began: here again was a new situation, never contemplated by the 1914 veterans in Scotland.

Section (iv): **Defeat in the West**

In 1914 that a decisive weapon could come from the air was not a serious possibility: what really counted were ground forces supplied by long-range guns and strange new metal boxes called tanks, which began to present a problem to the men dug in to the permanent lines of trenches. For defence of her actual shores if it were ever necessary, Britain would of course rely on her navy. Quarter of a century later the first blitzkrieg, a war of lightning movement, by the Nazi united air and ground forces changed all that as it burst through the Maginot Line of impregnable trenches. Within days of it starting on 10 May, 1940, there had been total victory in the Nazi blitzkrieg on Flanders and France. Within a month of the Scots Congress the British army was in full flight. The majority of them succeeded in escaping across the Channel, together with some of their allies, thanks to the Royal Navy, the Merchant Navy and anyone on the south and east coasts with any kind of boat, which could reach Dunkirk.

France made peace, with General Pétain heading the Government together with Pierre Laval, Chamberlain's fellow arch-appeaser.[4] They took over for the Nazi occupiers the repression of the underground resistance movement initiated by the French Communist Party, which had been declared illegal immediately on declaration of war in 1939. The new Churchill Government's response to the collapse of France was to ban export of all goods to French territories, and to welcome French and other refugee troops. Almost immediately the British seized French warships off the Algerian coast and moved on to Libya and Egypt to cover the Empire's frontiers through the Middle East to India, where the Indian national leader Nehru was arrested.

By summer Nazi air-raids began across the Channel and southern coast as far west as Bristol as they prepared their possible invasion plan for which their ships were not yet ready. But the powerful response by the Royal Air Force succeeded in preventing this during the August "Battle of Britain". The Fascist military forces turned away to Greece and the Balkans, where in several countries, notably Rumania, they found ready assistance from dominant sections of the propertied classes. Meanwhile they continued shelling from the French coast and heavy air raids on industrial centres in the Midlands and the

South. Continual raids on London lasted nightly for nine months; with mass evacuation of children and schools to Wales, the West and the North. Occasional raids took place over the Borders, at Belfast and Scotland. Indeed, just six weeks before the STUC met at Dunoon in 1941 there were two very heavy raids on Clydeside with some 500 killed and 800 injured and a second heavy attack there two weeks after Congress. Miss Agnes Richmond, Elger's assistant, was deeply involved; late at work preparing the printing of the Congress documents she was caught in the raid all night, as she vividly remembered forty years later.

With the fall of France, the retreat from France with loss of equipment, the effects of bombing, fear of invasion, evacuation and new production needs, the Government was frequently issuing stringent defence regulations. Where these were necessary and unavoidable their operation obviously needed safeguards, for the most part depending upon local initiative and watchfulness. When these were drafted the comparable effects in Scotland during World War I, not least Lloyd George's harrowing experiences at the hands of the Clydeside shop stewards, could not be forgotten. Now, however, the man with responsibility at the Ministry was an experienced trade unionist, Ernie Bevin; from dockland himself he was quick to adjust to the Glasgow dockers' early rejection of their registration scheme, for example. Eager to avoid a general build-up of trouble on the industrial scene, Elger on his own initiative invited Bevin to come to address demonstrations in Edinburgh and Glasgow. Bevin was more than ready. What were described as the "largest trade union delegate meetings ever held in Scotland" took place on 14 and 15 December 1940. At Edinburgh over 1,600 delegates handed in 99 questions to Bevin; at Glasgow 4,000 wanted answers to some 300 questions.

It took a long time, however, before there could be a completely "united front" between rank and file and top leadership, between the young men and the oldsters, between Scottish representatives and Westminster, after such a long, bitter and justified distrust of the hierarchy. In Scotland in particular the change to a Churchill who was remembered for his actions during the "great unrest" and after, was not to allay all alarms by his merely bringing into the Government amongst its previous place-holders some English Labour Movement leaders. On the other hand, the GC following British TUC leads was opposing support for the People's Convention, which demanded a workers' government. They also introduced a further tight jacket of rules and restrictions on trades councils activity. There was already an active body of shop stewards in Scotland, particularly on Clydeside in the shipyards, before the foundation of the formidable Engineering &

Allied Trades Shop Stewards National Council in April 1940. This was criticised as "unofficial" by the AEU's Executive and the GC followed suit. Yet in the war years ahead speedy and skilful shop-floor initiative and local quick consultation was universally recognised to be essential for effectively running the vital war production. In Scotland their many activities during World War II are frequently mentioned in their history.[5] But the time for that recognition had not yet come at the Dunoon Congress, of Easter, 1941.

Here at Dunoon more debating time was spent on the consequences of defeat in the West and doubts about whether the new Government meant adequate change, than in tackling the many practical problems; though these did sometimes come to the fore. On 5 June, 1940, the GC had issued a "manifesto on the national effort". This welcomed the Churchill Government, promising support "so long as it fearlessly applies" its promise, which was "to place services *and property* at the disposal of the State" to mobilise the nation's resources. They stressed, however, that "unions must remain strong enough to safeguard the workers and perhaps the Government against any reactionary elements that might arise". It finally concluded that strong trade unions would be "a decisive factor in maintaining that full and free democracy for which the people of Britain are today fighting".

This moderation together with the GC's new rules in the autumn to contain trades councils' actions and later expressions of hostility to the People's Convention and the shop stewards' movement came in for sharp criticism. Owing to British Auxiliaries in Govan provocatively sacking a shop steward, which must have reminded many of 1915 practices, a nine-week strike had taken place in the autumn of 1940. It led to strong feeling throughout factories, not only in Glasgow. This was expressed by the Trades Councils of Glasgow, Edinburgh, Aberdeen and Greenock through George Middleton, A W Brady, T Murray, W Brown and J McCormick. There were also emphatic speeches from individual delegates from the Railwaymen, Distributive & Allied Workers, the Engineering & Shipbuilding Draughtsmen and Guild of Insurance Officials. The Co-operative Union's fraternal speech from P J Agnew warned how democracy could be undermined by propaganda, referring to the BBC excluding J B Priestley from the microphone and banning "the Orpheus Choir because its conductor had a certain point of view" as a pacifist. The critics' points were that the GC's document was "leading them into the lap of the Churchills"; and that his Government "was not fighting for democracy but for British imperialism". Calling the manifesto "a real crawling document", George Middleton said the nation's resources were not being mobilised, with iron, steel and armament companies "making huge profits out of the war". Others complained that the Government refused to state war aims, the time being "not opportune", while using Labour representatives to do the dirty work of putting over encroachments on liberty. Another warned that the American Lease Lend would mean "a tremendous concentration of the power of finance in Britain and America". Delegates were perhaps more impressed by contributions from two other trades council delegates who spoke in favour of the GC's Manifesto. A Whipp of Dundee Trades Council said the "two sides in the Government were acting from different motives", the Labour side to safeguard "the possibility of introducing Socialism and the Tory element to preserve its particular interest. It so happened that both sides had something in common at present in their fight against Nazi-ism."

P H Cook from Bothwell Trades Council followed this by saying:

> If Congress weakened the war effort, the fascist groups behind Churchill would become the fascist government of this country and there would be no more STUC.

Within two weeks of this speech Hitler's chief assistant Rudolf Hess had flown to Scotland on a secret visit to gain support, or at least acquiescence, from the British hierarchy in the invasion of Russia, which the Nazis were on the point of beginning.

At Dunoon, general debate continued with a composite motion calling on Ministers to prepare post-war schemes of "economic and social reconstruction", which included that

> ownership of land and capital should be changed forthwith from private to public ownership by the transference of the essential industries and services, particularly mining, transport and banking.

It was moved by William Quin for the GC, clearly looking back to the disappointments of the First World War. Other veterans regarded it as "window-dressing", adding that "after the last war there was a time-lag of more than 25 years before any scheme of reconstruction was seriously considered". The major general debate, however, was on war aims, and that prosecution of the war would be aided by "a statement of war aims from the democratic powers". Many, however, spoke in favour of an amendment which was narrowly defeated, which said the STUC should formulate and circulate their own peace aims, and that the responsibility for keeping Labour's aims before Scotland must rest with the GC. Alex Sloan, MP, of the Scottish Miners said that when the Labour Party had entered the Government they had stressed aims must be stated at once. Despite pressure from the floor of the House of Commons, where he himself had put down a question, there was still nothing, beyond saying that the aims would be stated "at the appropriate time". In his view, Churchill was "Enemy No. 1 of the workers". Others referred to some of India's "outstanding geniuses" being imprisoned; and that the two outstanding aims should be:

> the complete expropriation of capital and closer co-operation with the government of the USSR.

Saying that "there was undoubtedly closer affinity between the Scottish workers and the STUC than there was with the British TUC", D Currie, the mover of the amendment for Glasgow Trades Council, went on that it was essential that Labour aims "should be clearly and repeatedly stated", in view of recent statements by the arch-appeasers, Vansittart and Halifax.

In a bitter closing speech urging rejection of the amendment, the Printer, James Crawford, for the GC fiercely criticised Sloan and considered that by signing the non-aggression pact with Germany, the USSR had "not hesitated to precipitate the present war and to embroil the rest of the world". At the end of Congress, however, when the Draughtsmen's delegate W Boyle and the Miner Will Pearson called for full support of unions and trades councils for the "policy of friendship with the Soviet Union", it was passed by a large majority, despite opposition on similar lines from the Scottish Bakers' delegate. Such attitudes were indeed to be different in future Congresses.

Section (v): **Practical Problems of Wartime**

In the new conditions a number of practical problems were already beginning to surface which were to cause concern. In the First World War there had been much anxiety about dilution, not least amongst the semi-skilled on Clydeside. Indeed, it was finally to emerge that correspondence on this had led to the Yorkshire shop steward John Mason being detained for months without trial or explanation under Defence Regulation 18B, intended to intern potential "Fifth Columnists". In Scotland the question arose early over the transfer of women workers to England, while English women were being compelled to come to Scotland. Young women were directed to go from Dundee and Aberdeen to Birmingham and Coventry and offered such low wages that overtime was unavoidable. Early on, Dundee Jute and Flax women refused, and were refused benefit in consequence. Yet they could have got munitions work in Dundee itself, but were not accepted. The GC intervened with the Scottish Secretary to get adequate living allowances and settling-in fees; but T M Ferguson said that 50 of his Jute and Flax women members who refused to go had still not received benefit. There were difficulties about representation on Food Control Committees looking after adequate supplies for specialist workers, works' canteens and rationing, on which there were no less than nine motions. There was need for adequate supplementary pensions; on this Abe Moffat for the Miners made his first intervention on the needs of pensioners, for whom he was to become acknowledged as the national advocate. Differences had to be sorted out between a number of unions over the responsibility for organising the many new sections of Civil Defence Workers, about which the GC had been much concerned for some six months.

A war problem, however, that most deeply concerned delegates was the consequences of bombing, air-raid shelters and abuses of fire-watching precautions for business premises. Incidentally, the anger of their mood emerged in the remarkable vote of 94-95 to protest against the banning under emergency laws of the *Daily Worker* and *The Week*. During the height of the bombing of London these journals were fiercely criticising Government policy, especially about air-raid shelters and lack of protection from raids; the same Regulation 2D was later used to threaten suppression of the *Daily Mirror*. When the bombing began, the fire-watching Order was made under the Defence Regulations; it required employers to keep a continual fire guard night and day at their premises, and employees were obliged to take part. Problems arose at once over lack of consultation with the trade union movement in preparing each specific scheme, pay, amenities and compensation rights. The Railway Clerk, P G Forrester, in his Glasgow experience said that "the whole fire-watching arrangements were in a state of chaos". D Currie of Glasgow Trades Council quoted an example which he said was typical "where a superintendent of a large institution went to his dug-out on an alert while the employees went on duty". For the Miners, J McKendrick described how workers in mining and iron and steel trades were called on to do a night's fire-watching "after a very heavy day's work and, as a consequence, losing very necessary sleep". Yet mine-owners refused to let them do fire-watching in substitution for their ordinary work. The Scottish Bankers' delegate, J McIntosh, described disputes with the Royal Bank of Scotland, both in Aberdeen and their London office over lack of consultation with the union. There was also a lively debate on the need for deep underground shelters from both Glasgow and Edinburgh delegates. There had been sites prepared for tunnels including one under

Calton Hill in Edinburgh. There were doubts even then whether many feet of reinforced concrete could withstand "an aerial torpedo" such as one delegate had witnessed in Birmingham, believing the spread of fire from incendiaries was the most serious danger. But delegates refused to have a motion referred back which demanded that Government and local authorities at once proceed with construction.

Much indeed was to change before they met the following Easter, by which time there had been immense developments in the prospect of reversing the defeat in the west and winning the war against Fascism.

References

[1] Some years before 1914, the author's grandfather, H E Stacy, would sing to her the "Three Blind Mice" street parody: Prices rise! prices rise! See how they mount! see how they mount! They've raised the price of our daily bread, and given us cruisers and guns instead! But what will it matter when we're all dead that prices rise!

[2] Of the 72 affiliated unions consulted, 27 submitted names, with seven refusing to nominate, being against the scheme. Of the 23 trades councils, no less than 12 refused.

[3] The Journal of the Labour Research Department, which received the STUC support, contains useful factual accounts, particularly in the October 1939 issue, entitled "War Origins".

[4] When the war ended in 1945, both were tried and found guilty of treason; Laval was executed in October and Pétain sentenced to life imprisonment.

[5] *Engineering Struggles: Episodes in the Story of the Shop Stewards* Movement, by Edmund and Ruth Frow (1982), Chapter 5.

18

The Nazi Army is Resisted

Before delegates were to meet at Rothesay in April 1942 there was a total change in the world situation, which altered the mood of the trade union movement. This happened quickly indeed in Scotland, with its concentration of heavy industry so vital to any serious war effort. The unique process began of trade union activists becoming drawn into the control of industry from the ground up. With this involving the need and experience of industrial planning, the basis was laid for the development of the trade union movement on a scale never before accepted, and from which no post war government would find it easy to retreat. For the Scottish TUC it opened the door wide for it henceforth to be taken seriously by any government. All that was needed was that this should be recognised and followed up by active new-thinking men and women from the factory floor, who were already learning it the hard way. By 1942 Congress, differences and divisions were hardly to be seen; the prevailing atmosphere of distrust was reduced to a minimum; and the movement's self-confidence grew with the belief that Fascism could now be defeated at home and abroad. First signs that a major change was coming could be seen within a couple of weeks of Dunoon. For while there was still speculation about the reason for the secret flight by Hess to Scotland in mid-May, the first sign of change was literally in the air; the nightly bombing of London stopped. While in April there had been 6,065 deaths from air-raids, by May these had fallen to 5,394, and then in June to merely 399, with not a single night raid on London for seven weeks. The reason became clear on 22 June, 1941: the entire Nazi war effort turned to the east and an invasion began of the Soviet Union.

Section (i): **Response to the Soviet Fight-back**

The way in which the peoples of the Union of Soviet Socialist Republics resisted the blitzkrieg and operated the "scorched earth" tactic whenever retreat was necessary had an overwhelming effect on public opinion. It proved that successful resistance was possible. Unlike Poland, Czechoslovakia, France, Finland, Hungary, Denmark and all the other countries of Europe over-run by the Nazi onslaught, here in the Soviet Republics there were no great landowners and hierarchy of Fifth Column military officers seeking to make common cause with invaders. The effect in the factories and at British grass roots was tremendous; within a week the Glasgow District AEU Shop Stewards' quarterly meeting called on the Government for full diplomatic, military and economic co-operation with the USSR, and warned against "influences at work in this country hostile to the Soviet Union". That was soon seen to be the general reaction in the factories: from the point of view of the Churchill Government the time had now indeed become "opportune" to declare their war aims. By the middle of August, Churchill had met President Roosevelt to agree peace aims in "The Atlantic Charter" declaration, together with a joint message of support to Moscow, suggesting a meeting there of the Three Powers. That was four months before the attack on the American fleet in Pearl Harbour by the Japanese finally brought the United States into the war against the Fascist Powers. Moreover, at the Soviet Union's request, war was declared on the Governments of Rumania, Hungary and Finland which had made common cause with the Nazi invaders.

Immense effort was put into the production effort; by early September a "tanks for Russia" production week was operating, together with considerable effort to support the men and merchant ships transporting weapons to Russia. Ten weeks after the invasion began the GC issued a statement congratulating "the armies and workers of the Union of Soviet Socialist Republics on their heroic and determined resistance" to the invaders. It continued:

> Scottish trade unionists are fervent in the belief that this vicious and obviously long premeditated attack will ultimately fail, and that the combined resistance of the British Commonwealth of Nations, the Union of Soviet Socialist Republics and their Allies and supporters will succeed in ridding the peoples of the world of Nazi and Fascist tyranny.

It pledged full co-operation "in this liberating war of humanity". On 10 October, 1941, the STUC, Co-operative Party and Scottish Council of the Labour Party put out a joint circular calling for local joint committees to be set up everywhere to explain the need for intensifying the war effort; with trades councils' help to plan demonstrations and conferences "to key up the national effort"; and to collect funds for medical aid to Russia, of which Elger was Treasurer. The Report describes that it was taken up "in an unprecedented manner". They also greeted Soviet sailors visiting Scottish ports. By early 1942 they laid on conferences in Edinburgh, Glasgow, Dundee and Aberdeen to greet visiting USSR trade unionists; delegates were appointed from 1,000 Scottish trade union branches.

Debates at the 1942 Congress were largely concerned with how to remove obstacles to production. How were they to make the new Regional Board of Production effective and put bite into the Joint Production Committees already active in the engineering and shipbuilding industry? There was much work to be done in all factory JPCs, to prevent them being reduced to merely disciplining absenteeism while separating manual and non-manual workers and ignoring management wastage of material and labour. There were strong complaints too of Admiralty waste and delays, particularly from Arnold Henderson of Clydebank, R Farrer and George Middleton of Edinburgh and Glasgow Trades Councils. Planning was "not simply a technical problem", said Middleton, "they had to have power to over-ride vested interests". He added that too many employers "were concerned with preservation of the means whereby they could ensure profit-making after the war". The forms of control "gave the impression that it was not the State controlling big business but big business very largely controlling the State", in contrast to what prevailed in Russia.

At a Production Conference in Glasgow at the end of 1941, attended by 800 shop stewards, they declared they were willing to take part in any production committees. This was certainly the practice throughout Scotland from the beginning, even if elsewhere some workers were slow to react positively at first to the existence of factory JPCs and how they could be used to advantage. According to A Maloney, attending for the AEU from Northampton, the reason members showed no enthusiasm for them was that they saw production "as a question secondary in character", the union's primary purpose being to look after wages and conditions. Yet with the new costs-plus system operating on Government orders, the employers temporarily lost any incentive to cut wages; and it became clear as time went on that alert members on JPCs could effectively accuse employers of hindering production when they were difficult about conditions. Some employers, however, remained slow to change attitudes, as Abe Moffat complained of the mine owners. Clyde shop stewards were already meeting to complain in July 1941 that production was being held up by waste, corruption and mismanagement; and that not only was there often a lack of materials but some employers were trying to undermine workshop organisation by attacking piecework prices and similar ploys. There was a continual campaign by west of Scotland shipyard shop stewards. From Greenock they led marches after work straight from the shipyards; on one occasion they ended in a demonstration addressed in the centre of the town by a member of the GC, D Carlin of the Transport & General. On another occasion they organised a total stoppage of the shipyards for half an hour, to bring matters home to the Admiral who was shipyard controller. The costs-plus system could also have its disadvantages. On some work there was much letting and sub-letting of contracts on a costs-plus basis which led to delays and abuse. H Livingstone of the Plasterers showed the very bad effects it had in repairing blitzed houses in Clydebank and Greenock. The view was expressed finally, after separate motions insisting that railways and all other public forms of transport should remain under Government control, in a composite entitled "Control of Essential Industries". Moved by J Stanley, General Secretary of the Constructional Engineering Union, it declared that the highest possible degree of planning and organisation could not be achieved while these were privately controlled. The Government should, therefore, use its powers "for the immediate control of all essential industries", which would also "render unnecessary" the costs-plus basis of letting and sub-letting contracts, which "lends itself to abuse and to the consequent retarding of the war effort". Supported by Glasgow Trades Council and the Operative Plasterers it was carried unanimously.

For the next three years of war at each stage Congress delegates continued to voice the scores of new problems with which the movement was so vitally concerned. Varied as these were in detail, basically they fall under two headings: firstly, those concerned with winning the war and then those concerned with winning the peace. As time went on, it began to emerge how interdependent were decisions in both areas.

Resolutions on restoration of post-war practices and that the STUC should use its influence with the British TUC and elsewhere to support the aspirations of Indians "for independence" and so remove "every remaining obstacle to British-Indian harmony", were carried unanimously. The only debate where there was any small measure of dissension which had so marred recent Congresses was when the Fire Brigades and Glasgow Trades Council demanded that the ban should be lifted on the *Daily Worker*. On this occasion it was opposed by the GC through D Robertson, the Railway Clerk, and J Watson, a Glasgow Distributive & Allied delegate, but it was eventually carried. After a similar vote three months later at the LP Conference, despite the opposition of James Walker, MP, who had been STUC Chairman in 1921, the ban was finally lifted.

Section (ii): **The Siting of Wartime Industry**

One other problem discussed brought to the fore what was to become the key question after the war for forty years: the future state of Scotland's economy. For it was already seen

> that the industrial post-war position of Scotland will to a considerable extent be affected by wartime development.

A resolution, therefore, urged that the Standing Industrial Committee for Scotland, set up in February 1942, should "give close attention to this". In moving this for the GC, W P Earsman, JP, the Edinburgh Trades Council Secretary, quoted important facts. He described how the loss of colonies abroad and "the telescoping of factories" meant many were "divorced from the industries they had been brought up to". Apart from the loss of raw materials suffered by Dundee, he stated that 600 had just been sacked from Edinburgh mills because of the lack of rubber; pottery had been affected at Bo'ness. Unless steps were taken it meant that

> at the end of the war Scotland would be left with nothing but its heavy industries and the rest of the country would be more of less derelict.

Some of the new industries arising from the war ought to be established in Scotland; and he pointed out that from 1932 to the beginning of the war, of the 12,600 factories opened in Great Britain, only 102 came to Scotland, which "suffered from unemployment to a greater extent than any other part". More attention to planning had been needed; and a long outstanding problem needing to be tackled was that of the Highlands and Islands. Alex Sloan, MP for the Miners said the drift south had become serious; first their industries were being driven south and following industry the youth and manhood; it would be no lasting benefit "to have new factories merely designed for the war effort". If industries had been established in Scotland the young Scottish women would not have needed to be sent across the border. This point was emphasised in another GC resolution, moved by Herbert Ellison, JP, of the Railwaymen about transferring women workers to England, with their problems of billeting, catering and social amenities, while there were empty factories in the north and north-east. Later, Sloan moved a unanimous resolution protesting at the jailing of two Scottish girls, "forcibly sent across the border" to work in Coventry for alleged breaches of the Essential Work Order. They had "to face the prosecuting counsel with no defence" before "hard-faced magistrates" in what was to them "a foreign nation". The only objection to the motion came from J L Brown of the Scottish Bakers, who said the women should have been in a trade union, and that the case of an 18-year-old engineering apprentice should have been included; he was jailed in Glasgow for 40 days for being late.

In their daily wartime struggle on the factory floor, in mines, shipyards and the JPCs about all the practical problems of production, a full awareness of the run down of Scottish industry, as well as its enormous potential, became very widespread indeed. It took on urgency, rather than remaining a "hardy annual" general question which the Scottish Development Council had been set up in 1931 to consider. Little had come of that: but in 1942 the new Secretary of State for Scotland, Thomas Johnston, MP,[1] set up a Scottish Council of Industry which meant action.

Johnston invited STUC representatives to a conference to advise "upon questions relating to the location of industry in Scotland". He told them he was troubled about "the industrial post-war prospects"; and

> the need for organised machinery by which, or through which, it might be possible to arrest industrial tendencies which, if allowed to develop, might have serious consequences to our Scottish people.

There was, he pointed out, a "very limited number of new industrial enterprises in Scotland being set up to manufacture products likely to have a post-war or peace-time market". Permanently serving on it from February 1942 were the Miner, Peter Henderson, T M Ferguson of Dundee, Textile Trades Representative, as well as Charles Murdoch, the Baker, and Elger from the GC. Peter Henderson devoted much of his 1943 Presidential Address to it. He welcomed the concern with Highlands and Islands and the Hydro-Electric Development Scheme which Johnston had brought to the fore. Saying that "Scotland too long had been subjected to accepting what was left of the trade of Britain", Henderson also stressed the need for proper housing, which "would be a tremendous contributing factor in improving the position of Scottish manufacturers". He spoke in some detail of that in connection with the Scottish Coalfields Committee, on which he represented the Miners, and about developing new sinkings in the East which would be necessary. The Scottish Council for Industry spent the next year working on how premises could be made available for new industrial enterprise after the war, restoring industries such as fishing and agriculture, how to co-ordinate transport by road, rail, water and air; about new building materials and how light industry could be built.

When Johnston spoke to the 1944 Congress in Dunoon, he could declare that he was "joyful to say" that the STUC "has played a prominent, noteworthy and most creditable part" in the Council's work, which aimed at

> encouraging and persuading by every means in its power business firms to locate themselves north of the Tweed.

But he stressed the difficulties of planning without public ownership:

> So long as business is privately owned and so long as private citizens are risking their capital in these businesses, it is almost literally impossible to direct or compel them to areas or locations where they do not wish to go. It is another matter, of course, prohibiting new industries from going to particular areas.

He gave a wealth of facts and figures from the past to the present, including the problems for the building trades of the "pre-fabs", the factory-built steel houses, whilst stressing the great importance of industry's future in tackling the vast Scottish housing needs. Housing came in later for especially sharp comments by delegates from Aberdeen, Edinburgh, Clydebank and Johnstone Trades Councils, with Electricians, Locomotive Engineers and Transport & General delegates taking part. But Johnston's address was received with acclaim: it laid the basis for struggles for decades of both the political and industrial future of Scotland. The first expression of this was soon to come; for it clearly influenced the thinking of the GC six months later when they produced a very full statement in October 1944, on the Government White Paper on Employment. In this, the Board of Trade had the responsibility of carrying out Government policy on the distribution of industry. The GC stated that having seen the disadvantages of "location questions being handled by centralised Government Departments having no real intimacy with Scotland either geographically or industrially", they looked for

> the establishment of a Scottish Department of the Board of Trade equipped with an expert staff in close touch with both sides of industry and working in conjunction with the Secretary of State for Scotland.

Approval of their attitude was accepted by the 1945 Congress despite the lack of Government mention of public ownership and with many examples quoted of acute difficulties now that the war in Europe was ending.

Section (iii): **Home Front Problems**

If location of industry proved to be the essential long-term home issue, there was nevertheless a very wide range of other home front problems covered in important debates at wartime Congresses which could provide a profound political education for activists in later years. While much had been learned, not least by the long-term unemployed now coming back to work or those never before in employment, sections of the ruling class had also learned fast. Having noted their disasters and difficulties at home during the First World War, they had adjusted to the changing mood from below by putting men like Tom Johnston, Ernie Bevin and other Labour leaders into the key positions. Not only did they keep in constant touch on matters of war production; there was control of consumption goods to cover adequate food and clothing rationing in this Second World War, including even the canteen system being extended into "British restaurants". Indeed, the Government had in fact to put forward, as an essential "peace aim", the basic structure of what was to be the future "welfare state". There was unprecedented attention paid to preparing and publicising immense post-war social improvements by means of the Beveridge and other Reports. Here therefore was the prospect of national public systems for the first time in health, education, housing and long-term pension and social insurance benefits. Some of the post-war gains, such as annual holidays with pay, seemed almost incredible to those who were young when the STUC was founded. In addition, public control, if not complete national ownership, of mines and railways which the previous private owners had found to be disappointingly unprofitable, was to be retained, with the prospect or expectation of extending the principle to other forms of transport and energy.

Not unnaturally often enough there were breakdowns in practice, inadequacy, failure to implement fully or to allow for changes due to new processes. To quote only one example: there was failure to recognise by equal pay the immense contribution made by women in war production. Indeed, it must be admitted that the trade unions themselves could be slow to recognise change, as evidenced in the late recognition by a craft union such as the Engineers that women should be admitted to membership. Scottish trade unionists were, however, alert to the dangers of certain wartime Defence Regulations being carried over into peacetime. One example was Defence Regulation 1AA against strikes, first introduced when the miners reacted against the owners' attitude on the Portal Award. Their fears were indeed justified about this Regulation being retained, while the need to abolish the 1927 anti-trade union Act was still ignored, and in Congress proposals were discussed which were in fact disastrously introduced 25 years later: "In Place of Strife".

Without constant alertness and ability to learn by the men and women at their place of work, both the current and the future dangers would increase and become inevitable. Indeed, at the 1943 Congress, the General Secretary of the Tobacco Workers, Percy Belcher, moved a resolution pointing out that in view of the important work shop stewards were doing and how subject they continually were to victimisation, they should be safeguarded; the STUC should press for legislation to force all employers to recognise them. Through James Crawford, Printers, the GC spoke against it, and an adverse vote was only avoided by the Renfrew Trades Council moving next business. The GC at the time consisted almost exclusively of full-time trade union officers, often with heavy commitment and responsibilities in London head offices which, like the factories themselves, had been widely dispersed. There remained a strong tendency amongst some to fear over-reaction at grass roots. In addition to direct moves to prevent general co-operation amongst shop stewards this was evidenced in frequent efforts by Elger to get Congress to alter Standing Orders and to introduce the block vote in order to reduce the representation and influence of the trades councils. Here Communists, ILPers and left wing LP members, agreeing on a wide range of topics, had considerable and growing influence. In his attempts to reduce the rights of the trades councils, Elger consistently had support from the Printers' and Bakers' representatives on the GC; the attempt was narrowly defeated in 1943 and again by Previous Question being moved in 1944. Elger himself was busy throughout the war with invitations to lecture to the troops, as well as attending a large number of other organisations, and conferences on behalf of the STUC.

How the future was to turn out for Scottish trade unionists as for the world itself, moving on towards a hitherto unimaginable nuclear potential, was to depend on the defeat of Fascism in Germany and elsewhere; how and by whom it was to be achieved; whether international peace could be speedily established, and under what conditions. Here we must therefore break off and turn to consider the conduct of the war and conditions of the peace and how the STUC was to develop.

Section (iv): **The Conduct of the War**

From the first, Hitler and the Nazi generals had feared that when they opened hostilities in the West they might be attacked at their back door in Eastern Europe. Hence before the blitzkrieg on France and the Lowlands in 1940 they had first broken the East European countries one by one, with Britain and France failing to check them. If they invaded the Eastern super-power, the USSR, would they have a Second Front opened behind them in the West? It was clear that Hitler was convinced that this would not happen: by September 1941 some twenty Nazi Divisions had left occupied France for the Eastern Front. The German command believed the Russian military forces would quickly crumble – a view shared by leading Conservative MPs for many months. Eden was sent to Moscow in December 1941 to discuss war plans; central to these was the need to open a Second Front in Western Europe and the promise was given that it should be opened during 1942. But the years passed with no landing, and British military forces were confined to defensive moves in the Middle East, North Africa and later Burma. Offensive developments came with the American-aided invasion of French North Africa, after which the fascist troops there were pushed back. By the summer of 1943 the slow progress could begin of landings on what Churchill called "the soft under-belly of Europe", through Sicily and Salerno and in co-operation with the underground resistance movements on the Mediterranean shores. It was to be another year before the Second Front was at last to be opened in the West following massive RAF and USAF bombing of Germany and German-occupied territory. This coincided with the immense advances of the Red Army, following the historic defeat of the invading Nazi army and its surrender by General Von Paulus at Stalingrad.[2]

As the Red Army was closing in on the home ground of the retreating Nazi forces and their fleeing East European Quisling aides, while the British, American and Canadian troops, helped by the underground resistance movement advanced at last, many new questions were arising. Where would the allies meet? Would there be a joint policy towards liberated Europe, and what should it be? How could provisional governments be helped until survivors could be released from concentration camps and displaced people returned?

While the STUC was meeting in Aberdeen in April 1945, the Red Army surrounded Berlin; further south the historic meeting between them and the Americans took place on the River Elbe, and Himmler asked the British and Americans to accept the German army's surrender – but to them alone. The GC presented a long emergency resolution demanding that the war criminals must be punished; and that during the Allied occupation the United Nations Governments should help to create democratic institutions, with the trade unions an essential part, to ensure "that no vestige of Fascism remains". Passed unanimously on the anniversary of the Guernica massacre during the rebellion of the Spanish generals, who had been carrying supplies to Germany throughout, it also demanded that "diplomatic recognition be withheld from those States which still have fascist governments". After John Sullivan, Transport & General, had moved it, E Mackintosh of the Fire Brigades, in seconding, said Germany "should have taken from her the power ever again to go on the road of aggression". He warned that "at the moment German Fascists were being left in control and this policy must be stopped. Every Nazi or supporter must be removed from office". On this point, Arnold Henderson, Clydebank Trades Council, thought the resolution not definite enough, saying:

> A lax form of control might allow similar elements to the Nazis to regain control. In Britain we had certain elements who would confuse the issue

On that point, therefore, "the trade unions should be decisive" about it. The following day Congress went on record as being "aghast at the gruesome and horrible depravity of the Nazis uncovered in the prison and concentration camps", about which a visiting Parliamentary delegation had just reported. Moved by Guild of Insurance Officials and Distributive and Allied delegates, it demanded

> that summary justice should be executed on all those who have been responsible for such unspeakable outrages against humanity.

Throughout the 1945 Congress delegates frequently stressed the importance of the decisions taken at Yalta in the Crimea Declaration of February at the last meeting of Churchill, Roosevelt and Stalin. Tribute was paid in his Presidential Address by James Young, of the Draughtsmen, on the death only two weeks earlier of Franklin D Roosevelt, saying "the United Nations in general having suffered a grievous loss in the passing of that great American". Indeed, both these events had immense significance for the future, in the conduct of the war both in Europe and in the Far East as in the post-war prospects for many years to come.

When they met at Yalta in February 1945 as the war in Europe was nearing its end, the three leaders had made vital decisions upon the following points:

1. Complete military plans for Germany's final defeat.
2. How to enforce unconditional surrender terms, with each Power

operating separate zones of Germany, co-ordinating through a Central Control Commission. This was to "disarm and break up for all time the German General Staff that has repeatedly contrived the resurgence of German militarism".

3. Germany was to pay compensation for damage in kind.
4. China and France were to help in joint sponsorship of a Conference at San Francisco, which was to work out what finally became the United Nations.
5. They agreed joint action to help liberated countries to form provisional broadly based governments pending elections, and boundary modifications for Poland.
6. Machinery was to be set up for permanent consultation between the three Foreign Secretaries; and they reaffirmed the common determination to maintain unity of action in the peace to come.

Three months earlier Roosevelt had been re-elected for a fourth term as President of the USA. From his point of view, the Crimea decisions were the culmination of the progressive anti-fascist policies he had so long and skilfully worked for. He had overcome opposition, both from isolationist attitudes typical of the descendants of emigrants from so many reactionary European countries, and also from the financial hierarchy, which indeed had other aims. At Yalta there were other decisions not announced publicly about the war in the Far East. On this, it was agreed that the USSR should open an offensive on Japanese-occupied Manchuria exactly three months after Germany surrendered: Roosevelt ruled out the use of the atom bomb, which was on the point of completion under US control. His successor, Henry Truman, was a man of different calibre, for he agreed with Churchill that the new horror weapon should indeed be used. The first atom bomb was, therefore, dropped on Hiroshima exactly two days before the three months after V-E Day were up and the USSR was, therefore, due to open hostilities against Japan in Manchuria. In his New Year message Roosevelt had made a significant point:

> I would express a very serious warning against the poisonous effects of enemy propaganda. The wedge the Germans attempted to drive in West Europe was less dangerous than the wedges they are continually attempting to drive between ourselves and our Allies. There are evil and baseless rumours against the Russians, against the British and against our own American commanders.

That his warning was not groundless began soon to emerge on very many other issues after his unfortunate death.[3]

The problems resulting internationally, and not least in economic affairs, were be to felt severely in Britain. This was despite the overwhelming defeat of Churchill and the Conservatives in the July 1945 General Election, which returned to power at last a Labour Government with an unprecedented majority on a programme for sweeping change. It found expression already at the first working-class conference to take place that year which was, as ever, that of the STUC. They met in Dunoon at Easter, 1946.

References

[1] A socialist of long standing, author of *A History of the Working Classes in Scotland* and former editor of *Forward*.

[2] A popular bitter crack describes Winston Churchill answering a telephone call from Stalin. The voice asked: "When shall I be seeing you?" Churchill replies: "Oh, yes . . . er. . . where are you speaking from?" Stalin replies: "Boulogne!"

[3] Two other American Presidents died in office when operating progressive policies: both were assassinated, Lincoln in 1867 and Kennedy in 1963.

19

They Face the Future

Delegates' first concern naturally enough was with the immediate difficult problems of transforming production to peacetime uses. This meant dealing at once with unemployment, not least amongst the women, caused by the sudden stopping of war factories and equipment, and even by permanent redundancy from the turnover; recovery of the interrupted flow of old raw materials, or finding new sources; adapting new technology and factory premises; catching up with Scotland's long-neglected housing needs, which the Government admitted amounted to half a million, speaking of the target being 100,000 within the next ten years. There were also anxieties arising over continuing controls on food, rationing and shop licensing, which the employers' politicians were not slow to exploit. The solution to these problems depended on unprecedented mass planning, public ownership and control. Over these measures delegates felt some confusion and no little anxiety lest there should be back-tracking on the structural charges which would be necessary to carry out the vast promised plans when the war both in Europe and the Far East was over.

Section (i): **How to Transform Production in Peacetime**

For the 1945 General Election, the Scottish TUC had issued a full manifesto. After saying that "the Japanese war must be strenuously prosecuted until no vestige of Fascism remains in the Far East", it went on to follow up their previous statements on employment policy and the Beveridge Report aiming to establish "the Welfare State". Their view was that Britain must have a government which would not only "co-operate fully with progressive forces throughout the world"; in addition "an equally progressive outlook is demanded in the realm of home affairs". To improve industries upon which the people's standard of living depended, Britain

> must depart from the nineteenth-century ideas of absolute capitalist control.

Pointing out that in coal, gas, electricity, water, iron and steel and inland transport "capitalist resources and methods are incapable of guaranteeing either maximum productivity or steady development, it was now a matter of vital importance to the whole nation" and its economic security that they should be publicly owned. Special emphasis was laid on Scotland's need for the control of the location of industry as well as prime necessities including housing:

> The weakening or removal of such controls will be followed by opportunities for the racketeer and the profiteer to exploit the nation.

With the war over, delegates were in support of this and looking, in broad terms, for its early full implementation. There were, however, already some differences in interpretation, and early signs of the possibility of the changes which could bring the then nascent "Welfare State" from its cradle to its grave. There were powerful and hopeful speeches from fraternal delegates and visitors, including Ebby Edwards, Miners' President from the British TUC and also from an International Labour Office Director. Most significant was a lengthy speech by George Isaacs, the Minister of Labour and National Service, together with one from the Parliamentary Secretary of the Board of Trade, who intervened in the main debates.

These were on Production Plans, Unemployment and Location of Industry. The GC's resolution, while welcoming the Government's attitude on getting full employment in the development areas like Scotland and approving the idea of trading estates to diversify industry, thought "the rate of progress is far too slow". Moving it, Charles Murdoch said that they needed industries to employ 150,000, which was Scotland's pre-war "permanent army of unemployed"; but Isaacs had said there were only plans to employ an additional 80,000. "That was poor comfort", especially for those in areas where there was only one industry, like Dundee and Lanarkshire. George Middleton joined in with an effective contribution on the examples Isaacs had quoted. He said that if they brought

> the motor car industry to Hillington, only 20% of the selling value of the car would be produced there, 80% of the value would require to be produced in the Midlands.

He added that there were too many instances like that of Prestwick, "where we had the airport but had not yet got the airlines". Most of the bodies set up to deal with Scottish questions were only advisory and some authority was needed; otherwise he felt "we would have a resurgence of Scottish Nationalism". Speakers from Paisley and Greenock Trades Councils stressed priority for Clydeside with its mounting redundancy in yards and engineering factories. From Dundee came the point that the Tay Road Bridge was an "indispensable item" in Scotland's economic development; from Aberdeenshire pleas not to close the Turriff Flax Factory, with Kirkcaldy Trades Council stressing how they needed linseed oil from it for linoleum production; while Dr Muir of the Scientific Workers spoke on the needed speedy and full electrical development in the Highlands, as well as the lack of enough grants for research facilities in Scotland. The Government's announced aim of taking control of public transport was welcomed; but road and rail delegates described the proposals as only "a limited form of nationalisation"; and as "all transport is purely a public service", they urged that "the ultimate complete nationalisation of every form of transport" should be kept in view. Indeed, all too soon the failings in this respect were to be felt strongly, not least in Scotland's industrial development.

In general terms, however, the GC put down a resolution strongly urging effective planning and organisation, to be recognised "by managements and workers alike", who both had "a special responsibility in securing maximum production": it was at this that Isaacs had aimed most of his intervention. It was also to this that the miners had put an addendum which called for a subcommittee to be set up "for the purpose of considering a National Wages Policy" and the Government to legislate for a 40-hour week. Speaking on this, Abe Moffat made it clear that for the miners a "National Wages Policy" was indeed remote from the "Wage Restraint" policy, which was to be first announced by Sir Stafford Cripps only a short time later. Moffat explained that what they demanded was "a guaranteed weekly wage for all". Supporting his view J Stanley for the Constructional Engineering Union pointed out:

> In many industries the lower-paid workers were placed below the lowest wage line and in his view the lowest grade should be at least 25% above the poverty line.

The incoming GC required the Scottish Miners to amplify their proposal before they would submit it to the British TUC; but before that was done there were to be major difficulties and changes. There was an extreme shortage of coal stocks, about which the Minister responsible and former STUC delegate, Emanuel Shinwell, had warned that summer. Stocks had been deliberately run down by the coal owners, with the National Coal Board due to take over on Vesting

Day, 1 January, 1947. With a desperately cold winter there was a major fuel crisis, putting concerns in many industries in danger of closing down, and causing havoc with Britain's dire need for building up exports.

Section (ii): **Problems in Their Jubilee Year**

In facing the future in the year 1947 when the mines had at least been taken out of the hands of the private owners, in the first of the measures for which the TUC's founders had fought so persistently, they had a number of domestic changes to note on their 50th anniversary. William Elger had died suddenly at the age of 55, to be replaced as General Secretary by Charles Murdoch. The Assistant Secretary, T F McWhinnie, had left only a month before Elger's death to join the staff of the World Federation of Trade Unions, to be replaced by James Jack. Two other GC members had left on their appointments to other posts, Peter Henderson becoming Labour Relations Officer for Fife under the Coal Board. The demand for experienced trade unionists to staff the many new administrative offices expanded fast: Charles Murdoch himself resigned within two years to take up such a post, as well as two other senior GC members.

Their Jubilee Year was indeed not a happy one. In Scotland they felt the difficulties already mounting throughout Britain after the abrupt ending by President Truman of American Lend-Lease. There followed unhappy discussions between the Powers at the Paris Conference and the American "Marshall Plan" with its embarrassing terms for "foreign aid" loans. American foreign policy was increasingly seen as world economic domination, including aims to corner rare raw materials from former colonial countries, which were all now involved in seeking independence from Britain, France, Holland and the defeated Germany and Italy. As the leading American official Acheson put it, one of their main aims was

> to push ahead with the reconstruction of those two great workshops of Europe and Asia, Germany and Japan, upon which the ultimate recovery of the two Contintents so largely depends.[1]

As their Secretary for Commerce Harrison admitted, their interest was "in the restoration of Europe as a paying market for U.S. goods".[2] The main "Marshall Plan" strategy involved excluding the Soviet Union and hampering any country attempting planned industrial and agricultural development under popular control. This inevitably led to resistance in countries as the invaders were defeated and the former occupiers and their adherents attempted to come back. The new line-up of "the West" as the years went by therefore finally involved the use of British, American, French and Dutch troops in Cyprus, Greece, Palestine, Persia, Egypt and North Africa, the Indian sub-continent, Malaya, Vietnam and China; and finally was the background to the threat by the American General MacArthur to use the atom bomb against North Korea's supporter, the new revolutionary Republic of China. There was already in sight in 1947 the growth of two "blocs" in the world, East and West, in what was to become known as "the Cold War".

The inevitable continuance of conscription for a number of years as a result made the grave economic problems all the more difficult; and step by step anxieties grew about whether the Labour Government's foreign policy could remain independent. When in Jubilee Year a Prime Minister attended an STUC Congress for the first time, Attlee and his then Secretary of the Board of Trade, Sir Stafford Cripps, KC, were to hear a debate about the need for "a radical change" in foreign policy, as well as a remitted resolution opposing "conscription being maintained as a permanent feature of British life under normal peacetime conditions". The major resolution, moved by Abe Moffat for the Miners, noted developments "since last Congress in relation to Greece, Spain, Palestine and our increased dependence on American Imperialism". It therefore demanded "a radical change" so far as to achieve "a real Socialist foreign policy in the interests of peace and progress". This would need "the fullest possible economic and political relations with the USSR and the Socialist forces throughout the world". Moffat recalled how the early pioneers always taught that once there was support by their enemies "it was time to examine the policy", adding:

> If we applied that logic we should find, in practically every occasion, those who opposed us prior to 1945 were the same people who were giving unqualified support to the present foreign policy, while on the other hand they took the opposite view when dealing with a progressive policy on the home front.

This appeared to be an indirect reference to Churchill's anti-Soviet speech in 1947 while at Fulton in America. In closing Moffat "reminded the delegates that the Movement, whilst supporting the Government, always reserved the right to criticise when that was necessary". It was seconded by George Middleton for Glasgow Trades Council, who stressed the role that should be played by the United Nations which was "still in its infant stages" where the mistakes of the

League of Nations must not be repeated. In his view the present trend was

> providing a close tie-up and alliance with American imperialism which would lead to undue dependence on the capitalist economy of the USA and would eventually have a serious effect on full employment prospects in Britain.

Delegates speaking in support of the resolution included J F Muir of Dundee Trades Council, deprecating "the American economic penetration in Greece and Turkey". Percy Belcher, General Secretary of the Tobacco Workers, had just been in touch with the Greek trade union movement, and deplored British support of the restored Greek Government using force against the Greek resistance movement which had openly opposed the German occupiers, while trade unionists were now "being arrested and done to death". J W Brown, AEU, also supported, especially on economic grounds of the need to expand trade with the Socialist countries and their planned economy, since a slump within two years was foreseen in the USA. Those who opposed on behalf of the GC included the Railway Clerk, Robertson, and the new General Secretary, Murdoch, and also J Benstead, Railwayman. Robertson denied "that we have become a mere satellite of the USA", adding

> Indeed, Ernest Bevin on several occasions has taken a different line from that pursued by America and this suggestion of an Anglo-American tie-up is mere wishful thinking on the part of those who, for their own ends, desire to see the creation of a Soviet-British bloc directed against the USA.

Benstead took the same line, insisting that there was "not the slightest intention of entering an American or Russian bloc". He added that "once we veer either to Moscow or Washington then you can condemn the British foreign policy". Murdoch said that nothing had changed since the previous year's support of the Government's foreign policy, and to pass the motion would "be tantamount to stabbing Attlee in the back" whom they had just received with enthusiasm. The vote was indeed close, it being lost by 166 to 158 with few abstentions.

Delegates listened closely to Attlee and Cripps who detailed the considerable difficulties facing them to get the essential maximum production needed to carry out reconstruction and all the Social Welfare measures. In major debates, however, delegates continued to express dissatisfaction at the slow rate of attracting industry to Scotland, calling for compulsory direction of industries. On nationalisation they called for workers' control on the Administrative Boards and at workshop level; and in addition a resolution was passed to examine "present methods of management within industry" to get machinery for adequate training to equip employees "to take a greater share" in management.

In the debates stress was laid on the need for heavy industries because of grave concern at the developing mass unemployment, with full maintenance for the unemployed. The background to this was the major strike of Glasgow dockers against redundancy. More than 3,000 of them were still out after a month. For nearly a year there had been a major dispute on Clydeside because after a local investigation 800 dockers were said to be redundant, owing to the Glasgow Dock Labour Scheme losing money. Under the threat of notices issued to 500 men some 3,000 Glasgow dockers came out on strike for 40 days on 24 March, supported by the Scottish Transport Workers' Union. They had offered to return to work if notices were suspended pending a further investigation, but this was refused. They were mainly interested in the proper pre-war allocation of workers being restored to the Clyde, having already seen 1,800 of the wartime dock force allowed to go. With 5,500 members affiliated, the Scottish Transport Workers Union thereupon sent a deputation to the GC, asking their help in bringing about a resumption of negotiations. With the Minister of Labour, Isaacs, saying that the question of redundancy could not be reopened nationally and the National Joint Council proposing reinstatement of less than half of those under notice, the strike continued. In a statement to Congress on the consultations which took place, Murdoch stressed the limitation of the STUC's powers; they "could not under any circumstances pass judgment on an industrial dispute". They believed that there must be regard to the established machinery in any industry, but "were willing to give assistance where possible". He said they had merely acted on the established principle that "the status quo should prevail until a settlement", and had attempted to get negotiations resumed, as they had been asked to do. However, W McGinniss, General & Municipal Workers, was "perturbed about the future possibilities of the STUC being asked to be judges in respect of any stoppage at work". The Conciliation Department of the Ministry of Labour was always available: "it would be dangerous procedure to take up the cudgels and be asked to deal with the merits or demerits of a claim". He stressed that "this Congress should not be turned into a seat of judgment". Approval of the GC's statement was accepted unanimously at the end of the debate, which was taking place in the presence of Sir Stafford Cripps, President of the Board of Trade, the next speaker. The day after Congress ended 2,000 London dockers came out in support of the Glasgow men, who finally returned to work shortly afterwards with notices temporarily withdrawn from all 500. The whole incident was an indication of awakening grass-roots anxieties in Jubilee Year, for similar problems were lying ahead even under a Labour Government.

In these circumstances and after fifty years it was perhaps also an appropriate occasion to consider any review of the Constitution. Beside the old but unsuccessful attempt to control grass-roots activists by trying again to introduce the block vote, a proposal was made aimed at democratising proceedings and cutting out unseemly bargaining at Congress. This was to elect the Standing Orders Committee after due prior nomination at one Congress charged with preparing both the Preliminary and Final Agenda for the next Congress. It followed upon an occasion at the 1946 Congress when a motion of the Scottish Miners had been withheld and not printed; on that occasion Elger's arguments in defence of his action were rejected by Congress. The proposed constitutional change was moved for Aberdeenshire Trades Council by James Milne, a young delegate who nearly thirty years later was himself to be elected General Secretary. On this occasion the amendment he proposed was to be defeated; it was to be nineteen years before the change was finally adopted.

Section (iii): **Steps Towards Change in Scotland**

For the next half dozen years STUC delegates had to concentrate on two main issues, which increasingly began to be seen to be interdependent. On the one hand there was the deterioration of international relations with their threat to peace; this had its worsening effect on the already dire economic needs. It was the economy which demanded urgent special action in Scotland and it was over this that the STUC finally came to be recognised as taking the principled nationwide stand. In doing so, it forced recognition that it was the organised working people who were the true voice of Scotland. The STUC itself could no longer be undervalued when it was seen to be able to unite compatriots generally in determined action. As we shall see this development coincided yet again with new thinking and new personalities. Before turning to the main process in detail, it is useful to see what were the real post-war preoccupations amongst Scottish working people.

An immediate concern when the many plans and Bills were being worked out was that the Labour Government's promised reforms in production and ownership of key industries should be implemented by being structured towards social change. That, after all, had been the aim of the STUC's founding fathers as against the British TUC Radical-Liberals. Now attitudes had changed with the times following the consequences of unity in winning the war against German fascism and its reactionary sympathisers elsewhere. The prevailing mood amongst Scottish trade unionists was that "now was the day!"; and that social changes to lay the basis for Socialism rather than merely far-reaching reforms in economic practices were immediately possible. Opponents of activists expressing this mood described them as "Impossiblists" and sometimes even questioned their motives. This in general might be regarded as the usual Right versus Left attitudes, or of the London official hierarchy ganging up against rank and file; but it has to be noted that in Scotland the new and potentially unifying factor was growing, which continued and developed long after the defeat of the Labour Government in 1951. This was the increasing and over-riding understanding of the need for a very considerable increase of employment opportunity to be opened up in Scotland, which it appeared was being by-passed. There was now no Labour Secretary for Scotland of the standing and with the background of Thomas Johnston who addressed Congress in 1944. National independence came to be seen as being at stake. After all, the struggle for national independence was to be seen in many former colonial countries in Africa, India, the Middle East and above all the Far East, where the Chinese People's Revolution was forcing the previous rulers off the mainland to the island of Formosa (Taiwan), despite the support of the United States.

At the same time, the break-up by the war of many countries' economies and their reconstruction, involving immense changes into developing imperialist multinational firms, raised the question, could any Government centred in Westminster be relied upon to take Scotland's needs seriously by practical measures? The old trend of the working-class movement to switch from reliance on political pressure when disillusioned with industrial direct action, and vice versa, could become overshadowed in Scotland by seeking measures to guarantee national independence; in this some supporters even lost sight of the whole class question by their ideas of separatism. To keep effective defence of both working-class interests and national independence which were recognised as interdependent, needed as a first step the widest recognition of the STUC as the authoritative voice of all workers north of the border. Hitherto for many years under Elger's leadership the STUC tended to be treated merely as an offshoot of the British TUC. Now there were new objective possibilities for changing this attitude. Wartime had accentuated the crucial importance of all trade unionists; now the need for filling countless positions in the new administrative boards, nationally and regionally, began to affect attitudes in the Whitehall corridors of power. The lure of governmental office under a Labour Government also tended to draw off some hard-bitten "Old Guard" representatives, usually with the enthusiastic support of their own Executives. If new leaders emerged capable of new thinking and adaptability there could be marked development of the STUC's reputation and influence. In the spring of 1948 Charles Murdoch and the Chairman, David Robertson of the Railway Clerks, left to take up full-time administrative posts, Murdoch joining the Gas Board. Elected to take office as General Secretary on 2 May, 1948 was George Middleton, for years the Glasgow Trades Council delegate; and James Jack remained his able Assistant Secretary, later to develop even further his considerable skills as a research worker. Middleton set about building up on the objective possibilities, being determined to put the STUC "on the map" in every way that could be worked.

The new General Secretary took office at an extremely difficult time for the Labour Government and when attitudes in general were changing at uneven speed, demanding no small measure of tact in handling and regulating response to events. The tightening of the "dollar strings" of the Marshall Plan, as it effected penetration of both Europe and the British Empire, increased the difficulties confronting the Government as it neared the end of its five years of office by 1950. Quite apart from the problems of the division between the two new States of India and Pakistan, foreign policy came to involve resistance to continued actions for independence by the colonial peoples of the Commonwealth, not least in Malaya, the Middle East and Africa: that was bound to mean that the detested conscription continued, with all its cost in financial and human terms, let alone the consequences of later rearmament. All this and the difficulty of recovering the essential export trade, which accounted for the policy of wage restraint, demanded as a minimum severe control of prices and of ever-mounting profits, if it were to be temporarily acceptable. Increasingly grass-roots reaction was that the Labour Government's guarantee on such control failed to be honoured. How, some asked, could that lead to the promised "social change"?

Amongst the activists in the trade union movement there had also been much surprise and anger at the peacetime use of the emergency powers created under the wartime Defence Regulations against the dockers when they went on strike. Again, it was repeated six months later when dockers took international solidarity action in support of visiting Canadian seamen: their union had been taken over by what they regarded as a gangster set-up from the United States, which co-operated with the Canadian employers. Simultaneously the beginning of the McCarthy witch-hunting process in America, as well as the Labour Government's apparent reluctance on political grounds to develop speedily east-west trade with the Socialist countries and the new China, were seen by many to be echoed in Britain at the Bridlington British TUC in September, 1949. Having withdrawn from the World Federation of Trade Unions, the British TUC's GC had also issued a statement, in almost unprecedented harsh terms, denouncing "the malignant character of Communist agitation and organisation". It referred to "evil machinations which threaten the economic recovery of the country"; and went on to urge all trade union committees and officers to "counteract every manifestation of Communist influences"; the process of "blacklisting" thenceforth also spread to Scotland. It was carried by a considerable majority: amongst the delegates present at Bridlington were some thirty Scots, including five GC members, who three weeks later were to go up to Aberdeen for their own long-delayed Fifty-Second Congress.

There were a number of reasons for the eighteen months delay between the Congresses. In 1949 Standing Orders agreed that the GC should be empowered to make arrangements to avoid clashing with municipal elections expected early in May, 1949. Drawing on the William Elger Memorial Fund, new offices were opened at 12 Woodlands Terrace in December, 1948, when the veteran, Charles Gallie, unveiled a portrait to William Elger, reading a special tribute by Vincent Tewson, the British TUC's General Secretary, "to his long and valued friendship" with Elger. It took George Middleton, the new General Secretary with a very different background, nine months to settle in, in every sense. At Aberdeen, after Middleton had reported that 394 delegates represented affiliated membership of 729,390, both the highest on record, Councillor William McGinniss opened his Presidential Address by referring to the election of the new General Secretary in the following terms:

> His application for and acceptance into membership of the Labour Party should dispel any doubts that may have existed in Scottish Trade Union circles as to his politics; and in the circumstances his appointment as General Secretary will, I feel, result in the continuance of the responsibility and dignity of the STUC.

Many delegates were aware that for some years George Middleton had occupied the position of industrial organiser of the Scottish Communist Party.

Section (iv): **The New General Secretary's First Year**

The preparation of the GC's Report was of course his responsibility, covering no less than eighteen months, during part of which he had also been Chairman, so there was not unnaturally much time devoted to discussion on it. Delegates certainly had complaints about failure to process forcibly or effectively the previous decisions in discussion on the need for more nationalisation and better methods of running industries already taken over. But it was also clear that there had been a great deal of tactful influence exerted to reduce contention as far as possible, with obvious awareness of the approaching General Election. Whilst some GC members tended to regard any voicing of criticism of the Labour Government as due to minds "warped by dictation from the Cominform", in the words of the President, there was evidence of attempts to avoid expressing such an attitude. This was to be seen in the number of GC motions compositing points from many submitted on key issues. In the forefront were those on Industry in Scotland and the White Paper on Scottish Affairs, on the pressure for Production and Exports, and above all on Devaluation.

This had just been announced after the GC had issued their motion on Production and Exports, bound now to be affected by the critical situation arising from devaluation, on which an emergency resolution was to follow. Their first resolution repeated their 1948 conditions to stimulate greater output and asked for "the utmost flexibility" in export trade: it included the Miners' welcome of the recent unconditional trade agreement with Poland, which should be extended to all willing to exchange "goods for goods". Indeed, it was so worded that James Carmichael, MP, Life Assurance Workers, said he "wondered how anyone could emphatically support or oppose every line of it. It had been framed to suit all manner of opinions." It did however give scope for many examples of difficulties to be raised, especially from Glasgow, Edinburgh and Aberdeen Trades Councils before it was passed unanimously. When the emergency motion on Devaluation was prepared, it was again very tactfully worded, compositing many suggestions from delegations; but the GC refused to accept one submitted by the Miners and it became an amendment. The GC's motion, while expressing "the utmost confidence in the efforts of the Government to surmount the present difficulties", remained "greatly disturbed at the probable effects of devaluation on the standard of living". It spoke in general terms of the need for the "strictest possible control of prices" and for legislation to deal with those who would be "increasing prices unnecessarily". To this Abe Moffat moved the

Miners' amendment of direct and emphatic protest "against the policy of devaluation and increased prices" as being "in complete conflict with the fundamental policy of trade unionism". He asked:

> What was the difference between a direct wage reduction and an indirect reduction on the basis of increasing prices?

He concluded that they should "fight the Tories now, during and after the election on the basis of defending the living standards of the working class in Scotland". Support for the amendment came from the Dundee, Glasgow and Greenock Trades Councils, the Boilermakers and the Electricians; and then Middleton came in with a tactful and successful intervention. He pointed out that devaluation was "already a *fait accompli*" and it had been taken "to meet a particular situation". Their concern now should be how to protect the purchasing power, which was "as implicit in the motion as in the amendment". He won a defeat of the amendment and final acceptance of the resolution by 235 to 88. The devaluation debate was immediately followed by a very long and skilful fraternal address from Harold Wilson, MP, of the Board of Trade, explaining that the return of another Labour Government would at least guarantee full employment. This pre-Election speech included nothing on which they would disagree, except perhaps in urging that negotiating on differentials should not follow increases to the low paid. Earlier the Secretary of State for Scotland, Arthur Woodburn, MP, had carried somewhat less conviction when dealing with Scottish industry, as we discuss in the next chapter.

There were other reasons seen for unemployment that 1949 Congress. In a first move in Scotland on the struggle for peace, which as we shall see later was to take on outstanding importance, a motion declared that

> our economic resources should not be wasted on rearmament but concentrated on the peaceful reconstruction

Moved by J C Hill, for Glasgow Trades Council, with support from the General Secretary of the Constructional Engineers, Jack Stanley, it was backed up with grim details of the local effects already felt from Councillor Arnold Henderson of Clydebank Trades Council. But it was defeated by 189 to 139, with Hill complaining that "the slightest criticism" of policy was treated as "an attack on the Government". This certainly emerged in a debate on reference back of the Report on how the Airdrie Trades Council had been disaffiliated when all trades councils had been told that they were not to attend a Conference in

October 1948 called by the Scottish USSR Society. Jack Stanley, General Secretary of the Constructional Engineers, pointed out that it was a similar body to the British-Soviet Society, "as during the war, the Societies were trying to promote better relations between the two countries" and that, a few years earlier, MPs, Cabinet Ministers and statesmen supported it. Delegates from Glasgow, Greenock and Clydebank Trades Councils all complained, and asked the reason the GC had "proscribed the Society". Middleton repeated his softly-softly style, saying that the GC had decided it would be contrary to the terms of the Trades Council Handbook, under which they were empowered to say whether or not an organisation was to be recognised. Again he won support from Congress, which rejected reference back by 170 to 104. The ban was still in operation the following year, and it was not until six years later that relations became normal, with exchange of Scottish and Soviet delegates beginning in 1956, at first in connection with expanding Scottish trade. Back in the 1949 Aberdeen Congress on the last day W Murray of Clydebank Trades Council moved a resolution urging the GC itself "to convene an early delegate conference", which should "determine ways and means of starting off a great Peace Crusade". He urged them to visit Clydebank to see "eight years after the blitz, the result of two nights' bombing, which had cost the town 1,100 lives". When Bothwell for the GC opposed it as being unnecessary, J D Hughes of the Shop Assistants (USDAW) said it "was up to them to establish a means by which a peace conference could be held without its origins being suspect. Irrespective of ideologies they should examine every possibility of peace." The motion was accepted; and how it was followed up we shall see in the next chapter, as in Scotland the hostility and division still apparent at Aberdeen began to be overcome. There was one happy note struck. H L Bullock, the visiting Chairman of the British TUC, presented its Silver Badge to Jeannie Spence, a foundation member of the Dundee Jute & Flax Workers Union, which was founded in 1906. She had recruited hundreds in her forty years' membership, before which she had been in Mary McArthur's National Federation of Women Workers. For two years in succession, she had been runner-up in the British TUC's Gold Badge Competition.

But before they were to meet at Rothesay in 1950, the Labour Government's big post-war majority was reduced to a minimum; and within eighteen months yet another General Election saw the Tories again in office, where they were to remain for thirteen years.

References

[1] *Times*, 9 May, 1947

[2] Quoted in a useful article "What 'Marshall' Means" in *Labour Research Department*, February 1948.

20

Defending Scotland's Industry and Peace

The shape of things to come for Scotland nationally, economically and politically after the immense changes enforced by World War II would have to depend upon how the country was to earn a living, whichever political party held office in Westminster. There had to be real progress away from the deadly pre-war story of mass unemployment, the devastating extent of which was masked by tragic emigration whether overseas or south of the border. The dislocation of the tremendous turnover from Scotland's wartime industrial base to the new peacetime economy was now on. Finally, only the STUC was to carry out the major consistent battle on this; at long last that came to be recognised. The vital point to note is that from 1949 the start made was never abandoned.

It required foresight, persistence, widespread education, a break with old methods of mere formal "processing" of decisions, together with practical proposals for new Scottish administrative machinery. At long last this began to be forthcoming, although there were to be all too many often ineffective boards, councils and authorities emerging after White Papers and Ministerial statements; to some delegates most of these came to seem only for the purpose of heading off criticism.[1]

But there was initiative shown by those whose Socialist background gave a basic approach to Scotland's problems. One of these was Tom Johnston, Secretary for Scotland during the latter part of the war. When in wartime total public control of production was operated through Regional Production Boards, with some degree of worker participation, Tom Johnston used his initiative to set up a "Standing Industrial Conference Committee for Scotland", where trade unionists were invited to advise him. This made it possible for trade union representatives on the Scottish Regional Production Board to see that action would be taken on decisions; when there were some determined to follow up openings, it could even put teeth into the "Scottish Council on Industry", which in pre-war days had proved so ineffective. Indeed, within two years, the STUC's 1944 President, the printer James Crawford (NATSOPA), had to praise the current activities of the Scottish Office under Johnston, saying that it was due to him that "the

Scottish Office did not function on the assumption that Scotland was a mere suburb of London". But Johnston was not to continue long in office and his successors were of different calibre. Yet the door had at least been opened for those who would push: it was high time, for redundancies had already begun by 1944 at Clydebank.

Section (i): **Would New Administrative Machinery Work?**

With the end of the war came a series of White Papers on Employment and similar titles and the Distribution of Industry Act, early in 1945, with the awareness of the consequences of the closing of the factories which had been dispersed all over Britain. It was under this that the Development Areas together with "collective sites", or industrial estates, were set up. The GC issued responses to the White Papers and various enactments, which were usually supported by Congress. Here was reaffirmed year after year the general policy on location of industry, in debates which brought out the manifold problems both in general and in specific industries.[2]

The basic argument which invariably arose was whether financial inducements would be enough, or whether compulsory direction of firms to open up north of the border was essential. Opponents of direction tended to claim from time to time that it was unnecessary; or, more basically, that it might involve also legal direction of labour. But it was soon seen that the pace of inducement was too slow. The selection of industry was unbalanced; firms accepted inducement to set up not their decisive headquarters but merely branches, which were then closed in critical times; financial advantage could be unscrupulously taken of inducement; and finally no "fair share" of the Government's own undertakings was allocated to Scotland. Sometimes it was strongly argued at Congress in the immediate post-war years that the GC and officers were failing to find new methods of pressure, merely accepting brush-offs and unacceptable answers from Whitehall. In such circumstances, new factors had to come into play. With colonial countries taking up arms for national liberation before their dire economic problems could be tackled, it would indeed have been surprising if in Scotland also nationalism should not come to be felt by some to be the crucial question.

The prevalence of the mood which was developing began to be expressed as early as the 1946 Congress in a debate on the slow rate of progress in view of the increasing Scottish unemployment, with the older men recalling "the chaotic position" after the First World War. Speaking then as delegate for Glasgow Trades Council, George

Middleton said that Congress should take a very strong stand, without which "we would have a resurgence of Scottish Nationalism". The next year it began to come up in mild form in motions submitted. Congress unanimously passed a resolution from the Scottish Horse and Motormen calling on the Government to consider setting up "a Scottish body, with special powers", with the aim of "a wider measure of autonomy". Speaking to it in the presence of Premier Attlee, the Railway Clerk, George Younger, said "we should not leave the question of Scottish autonomy to our opponents in Westminster". When after long delay they were told that it was "not opportune" to set up a Committee of Enquiry into this and the GC began therefore holding regional conferences, it was clear that the mood developed sharply. At the 1948 Congress it was agreed at the request of the Railwaymen that a resolution on Scottish Nationalism should be referred to the new GC. Its wording ran as follows:

> Recognising that Socialism is international, deplores the trend towards Scottish Nationalism which is revealing itself in the Scottish Trade Union Movement, and driving us to support uneconomic projects. Congress believes that Scottish culture and traditions will be preserved by their own strength and virility without the need for exploiting Nationalistic sentiments. Congress therefore considers the movement should only support and initiate projects which utilise the natural resources of Scotland and are economically sound.

When the White Paper proposed a merely advisory Scottish Economic Conference allowing "no provision for the outlet of Scottish initiative or full expression of Scottish views and desires in relation to Scottish affairs", a sharply worded resolution moved by Glasgow Trades Council was carried. It demanded "immediate administrative reforms", including: a Scottish National Planning Commission; new Departments of Trade and Labour with Under-Secretaries in Scotland for each; and

> a Scottish "Cabinet" consisting of the Secretary of State, the Under-Secretaries and the Scottish representatives of Government Departments.

In broad terms that was the mood frequently repeated in the next years, although with different wording and emphasis as the Scottish Convention movement grew or dwindled.

At the 1949 Congress there were complaints of insufficient response when the Secretary for Scotland totally rejected their comments on the White Paper, with Abe Moffat for the Miners adding that what was now needed was a major public campaign. Glasgow Trades Council and the Scottish dockers' delegate moved reference back of the GC's Report which covered eighteen long months. Complaining that there had been no effective follow-up deputation, they warned that there was a growing feeling that, lacking a "Scottish Cabinet", it would be found that "the final answer was a form of self-government". For the GC Middleton then assured Moffat that they would consider his "reasoned statement" for public campaigning, but he asked for rejection of the reference back. He argued that in what they did they "had to get rid of the idea that in giving consideration to Scottish affairs they were associating themselves with the Scottish Nationalists". He asked Congress "to appreciate that the GC were faced with a heavy responsibility when presented with a resolution so tightly packed with important matters of this kind". On this he won agreement. But a later resolution on Industry in Scotland was carried unanimously, moved by a progressive member of the GC, the Railway Clerk, J G Bothwell. It called for "a new approach" from the Government, detailing a number of specific economic issues.[3] In the debate on it, the main criticism was from Councillor Johnston of Glasgow Trades Council; for him "the whole issue hinged on the direction of industry", which he believed the GC were no longer pressing for, while the existing machinery for locating industry in Scotland "was largely negative".

This was certainly being emphasised by Scottish Nationalists; and at the 1950 Congress the GC felt it necessary to take the warning further. Congress was asked to reject a Glasgow Trades Council amendment to reaffirm the 1948 declaration on the White Paper and demand "a wider measure for self-determination"; and also a Miners' more explicit demand for "a Scottish Parliament to deal with Scottish affairs and to be linked up with the United Kingdom". Congress accepted by 243 to 78 a different emphasis. This stressed that while the STUC had "more than an ordinary interest in the movements purporting to espouse the cause of the Scottish people against their alleged domination by the British Parliament", it was economic security which remained "the primary factor for the Scottish people". This was

> inseparable from that of England and Wales and it cannot be imagined as a self-supporting entity.

It followed that the STUC "had no desire nor intention to farm out its responsibilities". Their foremost interest

> must be the creation of a healthy economic structure yielding good wages and attractive working conditions.

After the argumentation had been sharp and contradictory, the new General Secretary intervened to lay emphasis on specific issues, such as whether Scotland was getting her fair share of Exchequer grants to local authorities or paying more than her fair share in the uniform fiscal system. On such questions they needed widespread and clearer understanding. He also said that it might be necessary to

> introduce forms of administrative devolution, but not legislative devolution for Scotland.

This later was to be more fully spelt out and become the significant central point in the many future statements and declarations.

Section (ii): **The Highlands and the Royal Commission**

In point of fact Middleton was already setting on foot very considerable public campaigning and education. He concentrated on specific issues which could be won or at least upon which no British Government, of whatever complexion, could deny were essentially of Scottish concern, both urgent and incapable of solution without Scottish knowledge and expertise. There followed many important regional conferences; very much fuller reports to affiliates; a great mass of valuable research for which James Jack was responsible. As one result many local authorities began to find themselves deeply involved, regardless of what political party was in control. This indeed was the new pattern beginning; and it was soon clear to the various "advisory bodies" what they must henceforth expect. By the end of 1952 it was no longer possible for the government of the day to do other than set up a Royal Commission on Scottish affairs, if in very general terms.[4] To this the STUC's evidence was brief but definitive: in course of time it opened up the prospect of devolution being put on a realistic footing.

Their written evidence, submitted in January 1953, indicated their concern, expressed ever since the foundation by the many resolutions on the issues involved. They explained details of two with special point. Firstly that in 1899 they had urged the then government to set up a branch of the Board of Trade for Scottish Affairs, because of "differences existing in the industrial conditions between England and Scotland". Next, they pointedly quoted the terms of their demand as long ago as 1936 for a Royal Commission

> to enquire into the powers and practices of the existing authorities and

> into the advisability of establishing a national administrative and rating body for Scotland.

It was then believed necessary because the way public affairs were administered and the large number of local authorities was "both a drag upon efficient administration and an obstacle in the way of democratic development in our social and economic life". Indeed, at the 1936 Congress even that had been regarded by some trades council delegates as not going far enough. In seconding an unsuccessful amendment which doubted that the Chamberlain Government "could be relied upon to deal with the matter effectively", A H Paton, for Edinburgh Trades Council, had thought it "simply ragged-trousered philanthropy towards the governing class". After explaining that the then Secretary for Scotland, Walter Elliot, did not think there was "any general desire for an enquiry", the STUC evidence gave the facts about their resolutions on the 1948 White Paper on Scottish Affairs and the Economic Conference and its collapse and subsequent debates. They especially stressed the position of the Highlands, "a problem which has engaged the attention of many and varied interests". They commented on the later efforts to get a Highland Regional Authority with powers appointed, followed by the subsequent "Programme of Highland Development", submitted by the Secretary of State; but to carry through those measures in their view there was "need for some form of co-ordinating body"; they therefore asked the Royal Commission to "give sympathetic consideration", in this definitive statement:

> The multiplicity of authorities responsible for various branches of Highland development emphasises the need for the appointment of a Regional Authority for the Highlands or the creation of a small full-time Committee at St Andrew's House whose duty would be to co-ordinate planning and to investigate delays that hold up progress.

Just before the 1953 Congress opened at Rothesay, Chairman A D MacKellar and George Middleton as General Secretary gave oral evidence to the Royal Commission at Edinburgh on 10 April.

They answered questions elaborating their position on their three main points: the resuscitation of the long-inactive Scottish Economic Conference; more administrative devolution; and a Regional Development Corporation for the Highlands. They needed the Economic Conference for essential "interchange of information" on trends and developments economically important to Scotland. They had pointed out that the percentage of the insured population out of work in Scotland was twice that of England and Wales: also Scottish workers had a lower net output, due to less capital equipment behind them. This was "a serious impediment"; and "Government policy had restricted investment in new plant". They needed "an appropriate pattern of new industries", instancing chemicals, plastics, synthetic fabrics; and were "sadly lacking" in designing staff and production capacity. Shipbuilding Draughtsman, MacKellar was well-equipped to know about technical shortages, both from his own experience and from information supplied by the Scientific Workers through Dr Lilli Stein, soon to become a valuable candidate for the GC. They explained to the Royal Commissioners "that Scotland's deficiency in precision engineering acted as a brake on electronic and similar types of development"; and told them that what was needed was

> an industrial strategy about what industries we want and what assistance should be given to those already placed. Branches of parent firms in Canada, America or England were not very secure.

All of that, they argued, a revived Economic Conference could assess and the Secretary of State could then press for.

Asked about transferring functions of some Ministries to Scotland, they explained they wanted more bodies like the already established Scottish Departments of Agriculture, Health and Education, to give more administrative devolution in other fields. When the Commissioners, having had proposals from elsewhere about setting up a separate Scottish Parliament, asked their view of this they made firm reply: "Congress was very strongly in favour of the maximum administrative devolution, but not legislative devolution"; fiscal and trade policies made separation from England impracticable, they felt. In support of that they quoted the Catto Committee finding "insuperable difficulties in trying to devise workable methods of estimating Scotland's share in the visible and invisible trade".

Finally the STUC representatives returned to the problems of the Highlands and Islands, about which Lord Home had been obliged to give assurances that the Government would do all in its power to increase beef and mutton production and develop all agricultural possibilities there. But the main issue, their spokesman had said, was "who was going to be responsible for this development?" That was why they urged a Development Corporation for the Highlands, as in the new towns. It would be the over-riding authority financed by the Government "to carry through a specific job"; after which, it would withdraw and "responsibility would then revert to the elected authorities".

Congress welcomed the written and oral evidence given, and called for vigorous campaigning for its support. This was already planned; it was followed up by frequent area Conferences, not least on the Highlands question; the proposals for that stimulated campaigning in other especially deprived Scottish areas and industries. Moreover, of its nature it had to involve action amongst local authorities to counter the line the Government was to develop that many burghs would object to a Highland Development Corporation, even though its responsibility was seen only as temporary. When the Royal Commissioners finally made their Report it was clearly the Highlands proposals that they found greatest difficulty in resisting. On all the many specific issues which the STUC now began to campaign, this battle for the Highlands was the first breakthrough which was to point the way.

Meanwhile the whole issue of Scottish Industry and the administrative devolution to achieve it had played a big part in putting the STUC on the map. As the ex-President A D MacKellar at the 1954 Congress pointed out, referring to the Royal Commission, it was the STUC alone which submitted the proposal.

> which would justify their optimism in seeking to rehabilitate the Highlands. They believed in a planned economy and that a Development Corporation must be created. That was the only way in which they could restore to the Highlands some semblance of its past.

He was seconding a resolution on Industry, Trade and Employment; by then the STUC was forced to face up to the need for more international trade to offset reduction of exports, under the increasing cloud of wars and even threat to international peace. For by now British troops were, or had been, involved in hostilities in Greece, Malaya, Korea, Kenya and Tanganyika – and indeed more to come, including in the British Isles themselves, with the development of German rearmament.

Section (iii): **Peace Under Attack**

For the STUC to become recognised as the prime mover of all action for national progress did not solely depend upon its battle to build Scotland's economy on a new and effective basis. Their work for a new economy could not stand alone: it had to be linked with campaigning to prevent Scotland being drawn into yet another war. But it took years before the STUC would finally be recognised as a decisive force in Scotland taking the lead in the struggle for peace between the peoples of the world. For a long time there were mistakes, sad misunderstandings and political differences before this could be seen to be achieved. We must now study their reaction to the main issues developing over a dozen years.

The Americans had not yet dropped the world's first atom bombs on two Japanese cities when the 1945 Congress met at Aberdeen. Delegates were then clear about what must be done, when the German army was on the point of surrender. One emergency resolution demanded that all "war criminals must be punished", and steps taken to ensure "that no vestige of Fascism remains". In seconding the GC's motion, a Fire Brigades' delegate, E McIntosh said "Germany should not only be defeated in the field but should have taken from her the power ever again to go on the road of aggression"; and he warned that "German Fascists were being left in control". A second emergency resolution on the torture and concentration camps demanded that "summary justice should be executed on all those who have been responsible for such unspeakable outrages against humanity". Both were passed unanimously. Yet nearly 40 years later in 1984 the Jewish Documentation Centre in Vienna which had been attempting to track down those responsible for atrocities in such camps, was to claim that only some 50,000 out of 150,000 war criminals were ever tried; and that there were still some 15,000 living under false names, often in different parts of the world.

While at the STUC Congress in their Jubilee Year of 1947 the spokesmen for the Labour Government were denying that there was any question of the foreign policy driving Britain to become part of either a West or East Bloc, it was clear that the picture was fast changing by the early 'fifties. In less than ten years after those 1945 resolutions, delegates had cause to protest at the setting up in the Western zone of a new German army, soon to be part of the NATO forces. Indeed, the detested conscription was still in operation sixteen years after it was first brought in. At first the hostilities in which they were engaged were primarily confined to the colonial areas with countries seeking independence in the Third World and Palestine. But by 1950 the most dangerous war began in Korea. This certainly threatened a direct clash between the two blocs. For the background to the civil war in Korea, whose northern border is China's Manchuria, was the total victory of the new Chinese People's Republic over the old regime headed by the United States ally, Chiang Kai Shek: he had been forced from the mainland onto the island of Formosa (Taiwan). Ruling circles in the United States, which was much beset at the time by the McCarthy witch-hunting scares, feared that old-style regimes in all the previous colonies of the Far East would fall like "a collapsing line of dominoes". In 1945 American troops had moved into the south of

Korea to take over from the occupying Japanese forces. In the north of Korea the Soviet forces had driven the Japanese out, with Koreans thereupon setting up people's committees and beginning their own government; this was similar to what happened in East Europe beyond "the iron curtain" which Winston Churchill so described (borrowing the phrase from the Nazi propaganda Minister Goebbels). Efforts for reconstruction and to gain a united Korea were now at stake. Finally in June 1950 hostilities began between the North Koreans and the old regime in South Korea where an émigré from the USA, Singman Rhea, had been brought over and put in charge. The US troops then acted in support of the South Korean regime.[5] Years later it came to be seen by many as a pre-run of the disastrous US involvement in Vietnam. The four-year war was conducted by South Korea with military support of what were later to be known as "peace-keeping forces". In supreme command was the American General with major units, but in the name of the United Nations, from membership of which the Peoples Republic of China was still excluded. But since the United Nations' Security Council was designed to turn on the permanent members from the five great anti-fascist Powers – the USA, the USSR, Great Britain, France and China – its role as a peace-keeping authority was thus already deeply undermined. In deciding to deploy troops to support the South Korean regime the Security Council had acted outwith its rules, the Soviet delegate being absent and China represented only by the Chiang Kai Shek regime.

Delegates to the STUC Congress soon began to concentrate on the need for an early negotiated peace, whatever differences they might have as to the rights and wrongs of its origin. They urged that the hostilities should at least be confined to that area, as both India and China suggested. They pressed for a truce, which should not be negotiated by the generals in the field but by a conference of the countries involved. That the Chiang Kai Shek regime should be excluded and the Chinese Republic given its rightful place on the Security Council they began to see as essential for the survival of the United Nations itself and the maintenance of world peace. But that lay ahead.

The Korean situation underlined all the fear about the threat of international relations worsening in so many different ways, not only in the Far East but in Europe too. Reactions to it all were many and varied as the progressive unity achieved during the war indeed became disrupted at home and abroad, as "the Cold War" began to take all too firm a hold. Hopes of East-West trade expanding, for example, became disappointed, much to Scotland's disadvantage. Effects reached the collapsing Labour Government itself: Harold Wilson resigned from the

Board of Trade, and so did Nye Bevan, the popular left-winger, from the Health Ministry, because the cost of rearmament was putting in jeopardy his nascent National Health Service, the great post-war social achievement. There was the further development of nuclear weaponry, with the Soviet Union now achieving atomic power and the USA producing and testing the even more horrific H-bomb. Was it possible that cold war between the wartime allies could become a hot war, and one with unthinkable consequences? To counter this, with the United Nations so visibly ineffective, there came demands for mass action of protest at grass roots. The World Peace Congress developed, met in Stockholm and issued a petition to ban atomic weapons which rapidly gathered nearly 4000 million signatures throughout the world. But it had strong support from the Soviet Union and was, therefore, hotly denounced as a Communist ploy in some quarters.

The STUC was not to be free of the confusion and political disarray, with some strange results and intrigues emerging. But in 1950 the general tone was still for action to promote peace in a nuclear world. There was a strongly positive lead from the Miners' Secretary, William Pearson, in his Presidential Address, being the sixth Scottish miner to hold that position. When he closed his speech on the subject of peace, which he saw as "linked with the fight for higher wages and improved conditions", he spoke of the "deadly fear of the weapons of mass destruction" in the troubled world. He had never before "witnessed such a campaign as that which has been going on in the press and on the radio in this country". He added:

> Deliberate attempts are being made to create and foster the idea that the Soviet Union endangers the peace of the world and little attention is given to the positive proposals made by that country.

He quoted what the leader of the Russian TUC had told a visiting Scottish miners' delegation, of how "the Soviet people resent such foul slanders". Strongly recommending delegates to support the resolution the GC was putting forward on the "Maintenance of Peace", he added:

> We live in a world where powerful Imperialist forces still exist and are agressively active. If nothing is done to curb them, these Imperialists will involve the world in war in order to maintain their system of profit-making and their domination and exploitation of millions of men and women throughout the world.
>
> It is only madmen and criminals who talk about using the atomic bomb and they should be treated in an appropriate manner, and their

> power to incite war taken away from them. You cannot have progress and war at one and the same time.

The Clerks' delegate, J C Reedie, congratulated the GC "for being the first authoritative body to give a lead which might achieve the solution of a tremendous problem". The 1950 resolution had called for the British Government – still then Labour – to appeal to the United Nations "with the passion and energy which the danger demands" to get East and West to agree on three points:

(a) A ban on the manufacture of the hydrogen bomb and all atomic weapons.
(b) The destruction of all existing stocks.
(c) International control of the sources of atomic power and its utilisation for peaceful purposes.

In the main body of the resolution it was also decided "to discuss and determine ways and means of starting off a great peace crusade". It was passed unanimously. But two days later, when the ballot for the next GC was announced it was found that Pearson, who was a leading Communist, had been manoeuvred off it, which had never previously happened to a sitting President. When Percy Belcher of the Tobacco Workers deplored this in his closing presentation, Pearson's reply was characteristic. He said his only regret about his exclusion from the GC was that the Mineworkers were therefore not represented. He added:

> Whether or not they were in high office, each had a duty to his class and he warned Congress that the moment they allowed either political or religious discrimination to enter Congress it would have a serious and detrimental effect upon the unity and purpose of their organisation.

The much-respected Scottish Miners' Secretary did not stand for STUC office again: it was left to John Wood and Alex Moffat to represent the miners on the GC for some years.

But there were unusual events when the unanimous resolution came to be processed by the GC under his successor as President, John Lang OBE, the Scottish Secretary of the Iron & Steel Trades Confederation. For in his 1951 Presidential Address Lang struck a very different note. In his view the Soviet Union had "by endless wrangling, obstruction and boycott prevented agreement being reached" at the United Nations. Such a truculent and unco-operative attitude proved "how spurious and unprincipled are the 'peace campaigns' of the Communist Parties in this and other countries". Speaking at the first STUC Congress after the Korean war had begun, he thought the war there "could be ended almost at once and the problem of beginning the establishment of a united democratic Germany could be resolved within a few months if the Soviet Union so desired".

What, then, had happened when the new GC set about processing the 1950 Rothesay resolution, lacking both Pearson and the progressive James Duncan of the Constructional Engineering Union, who had also been ejected from the ruling body? When they came to "seek the observations of the Prime Minister and the Secretary of State for Foreign Affairs upon the terms of the decision", the Government spokesman's reply was merely that all their three demands must depend entirely on an international system of control which involved inspection. Following upon that, on 12 June, 1950, the GC circulated all affiliates that they had asked the Scottish Council of the Labour Party to join in area conferences to approve a joint declaration. But meanwhile there must be no association with any activities "at present being conducted by an organisation calling itself 'the British Peace Committee' ". In the GC's view, to become identified with that would cause "confusion in our ranks . . . and would perhaps vitiate the efforts we are making in co-operation with the Labour Party". Yet just after the Korean hostilities began, the Scottish Labour Party withdrew from the proposal in July; the GC therefore decided to prepare for an area peace conference itself in Glasgow in October, with Hector McNeil, MP, Secretary for Scotland, as speaker. But meanwhile they forbade the Airdrie Trades Council to hold a local conference in August as part of the 1950 call to start "a Peace Crusade". Middleton explained that the original suggestion of a "crusade", made back in 1949 by Clydebank was too vague; and that in any event a local conference was unnecessary in view of the intended area conference in October.

When this one-day area conference did take place in St Andrew's Hall, Glasgow, there were 1931 delegates present, with 33 unions appointing 173 officers and 23 trades councils appointing 44 delegates. The GC put a long motion before them saying the United Nations' "moral authority and prestige" had been "immeasurably increased" because of

> the swift and purposeful intervention of the United Nations to halt the aggression of North Korea.

It also remarked that it was "highly gratified to learn that the war in Korea is drawing to a close". This was indeed premature, with several more bitter years to go before that was achieved. Referring to the danger of atomic weapons it repeated the Government statement on international control and inspection. The one-day area conference endorsed this, after the Miners, Painters, Scottish Horse & Motormen and a number of trades councils had complained that there was not enough time allowed for questions and discussion.

Section (iv): **Grass Roots and Peace Campaigning**

Very considerable differences and confusion throughout the movement were expressed when the 1951 Congress met at Dunoon and discussed both this Report and another quite new GC motion. The Bevan and Wilson resignations owing to the cuts in the Health Service and other post-war gains had just become known, which further underlined how widespread were the differences; Middleton announced on the first day that the GC had withdrawn the invitation to Bevan, who was to be replaced by Alf Robens, later to be all too well-known to the miners. That the majority of the GC were not opposed to the news expressed in Lang's Presidential Address was soon made clear. They insisted that they would not accept the many motions and agenda on aspects of peace and international relations; instead, these could be covered only in a single composite amendment to be moved by the Miners.

During the discussion on the Report itself, J C Hill for Glasgow Trades Council had supported the Airdrie Trades Council's complaint and then raised objections about the October area conference. It was the beginning of conflict with a number of trades councils which was to go to very considerable lengths in the course of the growing grass-roots pressure for effective action on peace. Putting it in moderate terms, J C Hill said there was a sense of disappointment about the result of their Rothesay resolution. When the point of view that it expressed had been put to the Government, the reply "did not represent any advance". Yet the GC had accepted that "and incorporated two sentences of the reply" in the resolution submitted to the Glasgow area peace conference. But that was the only implementation of the call for a great crusade, and that was limited only to west of Scotland branches. They were also entitled to question bringing in Hector McNeil as speaker. Middleton could only reply that they had not organised a further peace conference because they were already committed to three regional conferences on industry and employment. He did not mention to Congress that there was already brewing a situation which was to bring about the disaffiliation because of its peace activities of the Glasgow Trades Council, of which he himself had once been the secretary. There was some sharp discussion about events at Dundee Trades Council, where the GC had suspended the chairman and secretary for receiving a speaker from the League for Democracy in Greece, and appointed two new people to replace them.

The main differences, however, emerged during the debate on "The United Nations and Preservation of Peace" and the composite amendment. The motion was moved for the GC by the Railwayman, F Donachy. With the General Election only six months ahead, in which Churchill was to oust the Labour Government, the motion dealt with the need to defend Labour's position on rearmament. It expressed a firm belief in the United Nations, the need to "contain hostilities in Korea" and welcomed Four-Power talks which had just been mooted; in general, it was more moderate than that put over at the area peace conference six months earlier. It was also moved in moderate terms by the Railwayman, F Donachy; he was well aware of many different points of special concern, all forced into the miners' composite, which some of the sponsors would have preferred not to support. The seconder of the GC motion, however, had no such qualms: John Brannigan, of the Scottish Horse and Motormen, was himself at the time deep in problems in the leadership of his own union, with both political and sectarian hostility playing a part. His speech was confined solely to opposing the miners' amendment, which he regarded as "burlesque". He hoped that

> Congress was not going to become the sounding board of the Communists, the fellow-travellers and others in Britain who talked about peace, who could help to make peace but who all the time submitted to the dictates of the overlords of the Kremlin.

He repeated that he hoped the Movement "was not going to be prostituted" any longer by people "who know equally as well as any member of the General Council that the greatest opposition to the peace of the world was not ideologies – it was imperialistic Communism emanating from Russia". He trusted Congress would "not be sidestepped or fooled by the wording of the amendment".

The Miners' amendment which so alarmed Brannigan stressed first the need for the Government to press for a cease-fire in Korea "on terms of equality of all participants"; it hoped that the Four-Power talks would be extended to Five-Power talks; and that then the United Nations, with "the Chinese People's Government being accepted as the rightful representative of China", should reach agreement on all-round reduction of armaments and the banning of all atomic power weapons. It "emphatically rejected" any suggestion of the rearmament of Germany, "both East and West", or of Japan; and closed by referring to the urgent need for material assistance to raise the standard of living "of the backward races of the East", which should be organised through the United Nations. For the Miners, John Wood said it was a tragedy that the GC had refused when he had asked, during the Standing Orders Committee discussions, to include some reference to banning the atom bomb; or that China should be admitted to the United Nations; or that Germany should be disarmed. Seconding the amendment for Glasgow Trade Council, J C Hill laid emphasis on Bevan's reasons for resigning from office, which he believed showed that more and more people "were realising that there was an alternative policy to all-out rearmament". He closed by restating "the fundamental attitude of the Socialist Movement on the question of peace and war". He put it in these words:

> The fundamental cause of war was Capitalism, but that did not mean that Capitalism and Socialism had to fight it out or that Social Democracy and Communism had to fight it out. They stood for peaceful competition between the different systems of society, which itself would decide which was the stronger force and the system under which the people would live.

In the long run the STUC was seen in later years to take its stand closest to the view expressed in 1951 by Hill. But there was still much confusion to be cleared up and a long way to go. D Maxwell of the Sheet Metal Workers' main standpoint was that "rearmament was not the Labour Party's policy: they were being dragged into it by America". For America "was causing grave shortages all over the world by stockpiling". They were establishing military bases all over the world, and "Britain was America's aircraft carrier". R Irvine of the Engineers complained that the wholesale compositing prevented delegates dealing with each of the motions as they thought fit: delegates were "in the invidious position" of having to support the motion because there were some things in the amendment with which they disagreed. James Lenon for Cambuslang Trades Council was perturbed most by the proposed rearmament of Germany and Japan, and by the occupation by American forces and Chiang Kai Shek of Formosa, which was an integral part of China. Then came a contribution from Bailie James Duncan, Constructional Engineers, who had lost his seat on the GC at the same time as Pearson. He said they had to "find a road other than rearmament or accept a tremendously reduced standard of living". When he looked at the wording of both the motion and the amendment, he "wondered why there should be disagreement". While the motion was "practically a statement of fact with which almost every delegate could be in accord", he asked Congress to support the amendment because it contained positive statements which were missing from the motion. He was the only delegate who referred to Brannigan's speech, which he described as "nothing more or less than the popular theme song of the moment". Speaking of Brannigan's reference to submission to "the overlords of the Kremlin", Duncan said he was quite certain Britain would never do that; but, he added significantly,

> neither, he hoped, would they submit to the overlords of the White House nor of the Vatican.

But R Calderwood of the Co-operative Officials hoped the "Scottish Labour Movement was not going to be dragged into supporting amendments which cut across the policy of the Government". Bailie Meldrum of ASSET agreed, thinking the amendment should have been withdrawn. He thought solving the question of Germany "was the key to peace". It was the "main danger spot at the moment", and he blamed Russia for breaking the Potsdam Agreement by stopping traffic between East and West Germany.

Mrs Smith for Dundee Trades Council supported the amendment because of the lack of control of guaranteed profits in the armaments industry; the armament drive and American stockpiling had brought shortages which had already put local factories on short time. After James Carmichael MP said the motion should be supported to give the Labour Government "every encouragement", President Lang called on Hector McNeil, MP, the Secretary of State for Scotland. He spoke for longer than all the contributors to the debate; a vote to close the discussion was then carried by 197 to 128. After a mild closing speech by Donachy the amendment was defeated by 215 to 114. But it was not the end of the controversy at grass roots.

Trades councils provided between 11% and 12% of the delegates; but far more than that percentage were their spokesmen in debates on international relations and peace in the early 'fifties, whatever particular aspect was being discussed. They virtually always spoke in favour of the STUC becoming more active about it; this was an expression of mounting concern at grass roots. In the early stages, when confusion and differences were rife, it resulted in the GC and its officers taking disciplinary measures, some of them going unusually far. It included reducing them to trade group status; disaffiliation; appointing new officers; and banning a trade union branch from electing a representative. As well as the Trades Councils of Airdrie, Dundee, Rutherglen, Kirkcaldy and, above all, Glasgow, there were other associations affected; such as the Clydebank Scottish Youth Peace Festival, and Edinburgh Labour Festival. Labour May Day Fêtes fell away, undermined as key expressions of unity as rival exclusive rallies were organised.

Most far-reaching, however, were the events affecting Glasgow Trades Council. Immediately after the 1951 Congress their Executive circulated a report to the 190 delegates, who then adopted a resolution on "The Preservation of Peace", which included endorsement of the Five-Power Pact of the defeated composite amendment. While the GC was already discussing disaffiliating them and setting up a new body, Glasgow made a protest about the interference by American troops at Innsbruck with young people on their way to a Youth Rally in East Berlin, and sent it to Prime Minister Attlee. The GC finally set up an Interim Committee demanding that funds and records be handed over pending reorganisation; and meanwhile asked trade unions to inform Glasgow branches they should withdraw representatives. A special Executive of the Glasgow Trades Council decided, with two exceptions, to apply at once for an interdict to prevent it. While the legal tangle dragged on, the GC called on the Interim Committee to hold a conference, during which Dan Kelly, long a Railwayman Branch delegate to Glasgow Trades Council, had created so much disturbance that Middleton could not make himself heard. Thereupon a new Glasgow Trades Council was set up which expressly banned Dan Kelly and all those who had signed the interdict from future membership. The end of this unsavoury affair did not begin to be in sight until the 1953 Congress. Here James Campbell, the General Secretary of the Railwaymen, moved reference back, speaking of his union branch being denied the right to appoint Kelly as their representative. After D McGibbon of the Shop Assistants had fiercely defended the GC's action, he disclosed that the new Glasgow Executive had asked, however, for the bans to be reviewed. With Middleton tactfully assuring Congress that he was sure the incoming GC would do this, the reference back was defeated by 164 to 203 – and Kelly was then seen to be in his place.

Clearly it was high time that the eyeball-to-eyeball confrontation should lessen; at the 1953 Congress in Rothesay one of the fiercest protagonists of the right wing, John Brannigan, was defeated and never re-elected to the GC. Within a few months Middleton began calling conferences of chairmen and secretaries of most trades councils in the Glasgow, Perth and Fifeshire areas. Out of the glare of publicity, at these were discussed some of the vexed problems and knotty points of policy the GC was developing. These included what the role of trades councils should be; whether every topic of a political character should in theory be left strictly to the local Labour Party unless there was formally agreed joint action; whether local May Day rallies should be dropped in favour of schools and discussions; how far should trades councils regard their duty as merely processing STUC decisions; whether if a delegate's attitude was disapproved, responsibility to take disciplinary action must be his union's alone; and whether bodies concerned with social problems, such as the Socialist Medical Association and the Union of Democratic Control, were political organisations, to which trades councils should, therefore, not affiliate. But also they came to cover the question that none could doubt was the proper business of trade unionists – the urgent need for economic development in Scotland to counter unemployment. It was this that Middleton himself was increasingly concentrating upon by skilful use of radio and television appearances.

Section (v): **Moves Towards Peaceful Co-existence**

Peaceful co-existence was not only needed internationally; it had to be reached also between trade unionists of different views if Scotland's economic development was to progress. Henceforth, more emphasis was laid on this in the debates about the urgent need to improve international relations. It was especially noticeable when James Milne, for Aberdeen Trades Council, moved a resolution calling for an

> end to all bans and restrictions on trade with the Soviet Union, People's China and the countries of Eastern Europe.

As he said, they needed "the fullest possible development of peaceful trade between Britain and other countries of the world, particularly the non-dollar countries". Quoting how "political considerations were a barrier", he pointed out that America apparently allowed

> Japan and Germany to trade with Russia and the East while Britain had imposed on her an almost impossible list of goods not for export.

He saw such increased foreign trade as not only a solution to the problems of iron, steel, shipbuilding and textiles; it also "might ease the present international tension". Strongly supported with details by the dockers' delegates, the Constructional Engineers' General Secretary, Vehicle Builders and Fire Brigades the only opposition came from the Boot & Shoe Operatives who believed the claims "exaggerated". There was no direct spokesman for the GC except the General Secretary, and that expressed in very mild terms. After saying that "the GC were agreed that the climate of opinion in regard to East-West trade was changing", Middleton said "it was wrong to become lyrical about its possibilities"; and that their main motion on Industry the day before had sufficiently covered it. In closing, Milne replied that "for reasons not produced, certain people at Congress were intent on confusing the issue and belittling the targets. The orders were there." His motion was carried 196 to 174: next day James Milne was elected to the GC. Top of the unsuccessful candidates was Dr Lilli Stein; moved by Dr A B Hart, her co-delegate from the Scientific Workers, a motion was carried unanimously welcoming setting up an Atomic Power Station in Dounreay, but with a clear-cut warning about the dangers. She said "they must safeguard Scotland and the people in Caithness and surrounding counties particularly from taking risks without getting any of the benefits". The power should be used for Scottish industry and not diverted to England; and it "should not be left to a privately controlled group of people to decide how it would be used". Then the Scientific Workers sponsored an emergency motion on the Hydrogen Bomb: the testing of this in the Pacific had caused the deaths of Japanese fishermen 90 miles away through its radioactive effects, and the sickness years later of British servicemen taking part. The resolution called for the three Great Powers to talk immediately, aiming to stop further tests; ban the bombs; control atomic energy; study peaceful uses of nuclear fission; and strengthen collective peace through the United Nations. Detailing its horrors, which meant that "there was no meaning to civil defence any more", Dr Hart asked Congress "to send out a call that would echo round the world uniting all races – all creeds; a call to new sanity and hope". Strongly supported by Dan Kelly for Glasgow Trades Council, Dr J Winning of the Medical Practitioners Union and the Railwaymen's General Secretary, James Campbell, it was passed unanimously. Their remarks were clearly in the minds of delegates who shortly after carried a resolution demanding that there should be "no German rearmament before further efforts have been made to secure the peaceful reunification of Germany". In moving it the Fire Brigades Union's Scottish Organiser, J McDonald, said:

> The great majority of leading Nazi criminals had been released from prison and were in positions of considerable importance. These were the people who were going to control the West German army.

When the next Congress met at Rothesay in 1955, the date of the General Election had been announced and the change in mood was speeding up. The Transport & General Scottish Regional Secretary, T B Meikle, noted in his Presidential Address, "the status now accorded our Congress throughout Scotland and the attention given to our views on the many and varied problems with which Scotland is faced". He itemised "the threat of the hydrogen bomb lying over us"; automation and changes in production techniques; and "the competitive factors of other countries". At this Congress there was indeed a considerable improvement with a marked decrease in the bitter factionalism, and with less confusion. On international affairs a very strong sense had developed about both the need for peaceful co-existence and that it was a practicable possibility; this was expressed in particularly well-informed contributions from the scientists, and also hard local facts quoted by Glasgow, Aberdeen and Paisley Trades Council delegates. Resolutions in all the sensitive areas were passed unanimously. These included that Britain should take the lead on nuclear disarmament and banning H-Bomb tests; prevent rearmament under dubious leadership in West Germany; and even the Miners' motion on recognising the People's Republic of China. There was no formal opposition expressed by GC members as such even to the resolution on Chiang Kai Shek being expelled from Formosa, which had "an overwhelming majority".

One sign of the times, and certainly itself a new factor already beginning to play a part, was the whole question of the exchange of foreign delegations; it was to become a permanent and important feature of the STUC. It had a bearing not only on peace but also on the key question of developing Scotland's trade and industry. In time, Scottish industrialists themselves, regional authorities and political parties were to recognise the leading role of the STUC in this. It had first been mooted as early as 1947 by William Pearson for the Miners in the form of the GC being instructed to arrange for "a delegation representing the Scottish Trade Union Movement" to visit the Soviet Union and then seek a return delegation; and also to invite trade unionists from Europe to visit Scotland to examine the work of the trade union movement. With the Cold War then just developing, however, nothing came of that for several years, although repeated arguments favouring it were heard from the delegates of such unions as the Miners, Railwaymen, Foundry Workers and Tobacco Workers, who had all already exchanged official visits with other countries. It was, however, decided to send a sizeable group of GC members in 1951 to visit Yugoslavia, after the rift had taken place between that country and the USSR. Later a formal delegation was sent to the Yugoslav Confederation Conference, while their General Secretary addressed the 1953 STUC Congress. But meanwhile, not only had individual trade unions begun exchanging visits with trade unionists elsewhere, but a demand from the STUC Youth Advisory was finally successful, asking that Study Tour visits of young trade unionists to Denmark and Norway should be assisted by the GC. They were headed by James Jack, the Assistant General Secretary, and were clearly of considerable interest to the younger people; and the Youth Advisory at the time included some who, like the Miners, Lawrence Daly and Michael McGahey, were later to be found in the top leadership.

Then in this changing atmosphere, at the 1955 STUC Congress, William Barclay for Dundee Trades Council argued that the STUC "should not lag behind the individual trade unions who had already sent invitations to Russia. Nor should it lag behind the Scottish Churches, who had invited a delegation of clergymen." Middleton replied that, provided his motion were remitted, the GC would "reopen the whole matter". This led to a visit there in October of ten members of the GC; it was pointedly accompanied by the Technical Secretary of the Scottish Council for Development and Industry to get some discussions on trade. The impressions of all the visitations were published in pamphlets, the Bulletin and Annual Reports. A return visitation came from the USSR in May 1956, and the door was opened to formal exchange of greetings, and finally came actual delegations to their respective Congresses. When the Soviet Union's General Secretary, Victor Grishin, addressed the STUC Congress in 1961 for the first time he received "a wonderful ovation". Whatever might be the differences in policy or approach, at home or abroad, they were henceforth to be treated by STUC delegates as topics for discussion between people sharing a common interest in peace and economic development for Scotland, rather than as target practice between exponents of rival blacklists.

References

[1] Scottish Development Council, 1931; Scottish Economic Committee, 1936; Scottish Regional Production Board, 1943; Standing Industrial Committee for Scotland, 1942; Scottish Coalfields Committee, 1942; Scottish Council on Industry; Scottish Regional Board for Industry, 1946; Scottish Council (Development and Industry), 1946; Scottish Tourist Board; Lord Catto Committee; Advisory Panel on Highlands & Islands; White Fish Authority; Royal Commission on Scotland, 1953-4.

[2] War factories to be adapted and reused; transport facilities improved; roads, bridges, rail tonnage rate; hydro-electric development; work for the closing industries; essential Scottish housing for new industrial development areas; trade union offices on estates; Prestwick airfield and the airlines; Clyde graving dock; scrap and new blast furnaces; diversification; alternative employment for transferred miners' families; agricultural and horticultural machinery; export trade outlets, especially East-West; Rosyth dockyard and ordnance factories to stay; many chemicals to process; Harris tweeds; fishing industries; work for north-east shipyards; crofters and alternative farming; afforestation; landlords misusing land; science research; precision engineering; loss of repair of Viking aircraft; locomotive rebuilding; plastics and light engineering; women's work and more adequate choice of work; shipping and ship repair; takeover of Coltness Iron Works; same of Glebe Sugar Refinery; redundancy at Clydebank, etc. etc.

[3] These included that there should be a National Plan, to go beyond designing

development areas to cover where there was undue dependence on a single industry; inadequate choice of employment, and not enough paid work for women; where miners' families could find additional employment; special remedial treatment for depopulated areas like the Highland and Border counties. It renewed the demand for positive direction of new industry; extended research facilities and Scottish trained scientists and technicians.

[4] "To review with reference to the financial, economic, administrative and other considerations involved, the arrangements for exercising the functions of Her Majesty's Government in relation to Scotland."

[5] An informative contemporary brief account is given in "New Light on Korea" (Labour Monthly pamphlet, 1951, No.5) by D N Pritt KC who quotes from statements by Sir John Pratt, former civil servant and adviser to the Foreign Office on China and the Far East.

21

Changing Attitudes in the 'Fifties

Scotland's economic health was in a bad way; and that at a time when it was argued that in Britain working people had "never had it so good", as a Tory Premier of Scottish origin was to describe it. Hitherto there had been arguments about whether there could be a magic cure. There had been those who had dismissed reliance on any British Government, seeking instead a purely nationalistic political solution. Others argued that all must wait until the return sometime of a Labour Government with a bumper majority like that of 1945. Some were to see the European Common Market as providing Scotland with security through a safe trading outlet, though others feared that could mean German economic penetration. Beyond these general considerations delegates had been divided about whether financial inducement by any British Government could be the sole solution, while others saw forcible direction as being the only cure. Finally opinion hardened into accepting the fact that there could be no real cure nor amelioration, whatever the immediate policy, without continuous public campaigning and explanation aiming at maximum popular active involvement. When this developed fully it could be seen that there was no other body in Scotland which could take the lead and unite interests of whatever persuasion. That was the road to it becoming the Scottish TUC of modern times, unique in argumentative but fraternal unity of action in Scotland.

Section (i): **Direction and "The Mixed Economy"**

A number of factors brought about the new gradual changes in attitudes and practice. But the decisive factor was that in Scotland the trade union movement as a whole finally was won for public campaigning on each and every issue. In the late 'fifties the return of two more Tory Governments, each with increased majorities, was not without its effect. Very important indeed was the continuing vigour of the major trades councils as they succeeded in overcoming arguments which could have seriously limited their strength and effectiveness. An example of this was their opposition to the instruction that they should have no dealing at all with any "political" questions, all of which must be left strictly to the local Labour Parties, whatever their strength. But without due balance between the two "wings" of the working-class movement, the bird could not fly, as the old founders were well aware in 1897; so that was soon ignored. Next it was argued that trades councils should be seen as merely local agencies processing Scottish TUC decisions; and that in particular they must be watchful against being drawn into interference in some individual union's business and committing the STUC to that. For example, this was argued in 1955 by the General Secretary of the Shop, Distributive & Allied Workers visiting from England. J A Birch opposed the miners who had demanded full support "to all trade unions in their efforts to secure wage increases"; that, he claimed, would risk bringing the STUC "into the active field of wage applications and negotiations". His view was endorsed by the Railwaymens' member on the GC, F Donachy, who stressed that there could be much conflict in some industries on what was a legitimate wage claim, with one union going on strike whilst another stayed at work. But soon the movement on the factory floor, leading on to major industry-wide action, put that attitude into the background in Scotland.

Even at this same 1955 Congress the arguments about direction of industry, especially those covering wide areas voiced by trades council delegates, were revealing. McQuilkin of Paisley Trades Council moved an amendment for it, noting slackening in engineering, the poorer prospects in coal and shipbuilding, vehicle building and fishing. He said there must be direction of new light industries, quoting the effect of the proposed transfer of Renfrew Airport maintenance base to London, the closing of Larkhall's Rolls Royce factory and fall off in orders for locomotives and vehicles. A Taylor from Falkirk Trades Council complained that the pre-war number of foundries there had been halved. From Clydebank Trades Council, Arnold Henderson said alternative employment must be provided to John Brown's, with its shipbuilding slumps and booms. As an instance of how inducement did not work he quoted a large site in Dalmuir laid out for new factories some years earlier which was now merely used by a Royal Ordnance factory as a tank track. Other delegates told of buses being ordered from England to replace the tramcars; that 170,000 had emigrated since the war; and that Scotland was not learning the new techniques of the automobile and jet plane industries. A foundry worker mentioned the falling proportion of light castings so suitable for use in the automobile industry which was then thriving in England's Midland counties. When the failure to increase the production of electrical power by the North of Scotland Hydro Board was mentioned, one delegate raised the old bogey of direction of labour, saying they might find Clydebank workers directed away to hydro-electric schemes. To that J Paterson of Clydebank Trades Council made the shrewd reply that there was

> a big difference between being directed from one locality to another and being directed from a factory to the Labour Exchange. Yet that was the alternative.

By the next year, attitudes to direction from officials had begun to change. As one of its fiercest opponents on the GC, John Lang, said: he had "come to the conclusion that if we could not induce industry to come to this part of the United Kingdom then we must insist on industry being directed". Four years later at the 1960 Conference a Miners' resolution "that the Government direct industry into Scotland to build a balanced economy" was carried unanimously with no-one speaking against.

A change in outlook indeed. And this came through at a time when there was considerable unease at the proposal by Attlee's successor, Hugh Gaitskell, to review the Labour Party's Clause IV of its constitution, involving "common ownership of the means of production", which raised controversy on the whole question of socialism and socialist planning. Would this conception of a "mixed economy" gradually moving towards socialist production be sabotaged if ever it threatened capitalist private monopolist interest? Both the need and total practicability of planning the economy had been underlined in the minds of the Scottish leaders since their exchanges with the Soviet trade unionists. In the Report available to the 1956 delegates on their own first visit to the Soviet Union they stressed several points which had particularly impressed them, all of which involved public planning and control. Outstanding was "the excellence of Russian technological training", which they regarded as "the fundamental measure of Soviet strength". Together with this was the fact that the young were to be found in highly skilled jobs; and also the part that women played in Soviet industry, especially in building, where they found them to "predominate". They stressed too the very high "technical development", mentioning especially metallurgical plant, steel strip, blast and furnaces and the caterpillar tractors. They were much impressed that the level of planning there enabled the Foreign Trade Minister in their interview with him to provide an immense list of over 80 articles they would be willing to import from Scotland, ranging from textiles to washing machines, minerals, gas turbines and locomotives.

Now was developing what became recognised in the early 'sixties as the drive which won popular support for the aim to totally re-industrialise Scotland in modern terms. It involved tackling formidable new problems, as well as the traditional difficulties of completely inadequate transport between remote centres of population, local dependence on single industries and resultant emigration of the skilled when each crisis arose. There was not only the major need to achieve national ownership of some key industries, but also the vital popular control to make them work effectively; the bitter struggle for their efficient funding; and later to prevent, or hinder, their deliberate destruction. There were the new questions raised by immense technical change, already seen by some to threaten a new industrial revolution without social revolution. Beyond Scottish frontiers there was the threat of continued rivalries and economic penetration, only to be complicated immensely by growing multinational firms being free to move unimpeded by effective challenge throughout what was indeed becoming their "Free World" This was to bring the newly developing Scottish economy continually into ferocious difficulties. With the break up of the British and French Empires, there emerged the extreme problems of the Third World countries, ranging from those of Latin and Central America, Africa, the Far East and, above all, in the oil-rich Islamic States. Early in the process came the shock of the disastrous Franco-British attack on Egypt over Suez alongside the threat to the new Caribbean regime in Cuba. The consequences of all this, together with the growing astronomical increase in the nuclear arms build-up, meant the disruption of potential international trade which lay heavy on Scottish prospects, as their plain speaking at conferences illuminates.

Section (ii): **Campaigning on Industrial Changes**

When the British and French troops moved in from the Mediterranean to prevent Egypt assuming full control of the Suez Canal through her territory, already under threat from Israel, the GC at once issued a statement deploring it. They saw the effects as likely to be disastrous "economically, politically, morally and in terms of loss of life and limb"; they urged trades councils to act at once with local Labour Parties "to engender the greatest possible public opinion" for an immediate cease-fire and withdrawal. The situation raised immediate problems for the progress of the campaign for revitalising Scotland's major industries both directly and indirectly, by the immediate oil crisis and by the long-distance transport now necessary round the African continent. The GC had to speed up the trend on which they had already entered of concentrating activity on the specific changes needed in the major industries, rather than confining themselves to generalised policy statements.

After much pressure from the STUC, the Steel Board had been forced to send representatives to Scotland to look into various projects in steel; that resulted in promises of the Ravenscraig blast furnace, with better loading and transport facilities to it; it also led to top discussion about steel strip needs and extending rolling mills. The GC were accompanied by representatives of the Clyde District of the Confederation of Shipbuilding and Engineering Unions in approaches to the First Lord both about the whole position on the Clyde and repair work in Aberdeen. There was unanimous acceptance of Greenock Trades Council's view that a large graving dock on the Clyde had become "a matter of first importance", referring to the "switch to large oil tankers and ore carriers" following the Suez crisis. Each year there was increasing cause for alarm at there being no integrated energy or transport policy. The GC was, therefore, concerned with the miners in important area conferences, drawing in the local authorities in Fife and Midlothian, regarding all the problems of the industry from closures, transfers, lack of housing and alternative employment. This became especially important when by 1957 the Government had decided that no centrally financed factory building was to continue. The GC played an important role in a major conference about retaining Renfrew Aircraft Maintenance Base, with many local authorities drawn in. With shop stewards from railway engineering seeking their help they took up the question of threatened redundancies over steam locomotives: orders for these from colonial countries were being lost to Germany, Japan and America while their export to Russia and China was being discouraged.

But the year before Suez there were signs that a major attack was contemplated against the trade unions, in view both of the economic crisis on the Western horizon and the new prospect for profit offered by the technological revolution to be ushered in by automation. The GC arranged for a film produced by the Ford Company on "Automation" to be shown in Glasgow to officers appointed by 38 unions, and then discussed. This was followed up at the 1956 Perth Congress by a resolution from the Miners and Scientific Workers welcoming the technical progress and need for new skilled workers "on an unprecedented scale", but making this important proviso:

automation in itself is no guarantee of a rising standard of living for the workers when such power is controlled by private enterprise.

It therefore demanded public ownership both of it and of atomic energy to ensure that these "are used not for profit but for the benefit of the people and of the living standards of the workers". It concluded that there must be measures to safeguard security of employment and earnings in the industries affected. Abe Moffat in moving it said "we could learn some lessons from the first industrial revolution", referring to child labour and the place of women in industry. "Remaining passive could have serious repercussions"; instead there must be a fight for increased wages as productivity increased, shorter hours, full wages for those thrown out and earlier retirement. J J Duffy of the Jute & Flax Operatives described how women previously attending two looms were now finding themselves looking after ten. After John Lang had asked for a remit instead of declaring a policy before respective unions had considered their attitude to it, it was nevertheless carried. This was followed up by discussion conferences on the impact of automation and the probable future of electronic computing, with its effect on employment and skills. Lectures were given by a scientist who had worked on preparing the Government report and by George Middleton dealing with the consequences for the trade unions. The conferences were designed for trade union officers, of whom 76 were appointed by 48 unions to attend at Edinburgh and 102 by 52 unions at Glasgow. They were regarded as highly stimulating, and 1000 copies of a duplicated report rushed out afterwards were snapped up immediately by the unions.

But when automation came to be discussed at the 1957 Rothesay Congress there had taken place an immense industrial struggle in shipbuilding and engineering which had considerable bearing on delegates' attitudes in all debates, not least on automation. The previous summer these employers had announced provocatively that it was no use submitting any wage claim because no advance would be considered. It seemed clear, as attempts to get negotiations going went on, that their attitude certainly coincided with Government policy.

Finally the unions within the Confederation, including the AEU, authorised a strike starting on 16 March, 1957, in shipbuilding and engineering which quickly began to extend. Marine engineering works on the Clyde stopped. There was immense support, extending to engineering generally: the Singer sewing machine factory at Clydebank, which was non-federated and only partly organised, had 10,000 out of 14,000 quickly stopping; and also MacNeils forge of Glasgow, which had worked during the General Strike of 1926. The

Scottish Miners were foremost in giving financial support. The Government was obliged to call in the employers to begin talks; and a Court of Inquiry was set up after the employers had proved stubborn. The strike was called off early in April as soon as the Court was in session, just before the STUC conference began at Rothesay. Clearly industry at large was affected; the threat could extend and so could the mood for strike action.

The fraternal delegate from the British TUC that year was Sir Thomas Williamson, the General and Municipal leader. He said he considered it "the most serious industrial dispute since 1926". He added:

> Certain industrial and engineering employers had decided to fight the unions; to use the assets of their industries to bring them to their knees, to cripple them and then to be able to dictate their terms for the next 15 to 20 years.

But, he added, "to have carried on the strike, with all the possibilities of an extension to other fields, would have been the utmost folly for the Trade Union Movement"; in his view they could not afford to have a serious upheaval forced upon the nation. But Scottish delegates saw it in other terms, not ignoring the general effect on wages nor Government and Opposition leaders' attitude to wage restraint. Moving a GC motion on the cost of living, in which "the upward trend of prices in a whole range of commodities" had reached the point of "making 'wage restraint' almost meaningless", the Scottish Baker, W Mowbray, stressed that employers had been led "to believe that the Government would be solidly behind resistance to wage claims". But the Government and employers had been shown what was the "attitude of the united trade union movement in any further attempts to destroy the purpose and solidarity of collective bargaining". Guy Stobbs seconding for the Miners referred to "the avowed intention of the employers to have a pool of unemployment designed to undermine the strength and unity of the working class". James Milne, Pattern Maker, for Aberdeen Trades Council spoke of his pride "that his workmates in the shipbuilding industry had decided to a man that they would answer the call of the unions"; and he added that "they were fighting on behalf of every organised worker in the country".

An emergency motion recorded their "appreciation of the magnificent response" to the strike action which "forced the shipbuilding and engineering employers away from their negative approach to claims". It "congratulated the workers in putting the brake on wage-freezing", which reaffirmed the STUC "policy of opposing any wage freeze". Moving it for the Boilermakers, W F Whitley spoke of the hundreds of letters and telegrams of support from all over the world received by the Confederation. Seconding it the Blacksmith, Jimmy Jarvie, said it had "removed the last pockets of resistance to trade unionism in shipbuilding"; had influenced the course of wage claims in other industries; and that the mass of the working class realised that the shipbuilding workers' problems were also theirs, and "that its solution was the solution to their own wages problems". Patrick Connor of the AEU thought this "deliberate challenge" by the employers "was the precursor of possibly even greater battles to come"; he quoted the engineering lockout of 1922, and the 1926 General Strike which followed. He specially mentioned how scandalously treated in the industry were the women workers, and also the apprentices. The electrician, George Scott, describing the "intransigent, arrogant and cynical attitude of the employers", underlined "the lesson that unity of the trade union movement could bring any set of employers to heel". The resolution was carried unanimously. Hugh Gaitskell, MP, bringing their fraternal greetings as leader of the Labour Party to Britain's first major trade union conference of the year, was left in no doubt about what Scotland thought of any wage-freeze policy.

But would automation and redundancy put a new weapon into the hands of employers in some industries? And were the unions capable of finding quickly a united answer? The debate on it showed some doubts and anxieties. The Electrician, George Scott, moved a resolution repeating that the benefits "can be secured only by and through the nationalisation of the major industries" operating within a national economic plan; and then went on to demand specific safeguards, which included "negotiations at all stages and all levels", full wages until alternative employment where there was redundancy; employers to pay for suitable training; shorter working week, and increased wages alongside of increased productivity. He strongly stressed the need for prior trade union consultation: if they "allowed uncontrolled automation within the present industrial set-up they were tacitly accepting progressive unemployment". Quoting disputes currently in the car industry he said it was "even now a life or death matter for many engineering workers". Seconding it for the Blacksmiths, Jimmy Jarvie believed they "could not afford to wait much longer to forge a policy which would meet the social implications" of what was already a fact of economic life; for employers already looked at it "as something that would meet their ideal of ten men looking for nine jobs". But for the GC, W McGinniss moved an amendment which cut out nationalisation and almost all the specific detailed claims. He said the purpose "was to try to keep Congress in line with general policy": they were very conscious of the occupations and industries where automation did not yet threaten. Seconding the amendment, the Shop Assistants' E W Craig said their decision could be no more than a guide for such unions as would be affected. Delegates of Supervisory Staffs and the Clerks agreed with the GC's view; and what Scott described as the GC's motion of "airy-fairy generalities" was carried on this occasion by 178 to 145, with more than a quarter of the delegates not voting.

Section (iii): **"The Three Wise Men's" Threat**

But the changing mood was there in Scotland with the crisis on the horizon already bringing a sharp increase in unemployment. Some began at once to take vigorous action; in Dundee 10,000 went on strike as Government action threatened the jute factories whilst elsewhere Government establishments were closing. A significant example was the Torpedo factory which was moved south to Portland, where there was actually a shortage of the necessary skilled labour: that was merely one straw in a hurricane. With unemployment always so much worse in Scotland, even before the failure to expand the shipbuilding industry turned into a refusal even to maintain it, Scots were not slow to recognise the craft and cunning of a document commissioned by the Government, giving a foretaste of employers' intentions. This was from the Council on Prices, Productivity and Income, consisting of Lord Cohen, Sir Harold Hewitt and Sir Dennis Robertson, and was soon to be known bitterly as the "Three Wise Men's Report". The Council was set up to "keep under review changes in prices, productivity and the level of incomes". It was published in February 1958 just before the STUC met at Aberdeen, and included the statement:

> It is impossible that a free and flexible economic system can work efficiently without a perceptible (though emphatically not a catastrophic) margin of unemployment.

It went on to declare that "wage increases in the past few years have not only exceeded the rise in the cost of living, but have gone beyond what would be justified by the average increase in productivity". The GC issued a statement about "this highly political document" which echoed "in almost every respect" the views put forward by the Government, of which it had "blatantly shown itself to be the mouthpiece". For it gave "unqualified support to the policy of monetary techniques" and had rejected price controls, planned investment and adequate fiscal measures, which the GC believed were "the only effective way whereby the Government can deal with the present situation". A very blunt emergency motion repudiating it was put down by the Blacksmiths' delegation in these terms:

> It promotes unemployment in order to reduce real wages. It impudently advocates wage restraint for the Trade Unions, while rejecting dividend limitation for the employers.

Pointing out that it put "the burden of sacrifice upon the backs of the workers" they called for the movement "to utterly reject and actively combat this policy". But time was short and it was remitted with many other resolutions, including one calling for a vigorous campaign for a shorter working week. This the GC circulated to affiliated bodies together with a sharp statement, when the second report of the "Three Wise Men" came out four months later, demanding that on the contrary:

> Greater public investment is called for; and we should expedite the modernisation plans of the nationalised industries.

These were the opening shots of the attack by the employers which was to result in frequent interruption of production. It was also to lead to attempts to undermine the power of the unions; this was to find those who advocated wage restraint in a mixed economy out-manoeuvred, and in growing confusion, with mounting disfavour felt at grass-roots level.

Scotland's economy needed special campaigning on many fronts if only to get her "share of short-term policies", as Middleton put it, in an important debate at the Dunoon 1959 Conference. Two months earlier the Scottish Miners had gone down to London to demonstrate in impressive force against frightening proposals for 36 pit closures throughout Britain, with twenty of them destined for Scotland. Their delegate, W Moore from Shotts, detailing some of the gains, said it had wide public support, and was the biggest "seen in Scotland since 1922". He added that if other Scottish unions "had taken up the same attitude as the miners in organising the London demonstration, the position would have been better than it presently was". But action had not been confined to a single industry. The Miner, Alex Moffat, in his stirring Presidential Address, referred to "the magnificent campaign" conducted by the GC in shipbuilding and engineering to bring strip mills to Scotland.

Section (iv): **Active Campaigning**

The whole line of future confrontation against the unions and the labour movement to counter the post-war high hopes was now already foreshadowed; it meant major new battles in the 'seventies and reached crisis proportions in the 'eighties. More and more frequently the initiative was to be taken in Scotland, with miners and shipyard workers in the lead. Throughout it all the STUC began increasingly to be seen playing an important role as co-ordinator. This was due to their increasing ability and willingness to encourage active campaigning at all levels.

Throughout 1959 the Scots had continued to increase their activity. Frequent deputations and statements were issued in view of the growing and disproportionate unemployment in Scotland. One striking example was against redundancies in Rolls Royce, where shop stewards had been campaigning with vigour: when all the unions then approached the STUC, the GC met the management on their behalf. Relations with trades councils had improved with Middleton addressing a Conference on unemployment called by Glasgow in the Trades Council's Centenary Year of the district committee of each trade union. There had been frequent approaches on aspects of this and co-operation with local authorities in Dunbartonshire, Ayr, Dundee and Aberdeen, and over the Montrose shipyard closure which was threatening Tayside. A particularly striking STUC regional conference at Hamilton brought together trade unionists with representatives of no less than forty-two local authorities; campaigning also continued over the Highlands and in Aberdeen, where the Trades Council opened impressive new premises.

Other topics debated were pointers to the way ahead, when delegates spoke of the drift "into a technocratic society". As the Supervisory Staffs General Secretary, Harry Knight, put it:

> More and more control of industry was getting into the hands of the accountant, the statistician and the economist. This unholy trinity was, in fact, making most of the major decisions in industry today.

The Blacksmith's delegate, Jimmy Jarvie, pointed out that since "the First World War, new techniques had revolutionised engineering. Today it was the era of the machine tool." He was one of many delegates strongly stressing how essential it was to press for a shorter working week. Problems with foreign employers came up in an engineers' resolution exposing persistent refusal "by American firms to recognise normal negotiating procedures", naming some where there was already trouble.[1] The link between foreign policy and international relations with the economy was brought out in a powerful speech by Jimmy Milne, in moving for the GC an end to nuclear tests as "a vital first step", and calling for British initiative to break through the "tardy progress" with fresh proposals "to build lasting bridges". He said this to those who thought more industry for Scotland should be occupying most of their time:

> All the new industry and the building of new factories in Scotland would give them nothing if they could not win the major battle – the battle for peace.

This was underlined by a unanimous resolution that all restrictions on East-West trade should be removed, moved by E Stewart of Greenock Trades Council. Every speaker was from a trades council, with many examples given. Delegates from Renfrew and Clydebank described what it could mean for shipbuilding and engineering in their areas; Gordon Massie for Cambuslang described how redundancies would hit several hundred with the closure of Pickerings, because they could not build railway wagons despite orders from Hungary. An order from India for metal-cutting machinery had been lost to Poland. In another debate Abe Moffat, the Miners' leader, said that the "strategical list" imposed by the American Government was ridiculous, with many of the commodities on it now "being exported to other countries by the Soviet Union themselves". Middleton said that with the Government about to send a trade mission to the Soviet Union, he thought they should call upon the Scottish Council (Development and Industry) to do the same. While there were some differences of degree in their attitude to the Common Market and the failure of the European Free Trade area, they were unanimous in their anxiety about the effect of the war danger on their economic problems.

The campaigning by Scottish trade unionists throughout the year on many points, from grass roots to the GC itself was both an indication of the changing mood and also contributory to it. For example, the Miners won support, including donations, when they took their 600 deputation by special train to London to lobby against the National Coal Board's pit closure plans, affecting 20 pits in Scotland, as well as 16 elsewhere. Aid to them came from co-operative societies in Ayrshire and Lanarkshire and also some town and county councils: officials of miners' branches in different areas set up campaign committees to explain the case. In one area a minister of the local Presbytery was appointed to go with them. Branch representatives from miners' lodges came to leaflet the Dunoon STUC delegates. In addition representatives from shop stewards' committees at Remington Rand, Metro Vickers, Rolls Royce, Harland & Wolff, Barr & Stroud and King Aircraft did the same. Inside Queen's Hall at Dunoon the last item at the 1959 Congress was a skilful electioneering speech in a Labour Party fraternal address from Harold Wilson, promising "a resounding defeat for the Tories" and a new Labour Government pledged to raise Scottish living standards. But six months later the result of the General Election was yet another Labour defeat. Some had feared it. The editor of *The Draughtsman* J E Mortimer, wrote at the time:[2]

> If however the electorate feel that Labour is lukewarm about the extension of social ownership, it will be all the more difficult for us to convince them that we can offer a better economic future than the Conservatives. The question before them will be, who can best manipulate the existing system, instead of the more fundamental one of how to rid ourselves of the main source of economic instability and unemployment.

But in Scotland there was no swing to the right; and Labour gained four seats at Glasgow Craigton, Glasgow Scotstoun, Ayrshire and Lanark. These were all areas where trade unionists' campaigning over the years of late had been strong.

Section (v): **Scottish Youth on Strike**

Now there were to begin major industrial struggles, including a seven-weeks' strike in the general print industry, where a demand for increased wages, given new technology, was united with a demand for shorter hours; that was a direct challenge to the policy laid down by "the Three Wise Men's Report"; and part of the campaign was resistance to attempts to break craft practices and introduce dilution. The action was another indication of the attitudes ahead; for there was ferocious police violence used against picketers, although nothing approaching the appalling events to come in the 'eighties.

Even more remarkable, however, was an immense action by shipbuilding and engineering apprentices, after more than two years' negotiations for improved conditions had brought nothing from the employers. This started on the Clyde – thousands of Clydeside apprentices came out on a one-day token strike on February 24, 1960, to speed the long years of fruitless negotiations.[3] When employers suspended some, workers at Singer's in Clydebank and six shipyards stopped work in protest. The young people came out once more at the call of the Clyde Apprentices Committee, and at one time there were no less that 36,000 out in Scotland. They decided to extend it. As their young Blacksmith Secretary, Don McLaren, wrote some months later.[4]

> After the first turmoil of thousands of apprentices pouring out from every yard and factory on Clydeside, we in the Clydeside Apprentices Committee settled down to plan a campaign that would ensure ultimate success. Finally we agreed on a line of action around this idea. First stage: 100 per cent apprentices out in Scotland. Second stage: winning adult support, both financial and militant, first on Clydeside, and then nationally. Third stage: 100 per cent apprentices out in Great Britain.

Their tremendous enthusiasm and militancy won through, after they had travelled all over Britain, and McLaren was even invited to address the Confederation's Annual Meeting. At the 1960 Perth STUC in speaking to a Draughtsman's motion on the shipbuilding industry which demanded a "scrap and build" policy, Ted Hill, the much respected General Secretary of the Boilermakers, spoke of the apprentices. He congratulated them "for the grand stand they had made for bigger wages and better working conditions".

Some of these young people were to play an active part a dozen years later in the great Upper Clyde Shipyards' work-in on Clydeside. They had learned much and fast during their struggle. As Michael McGahey, the former secretary of the Scottish Miners Young Committee wrote:[5]

> in their enthusiasm and unity (they) broke down the resistance of the employers – and the slow-foot indifference to their claims of some within the trade union movement itself.

It was he who had sponsored the sucessful resolution at the Miners Conference for the right to vote at 18.

References

[1] Burroughs; Westclox; International Business Machines; Caterpillar Contractor Co; Euclids; Sunbeam Electric.
[2] *Labour Monthly*, October, 1959.
[3] *The Blacksmiths History*, "The Apprentices Make History", by Angela Tuckett.
[4] *Labour Monthly*, October, 1960, "My First Strike", by Don McLaren.
[5] *Labour Monthly*, August, 1960, "The Vote at 18", by Michael McGahey.

22

How Scotland Faced the 'Sixties

The 'sixties was to be an unhappy decade of mounting struggle with new problems for young and old trade unionists. There were to be ever-increasing doubts and confusion, sometimes even on aims, but primarily on how Governments could be persuaded, relied upon or forced to respond to ever-pressing economic needs. While in Britain as a whole attitudes and action although often vigorous were uneven, and efforts by each section failed to be co-ordinated, in Scotland this was far less the case. North of the border there were still many unions whose chief officers were locally based and more readily and quickly responsive. With the strong unifying influence also from trades councils the Scottish TUC showed far less hesitation to reach decisions and to campaign.

Their developing active and independent campaigning did not go unnoticed in the corridors of trade union power south of the border. The practice began of National Presidents and General Secretaries to come north frequently to observe the Scots in Congress; many came in 1962 to Aberdeen. There remained moreover some anxieties locally as to whether the STUC's campaigning could ensure sufficient unity in action from members of unions whose power base was in the south. This may well have been the background to a change in Standing Orders which in one respect broke the Scots' traditional practice maintained for over 65 years. In 1962 the introduction of a card vote entitling affiliates to one vote for every 500 members was moved by William Mowbray for the small Scottish Bakers Union. He emphasised how low was representation from some of these big unions, with the Engineers only 7% and the Railwaymen 11% of their entitlement. Seconding on behalf of the GC, the Scottish Regional Secretary of the Transport & General, William Scholes, went out of his way to stress that it would benefit trades councils, who would be given a voting power as though each had 1,500 members. After the Miners had unsuccessfully moved the previous question, the change was carried by 266 to 192. It did not, however, hinder the STUC from increasing their remarkable campaigning, as we shall see.

Section (i): **The Right to Revise Their Tactics**

The final decline of the empire "East of Suez", with resulting balance of payment problems, financial crises and doubtful markets was seen as likely to bring prospects of "full employment" to an end. The Tory Government re-elected in 1959 under Macmillan then began with softly-softly methods, showing that there were some major employer and City interests on whom the lessons of the mid-twenties and early thirties had not been lost. They moved at first with carefully thought out step-by-step tactics to undermine the expectation of rising standards. They followed this with skilled propaganda about traditional trade union practice being out of date. Perhaps fundamental was their apparent adoption of the cherished aim of "social planning" which might be "in the national interest"; but their real aim was that it should be used to avoid public ownership. The questions they raised included:

> What could the country afford? How could productivity be increased? And must not incomes depend strictly on this? Should negotiations now concentrate on wages determined at an industry's national level? Or through workshop agreements in the new combines? Should the role of shop stewards be reconsidered and codified? Were hourly wages or weekly wages the key question? And how could hours of overtime be controlled? In any event during the present "temporary uncertainties" should there not be a "temporary pay-pause"?

Meanwhile parallel to this there was the tendency of some sections in the top leadership both of the British TUC and the Parliamentary Labour Party under Gaitskell's successor, Harold Wilson, to seek to avoid confrontation; they became convinced that current economic circumstances did indeed make it advisable to reduce "unrealistic expectations" to what had been described fifty years earlier as "slow reform that heals".[1]

By the end of 1962 the Macmillan Government had set up the National Economic Development Council and the British TUC was induced to be represented on it. A National Incomes Commission began pouring out reports on wages and hours in different industries, including a general extension of the "pay pause". In addition "Beeching the Butcher" and "Robens the Robber" were put into the nationalised railways and mining industries to cut these down to suit private enterprise in road transport and in other forms of energy. There was a steep rise in sectional strikes, and many instances of provocation.

There followed the long drawn out and disastrous case of *Rookes* v *Barnard* decided by the House of Lords against the Draughtsmen's Union, drastically limiting the right to strike. As these trends and reactions continued, when it came to the General Election of 1964, Wilson could head a new Labour Government, after more than a dozen years in opposition, though by a bare margin of four seats. After passing a Trades Disputes Act in 1965, which was welcomed, to reverse the effects of *Rookes* v *Barnard*, some other problems were put into cold storage by a Royal Commission being set up on Trade Unions and Employers Associations, under a former Labour MP, Lord Donovan. This enabled the Wilson Government to hold a General Election in March 1966 and gain a somewhat larger majority.

Under the new Labour Government, however, things quickly went from bad to worse. A divisive "Statement of Intent on Productivity, Prices and Incomes" was set up calling for the unions to decide to keep wage increases down to 3 per cent. A "National Plan" had to be dropped: soon there was yet another White Paper called "Prices and Incomes Standstill; Period of Severe Restraint", which stopped all advances. When the Donovan Commission[2] FN1 came out, it continued proposals for changing trade union structure and powers; these were finally taken further and made explicit in the proposals produced by Barbara Castle as Employment Minister in the fatal document "In Place of Strife".[3] This document gave any future Government power to order a twenty-eight day suspension of strike action, if it thought fit, with financial penalties enforced by attachment of wages; power to insist upon a ballot before a strike could be lawfully called; that there should be a new Act requiring all unions to register, with the Government able to decide which of their rules would be unacceptable. This disastrous document was to result in an "Increase of Strife", as some nicknamed it, which guaranteed a Tory Government being returned under Edward Heath. It not only provided him with a model for his Industrial Relations Act of 1970 and ensured that chaos would result. It was also to lead to the new and biggest action of all, as we shall see, when the Scottish trade unionists were to head the whole British working class in action from the banks of the Upper Clyde.

Section (ii): **The Scots' Response is Determined**

How Scotland's response to the difficulties of the decade at each stage was to be determined could be seen as early as the Aberdeen Congress of 1960. They were to find their way to major and consistent campaigning. The factor which dominated the STUC's activities was their concern about the need to create employment opportunities and to counter redundancy. There was the grimmest position in the coalfields; but Scotland's "greatest employing agency", shipbuilding, was in the doldrums. For many months before and after the 1959 General Election the GC had kept up insistent pressure by every means on this, under the current Chairman, Jimmy Milne. It was twenty-six years since any trades council delegate had been elected STUC Chairman, which had happened so frequently in its early days: a Patternmaker, until recently convener in an Aberdeen shipyard, Secretary of the Trades Council there and President of the District Committee of the Confederation, Milne was in close touch with the needs in this crucial industry.

Immediately after the 1959 Congress a telegram was sent to Prime Minister Macmillan which resulted in a meeting with him, the Secretary of State for Scotland and all the senior officials and Regional Controllers. At this the GC were indeed emphatic about the hard core of unemployment, far worse than elsewhere in Britain and not least amongst school leavers. Their research officer, Jimmy Jack, provided formidable documentation on all industries, not least shipbuilding, where far more was needed than the promised steel strip mill at Motherwell, with some public funding. Throughout the year they kept following Macmillan up, as when he proposed a new Local Employment Act which they considered fell far short of what was needed. They kept up insistent pressure on the Scottish Council, Scottish Board for Industry, on Whitehall, and deputations to firms threatening redundancy; they also used to the full press, radio and television, on which George Middleton proved very adroit. They were constantly in touch with trades councils; amongst these Glasgow suggested a conference of the main chairmen and secretaries. This was held after first getting written assessments of the position in each locality. Thus on 22 November, 1959, Milne presided over a conference of 56 officers from 32 trades councils meeting the GC. There was "a most lively and informative period of questions and discussion". Milne and Middleton said it had provided "a sharper and more up to date picture"; its report was circulated to all trades councils.

From ground floor activists to Westminster itself there was no let-up. Two weeks before the 1960 Congress delegates met, the GC initiated what proved to be a historic meeting in the City Chambers in Glasgow. Delegates described it as "a master stroke", proving the STUC to be "the only constructive force within the Scottish economy to give a lead". Here on 2 April, 1960, Jimmy Milne presided over a summoned conference of Scottish MPs with 49 from all parties in attendance. From it an all-party deputation was elected to interview

Macmillan about many aspects of the Scottish economy. On 31 May, therefore, three Conservative, three Labour and one Liberal MP, together with the GC's Chairman, Treasurer and George Middleton as Secretary, were duly received by the Prime Minister in London for a joint report and discussion. Middleton later described the interview as "a fairly satisfactory one", with Macmillan applying "a fairly receptive ear" to the submissions; it certainly provided possibilities for follow-up. The first immediate result was that the GC induced the Scottish Board for Industry to call a conference of over 300 firms to discuss their ability and readiness to produce components for the car industry. With the Carron Company in the picture for laying down new foundries for castings, the use of sheet metal from Ravenscraig, with Rootes and Pressed Steel active, the British Motor Corporation could develop production north of the border, and Bathgate and Linwood could see important expansion. Even this measure of winning some share for Scotland of the motor industry could not have been achieved without "persistent efforts and unwavering confidence", said a GC statement welcoming it; and this industry could attract more jobs to Scotland beyond mining, shipbuilding and marine engineering, and "supply the dynamic" Scotland so much needed.

Many other reports were published working out how orders for Cunard's new *Queen Mary* liner should be placed with John Brown's at Clydebank; pursuing the Government's delay and silence on it; moving too on Clyde graving dock. One immediate achievement was to prevent the Admiralty from selling the whole of the Naval stores at Carfin merely for use as a whisky store. They also moved fast to press the Scottish Board to induce Imperial Chemical Industries not to shift their factories from Linlithgow and Grangemouth to south of the border. They raised sharply both employment difficulties at Beardmore's Parkhead Forge and also redundancy from Babcock and Wilcox at Renfrew and Dalmuir. There was also much correspondence with the War Office and electricity authority about lack of orders for bridging, pontoon and power station boilers from John Brown Land Boilers. Many similar issues were taken up, including those affecting aviation, where there were charges of "graft"; the Crimond nuclear power station; Scottish roads programme; and the future of the rails and locomotive building. Nor indeed had they been idle on continuing and expanding their campaign about Highland development, which they alone had initiated. At their fourth major conference in Inverness 88 public bodies were represented, besides 120 delegates from the trade union movement: universally firm approval had been won since they first put forward the conception of a Highland Development Authority with full powers: they hotly followed up Macmillan on this which he had still failed to accept, pointing out that there was "not the slightest sign that the tide of emigration is likely to be stemmed by the Government's present policy".

After this long and ever-persistent effort in so many fields there could be few Scottish trade unionists who doubted any longer that nothing short of government direction would work. But before direction on the necessary scale could be won there were related points on which doubts could and did remain in the early 'sixties. The first requirement of course was that the government of the day must be won to a conviction of Scotland's paramount deserts and capabilities. Given a full recognition of that, would any powers of direction in fact prove practicable, with American, Canadian and British large firms having an eye on inducements the Common Market might offer? Some like W R Hattan, Public Employees, regarded direction as only "a negative policy", with the lasting solution being intervention by the State in production engaging in "direct labour". Would it not necessarily require, the vast majority felt, taking into public ownership at least the hard core of the basic industries? They were unanimous on that at Aberdeen. Yet that was far from probable under a Conservative Government which was then appointing the Beechings and Robens to cut back the industries already in some degree of public ownership because of their "lack of profitability"; twenty-four years later the phrase was to be "uneconomic".

This again raised a further difficulty. For there was some dissatisfaction amongst the uninformed public about lack of progress in these industries. Only those working in or dependent upon them could fully understand how much difficulty was due to the terms on which they were taken over, already bankrupt yet with excessive claims for compensation; and also lack of popular control over their management. There had just been much media propaganda that the Labour Party's failure to win the recent election was due to it being thought that their victory would have meant more of the same. This was giving strength to those forces within the Parliamentary Labour Party turning more to a policy of continued "mixed economy" rather than expanding speedy and effective public ownership. Over this there were likely to be further difficulties and disunity all through the decade in Britain as a whole: but this was to have very little effect in Scotland.

The attitude became clear in the 1960 debates at Aberdeen. They were unanimous for the motion moved by Abe Moffat "that the Government direct industry into Scotland to build a balanced economy"; and equally so on the General Council's demand for "conscious planning and intervention by the Government", criticising the weakness of the Local Employment Act. But the really sharp speaking came in the unanimous support for the motion calling for the next Labour Government to nationalise basic industries and meanwhile for the Labour Party "to publicise and popularise this fundamental principle in every possible way". When he moved it, Alex Kitson, General Secretary of the Scottish Horse & Motormen's Association, said bluntly: "The only basic industries which were not subsidised nowadays were the nationalised industries", giving scathing details of the working of the "so-called mixed economy" which road transport workers had endured. In seconding, W Simpson, Foundry Workers, said: "At present the private sector was master, the public sector was servant." He added that "the nation did not control the commanding heights of the economy": and a Government could not control the economy "with the present mixture of public and private enterprise". George Scott, Electrical Trades, saw them "faced with a growing concentration of capitalist monopoly power in private hands. The giant combines were the force behind the Tories. They were the enemies of the people." Less strong feeling was expressed only when George Middleton said he "believed that we did have a situation where monopoly capitalism and common ownership could grow together". He added in his characteristically soothing manner:

> It had to be remembered that the road to Socialism would be easier if we were required to tackle a comparatively small number of large enterprises rather than a vast number of small ones.

Ever anxious to concentrate on issues which he believed to be readily achievable, Middleton was to resign three years later, but remained in touch on his appointment to the Scottish Board for Industry in Scotland and as chairman of the Herring Industry Board and other public positions.

The question remained after the 1960 Congress: in the next decade, where should the Scottish trade union movement concentrate its public campaigning, on which it had first ventured in the Highlands and Islands in the 'fifties? Should it aim to campaign simultaneously on direction, public ownership and bringing in a Socialist Government? Or should it devote its major efforts only to issues which would ensure maximum unity amongst the different Scottish political and social interests, and which might therefore perhaps be readily achievable? Seventy years earlier when the STUC was founded in the general climate of Radical Liberalism this would be no new problem to delegates. Now, however, the movement was more mature and infinitely stronger. Virtually the whole GC was already and increasingly committed to maximum campaigning in a balanced way, and not merely passing and formally "processing" hardy annual resolutions.

There were other spheres and areas in which the interests of the Scottish people must be advanced as well as the particular needs of sections of the economy. On expanding trade, colonial and international relations and above all the preservation of peace, the STUC was also active in campaigning during these taxing years. Moreover, in this era of technical change at immense pace involving new techniques, changed structure and everything implied in off-shore oil development, the social questions of education and housing demanded insistent attention and new emphasis.

Section (iii): **Industrial and Political Campaigning**

After Macmillan's meeting with the Scots, his Government took some steps to exert added pressure in certain directions; but it was not long before it became clear that these were quite inadequate. He was doubtless relieved when the Toothill Committee, set up in the period of the 1959 General Election to study the future of Scottish economy, stopped short of advocating direction of industry when they came to report in 1961; instead they favoured increased Government grants and financial concessions to private enterprise. Inevitably the STUC campaign to prevent further decline was seen to involve the whole political aspect. Thus in the first half of the 'sixties the trade union movement realised increasingly that it must rely on the return of the Labour Government capable of resisting the pressures from major financial and business interests and their representatives at Westminster. In Scotland there was quick response as the Macmillan Government began preparing for the disappearance throughout Britain of "full employment", with steps towards privatisation and methods to limit trade union functions, such as setting up joint consultative bodies to introduce "pay pause" by agreement.

Inescapably, different industries were in the forefront at different stages, but all responded strongly with strikes, demonstrations and other protest actions. They included builders, miners, workers in road transport, railways and rail shops, aircraft, textiles, the motor industry, steel and of course every form of shipbuilding and engineering. All were linked in remarkably united action through the campaigns on behalf of each and the activity on the general economic position which the STUC was now uniquely equipped to generate. As Middleton pointed out during the main 1961 debate at Rothesay, the GC "had issued more statements about the economy of Scotland than any other organisation", arguing the case and proving "just precisely" what was needed, while gaining much publicity for it. He added that being associated with so many deputations, conferences and meetings it was clear that Congress "could claim to be a social as well as an economic organisation". Particularly bitter remarks were made on how vulnerable Scotland was because of its transport deficiency in the debates on that and on the Beeching destruction of the nationalised railways. The Government's plans to destroy any co-ordinated system of road and rail transport Alex Kitson said bitterly was "the final act of sabotage". He pointed out that the lucrative British road services were "now being built up to hand back to the financiers because of the profits that could be obtained from road haulage". Privatisation was to go ahead fast after much public expense to make it profitable for private owners. Meanwhile no less than 102 branch lines were to be closed by Beeching who in future would be known as the "butcher of Scotland", said R W Paterson, the Railway Clerk. They also passed unanimously a resolution which deplored "increasing reliance on oil", and demanded the preparation of a comprehensive long-term national fuel and power policy, with adequate research "into coal uses and smokeless fuels".

Action by railwaymen was greatly strengthened by Scots Miners once again engaging in an immense campaign against further closures of "uneconomic" pits: pit closures inevitably involved closures of the railway lines carrying coal. The 16 pit closures threatened for 1962 underlined the miners' experience of how false were the promises made during the 1959 closures of permanent work elsewhere. So the Scots Miners decided

> to refuse to co-operate in closing so-called "uneconomic" pits; to insist on the fullest consultation in accordance with our rights within the industry; and, finally, to demand a public inquiry into the administration, financial planning and mechanisation policies.[4]

Once again, the Scots were in the lead in demanding what was to become the "Plan for Coal". Although the British Miners' Executive objected to an inquiry, even though they had the support of Yorkshire and South Wales miners, in Scotland they won immediate support for an inquiry even from the Presbytery of Ayr. It was largely the Scots Miners' campaign which encouraged the GC to call an important conference on the Scottish economy in Glasgow with an extremely wide representation of 1,200 delegates on 18 February, 1962. The Scots Miners, supported by the Railwaymen's Unions, followed this with an immense Parliamentary Lobby on 8 March. With over 700 descending on Westminster only a sudden outbreak of smallpox locally prevented a mass delegation joining them from South Wales, the other coalfield to be most gravely hit by threats of "uneconomic" closures.

This took place just before the annual STUC Conference: against this background and with the publication of the feeble Toothill Report on the Scottish economy, delegates at Aberdeen in 1962 sharpened their tone considerably. For unemployment was worsening, and the same week had already seen major demonstrations by Rolls Royce workers against their redundancy. As Jimmy Jarvie of the Blacksmiths put it, the position "would have been catastrophic" without the investment of some measure of public money, through the campaign for which the STUC had been "the main driving force". Congress unquestioningly resolved that "positive direction" of industry had become essential; moreover, they unanimously instructed the GC to organise demonstrations everywhere, to explain the STUC policy to educate and win active support for it. The Miners thought that they must also spell out definite proposals about just what should be located and where. Will McLean promised that if the STUC undertook to produce such an exact plan, the Miners would donate £1,000 towards the cost; already miners were being moved for the third time, now down over the border to Yorkshire and the Midlands. One delegate stressed how important it was that their main resolution should also become the policy of the British TUC and the Labour Party. He may well have had his eye on the score of General Secretaries and National Presidents who had come to Scotland for the Congress, some for the first time, including Frank Cousins of the powerful Transport & General. Delegates from many industries brought forward their own special problems, as did the Railwaymen's General Secretary, Sidney Greene. He moved a composite on Scotland's need for integrated rail and road services, deploring the closure of branch lines: it declared that "stronger measures were needed than mere expressions of opposition", and that there must be support for any steps the transport unions might take. This was in fact in anticipation of the coming railway strike which won major support in Scotland.

Many of these national leaders spoke out very strongly in the debate on the Macmillan Government's new measures; these Patrick Connor, the STUC's first AEU President, had described in his opening address as "blatant interference in negotiating machinery". His remark that it had had the effect of uniting indignant non-manual with other workers was borne out in the subsequent debate on the National Economic Development Council (Neddy) and the "pay pause". The Boilermakers' leader, Danny McGarvey, moved a unanimous composite on this "unilateral arbitrary interference with negotiating machinery". It declared support for any union taking action in defence of its members' standards. It was seconded by a Civil Service Union delegate and followed by a General & Municipal Worker. Then Frank Cousins said that the trade union movement would not accept what "Neddy's" task was to bring in by way of "any policy of wage restraint, either in that body or out of it". What they needed was

> higher wage levels spreading the production cost over a greater output, a reduction in the profits taken out of industry and, above all, the opportunity to have free negotiations in a free society.

Clive Jenkins, the Supervisory Staffs' new General Secretary, said that in its policy the Government was "acting in concert" with other nations, "particularly those of the Common Market, to effect a reduction in purchasing power throughout Western Europe".

The GC followed up the instructions to organise demonstrations by a "Jobs for Scotland Campaign". After discussions with the Development and Industry Council, the Scottish Board and MPs, and finding their approaches to Ministries remained abortive, in the autumn they held nine regional conferences about the rapidly deteriorating general economic situation. Attendance at these ranged from 144 in Dumfries to 914 in Glasgow, numbering 3,369 in all, which included "a very large number of local authorities". In what was to be his last report, Middleton said that many of these "openly associated themselves with the resolutions passed"; he described the conference as "amongst the most successful ever held". From these emerged a memorandum to Macmillan outlining "the long-term aims", as well as some of the "short-term needs", in shipbuilding and marine engineering, iron and steel, coal, transport and rail shops. They followed this with considerable detail, including points on such issues as the Atomic Energy Authority programme. This forced Macmillan to receive the GC representatives in January 1963 for the third time, after they had got much useful information from the Confederation as well as having been directly involved in protest actions. They had some difficulty with the Executive of the Scottish Labour Party whom they found uneasy about direction, preferring the phrase "planned location of industry". Throughout, a central point had been the need for the Government to set up "a Scottish Development Agency armed with the essential finance and power to plan the development of the Scottish economy", and as a first step to revive the post-war Scottish Economic Conference. Then just before the delegates met at Dunoon in 1963, this being one of their representations which the Secretary for Scotland had ignored in an "offhand manner" since his appointment in July, they made a fierce complaint to Macmillan. In the press statement they issued about it they said the times were too difficult and

> the issues so important that Scotland can ill-afford a Secretary of State who surveys the industrial scene like a shepherd on some distant hillside.

More and continuous pressure was needed.

There had been important grass-roots action, such as demonstrations by Cowlairs and St Rollox rail shopmen. There was also deep suspicion about "Neddy's" new offshoot: this was the National Incomes Commission, known as "Nick", which some thought Rabbie Burns would have described as "Auld Clootie". Its first victim was to be the Scottish builders' activities, reacting to the effect on employment by the Government's monetary policy in wholesale slashing of grants to local authorities for school-building. For "Nick" was to describe the Scottish builders' agreement to cut the working week as "against the national interests". While approving the GC's general campaigning efforts, Dunoon delegates stressed that more was needed, that call coming especially from the four trades council speakers in the main debate there. From Cambuslang, for example, Gordon Massie said the GC should give greater support "to militant mass rank and file action", and active encouragement "to all demonstrations and stoppages organised by any" against redundancy. In the climate of growing anger there was a huge Mass Lobby for Jobs of Parliament that spring, organised by several Federations of Trades Councils. It was supported by the Northern Ireland Committee of the Irish Congress, and also by the STUC, despite what Massie described as "a negative attitude" in some of the top leadership. Some showed only "grudging consent" to such forms of action; but Congress had now armed them with powers "to develop a massive campaign, co-ordinating centrally all efforts of affiliated organisations".[5]

Section (iv): **A New Labour Government**

In the busy year running up to the General Election which narrowly returned a Labour Government under Harold Wilson, the GC did continue its "Quest for Jobs" campaign; it included regional conferences for trade union and local authorities' representatives in the main areas; visits to 45 trades councils; and a conference with the latest Tory Premier, Sir Alec Douglas-Home, together with Edward Heath and with 36 MPs of all parties. There were also no less than four major meetings with the Secretary of Scotland before the General

Election, at which they bluntly dismissed the "White Paper on Central Scotland Growth and Development" as being no real plan.

The 1964 delegates to the Perth Congress unanimously praised their policy statement, which James Milne for Aberdeen Trades Council described as "the most complete" they had ever issued, and they did not stop there. Welcoming the "persistent quest for jobs" they called on the GC "to step up their public campaign". Of the five other speakers from trades councils once again Gordon Massie stressed that they

> had come to the conclusion that the only effective means of getting a substantial change in Government outlook was to organise mass rank and file demonstrations and send lobbies to Parliament.

Calling on delegates to redouble their efforts to return a Labour Government, he added that "such a sustained campaign of demonstration would also be useful in making clear" to a Labour Government what Scottish people were demanding.

Throughout 1964 they found themselves deeply concerned in dealing with closure after closure of factories and workshops in engineering, mining and textiles. By the autumn they had to repeat their case to all the Ministers of the Labour Government; from them they soon had at least one innovation to welcome warmly. This was the Highland Development (Scotland) Act bringing "to fruition the policy" which the STUC had advocated for so many years. But at Rothesay in 1965 they did warn that it would "not be really effective without powers of land acquisition", and co-ordinating the activities of other statutory bodies there.

Much was hoped for from this first Labour Government since the early post-war years; but as they had less than a half dozen majority, there was a widespread feeling that they should be given time and not unduly harried in their early days. As the STUC's new General Secretary, James Jack, said in introducing the main 1965 Report on the economy to the Rothesay delegates, the press had been speculating "as to whether Congress would be as vigorous in their demands to the new Labour Government". In fact over the main areas of the economy they continued strong insistence on their basic policy. There was no hesitancy on direction; re-nationalisation of steel; a national fuel policy and a halt to rail closures. The previous year's President, F H Stephen of the Draughtsmen, sharply warned that in shipbuilding, where so much diversification and modernisation was needed, "while the trade unions were seeking nationalisation the employers themselves were 'rationalising' the industry". He described how Barclay Curle's design department was transferred to Tyneside, other firms failed to invest, seeking instead to sell off at a profit, quoting the dredgers' yard, Simon Lobnitz and Harland & Wolff's Foundry. There were equally strong statements on the havoc the monetary policy had worked on Scottish housing, education, health and pensions; here already was beginning the trend to undermine the "welfare state".

But the STUC meeting as the first major conference of the movement for the year was also to be the scene of a trial run for the Labour Government's form of wage restraint. The Minister for Economic Affairs, George Brown, came to make a long speech just before the Joint Statement of Intent on Productivity, Prices and Incomes was debated. He provided a variety of statistics aiming to show why wages should be chained to productivity. It was the first time for three years that Harold Wilson himself had not attended. The following morning six resolutions and amendments were composited for debate on Incomes Policy. After calling for measures to curb prices and restrain profits and tax evasion, the composite went so far as to say that it could not "support any policy that will stabilise wages at their present level", although ready to support efforts for economic planning. But when H R Nicholas, the incoming General Secretary of the Transport & General, George Brown's own union, called for a remit, a majority accepted this, with only Alex Moffat and the Railwaymen's delegate speaking strongly against that. The argument used was that a fortnight later there was to be a conference in London of the Trade Union Executives to discuss their attitude. This had already been hinted at by the Regional Secretary of the same union in the Presidential Address; William Scholes mentioned the conference and said they must be sure "the trade unions speak with the same voice".

But if speaking with one voice involved agreeing to wage restraint in any form there was little chance of it being accepted in Scotland; that the STUC made very clear indeed, when it met within a month of the second General Election which confirmed the Labour Government in the spring of 1966. So while there might be leading figures as elsewhere who at first believed that with the small majority it was essential not to appear to be going too far and too fast if a Tory Government were to be kept out, this was quickly rejected by the Scots: they wanted further and faster action. Moreover, when measures began to be taken to restrict the unions' powers for fear they would respond to indignation from their grass roots, the Scots were amongst the first once again to show strong disapproval.

But before following the fate of these policies which in fact brought about the defeat of the Labour Government at the end of the decade, it is necessary to look at other features which had a profound effect on the attitude expressed by the STUC.

Section (v): **Response to International Problems**

With their cultural awareness, historical experience and sense of economic discrimination and neglect, Scottish trade unionists continued to be highly responsive to internationalism's links between peoples and the value of unity. They were, therefore, not slow to react against racialism, whether of Italian Fascism, German Nazism or attitudes characteristic of imperialist rulers towards colonial peoples. In the fourteen years of continuous Tory rule in the 'fifties and 'sixties there were increasingly all too many occasions for their anxieties to be expressed; for these were the years of the break-up of the British Empire.

These were times when unprecedented problems of change and division were emerging fast. Indeed, change was expressed even in the terms describing the inhabited globe. It was no longer described as "One World": it had even ceased to be regarded as two worlds – the competitive, capitalist free enterprise world and the co-operative, planned socialist enterprise world. For now it was recognised that account must be taken of the "Third World" of immense populations, largely kept undeveloped when dominated by the former colonial powers of Europe. As they began to achieve a measure of independence, many tended to look beyond at the two super powers of the USA and the Soviet Union for help or hindrance. High hopes for the United Nations were soon dashed by the United States insisting on the new Republic of China being excluded; moreover, while China sought her own specific form of development, there was some degree of lack of unity between her and the Soviet Union which tended to keep progress slow. Meanwhile there was no continent without its deep divisions.

But the vastly uneven level of economic and social development now thrust into the foreground was further complicated by the spreading effects of technological change of which the divided world had never seen the like. Experiments following the development of atomic theory had already started revolutionising energy, communications, transport, health and everything capable of automation. Technological change saw the first man in space, when on 12 April, 1961, Yuri Gagarin signalled back his first words to mankind's advance base: "How beautiful the world looks!" Seven days later the Rothesay STUC delegates passed with acclamation an emergency resolution of congratulation to this son of a carpenter, for

> being the first man to enter space and the service he has rendered for this greatest scientific achievement in the history of man.

In moving it Abe Moffat said it "transcended all political and racial barriers"; and he recalled that at the sputnik's launching the Soviet Union had "declared that they would place it at the service of all people in the name of progress, happiness and the well-being of everyone". Seconding this Jimmy Jarvie, the Blacksmith, said it could mean for all "an era of peace and progress"; and described the kinship they felt because it was "a working man who broke the new barrier and opened up the new vista of history before us".

But this use of the development of technological change had to be set against the terrifying nuclear arms race between the super powers. This had started when the capacity was used sixteen years before Gagarin's achievement to drop the first nuclear weapon from an American aircraft to wipe out a Japanese city at a single blow. After the Soviet Union had next developed a similar capacity this began to be followed by all the main European powers. Finally there was nothing that could stop final weapons of mass destruction coming into the possession of the warring countries of the Middle East, of Latin America and of Asia. Step by step over the years what nuclear war must finally mean became increasingly clear. The Scots were not slow to react. From the very first they were to express all the arguments: for and against banning; for unilateralism; for nuclear-free zones; for agreements against first use; against foreign bases; and against the increasingly horrific foreign missiles being based on Scottish land and in Scottish waters.

At first concentration was on trying to prevent both the spread of the ownership to more countries and the development of even worse weapons by agreement to ban further scientific testing, both above ground and also later below ground. On this the super powers were at odds over how tests could be inspected; must inspection be on site? If so how many, and conducted by whom? It was not until some time after scientists had proved that site inspection was not needed that a partial ban treaty was agreed in general terms. Meanwhile there had been horrific testing of the H-bomb on remote Pacific islands.

By 1959 a unanimous resolution, "deeply conscious of the cataclysmic character of future war", demanded more effort to achieve summit talks between the main Powers, to concentrate on stopping the tests. Welcoming the Geneva experts' conclusions that means were already available for detecting tests, they deplored "the tardy progress" in reaching agreement. Discussions around the effects of the tests were winning widespread attention. By the following year at the STUC there were frequent references to the growing massive protest marches to the military nuclear scientific centre at Aldermaston by Salisbury Plain in the far south. These Easter demonstrations taking place each year when STUC delegates were assembling, "highlighted the desire for peace which united wide sections of public opinion", said the Miner Guy Stobbs at Perth. As the Railwayman delegate A Kirkwood put it bitterly, he had been "unfortunate enough to see Hiroshima and the effects of the first atom bomb used"; now photographs should be shown on television to "remind people with short memories" what it could mean, if they failed to achieve total abandonment of test, manufacture and use.

At the same time they now came out more strongly on preventing German rearmament and supplying atomic weapons to West Germany where there were so many of the old gang in charge. John Horner, the General Secretary of the Fire Brigades, described German peace supporters taking part in the immense demonstration in Trafalgar Square with their banners "pleading that we should not give them nuclear weapons". The reference to German rearmament was keenly supported from Clydebank especially, with its own memories of German air-raid casualties. Delegates welcomed strongly the proposals then being broached for at last developing Summit Talks which had failed so dismally in 1955. But hardly had the 1960 Congress ended when these hopes were dashed to the ground. For on 1 May, 1960, the Pentagon wrecked the proposal by sending a U2 spy plane which connected NATO bases in Turkey and Pakistan with Norway, over Afghanistan into the Soviet Union; photographing military objectives. It was brought down in the Urals whilst the GC delegation were still on their visit to the Russian unions and seeking trade for the Scottish shipyards. The pilot of the U2 survived and the plane's equipment was put on public display in Moscow. It was only then that Washington was finally forced to admit the facts.[6]

Section (vi): **The Final Weapon in Scotland Itself**

But when they met at Rothesay in 1961 anxieties had indeed widened; for during the autumn the threat had now come right on to Scotland's own doorstep. The Tory Government had decided to give facilities at Holy Loch for a base for US submarines armed with Polaris nuclear missiles. The GC was called upon for action by many affiliated unions and trades councils; as a result they issued an important statement of concern "to alert every trade unionist in Scotland to the meaning and seriousness of this step". They pointed out that while it might be accepted that NATO was a collective security system and might have to give a decision to use atomic weapons from bases in Britain, "the Polaris submarine operations are clearly in a different category". The base was ceded to the USA and the right to question its use was surrendered; a missile-carrying submarine could set out from the Clyde into Russian waters and involve Britain in responsibility for war; a submarine could be blown up in the Clyde "with all the horrible consequences". The statement also made these points: Polaris was not a defensive weapon; it would not be included in any agreement for NATO prior consultation; it was "an open invitation to retaliatory measures"; and that the manning of the base by American servicemen would bring trade was the "discredited slogan that 'war brings work' ". Issued on 8 November, 1960, they went on to try and involve the Scottish Parliamentary Group and convened a special meeting of the Joint Committee with the Labour Party for 25 November, to direct a campaign. But the Scottish Council of the Labour Party refused to take part until the tripartite national leadership in London should come to some decision: in fact by February they were still held back by the Labour Party National Executive. Meanwhile, responding to the request of the Glasgow Trades Council, City Labour Party and District Co-operative Association, the STUC held the first major public protest campaign in Glasgow on 18 December, 1960. Trades councils from all over followed suit.[7]

When the Tory Government's only reply was to insist that all these measures, including Polaris, were needed for a balance of nuclear power which was what prevented war breaking out – an argument repeated for so many years – the GC replied strongly. They emphasised their alarm that bases were now to be available as refuelling points for German U-boats, whether at Rosyth or elsewhere; that integration into NATO was no safeguard. While demands for a moratorium on nuclear testing as a first step towards banning the use of "this frightful instrument of destruction" were continued, it was Polaris which now remained central to their fears, together with their distrust over German rearmament, the non-recognition of East Germany, and the costly continuance of British troops in Germany.

When Frank Cousins, visiting General Secretary of the Transport Workers, moved the basic peace resolution at Aberdeen in 1962, the question of unilateralism was implicit; but by 1963 it was already in the open at Dunoon. Here the composite resolution included the statement that

> Congress opposes in every way the Government's efforts in having an independent nuclear deterrent. It views with disgust this hideous investment in Polaris submarines by the Government whose only

possible use is the massacre of workers and trade unionists in other lands.

Moving it for the Miners, Michael McGahey referred to "the terrible disaster which befell the nuclear submarine *Thresher*"; the failure to make contact with it showed that with a breakdown in communications "the world could be launched into nuclear annihilation". It was strongly supported by the Scientific Workers, Tobacco Workers' General Secretary, the Draughtsmen, Blacksmiths, Transport & General, and the Paisley, Clydebank and Renfrew Trades Councils. The only delegates to speak against it were from the Clerks and the Civil Service Clerical Association; their unions opposed the policy of unilateralism. The Clerks' General Secretary, H G Chapman, said "unilateral action could only weaken the voice of Britain", and might "well increase the dangers of nuclear war". But the motion was passed by a substantial majority.

With the approach of the 1964 General Election and when the three powers meeting in Moscow had agreed on a partial test ban agreement, the GC "warmly welcomed" it while still stressing the need for the removal of Polaris and foreign troops from all other bases in Britain. This was followed up three months later at the Perth Congress by a composite moved by Willie McLean for the GC. The partial ban should be extended to underground tests; there should also be admission of China to UNO; establishing a European nuclear-free zone; and a non-aggression pact between NATO and the Warsaw Powers. It had, however, opened with a demand for all nuclear foreign bases to be removed, because with Polaris their concentration in Scotland "places us quite literally in the centre of any nuclear battlefield of the future". This the Clerks' delegate once again wished omitted as being "contrary to Labour Party policy", which would embarrass the visiting Harold Wilson and "harm Labour's cause" in the General Election. But it was carried unanimously.

Section (vii): **Labour's Policy Overseas**

Having got little change on this from the Tory Secretary for Foreign Affairs, they repeated it to his Labour successor after the Election. But the nuclear-free zone and non-aggression pact were rejected on the ground that they "could only lead to a false sense of security and perhaps to uncertainty in the Communist world about the West's readiness to defend its vital interests". Nor was the recognition of East Germany accepted.

But as they met at Rothesay in 1965 they had seen the appalling intervention by the United States in Vietnam, using napalm bombs and gas. When Jimmy Milne for Aberdeen Trades Council moved an emergency resolution, with strong supporting speeches from trades councils, Miners, Scottish Motormen and Draughtsmen it was carried unanimously. It was also foremost, in the main debate. Peace and Rearmament he moved for the GC, referring to the dangers of "escalation of such hostilities" as Vietnam and Malaysia, in the twentieth year of UNO. It reiterated their basic points, adding denunciation of the new scheme of the so-called Multilateral Force to bring West Germany into operating the nuclear arms of NATO, while refusing recognition to East Germany. Although there was strong support and the motion was carried, the Shop Assistants' delegate opposed on the usual ground that recognition of East Germany was against the policy of Labour Party, British TUC and the new Labour Government.

On issue after issue the STUC was showing marked independence in its attitude now on international relations, overseas and colonial policy; on all of these subjects remarkable speeches by their leaders were made year after year at the Congresses.[8] It was also unwilling to accept, or to await, the lead from the British TUC. Whatever were the traditional hopes from a Labour Government it would not be spared criticism on what were increasingly felt to be life or death issues. Polaris and foreign bases in Scotland together with the staggering use of terror weapons in Vietnam and their threat elsewhere, with no certain barriers against the final nuclear weapon, remained unacceptable. Meeting in Aberdeen shortly before the 1966 Election had brought Harold Wilson back as Prime Minister, and just before he himself came to the rostrum, Congress passed a resolution calling on the British Government to dissociate itself from the American actions in Vietnam and stop all bombing. They also called on the Labour Government to abandon its "East of Suez policy", close down military bases, withdraw British troops and aim for "freer relations between the peoples of Africa and Asia". One delegate said it "was tragic that a British Labour Government had taken upon themselves the role of America's junior partner". But in his speech to them Wilson made virtually no reference to foreign policy.

While Vietnam with the napalm bombing and use of gas brought things sharply to the fore, on other events "east of Suez" and in Africa there had been no few occasions during previous governments when problems in former colonial countries had to be raised. There were frequent protests about repression in Nyasaland, the Rhodesias and Central African Federation. With the murderous attack in South Africa's Sharpeville, and the refusal of rights to Namibia, there were frequent demands for Britain to operate and rigidly enforce the United Nations' declared arms embargo against this "fascist police state policy". Full support for a popular boycott on the import of South African goods was supported when this was called for by the victims of racial persecution and the death sentences there. When President Kennedy attempted the invasion of Cuba the 1960 STUC demanded an immediate meeting of the United Nations' Security Council. Two years later in 1962 they had before them a resolution affecting events nearer home. The visiting Secretary of the Irish Congress of Trade Unions, Ruadhri Roberts, had complained how the Northern Ireland Government had refused to recognise, consult with or adopt unemployment policies put forward by the Northern Committee of the unions. A resolution expressing "deep regret" at what it described as both "absurd and unjust and is totally out of harmony with current industrial procedure", was passed on to the main body in Ireland.

With many motions having to be remitted to the GC without discussion through lack of time, including those on nuclear weapons, a German Peace Treaty and Rhodesia, all through 1966 patience was beginning to run out. Having already denounced the Labour Government's Prices and Incomes Bill and shown alarm at the prospect of lack of restraint on prices and dividends by 1967 at Dunoon there was a very sharp turn. The STUC had occasion to issue the first early warnings which the Wilson Government would ignore at its peril. These arose both on home and foreign affairs, and especially on the absence of a decisive change in attitude to Scotland's economy, which was under dire threat.

References

[1] "Call upon the wheels, master, call upon the wheels! Steel is beneath your hand, stone beneath your heels, Steel will never laugh aloud, hearing what we heard, Stone will never break its heart, mad with hope deferred! Men of tact that arbitrate, slow reform that heals – Save the stinking grease, master, save it for the wheels". (By G K Chesterton about the 1911 railway strike: " 'The Song of the Wheels" written during a Friday and Saturday in August, 1911".)

[2] See *The Donovan Report*, Labour Research Department Publications.

[3] Cmnd 3888 HMSO.

[4] Guy Stobbs, Ayrshire District Secretary, described the Lobby in *Labour Monthly*, April 1962, "A Shout from the People"; it included accounts from three others on the Lobby and also a poem written by a Clydach miner during the 1910-11 struggles in the Rhondda, which included these lines:
"When they introduced conveyors Half our wages then they stole. Now they say the Pits aren't paying And they've thrown us on the dole".

[5] Contributing to "Trades Councils and Jobs", in *Labour Monthly*, June, 1963.

[6] Earlier it was claimed that this was only a weather plane, merely flying over

Turkey; that the pilot had oxygen mask trouble; that he was probably unconscious when the U2 went off course. Somewhat similar statements were made twenty-three years later when an American plane was shot down over the Soviet Union's Far Eastern naval waters. Since it was lost in the sea there was no equipment to put on display, though both parties sought it diligently for many weeks.

[7] Middleton spoke at public meetings so organised locally at Paisley, Dundee, Airdrie, Edinburgh; J Jarvie at Vale of Leven; Alex Kitson at Kirkcaldy; Wm Scholes at Govanhill; F H Stephen at Cowdenbeath.

[8] Those making remarkable speeches in the 'sixties included Alex Kitson, James Milne, Patrick Connor, Frank Stephen, Will McLean, Lawrence Daly, Michael McGahey and Enoch Humphries; and many Trades Council leaders like Hugh Wyper, Gordon Massie, Arnold Henderson, W McQuilkin, Dunky Waddell and others. Visiting General Secretaries from south of the border also often took the opportunity to respond warmly; amongst these were Frank Cousins, and Harry Nicholas of the Transport Workers, Percy Belcher of the Tobacco Workers, Ted Hill, Boilermakers; Clive Jenkins, Supervisory Staffs.

23

In Place of Peace

With increasing closures, redundancy and short-time working in engineering and especially in the shipyards, Scotland had soon to scrutinise sharply the new Labour Government's legislation and proposals for industry, including the Geddes Report which showed no guarantee of early shipbuilding nationalisation. There were already grim total failures of privately owned shipyards at Fairfield and Lithgow, necessitating their rescue by Government financial intervention which, however, lacked appropriate controls. Introduced as the period of "full employment" was already fading, the Redundancy Payments Act of 1965 was to have a long-term effect throughout the whole movement. While it put forward the conception of individual ownership of a job in workshop, yard or office entitling a redundant person to an individual "golden handshake", as a retiring director for so many years had been getting, in Scotland it was quickly seen what could happen. For although the prospect of a redundancy payment "helps to soften the blow", as Sam Barr, convener in a Clydeside shipyard, wrote[1]; it

> adversely affects the campaign being set up by the more militant workers to oppose closures and sackings.

Apart from misgivings on this, there had been the Labour Government's unprecedented ban on any wage increase for six months, announced on 20 July, 1966.

Section (i): "Pay Freeze" and Job Loss

The impact in Scotland was immediate. In the words of their report to the 1967 Dunoon Congress the GC considered it a day which "will neither be seen nor readily forgotten". This inroad on the powers of trade unions added point to anxieties about the Royal Commission in progress under Lord Donovan on their future functions. It meant an extremely busy year for the GC under the chairmanship of Willie

McLean, soon to succeed Laurence Daly as Secretary of the Scottish Miners. There were frequent discussions with Ministers, including the Premier, and conferences of full-time officers with Margaret Herbison and Tony Wedgwood Benn on the role of their new Ministries of Social Security and Technology. The GC also submitted very impressive evidence to no less than two Royal Commissions on Local Government in Scotland, and the Royal Commission under Lord Donovan on Trade Unions and Employers' Associations. Their evidence to these was published as an Appendix to the 1967 Report, in which it was stated that it was felt that both contributions "can be counted as not unworthy additions to the long list of Congress documents which have been presented and published over the years". Each document provided the historical background, description of the differences and the STUC's standpoint, with detailed proposals of how the seven regions they recommended should operate. Their written evidence to the Royal Commission on Local Government in Scotland followed up the Government's Regional Economic Plan for Scotland: subtitled "A Plan for Expansion" it had proposed within five years to create 130,000 new jobs, reducing loss from older industries and migration. But as McLean said in his Presidential Address five months later, the "position today is, to put it mildly, very far from encouraging". But in fact unemployment had increased by a third, which he saw as substantially due to the "Freeze" policy. The Government in 1964 resisting the policy of direction had said that if private enterprise failed to come to Scotland, the Government would establish State-owned enterprises; it was indeed time. He added that the Scottish Economic Planning Council had neither money nor authority, and repeated their emphasis on communications and transport problems, the need to halt rail closures and integrate transport. He emphasised that housing required "most drastic action", and it was essential to encourage local authorities to increase house-building and at reasonable rents. Yet the results of the Plan were meagre; it was the Defence Estimates, for which a number of Labour MPs had refused to vote, which were indeed drastic. On Polaris his view was that the Government should tell the USA "to take the base lock, stock and barrel back to American waters".

Congress delegates showed themselves in basic agreement with all that he was saying, including voting by four to one against going into the Common Market. In this, the seventieth year of their foundation, they were in a new and angry mood; and Jim Callaghan attending as Chancellor of the Exchequer was left in no doubt about where they stood on incomes policy and the position of the union movement. The debates were on many subjects and discussion was lively. There was congratulation for the GC about the efforts they had made to encourage Scottish trades councils, the report containing the results of a referendum following a conference of their officers; Glasgow's opening of their Trade Union Centre and Social Club; and Kirkcaldy's decision to organise a special Festival of Trade Unionism at Glenrothes.

The following year was indeed to witness further development of their mood, with increasing insistence on urgent action: it saw further close attention by the GC to trades councils and the first of what came to be the annual weekend conferences of their officers. While the British TUC in its centenary year was voluntarily accepting the policy of pay freeze, arguing that legislation might then be avoided, delegates to Aberdeen in 1968 showed a much sharper attitude in every debate. It is perhaps significant that although they did concern themselves with two important centenaries, no delegate referred to that of the British TUC. First there was a warm welcome for the centenary of Aberdeen Trades Council, where James Jack had recently opened a Social Club. Then they went on to approve the proposal to commemorate the birth of James Connolly, which Alex Kitson had first suggested when as a delegate he attended the Irish Congress of Trades Unions some months before. John Henry as Secretary of the Edinburgh Trades Council described the week's programme they were planning, during which a commemorative plaque would be unveiled on the Cowgate Arch of Edinburgh's South Bridge, close to the birthplace, when the Irish Congress of Trade Unions would also be present. This announcement was warmly welcomed by the Irish Vice-President, James Dunne, of the Marine, Port and General Workers' Union, in his fraternal speech.

He expressed "great pleasure" at the plan "to commemorate the birth of a great Irishman, who was also a great Internationalist – for if James Connolly died before a firing squad for Irish freedom, he also lived in the battle to establish the human dignity and imperishable rights of workers everywhere". As applicable to Connolly, he quoted "words penned by a young Irish poet two days before he died in France" fighting in British uniform for the "Freedom of Small Nations". The young poet had

> died not for Flag – nor King – nor Emperor,
> But for a Dream – born in a herdsman's shed
> And for the secret scripture of the Poor.

To immense applause he ended by saying: "We must not rest until our Movement and our peoples have attained their full stature in a state of society more truly dedicated to the common good and welfare of all of the people without distinction of class, creed or colour". When next Dunne came to the STUC two years later, not only were Scotland and Ireland sharing the same economic and industrial problems, in the Six Counties the tragic civil rights struggles had begun, marking a new phase.

Two days after Dunne had spoken came the outstanding debate on devolution, following the Scottish National Party having won a by-election in the current atmosphere of frustration. There were two contrasting resolutions, the Miners' advocating a Scottish Parliament, "ultimate form and powers of which should be determined by the Scottish electorate"; the Foundry Workers stressed concern at "the rise of nationalism", and against "total devolution". Arguing for the Miners' motion, Michael McGahey stressed that Scotland was "not a region of Britain, nor a district, but a nation in its own right". They were therefore, "entitled to decide the form and power of their own institutions". He was dismissive of the Scottish National Party as not being "the custodians of true Scottish nationalism". The best guarantee of being properly handled "was for the STUC and the Scottish Labour Movement to take up the question of nationalism, challenge the chauvinists and deal with the issues concerned in a proper working-class fashion". He made it clear that the Miners not only rejected the theory of totally separating Scotland from the United Kingdom, but also "the theory of a classless Scotland at the present stage". For, he argued,

> they had more in common with the London dockers, the Durham miners and the Sheffield engineers than they ever had had with the barons and landlord traitors of that kind in Scotland.

He closed by saying that socialism meant "decentralisation of power in order to involve the people of a country in the operation of power at every possible level". The Miners' view was supported by Glasgow and Clydebank Trades Councils, the Draughtsmen and Alex McCrindle for Actors Equity. R Garland moved the Foundry Workers' motion "against any attempt to secure total devolution". It went on to state that a "viable and socially secure Scotland can only be achieved within the economic framework of Great Britain", with pay and conditions no less favourable, to be "secured by national joint machinery covering Scotland, England and Wales". Most of his speech was taken up with detailed criticism of the Scottish National Party's slogans and its absence of "a coherent economic policy". He was supported by the Local Government and Painters' delegates. After the Engineers and Shop Assistants had expressed doubts, thinking it would be best for the

General Council to study the whole question in depth, James Milne read a carefully worded General Council statement. It regarded the Miners' as too general in its wording, while the Foundry Workers' attitude of concern at "the rise of nationalism" was thought to be completely out of sympathy "with the present trend of opinion", and the whole history of measures for extending planning of Scottish economy. He, therefore, asked both to remit. The Miners agreed but the Foundry Workers would not until a card vote was taken. The next year the General Council came up with an interim report only on the sort of measures needed for a Scottish legislative assembly; but with the setting up of a Royal Commission which did not report until 1973 there was little further decision for six years.

There was one other anniversary mentioned during the Aberdeen Congress: that was the fiftieth anniversary of women having first achieved the right to vote. It was, therefore, timely for the Engineers to move a resolution on equal pay for work of equal value, following a lively debate on it the previous year. Now it was supported before being passed unanimously by men representing the Foundry Workers, Tailors, Civil Servants and Paisley Trades Council. Of the 22 women present amongst the 471 delegates two came to the rostrum. Mrs V D Donald of the General and Municipal said that "in all of the fifty or so statements issued by the Prices and Incomes Board, the subject of equal pay had scarcely been mentioned". It was up to the women themselves to organise strongly in their unions and seek legislation. Agnes McLean of Glasgow Trades Council asked, "did Congress know what was really happening in the electronics industry? Hundreds of women were entering it at the women's rate of wage." She added she was "totally fed up with the mood of pessimism and gloom which had overtaken so many trade unionists on this issue". She added that in her many visits to factories in the West of Scotland she had "seen women coming out and fighting for equal pay whenever a proper lead was given them". Later that day Congress elected to the new General Council of 17 members the first woman since 1943; this was Betty McIntyre of Hosiery and Knitwear, and six years later she was to occupy the Presidential chair.

Just before they had met in Aberdeen there had come what could be seen as the beginning of a breakthrough for the vital Scottish industry of shipbuilding, recently beset by so many bankruptcies and job-losing mergers. They had long been concerned at its collapse under private ownership's failure to modernise, as their major campaign of support to save the Fairfield Yard in particular had shown. Now in February 1968 the Shipuilding Industry Board, set up following the inadequate Geddes Report, had just promoted the Upper Clyde Shipbuilders. In this consortium the Fairfield Yard joined the 200-year-old Stephen Yard, together with John Brown's, Connell's and Yarrow's. With its interest-free loan of public money, but always crippled with shortage of ready capital and inadequate management which lacked the stimulus of worker control, this was not the socialist public ownership they had sought for so long. But in its future development, with historic events only three years ahead, the STUC was to play an honourable supportive role. Before that unique action of the UCS work-in, however, they were to be primarily engrossed in resisting the attacks on the trade union movement, unprecedented since the beginning of the century.

Section (ii): **Attacks on Union Rights Begin**

The historic action at the Upper Clyde Shipbuilders was to happen in the climate of the Conservatives' detested Industrial Relations Act, after they had defeated the Wilson Government in 1970. Prime Minister Heath set about codifying and adding to the measures first advocated by Barbara Castle, Labour's Secretary for Employment and Productivity, in the ill-fated White Paper, "In Place of Strife: a Policy for Industrial Relations". The ground for what was quickly regarded as a very serious attack on trade union rights was prepared when the Donovan Royal Commission's report was published in June, 1968, two months after the delegates left Aberdeen. Whilst softly worded in a number of respects, with useful references to points from trade unions' own evidence, the Donovan Report's main object was to "assist an income policy to work effectively". Thus it wanted to restructure the wages negotiation system, tying it to productivity with existing national agreements replaced by "productivity agreements". By extending State intervention in the internal affairs of trade unions, it would restrict shop stewards' powers to bargain at shop-floor level on take-home pay. This was at a time when vehement action was in progress in many industries, from engineering to building trade projects like the Barbican, with prices and taxes rising fast while profits remained uncurbed. At first the Donovan Report caused confusion and illusions in some quarters; at the next STUC Eddie Marsden, General Secretary of the Constructional Engineers, called it "the typical sugar-coated pill with the main aim concealed under a number of well-chosen popular seeming reforms". But Congress did not accept its reaction, lock, stock and barrel; for by the spring of 1969, anxiety about it was completely replaced by anger over the White Paper, "In Place of Strife".

While Donovan relied for the most part on alterations to disputes machinery, the Labour Government's own White Paper proposed adding some very serious legal restrictions. What it described as "unconstitutional strikes", called before procedure was exhausted, were to be prevented by legal measures. A Minister would be able to demand a ballot in any particular case, and even impose a no-strike order for twenty-eight days, with individual penalties by wage attachment. There was also to be compulsory registration of agreements controlled by a Commission of Industrial Relations, with an Industrial Board set up as the executive arm to deal with disobedient trade unions, whose own rules would be strictly controlled by law.

Published in January 1969, this onslaught was too much. As Enoch Humphries, of the Fire Brigades, pointed out in his Presidential Address:

> Recourse to legal action against trade unions only *creates* strife.

That was what this White Paper indeed led to. The Scottish Miners were in conference at the time it appeared and immediately demanded that a special British TUC be called. They urged full support for a major lobby to be held on 27 February, when the British TUC did call a conference of trade union executives at least to meet at Croydon. Willie McLean, the Scots Miners' Vice-President, said it could "be described as an historical day in the history of the British trade union movement, when thousands of workers were involved in what can be rightly described as political strikes".[2]

On Clydeside 40,000 stopped work, with every shipyard closed, difficult as their own problems were. There was strong reaction throughout Britain, including the Midlands, and in the motor industry Fords and Rootes, who were also in dispute against attempts to impose "measured day work". While the White Paper was going through the House of Commons on 3 March nearly 100 Labour MPs had voted against it or abstained, although the Labour Government had full support from the Tory Opposition. By the end of the month the Labour Party Executive had disapproved of it. Sid Bidwell MP referring to the Donovan Report then wrote: "What might have been a mixed reception now turned out to be an almost united all-movement resistance."[3]

It was not until June 1969 that the British TUC did finally call a special TUC, the first for forty years; it rejected the penal provisions. But two months before when meeting at Rothesay the STUC was indeed blunt in its total rejection, despite Barbara Castle attending to defend it. By nearly two to one, and on a card vote, the STUC passed a composite motion of the GC amended by the Miners which declared it "the most serious threat to British Trade Unions for many decades". Listing the five points which Congress could support in principle, which were "long overdue rights and should have been implemented decades ago", it continued that these could not "now be used as bargaining points for other measures which mean relinquishing the fundamental rights of trade unionists". Moved by Ben Smith, the Scottish Officer of Local Government Officers, it was seconded by Michael McGahey. The composite had been thrashed out in the General Council by a majority of 9 to 4 on the Sunday as Congress opened; but it was not to be reached until the day after the Chancellor of the Exchequer, Roy Jenkins, in his Budget speech, had stated that legislation to operate the White Paper proposals would be pushed through immediately. This meant that many delegates, no longer seeing it as a White Paper but a draft Bill likely to become law long before they next met, added an emergency resolution. It called for total rejection, saying "some long overdue reforms" in the White Paper "could no longer be debated". It came in the names of the Miners, Draughtsmen, Transport & General, Commercial Motormen, Sheet Metal Workers, The Supervisory Staffs, Cine and Television Technicians and seven trades councils. Both resolutions were carried by card vote after some fierce speeches. Those with doubts usually wanted discussion of reforms to continue, confining opposition to penal clauses; these spokesmen were from the Electricians, Shop Assistants, General & Municipal, Local Government Officers and Painters.

Even before the Budget disclosure, the tone of the debate was already set in his Presidential Address by Enoch Humphries, deeply regretting that "in their central economic strategy the Government has adopted the advice of the orthodox economists and opted for policies which regard unemployment as a legitimate regulator". Those present were to show in other debates that they were very much aware of his point that although they had suffered further unemployment still there was

> not one single state-owned new industry anywhere in Scotand; and, to cap it all, we have needless proposals, the most obnoxious of which is that to levy fines on trade unionists engaged in industrial disputes.

In the debate itself the General Secretary of the Supervisory Staffs, Clive Jenkins, seconding the composite rejection, made some satirical remarks in his characteristic style, saying that "cooling-off periods should be treated with derision. A cooling-off period usually ended up in a hotting-up process". He hoped they would be "unwilling to be foot soldiers for Major Barbara's conscript army", because this would in fact mean the political management of the unions. If these propositions were put forward on the basis that the unions could submit their alternatives, "it was rather like being invited to take a hand in the construction of a scaffold and being offered the privilege of tipping the headsman". A strong rank and file note came from the Glasgow Trades Council delegate, a shop steward for over twenty-five years. Speaking of the propaganda on "unofficial strikes" and "informal negotiations", Agnes McLean said that workers having control of production, through the medium of their shop stewards were using their power to maintain the standard of living. She added: "If Barbara Castle was bursting to pass legislation, she should pass it for equal pay".

A strong case was argued by the Commercial Motormen's General Secretary, Alex Kitson, himself a member of the Labour Party Executive. He answered those who, like G A Drain for Local Government Officers, opposed both resolutions, because they should rather stress the need to continue to strive for the good features in the White Paper, which they had argued for on the Donovan Royal Commission. Kitson replied that if the trade union movement were prepared to unite, they could get all those good things "without any legal assistance at all", without any Government interference. The "great debate" was already finished, with legislation to come that very session. He believed that trade unionists themselves "had to close the ranks and provide the alternatives". He thought the structure of the STUC itself should be changed to give it more power, by setting up machinery to deal with all disputes and dictate how they should be solved. The following year he was successfully to move the General Council's proposed changes to the Constitution on these lines, just before the 1970 fall of the Labour Government faced them with the use of legal powers to cripple the unions by the Heath Conservative Government's Industrial Relations Bill.

Section (iii): **The Fight-back**

Hardly had they left Rothesay in 1969, however, than there was a protest strike of over quarter of a million throughout Britain against "In Place of Strife", which stopped the whole press. The British TUC was obliged to call a historic special Congress in June 1969 and prepared an alternative Programme for Action rejecting penal legislation. This won delay of the Bill. But the operation of the incomes policy was creating more stoppages, denounced as "wild-cat strikes", and by-elections showed Labour defeats during the run-up to the General Election in the summer of 1970.

In Scotland there was much activity, with the added concern of the growing battle against closures and redundancy. There was action at the Rolls Royce's threat to sack 3,000; at the Albion Works; Inverurie Locomotive Works; the closure of the RN Torpedo Factory at Alexandria; the run-down of the RN Air Station HMS Condor with consequent loss of civilian work at Arbroath; over Dounreay and doubts of the effect of the Ayr Re-zoning Development Plan; in steel about expanding Ravenscraig and the successful drive in the Clyde Estuary for the Hunterston ore terminal. Throughout there was also mounting anxiety in shipbuilding where the storm clouds were already gathering in the Upper Clyde over the Yarrow and Fairfield yards, as well as in the Lower Clyde. In all these, the General Council was usually quickly and deeply involved.

Indeed, the General Council had become increasingly responsible for major new and heavy responsibilities. Following up Jimmy Jack's long record for valuable research as well as the additional duties of his office, it now became necessary to make further appointments. The important new post of Assistant General Secretary was created, with James Milne of Aberdeen Trades Council elected. Another General Council member, the Draughtsman F H Stephen BSc, was appointed Research Officer: he was responsible for drafting the important evidence given by the STUC to the Select Committee on Scottish Affairs, including the topic of Industrial Training and the Shortages of Skilled Labour, followed by oral evidence.[4] Their big report to the Oban Congress in 1970 reflected "the continuing and ever-expanding participation of Congress in national and community affairs"; and also it showed the growing capacity "to support by extensive documentation its views upon the major issues". They had many interviews with Ministers on health, education and housing as well as the economy; they also organised many regional discussion Conferences, as well as a major delegate Conference of 1,200 delegates on National Superannuation, with Richard Crossman MP as the Government spokesman. They kept in close touch too not only with trades councils affected but also by calling a meeting of delegates from 12 unions involved in the Upper Clyde problems, as well as members of the Joint Works Council of the Upper Clyde Shipbuilders. Responding to expressions of concern by a number of trades councils about the situation in Northern Ireland they kept in constant touch with the Irish Congress and sent their Assistant General Secretary, Jimmy Milne, to a Belfast special Conference in October 1969. They also offered full co-operation and support to the 1000 Engineering &

Foundry Workers Union men and women on strike for union recognition at BSR, East Kilbride, which was finally won after police had dragged away 200 pickets, and 200 women marched in protest to the police station.

With the return of a Conservative Government under Ted Heath in the summer of 1970 a tremendously heavy work load for the STUC developed as they moved into a period of years of industrial strife. Jimmy Jack's Report to the 1971 Aberdeen Congress described it as "one of the most trying and demanding" of the post-war years. At first their prime concern was the massive unemployment, threatening to rise to the 'thirties level and already close on 10 per cent in Glasgow. This was complicated by the new Government aiming to run down and hive off the publicly owned industries in mining, steel and rail. Unemployment was not confined to one industry or area: while there was contraction in mining, transport, shipbuilding, heavy engineering, agriculture, print, jute and textiles, it was also in building, so essential for Scotland.

The General Council had many meetings, not only with Ministers, but with the unions and shop stewards, particularly in shipbuilding, steel and the car industries. It included in December 1970 a mass conference in Glasgow, which was to have been followed by regional conferences on unemployment. But this programme was interrupted: for in the first days of January the proposal to introduce the Conservative Industrial Relations Bill was announced. Designed to create "tame" unions under the threat of very severe legal penalties, it would put the movement back a hundred years. Its main provisions would be that only if registered with the Registrar of Friendly Societies, with its rules approved, would any organisation have the status of a recognised union. Unregistered unions would be at major risk. There was to be a new offence of engaging in "unfair industrial action", such as inducing others to break contracts of employment; it would entail unlimited damages for an unregistered union. Other offences included insisting on a closed shop and discrimination against non-unionists. There was also power to impose a cooling-off period of sixty days and to order compulsory ballots.

The STUC action on Scotland's unemployment problem had to be broken off to concentrate on the campaign throughout the United Kingdom against the Bill. This included organising a Petition to Parliament and many special seminars and conferences. Summaries of the proposals were sent to all trades councils and an immense conference was held on 24 January, 1971, in Glasgow with 1,150 delegates. A conference of full-time officials had already been held there on 23 December addressed by Professor Miller of the Department of Law at Strathclyde, together with Jimmy Jack. Major demonstrations were held all through January and February in Edinburgh, Aberdeen, Dundee, Inverness and Dumfries, organised by the trades councils and with demonstration marches supporting them. The General Council also supplied speakers for meetings at Cumbernauld, Falkirk, Fort William, Kirkcaldy, Paisley, Perth and Stirling. Finally came their demonstration rally at Green's Playhouse, Glasgow, with an overflow meeting; this on 7 March, six weeks before Congress delegates met in Aberdeen.

When they debated it no less than twenty-three motions were composited, there being wholehearted opposition to the Bill, although some difficulties on how to maintain unity in methods of opposition appeared. The composite, finally carried by an overwhelming majority, affirmed its "complete opposition"; that no trade union should register; and that opposition should include "industrial struggle in places of work" as well as Parliamentary opposition. Both these points went beyond what the British TUC had decided. In moving it for the General Council, Ben Smith said the STUC was able to back industrial struggle at work to oppose it "not only because of representation on trades councils but also because of the number of delegates close to workshop life". He added that it was extremely important that when employers pressed for legally enforceable local agreements "workers at local level should not succumb to such pressures". Ben Smith was just on the point of retiring as NALGO's Scottish Officer, and was himself in a difficult position. His own union had joint negotiating rights alongside a large number of professional bodies and specialist trade unions not affiliated to the British TUC and which would in all probability register. As their delegate G A Drain explained, it would "hazard the strength of their bargaining position; at this stage therefore they would sadly have to abstain". Congress delegates listened in sympathy to this position and paid due attention to Ben Smith's stress on workshop resistance, and that if they studied the complexities they could find a "host of ways" to maintain rights within the law, and frustrate the aims of its sponsors. W Hutchison, Engineers, said the sole purpose of "their common enemy" was to make the trade unions a "toothless tiger". H D'Arcy of the Building Trade agreed that it "was a blatant attempt to strengthen the hand of the employer". With the defensive Acts from 1871 to 1965 which had stood them in good stead wiped out at a blow,

> the trade unions were to be at the mercy of the High Court judges. These judges were specially selected, highly trained, highly educated, highly paid servants of the British capitalist class, and their motto was:
> 'God please the Lord and all his relations
> To keep the rest of us in our proper stations.'

Then H K Penman of Public Employees moved a unanimous resolution deploring the destruction of independent arbitration and interference in pay negotiations in the public sector. This was supported by Charlie Donnet for the General and Municipal, whose brother Alec, their Scottish Secretary, was presiding over Congress.

In his Presidential Address he had spoken bitterly of the Government's denial of Scotland's needs, however much the Ministers, including the Premier himself, had been apparently willing to meet and listen to them. During his chairmanship the subcommittee which had so long been considering Scottish self-government developed a new approach. It still stood quite firmly by the principle of non-separation, as had appeared in the Interim Statement to the Scottish Panel of the Royal Commission on the Constitution. But the immensely complex problems of the exact form and powers of a workable legislative assembly proved extremely difficult when studied in depth; they felt some review was necessary. One month after the 1970 General Election, therefore, the STUC representatives appeared before the Royal Commission under Lord Crowther, sitting in the New Senate Room of the University of Glasgow, to give oral evidence with a new emphasis. Having made it clear that they remained totally against separation, they raised the problem of how it might work if the assembly were not to be "powerless or purely discussive" nor merely dealing with the Committee stage of Bills. Then they put forward an interesting comparison from the experience they had gained of the position of their own unions affiliated to the STUC while based south of the border. While the general policy of these was still settled at all-UK level, at "operational level" their Scottish Districts could have considerable powers, with their officers "being responsible, in large measure, not to the national executive, but to the Scottish Committee". It was "along these lines they would wish the Royal Commission to move". They were therefore proposing a deliberative assembly, directly elected, in Edinburgh, "which would exert control and give direction to the Government machinery of the Scottish Office". There would be 142 members, elected at the same time as Parliament, supervising the administration "within the broad bounds laid down by Westminster legislation". While not having its own over-all budget, it would decide how to spend the allocations for health, education and so on. There was no immediate follow-up; but with the vastly mounting special Scottish economic problems, the STUC itself was soon to begin the practice of calling the unique Assemblies on specific subjects. The first on Unemployment, in October 1971 was already timely, arising from the historic UCS work-in.

References

[1] *Labour Monthly*, December, 1966; "Scotland and the Freeze", Sam Barr.
[2] *Labour Monthly*, "Trade Unions and Government", William McLean.
[3] *Labour Monthly*, "Trade Unions and Government", Sid Bidwell MP
[4] See Appendices A, B, C and D to the 1970 Annual Report.

24
Scotland Takes the Lead

The historic occupation of the yards by the workers of the Upper Clyde Shipbuilders and the beginning of their work-in set a new form and pattern of class struggle. At once it became known, respected and also frequently followed up far beyond the boundaries of Britain. The hideous growing unemployment in this basic industry and amongst the subsidiary occupations dependent on the yards, the greed and incompetence of the shipyard owners, and the evasive Government trickiness and lack of funding could no longer be endured by the highly skilled and spirited Clyde shipyard workers. For years there had been efforts at grass roots and local union offices to save yard after yard, fully supported at each stage by the STUC. It was as a result of persistent campaigning over the years that the Upper Clyde Shipbuilders consortium, having some measure of Government finance, was set up in 1967. The Heath Government was now to allow it to become bankrupt, with yards sold off or closed, causing catastrophic unemployment. The long and disgraceful history and the fight-back story of the heroic work-in[1] cannot be told in detail: here there must be concentration on some details of the supportive role of the STUC, which year after year had shown no small concern.

Section (i): **UCS Workers Decide: "Here We Stay"**

For some years already the shipyard workers' mood had been sharpened by the campaigns, in which the STUC had played a creditable part, on the anti-trade union measures, from the Donovan Report, "In Place of Strife", to the Tories' Industrial Relations Bill, due to become law in August 1971. Industrial action against this and the pay freeze through one-day rallies and strikes with official support won in some engineering, public service, and transport unions, had built up a militant mood; shop stewards and their whole-hearted supporters were united alongside local full-time officials. In making this unity possible no small part had been played by the STUC coming out for industrial action to oppose the measures against the unions in 1971 at

Aberdeen: in the same city thirteen years later they were once again to give a decisive lead to the whole British movement in the battle to stop the mines being closed.

Less than two months after the STUC delegates had left Aberdeen, Scotland was plunged into an unprecedented confrontation with those in the corridors of power commanded by the Tory Prime Minister, Ted Heath. For the STUC its 75th year was to be an extraordinarily fruitful and informative period. From the first the STUC was seen to be in close touch and support of the fight-back actions of the Clydeside shipyard workers in their defensive battle. While there was of course no question of any attempt to dictate to the work force, with its many unions involved, the STUC's response was immediate and supportive throughout. The GC was much aided in quick reaction by the fact that one of their number was himself intimately involved in the struggle day by day. For the Engineer, Willie Hutchison, former convener at Rolls Royce but now Regional Officer of the AUEW and a UCS union representative was one of the key figures in the fight. It was a tragic loss when he died before it was over, as did the STUC's outstanding Vice-Chairman, Bill Tweedie the Boilermaker: both of them were on the Economic Committee of the GC.

On Friday morning, 11 June, 1971, the UCS management called shop stewards and union representatives together and told them that they had just informed the Government that, lacking immediate further financial support, the UCS was going into voluntary liquidation. That same afternoon Hutchison contacted the STUC office informing them of this and of a mass meeting of the work force organised for the evening of the next working day, Monday, 14 June. Thereupon GC representatives flew down to London, as did shop stewards and Hutchison himself, and told Government Ministers that lack of support for UCS was "unthinkable". After hearing the announcement in the House of Commons that nevertheless no resources would be made available, they flew home to attend the UCS workers' meeting that night, accompanied by some Scottish MPs and Tony Wedgwood Benn. After Hutchison had spoken, the decision was taken to occupy the yards, so that the Liquidator could not remove ships, material or machinery. It was then that Sammy Barr, Connells' convener, first suggested the work-in, which was to be adopted six weeks later at the next stage of the Government's manoeuvres.

The same day the Clydebank Town Council had held a special meeting and chartered a special train to London for the following day, Tuesday, 15 June; with the Clydebank Councillors went 450 delegates and shop stewards from the yards to lobby the Prime Minister. Following this Heath invited a delegation from the STUC to meet him on Monday, 21 June. The GC had already decided when it held a special meeting on Tuesday, 15 June, to remain in continuous session; their purpose was to run a major campaign demanding that the Government must give the Liquidator the necessary resources to keep the UCS operating fully and that the UCS should be taken into full public ownership. In the first statement to the media they stressed the appalling threat to employment throughout the whole Clyde and expressed their support of the workers to occupy "and ensure that the yard remains open and in production".

After that first meeting declaring the intention to occupy the yards, the STUC was always in close touch with the UCS Shop Stewards Co-ordinating Committee, of which the Chairman was Jimmy Airlie, the engineer who had previously, as convener of Fairfields, fought so hard to save the yard. When on 23 June there was a huge protest industrial stoppage of some 100,000, with half the demonstration then rallying to Glasgow Green to hear Jimmy Airlie report for the UCS workers, the Assistant General Secretary Jimmy Milne spoke to assure them of the STUC's support. It was a happy choice, to send this former shipyard convener from Aberdeen, to cheer those on Clydeside. Amongst his fellow speakers was Wedgwood Benn, who backed the key policy points of the STUC, regretting that he had not nationalised UCS when in office. The day before this impressive demonstration, the GC, after meeting the Shop Stewards CC, had decided to call a Special STUC Congress where, amongst the many important decisions taken, there was one which opened new prospects for Scotland attaining independence.

Events were moving thick and fast. After the Prime Minister had been obliged to come up to Scotland, where the STUC were amongst those who warned him of what were the likely consequences of his policy, an Advisory Group on Shipbuilding was appointed, ostensibly to examine the UCS's actual financial position. The STUC met and argued with the Committee of Enquiry, which consisted of three Scottish magnates, together with Lord Robens, who had attempted to leave his mark on the nationalised mining industry. While "the Four Wise Men" were sitting, all but John Brown's yard were on holiday. But, anticipating what the decision would be, the shop stewards came back to the Clyde to be at the ready. When after much juggling with figures it was recommended that UCS be ended, and a successor company entitled Govan Shipbuilders set up to replace the consortium, hiving off the rest and involving wage cuts, it was the last straw. Immediately there was a mass meeting in Brown's yard: the Co-ordinating Committee of the shop stewards from the four yards made the historic announcement. The work-in began on 30 July, with the shipyard workers declaring: "Here we stay!"

Section (ii): **STUC Goes into Action**

On Monday, 16 August, the STUC's Special Congress was held at Partick Burgh Hall with 400 delegates present. Large numbers both of long-term and short-term proposals on the state of the Scottish economy were adopted, all starting from the Government's attitude to the UCS struggle. They ranged over problems in the steel, power, transport and car industries; investment incentives; economic planning machinery; and public expenditure on housing, training and other social needs. The GC immediately began to process these, and in doing so took two important new steps. First it set up an STUC Committee of Enquiry in response to the Government's four-man "advisory". It was to consider

> the wider social and economic consequences of the decision to run down UCS Ltd.

Arising from its decisions the GC was then to organise the first and unprecedented Scottish Assembly to consider unemployment and its effect on the Scottish economy; the Assembly's meaning and character we shall consider after following up the gains of the work-in.

The STUC's Committee of Enquiry proved of considerable and immediate value: and it was indeed on the spot, for its first meetings on the first three days of September took place in Clydebank Town Hall. The three men concerned were Professor Raymond Illsley of the University of Aberdeen; Frank Cousins, the recent General Secretary of the Transport & General Workers' Union and George Perry, Managing Director of General Motors (Scotland) Limited. They rapidly took evidence from nearly fifty men and women, mostly with expert knowledge in some field; these included Tony Wedgwood Benn, Ken Douglas, the managing Director of UCS, Sir Iain Stewart, once Chairman of Fairfields, as well as six trade unionists, many economists and regional social workers. Perhaps the most startling written evidence was a document produced by the spokesman for the UCS Shop Stewards Committee, Jimmy Reid,[2] who became widely known during the action for the effectiveness of his contributions on the media. Dated 1969, marked "Private and Confidential" on House of Commons paper, it appeared to be personal notes of meetings with the UCS Directors and Sir Eric Yarrow, owner of Yarrow's. It immediately became known as "The Ridley Documents", having been written just before the General Election by Nicholas Ridley MP, who then became the Under-Secretary of State for Trade and Industry. "The Ridley Documents" expressed the view that the UCS should be "butchered", Government holdings sold off and Yarrow's yard detached. The Interim Report was issued by the end of the month and together with the whole Enquiry provided valuable ammunition for the battle, which ended with the yards not closed, although redistributed. The Government also had been given due warning to go canny. True, there was no question of taking the whole consortium into public ownership; nor were negotiations quickly completed for the sale of the Clydebank Division to the American firm, Marathon Manufacturing, backed by a Government loan. But the essential thing was that the yards had not been closed.

It was therefore hailed as a great victory indeed, when delegates met at Dunoon for the 1972 Congress. There were few debates in which the UCS struggle was not mentioned. For as Ray Macdonald said in the speech closing his tremendously busy year as President, the

> unions are where they have always been, right in the front line of the industrial and political battle.

It was their members who were in the firing lines; and he went on to

> salute our shock troops – the men of UCS, who wrote indelibly into our history the right to work.

All had depended on unity, and that had been "a living and victorious reality". When moving the GC's main Scottish Economy resolution, Alex Day of the Supervisory Staffs (ASTMS) spoke of the immense potential force which could change the whole structure of society, the working people "banding together in their strength, as did the miners and the workers in the Upper Clyde shipyards". Indeed, as he spoke the railwaymen's leader too had just announced that no trains would run the following Sunday. Alex Kitson said "new thinking had been established by the UCS shop stewards", which the Patternmaker A Dorrens followed up, saying "the lads there lead the way - they showed us new perspectives". But, he added, it should have been taken into public ownership. For it was "a scandal to think of UCS having to depend on an American company coming over to rescue one of this country's greatest assets". Some dozen years later, under another Tory Government, the workers of Scott Lithgow further down the Clyde would say the same.

Later R Hutchison for Greenock Trades Council and Eddie Marsden, of the AUEW Construction Section, moved a resolution calling for immediate nationalisation of shipbuilding,

> as the crisis on Upper Clyde reveals the intention of this Tory Government to sacrifice the industry.

Immediate action was needed if it was to survive. This brought an important supporting speech from a Boilermakers' delegate, himself a member of the UCS Shop Stewards Co-ordinating Committee: Sammy Barr thanked Congress and the whole movement for support against the Government policy of butchery. The lesson they had learned was that "where there has been the unity and solidarity, then the struggle they were in at the present moment could be successfully concluded and victory achieved". Detailing the heavy subsidies given in other countries to shipbuilding, he said that the UCS "had brought the problems, especially the financial problems, of the industry to the surface". He ended by saying that the UCS workers had

> demonstrated that they had the knowledge and know-how to run a highly complicated industry. They had destroyed the myth that workers could not run industry.

From Clydebank itself, A E Henderson for the Trades Council and a most active Communist Clydebank Councillor, gave a veteran's view of unemployment in the "hungry 'thirties"; and then went on to describe how the Trades Council, with the support of the whole community including the Clydebank Town Council, had led a deputation to Parliament in 1945 to prevent the Royal Ordnance Factory at Dalmuir being shut up. Since then they had witnessed closures of Babcock and Wilcox of Dalmuir and other workplaces run down. But when the UCS was attacked there was to be seen "a marked contrast to the 'hungry 'thirties' ". For these lads had learned from the lessons of the past. They accepted the militant and responsible leadership of their shop stewards and refused to be sacked, with the full support of all sections of the community. Another trades council delegate, C Betts of West Lothian and a British Leyland worker at Bathgate, described how in their own nine weeks' struggle over measured day work, they were inspired by the UCS and miners' fights, which had been two such "significant struggles that year past". D Campbell from Dunfermline Trades Council pointed out "the fantastic sums, never seen before in peacetime" being spent on defence, whilst the Government was preparing to let "highly productive industries such as UCS go to the wall". But there they had taken the initiative, saying: "No more; you are not on. We are taking over." He concluded: "they had given a lead throughout the whole of Scotland to other sections of the movement to do likewise". They must win "a Government with the strength in their leadership to create a socialist policy and to work towards socialism with the rest of the world".

James Jack gave a lively description of the highlights of the campaign, the events and the people associated in all the moves. He paid special tribute to the late Willie Hutchison and "the tremendous strain and anxiety" he had gone through. As he said, it was through Hutchison that "the GC were from the first on the scene", and they then became involved in every stage. It was on Jack's Report that another member of the UCS Shop Stewards Co-ordinating Committee spoke in praise of all the GC had done in their support. The Boilermaker, W Clydesdale, said he had come to the rostrum to "let them know that they had done a tremendous job of work", adding that both Jimmy Jack and Jimmy Milne had contributed "in a lot of different ways not even mentioned in this Report". All the UCS workers felt they had learned a lot. Most delegates present must have been visited by a UCS shop steward either in their branch, trades council or at their factory gate; for that was where they had begun.

> They would remember what was said, mostly at the end of these speeches, that the only way they could be beaten was if the trade union movement let them down.

He had come to tell them as its representatives, that "the Trade Union Movement in this country had not let them down, and that they in the Upper Clyde Shipbuilders would not let *them* down". From the chair the President thanked him for his speech.

Section (iii): **The Scottish Assembly**

It was clear that the struggle on Clydeside had generated immense support and unity throughout Scotland and the part played in this by the STUC was handsomely acknowledged. But it had also provided the STUC with a political and social opportunity for uniquely widening its activities and involvement; it could be seen to be giving national leadership within the whole Scottish community as never before. For its involvement took it far beyond the immediate industrial and economic struggle on the Clyde, vital as that was. As a direct consequence following the Special Congress recommendations, it had

The March in support of the Upper Clyde Shipbuilding Workers, 1973.

Front row (left to right) – Roddy McKenzie (UCS Treasurer), Alex Murray (Scottish Secretary CPGB), Bob Cook (UCS Govan), William McInnes (Linthouse), Vic Feather (General Secretary, TUC), D. McGarvey (President, Boilermakers), Hugh Scanlon (President, AUEW), James Airlie (UCS), Tony Benn MP, J. Reid (UCS), William Ross MP, Sam Barr (UCS Scotstoun), Bob Dickie (Clydebank), James Jack (General Secretary, STUC).

first held its own very widely based factual enquiry. Following the successful working of that it had gone on to organise the Scottish Assembly under its own chairmanship. This could become a type of gathering where working-class and national needs and aspirations were found united, and seen as bringing a new dimension to the case for devolution.

The GC had decided upon this new type of all-embracing gathering at their October meeting immediately after their Committee of Enquiry's Interim Report. It had been in their mind earlier in the year, then discussed with UCS shop stewards; finally after the widest possible circularisation of Scottish opinion 700 invitations were sent to local authorities, educational establishments, the Scottish Council (Development and Industry), the Confederation of British Industry, trade unions, Churches, political parties and MPs. The plan was to put forward a lengthy Charter of Proposals: a Standing Commission should be appointed to follow these up, and

> to be responsible for continuing consideration of Scottish economic issues and also for making direct representations to the Prime Minister.

It proved a unique event, bringing together a breadth of Scottish opinion "that it would be impossible for any Government to ignore", as the Report on the 1972 Dunoon Congress put it. Amongst the 1,549 at Edinburgh's Usher Hall on 14 February, 1972, were 57 churches, 39 MPs and five political parties as well as employers' organisations, trade unions and educationalists. There were 38 who addressed the Assembly, from every sphere; Charter and Commission proposals were unanimously adopted.

When the Commission it elected proceeded to process its decisions at top level, however, there was some anxiety felt about the lines on which such a wide body might develop. This may well have been behind a resolution moved at Dunoon by the TASS and Ayr delegates. Expressing fears of over-concentration on mere pressure on Downing Street rather than fullest encouragement for direct action at grass-roots level, their composite only fell when previous question was carried. But by the 1973 Congress at Aberdeen, the situation of the first Scottish Assembly had admittedly somewhat changed. On 15 January, 1973, the Standing Commission itself, and not the STUC, called an Assembly, attended by considerably fewer delegates. To this the Commission put forward a different charter of proposals. This led Congress to pass unanimously a resolution which, while congratulating the GC for setting it up as a public forum, viewed "with

Special Meeting held in Glasgow on 17 and 18 March, 1975, with the Prime Minister, the Rt. Hon. Harold Wilson and seven members of the Cabinet with the General Council of the Scottish Trades Union Congress on issues relevant to the Scottish economy.

concern" its future. Its mechanics should be reviewed because the STUC had "not set up a platform for the monopoly of one particular group of people". This was a reference to members of the Scottish National Party who had tried to monopolise discussion. In seconding, J Stewart of Angus Trades Council described his "feeling of great elation" at the First Assembly, with enough done for delegates to conclude that "a very small step had been taken along the difficult road to self-determination". But he went on to say that "unfortunately the Second Assembly was a lesson to all of them". From the first the success of the great gathering could be seen to "depend entirely on the amount of political activity carried on between Assemblies", if it was to be nothing more than a talking shop.

In later years the Scottish Assembly, under the guidance of the STUC, could often show real strength in dealing with a single issue or specific problem. There was to be no lack of problems. Within days of the delegates leaving Aberdeen there was a major May Day stoppage throughout the United Kingdom. Soon the whole working-class movement was to become locked in struggle in a sequence of events which were to bring about the downfall of the Heath Government. In the immediate wake of the heartening UCS struggle there were major battles over the use of the Industrial Relations Act. Later came the bitter resistance, above all by miners, to attempts to impose incomes policy. For the Scots in addition there was special concern over entry to the European Common Market and its relation to the devolution question. They also had to face the amazing contradiction of oil-rich Scottish waters producing immense private wealth not used to enrich Scottish land and people. Instead, privatisation and de-industrialisation were what the 'seventies threatened, and always with the growing threat of war.

References

[1] *The UCS Work-In,* Willie Thompson and Finlay Hart, Lawrence & Wishart Ltd. *"UCS" The Anatomy of Bankruptcy,* Robin Murray, Spokesman Books.

[2] Reid gained so much personal success for his television appearances on behalf of the UCS workers that it opened up a new career for him in the media. In the 'eighties he was a feature writer in the *Daily Record*, noted for extreme hostility to the unions during the struggle against pit closures led by the miners.

25

Deepening Conflict

There were crucial lessons to be learnt throughout the 'seventies and beyond, during the deepening conflicts between the trade union and labour movement as a whole and their opponents; and the increasing dominance of the multi-nationals lacking any homeland was becoming apparent. Three periods can be seen in a decade of considerable industrial struggle and revival both of hopes and disappointments in reliance primarily on political methods, which covered no less than four different governments. The issues involved new development in technology in the computer age; permanent mass unemployment; the use of that, of the law and curtailment of traditional civil rights to break the defences of the trade unions. This was against a background of an economy increasingly distorted also by unprecedented production and import of weapons for nuclear war purposes and the destruction of traditional markets. To come under fire was public ownership of shipbuilding, steel, mines and the transport so essential to Scotland's economy, with already visible moves to hive off and "privatise", as the process was later to be described.

Would their opponents or the immense numbers in the trade union and labour movement learn the faster? And who would prevail? The Scots were quicker than many; and prominent in learning new ways was the STUC, following their supportive action over the Upper Clyde Shipbuilders' Work-in, their all-inclusive Special Congress and the first Scottish Assembly on Unemployment. As the General Council's report to the 1972 Dunoon Congress put it: "Quite clearly the character of Congress is changing". Already there was

> an intensification of responsibility, a widening of activities and an involvement in the Scottish community such as has never been so obvious before.

Later events were quickly to increase the trend further, laying the basis for winning wide acknowledgement and respect, and earning a considerable advance to unity within their own ranks. Conferences of trades council officers now became an annual event, taking place well before Congress met each year, with GC and officers thus kept in close touch and up to date with grass-roots attitudes, and what response might be expected from them. An agreement was reached for trades councils to accept representation from unemployed committees. Again, there was tactful treatment of their affiliates affected by the divisive clauses of the Tory Industrial Relations Act. Early on inter-union problems had arisen by the Act's requirement that any organisation must be registered under it and their rules approved before it would be legally recognised as a trade union. The STUC had decided to reject and oppose the whole Act by every means, including industrial action: but what if a union should register under it? Twelve unions affiliated in Scotland, including the two Scottish teachers' associations, the Scottish Bakers and the Powerloom Overlookers, did register, being eager to gain recognition and hoping to achieve a closed shop. Yet unlike the British TUC, the STUC decided not to disaffiliate them immediately, but to give them more time for consideration.

Section (i): **The STUC's Response to Anti-Union Laws**

Later came the enormity of the ferocious fines on unions imposed by the Act's newly-created National Industrial Relations Court and sequestration of funds which followed. This called for maximum unity, which was quickly forthcoming in Scotland. The STUC played a full part in opposition to the use of old and new laws against trade union actions, fully supporting the British TUC's call for a day of action. It denounced the attack both on the Transport & General and the Amalgamated Engineering Unions' funds by the courts and also spoke very strongly indeed against the use of the 1875 Conspiracy Act to send building trade union pickets to gaol for their picketing methods. They also demanded fullest support for the Miners' strike which within weeks forced the Tory Heath to call a General Election which brought back another Labour Government. The wording of these resolutions was indeed representative of feeling in Scotland consistently throughout the decade; all were on issues which were to be reintroduced by a later Tory Government under Heath's successor, in a far more developed form, to be pursued ten years after Heath's Act. It is useful here to turn to some of the Scots' debates in a little detail.

At the Dunoon Congress of 1972, for instance, there was unanimous support for "all forms of pressure, including industrial action" and that all affiliates should "initiate immediate action in support of any trade unionist or affiliated body victimised" under the Industrial Relations Act. It also called for the Parliamentary Labour Party to be advised that

> a policy of total rejection of the Industrial Relations Act and restoration of trade union rights in full is a prerequisite for guaranteed support in any future Parliamentary election.

A McAlpine, of the Engineering Technical and Supervisory Section, in moving pointed out that profits in Britain "were still not high enough to satisfy investors and big business", hence "the Tory solution was to attack wages and working conditions"; he referred to their encouragement of dissidents to set up opposition unions, both against the Transport & General Workers and his own union.[1] He also moved an emergency resolution welcoming "the firm stand" by the T&GWU refusing to pay a £55,000 fine imposed by the National Industrial Relations Court for being "in contempt of court" by ignoring it. There were nine spokesmen from trade unions, with Graham Steel (Miners), John Walker (Footplatemen) Enoch Humphries (Fire Brigades) and Alex Kitson (T&GWU) speaking particularly forcefully. From the spokesmen for five trades councils there came some very sharp points. Bill McQuilkin for Paisley called for instant reaction if any worker or shop steward were attacked, adding: "The slogan 'Labour is invincible' should be made an effective reality". S K MacMillan from East Kilbride quoted a speech by Hitler on trade unions, and added:

> Fascism can come in slithering through the legislature as well as to the tramp of the jackboot. It would not be the first time that trade unionists had sounded the alarm in advance of public realisation of impending disaster.

From Kirkcaldy, the engine driver C Rodgers said the most heinous crime for him was to pass a signal at "danger": in his view "the learned judge had run past more signals at danger than any engine driver ever would". He concluded that "this was 'Big Brother' all over again".

But neither the Heath Government nor "the learned judge" took note of their danger. When AEU members under discipline tried to gain their ends through application to the National Industrial Relations Court, the union refused to attend, being unwilling to "put their rules up for debate". For this they had to face not only the fine of £47,000 which they refused to pay, but then the total sequestration of their funds was threatened. Then came an action which aroused immense grass-roots indignation, not least in Dundee, where the Michelin Construction project had given rise to difficulties arising from the ploys of contractors and subcontractors. For at Shrewsbury there was an official dispute in the building trade, with some two dozen prosecuted for their methods of picketing the lump labour employed. With the Conspiracy Act 1875 used against them, three were sentenced to more than a year's imprisonment. In an emergency motion at the Rothesay Congress of 1974 the Scots unanimously deplored "the savage sentences" which they saw

> as an attempt to erode the democratic rights of workers to picket in pursuance of improvement of their wage and working conditions.

These were only some of the events and manoeuvres which could lie ahead, whenever vigorous and united action was lacking. But in the 'seventies this was quickly to the fore.

From Scotland there were congratulations and very full support for British TUC's call for a Protest Day of Action on 1 May and also the BTUC Special Congress on the Act on 5 May, 1973. There were major strikes in many industries and places of work, including the railways and the Glasgow firemen, with immense demonstrations over the threats to miners and power workers. Joint STUC and Miners' demonstrations were held in Glasgow, Edinburgh, Aberdeen and Dundee. There were many thousand leaflets on this and the miners' overtime ban, with the STUC issuing 500,000 of their leaflet "Don't Blame the Miners" in December, 1973, when the Government had restricted fuel and power to bring in a three-day working week. Within ten days of the miners' strike beginning, Heath had to dissolve Parliament and the General Election of 1974 followed, in which the Labour Government was returned, with at first Harold Wilson again as Premier. The GC, of which the Textile Workers' leader Betty MacIntyre was President, immediately issued a series of press statements and three powerful leaflets concentrating on the Heath counter-inflation strategy, the importance of nationalising the North Sea Oil operations and urging "massive support for Labour". It was indeed to be a heavy year, with Betty MacIntyre as only the second woman at their head in the STUC's 77 years.

Section (ii): **They Look to a Labour Government**

Two years earlier, her predecessor in office, Raymond MacDonald of the Transport Workers, had shown how "massive support for Labour", despite the disastrous Labour "In Place of Strife" policy, had come to be seen as essential. In his Presidential Address at the 1972 Dunoon

Congress, he asked what could they expect of the Heath Government, "relentless in its pursuit of inequality"?

> What else can we expect when workers strike and picket, when people demonstrate resistance to injustice, but dire warnings about dark conspiracies, or threats to democracy, of violence menacing our British way of life?

Then he described what he called acts of violence:

> What of the violence of a Government which permits more than one million unemployed, steals milk from school children, robs young people of jobs, persecutes thousands of the people with the privations of poverty, forces up house rents which daily accentuates the gulf between rich and poor?

Then he quoted Benjamin Franklin's famous saying that unless all would hang together, all would hang separately, adding that the Heath Government "is determined to hang us, to suspend us with legal red tape from the scaffold of the Industrial Relations Act", and that law had "no real place in industrial relations", and that "legal terminology is not the language of the shop floor". Heath's language did not then go so far as another Tory Premier's twelve years later, who included active trade unionists amongst "the enemy within". Yet in 1972 this was the mood in which industrial and political action was seen as the Heath Government was thrown out and replaced by a Labour Government again.

With the Heath Government in the process of being defeated after provoking such immense resistance culminating in the miners' strike, the STUC were obliged to become even busier. Increasingly they were tackling the major economic problems affecting Scotland. Amongst these was not only decline in industrial production and increasing unemployment, despite the factor of North Sea Oil with its complications: there were also all the social problems of housing, education and health. With all these preoccupations it was essential that there should be considerable advance of good relations with the Scottish Council of the Labour Party; but for some time past this had been somewhat lacking, despite the GC being on effective terms with the Scottish Labour MPs. With the early prospect of the Heath Government being thrown out, there was considerable anxiety in Scotland following the experiences of miners, shipyard workers, steel and rail workers about how far and how fast a new Labour Government would be ready to go; they had not forgotten the earlier "In Place of Strife". This had been vehemently expressed at Dunoon in

1972. First Michael McGahey won unanimous support for a resolution totally rejecting "the propaganda of 'Incomes Policy'", and calling upon

> the next Labour Government to drastically redistribute the nation's wealth in favour of the wage earners, pensioners and the under-privileged.

This was immediately followed by a motion on "Relations with the Labour Party"; on this there were vigorous speeches from delegates from both the Engineering, Construction and Technical Sections of the AUEW as well as Shop Assistants and the Electricians. Fears were expressed lest the BTUC and Labour Party nationally would in fact be meeting "to hammer out" what one speaker described as "a blank cheque for an Incomes Policy". It was agreed to remit the motion with an even more sharply worded amendment to the GC, who decided to discuss it on the Joint Committee with the Labour Party, which had not held a single meeting since July, 1971. However, the Scottish Council of the Labour Party, which had had reservations about the GC having taken the initiative in calling the comprehensive Scottish Assembly on Unemployment, replied in August, 1972, that they were unwilling to meet unless all the representatives from the GC "were eligible for membership of the Labour Party".[2] This restriction the GC felt unable to accept and much correspondence on the point followed. Finally in February 1973 the GC, with Alex Day Chairman, agreed to a suggestion that no such restriction should apply to *ad hoc* meetings, of which it was essential that there should be many. Thus the standing Joint Committee was abolished and GC members and staff met the Scottish Council of Labour on specific issues whenever necessary, which was indeed often.

Section (iii): **Could the Lessons be Quickly Learned?**

In the period after they had humiliatingly defeated the Heath policies the Scottish TUC continued to grow in status, although a time of increasing crisis was beginning. Once again new thinking was needed: for predictably alongside massive unemployment threats were already in the offing of employers' newly devised pressure against trade unionists' advance. Both in the economic and political sphere they needed to be on the alert now, when the latest Labour Government had at least a small majority. The STUC received important new recognition during the last year of office of J Jack as the 1975 Congress approached. For on March 17 and 18, 1975, the Prime Minister, Harold Wilson, and seven Cabinet Ministers came to Glasgow to consult with the GC on the vital economic and political issues facing Scotland. As well as the state of the Scottish economy as a whole, these included the social services and Scottish devolution. The GC were given the promise of a Scottish Assembly with legislative powers. This their Conference a month later urged should be implemented within two years, whilst at the same time strongly condemning Common Market membership and rejecting any renegotiation of entry terms as the referendum approached: some saw the two questions as closely linked. All through 1974 and 1975 a very large amount of oral and written evidence was submitted on these issues, especially on steel, North Sea Oil and the energy crisis, as well as on peace and international questions, with detailed criticism to the Royal Commission on the Press. From now on the "Summit" consultations between the GC and key Labour Cabinet Ministers, headed first by Wilson and later by James Callaghan, were to become a regular feature. For this purpose many highly informative documents were produced and later published with an account of how they were received, in the Annual Report.

Throughout their service when each was Deputy General Secretary both Jimmy Jack and Jimmy Milne had been responsible for providing STUC spokesmen with outstanding research material. Now the work needed the attention of a permanent special department. When Jimmy Milne took over as General Secretary on Jack's retirement in December, 1975, an unprecedented greater mass of work lay ahead needing a larger staff. This involved moving to larger premises at 16 Woodlands Terrace: its purchase was achieved largely through major campaigning efforts by their Treasurer, Alex Kitson, before he left Scotland to become Deputy General Secretary of the Transport & General Workers Union. This made it possible to build up the small staff to cope with the ever-widening responsibilities as the STUC moved through the three years to reach their 80th Congress in April, 1977. They were not all new faces in the new staff at the newly named Middleton House. The position of Deputy General Secretary was occupied at first briefly by James Kirkwood and then by John Henry, both active members of the GC representing the Post Office Engineers and Edinburgh Trades Council respectively. The reorganisation included two Assistant Secretaries with special responsibilities: Helen Liddell took over Economic Research before she went on to become Secretary of the Scottish Labour Party, on behalf of which she addressed the 1977 Conference, while Gordon Craig attended to the Social Services side; both were soon replaced by Douglas Harrison and William Speirs respectively.

The immense increase in responsibilities was reflected in the greater number of working committees, such as those for Scottish Education and Training; Entertainment and Arts; Devolution; Transport; Energy; the Health Service; and Local Government. It is highly significant that a large number of activists from other organisations became represented on these committees, as observers, advisers and finally full members. Most happily the previous somewhat anomalous relationship with the Scottish Council of the Labour Party was fully overcome. It moved from mere *ad hoc* co-operation on special subjects to regular quarterly meetings of a Tripartite Liaison Committee by 1975 with both the Scottish Labour Party and the Scottish Parliamentary Group, finally to a situation where Labour Party observers attended all the major committee meetings of the GC. The STUC were well on the way to becoming the acknowledged centre for all Scottish people's problems. Ten years later, just short of their 90th anniversary, it was taken as a matter of course that the STUC should head a delegation of the Churches, the Lord Provosts of the four main cities and the Miners' Union to the Secretary of State for Scotland to demand negotiations for the expansion of the Scottish coalfields' existing capacity, rather than the National Coal Board's plans to axe more than half the pits.

Section (iv): **Had the "Good Times All Gone"?**

Central to these three years was a growing dread which had to be countered that "the good times are all gone", amongst those who had come to maturity in 1945. The post-war expectations universally had been that there would be speedy liberation in Britain through advance to the shared security and progress for all which had been the aim inspiring the STUC's founders, their grandfathers. With permanent full employment and rapidly achieved public ownership and control, private misery could be abolished for ever, and never again need Britain see economic action of the Upper Clyde shipyard workers and the miners which had had such a political effect. Could the important lesson now be learned of how such economic victories were to be carried into the heart of the political sphere to transform it? And, above all, at last to transform society? It was clear that in any major transformation of society there would certainly need to be a "Social Contract" agreed, about what incomes levels should be and any balance between skilled and less skilled wage packets. There were certainly still those who believed that on the way towards gaining the "commanding heights" while guarding the gains already achieved, it would be wise to make haste slowly. But this had happened all too often in Dad and Grandpa's past experience, under different guises, and it was regarded with deepest suspicion by many. At STUC conferences in the late 'seventies different opinions began to be expressed, at first less as to direction than as to speed. The key points centred on "incomes policy" and "alternative strategy", as we shall see. Midweek of each Congress, delegates were thrown into the deep end by the need to respond in an emergency debate on the Budget which Denis Healey introduced; each one came as the Cabinet reacted to the Treasury's dire threat of further crisis and its consequences.

But just how could this immense new economic crisis be defeated politically? Consciously part and parcel of the community and always in close touch with the men and women at the base of it, employed or unemployed, most STUC leaders were aware not only of the great possibilities of advance but also of the need to carry it further and to guard against disillusionment. For that they knew it was necessary to be actively concerned in consultations on every case of threatened redundancies, closure, cutback or lack of development; and to ensure that knowledge of it was carried outside the walls of any individual place of work, so that there could be the widest involvement and lessons learned from it.[3]

In their 78th Congress in Aberdeen, Jimmy Dollan (Journalists) in his Presidential Address was delighted by the "major response" after the two-day "Summit" with the Premier and his Ministers, in what was henceforth to be "a continuing dialogue" annually. He stressed that already the Government had wiped out the Tories' first post-war attempt to use the law to break the strength of the trade unions by repealing the Industrial Relations Act; pensions had been increased; and food subsidies introduced "in a bid to halt spiralling prices". He also highly approved of the proposed East-West trade deals. Having himself just been on delegations to the USSR and Czechoslovakia, he thought such moves should be further developed instead of the Common Market, of which he was a strong opponent. In the International Women's Year while he was already somewhat doubtful whether the Equal Pay Act would be fully effective, this was another measure which he praised the Labour Government for introducing.

However, he was speaking two days before Denis Healey introduced a Budget about which delegates expressed themselves as "appalled", followed with much alarm about the Government's new attitude to the vexed question of "incomes policy". On the Budget the GC itself put forward a very sharply worded resolution, moved by the incoming President, Andy Forman, which was passed unanimously. Not only was it "a serious attack on the standard of living" by increasing costs, and would have "a disastrous effect on unemployment prospects", they regarded it as

> totally irrelevant to the nation's needs and will do nothing to solve our basic economic problems.

Their resolution denounced the cutbacks in public spending on essential services and "swingeing increases in taxation" as starkly contrasting

> with the miserable three per cent reduction in arms expenditure announced by Mr Healey. The Government have, undoubtedly, responded to the pressures from big business and to the advice of the Treasury.

The continuing "assertion that wages are the major cause of present inflation and the deliberate attack made by the Chancellor on earnings" made it imperative for the trade union movement to react sharply. It closed by urging

> the Government to think again. It is imperative that their economic stragegy be immediately reviewed and that policies designed to protect the interests of the working people who elected them to power be put in hand.

In moving it for the GC, Andy Forman, the incoming President, described it as "a businessman's budget", with every attempt to "mollycoddle big business at the expense of the workers". There was no disagreement; Mick McGahey when seconding for the Miners praised those Labour MPs who demonstrated against it. Both J Walker of ASLEF and J Thomas of Supervisory Staffs prophetically expressed fears that what the Budget did was "to pave the way for a Tory comeback". J Langan of ASTMS added that he found "it amazing how successive Labour Chancellors fell into the same trap"; it was "economic and political suicide".

Subsequent debates led to very considerable pressure being developed on the public spending cuts and on the appalling "upsurge in redundancies and short time in Scottish industry". It led to consultations and subsequent involvement in the concerns of no less than 46 companies.[4] The STUC itself organised conferences on unemployment in Glasgow, Edinburgh and Aberdeen and were represented at many special demonstrations and meetings, mostly organised by trades councils. It also dealt with regional needs, involving the GC visiting the Outer and Inner Hebrides, as well as a useful conference with Tony Benn on North Sea Oil and Energy Policy. There were also important consultations on shipbuilding and the need for it to be nationalised and have adequate grants. A special GC meeting was called to follow up demands on the steel industry which resulted in a conference which saved it from worse disasters in several areas. The Women's Advisory Committee organised an important conference on equal opportunities, noting the weaknesses of the Acts and adopting the ten-point Working Women's Charter.

For the next two years the main preoccupation was "the completely unacceptable levels of unemployment", which called for a review of the Government's priorities during the "Summit dialogue" continued by James Callaghan and his Cabinet. To this was related the cutbacks in social services and failure to nationalise or subsidise under effective public control key industries. Each budget gave rise to emergency debates, which showed great anxiety but also some measure of difference of opinion as we shall see. The Presidential Address of Shop Assistants' Divisional Officer, Andy Forman, to the Perth Congress in 1976 gave clear expression to the basic problems confronting them. Their major activities that year had, he said, been

> concerned with the consequences of a catastrophic inflationary situation, and the worst trade recession since the end of the 1939-45 war.

However, the trade union movement could "take credit for the fact that the unemployment situation is not worse". He put that down to their "ceaseless and constructive pressure" on Government, which had resulted in short-term measures such as job creation programmes, training services agency schemes, employment premium and investment incentives which had kept in employment many workers at risk. But with private industry carrying on what he described as their "investment strike", even more Government intervention was necessary. It should use public ownership to end "gross misuse of scarce resources" he said, quoting the "wasteful competition between banks, building societies and insurance companies." Unanimously the Perth Congress decided to press for immediate reflation, with priorities to increase public spending, specific import controls and the outflow of capital, with stringent industrial and regional planning and research, while finding methods to subsidise shipbuilding.

Represented on no less than 90 Government and other Committees, ranging from the Standing Conference on North Sea Oil to the Open University, the GC plunged into a challenging year of activity. It organised and supported major conferences and demonstrations on unemployment, especially those caused by public expenditure cuts, for there were by then nearly one and a half million out of work. There had been conferences on devolution and seminars on equal opportunities legislation, with both the Women's Advisory and the Youth Advisory Committees fully active. They had also started the annual residential summer schools at the Treesbank Trade Union Educational and Recreational Centre at Kilmarnock, which had been opened by the British TUC General Secretary, Len Murray, when he came to open Middleton House.

Section (v): **Results of the "Summit Dialogues"**

Perhaps the most impressive of all work described in their 1977 Report to the 80th Congress are the papers relating to the discussions at summer and winter "Summit Dialogues" with James Callaghan and his Cabinet. Highly informative, the topics included devolution with a detailed background paper on the Scotland and Wales Bill which it was still hoped might be passed; and all the basic economic problems and crises. There had been some fruitful discussions, especially with Tony Benn on integrated fuel policy and the coming "Plan for Coal", the defence of which was at the heart of the miners' historic struggle seven years later. But the GC's closing comments had had to be that nothing in Callaghan's final remarks at the "Summit" had led them to believe "that the Government was doing anything positive to reduce unemployment"; moreover they regretted that the present policies unfortunately "could have an extremely adverse effect on the future continuation of the Labour Movement". They saw the Government's economic policy as showing "increasing evidence of the influence of the monetary school of economics on Government thinking and policy". Their statement added:

> The indications are that previous adherence to full employment is no longer with us, and that unemployment is more and more used as a means of controlling the economy.

The GC regarded the Government's policy as summed up in three sections: (1) drive for exports to strengthen the balance of payments; (2) increased industrial investment via increased profits for industry; (3) a consumer boom over an "indefinite period at home". But the GC "fundamentally disagreed" with the economic strategy, "principally on the question of certain aspects of policy and timing".

When delegates came to Rothesay three months later how did they respond? It was a record-making and record-breaking occasion. For on their 80th Congress well over a million were represented from 78 affiliated unions, and with those from 43 trades councils there were in all 508 delegates.[5] They were meeting shortly after Labour had lost several by-elections, in one of which much racist propaganda had been poured out. Similar trouble exploiting the mass unemployment had been experienced earlier in Glasgow; James Milne was an eyewitness and gave evidence in defence of members of the Glasgow Trades

Council when they opposed National Front violence at Kingston Halls in 1975. In a hard-hitting Presidential Address the building trade worker Hugh D'Arcy noted this "serious setback" of the latest lost by-election, with its "foul stench of racialism as Fascism emerges from the sewers of Britain under the name of the National Front". He remarked that "some of us have repeatedly warned that the cuts in social services and worsening living standards were the road to disaster for Labour". Strongly attacking the Common Market and its agricultural policy with butter and beef mountains, he said the consequent "rocketing of price increases are a crying scandal". Since the previous Congress, he pointed out,

> prices have gone through the ceiling and inflation is still raging ahead while wages have been held back.

With over a dozen GC members of the British TUC present, he went on to anticipate some later economic debates, setting out a six-point list for an alternative policy through reflation, to make an "impact on the completely unacceptable levels of unemployment". He also made clear his own view on the subject where there was to be disagreement in Congress: it was

> the tenth time in 27 years we have been urged to accept wage restraint by successive Governments, and it has failed every time and only made the crisis more acute.

After covering the wide range of topics before them, he ended by expressing hope for "the utmost support" to be given to the Northern Ireland Committee's call for "A Better Life for All Campaign"; and urged strong opposition to the Scottish national football side being called on to play in the stadium at Santiago, place of torture and execution of thousands by the upstart new general's regime in Chile. On both subjects Congress later passed unanimous resolutions.

Differences over wage restraint had emerged the previous year with a disappointing Budget by Denis Healey. At the close of the eightieth year of their founding under the influence of Scottish Socialists who had created the Labour Party knowing it to be the only way to defend the interests of working people in crisis, there was no hesitation about having the same general aims. But there was serious doubt amongst delegates as to whether the Labour Government's current policy was adequate to change the ghastly and growing unemployment in Scotland. Differences began to emerge on what the immediate changes should be, especially in relation to incomes policy and the Social Contract.

In 1976 at the Perth Congress it was the background to many debates on Scotland's economic problems, even before the main incomes issue was discussed. Early on a very sharply worded motion on unemployment from Stirling Trades Council included a demand for "an end to incomes policy measures like the £6 wage limit". Jack Jones, General Secretary of the Transport & General Workers Union, urged its rejection, because he regarded it as representing "a clear attack on the millions of workers who have democratically accepted the £6 policy", and it was defeated on a card vote of 632 to 1,107. The problem emerged again over the Budget, which was always announced in the middle of the Scottish TUC Congress week, often with the top brass of unions nationally being caught unprepared without an immediate reaction. At Perth it fuelled protest; nor were delegates pleased when one leader raised a doubt as to what the role of the STUC should be when the British TUC itself was far from unanimous. The GC's emergency motion on it was moved by the builder Hugh D'Arcy (UCATT), speaking immediately after a fierce debate on devolution and the Scottish Assembly. He regarded Healey's scheme of "fringe benefits on tax if we accept the 3 per cent" limit on wage demands as "a baited hook to trap the unwary". This tax concession proposal, which a Tory Government years later was to pursue, was described by employers and the press as "brilliant fresh new thinking"; but as D'Arcy warned, its benefits would be wiped out by rising prices, which were far from being controlled. The motion regretted that the Government had "missed the opportunity of pulling Britain out of its recession" by not introducing selective import controls nor easing hire purchase restrictions. Their main concern, however, was

> the introduction of "conditional proposals on taxation" as a means of securing agreement from the trade union movement on incomes policy.

This was seen as a device "comparable to using increased provision for social services, as was used in the Social Contract". Yet the recent "cuts in public sector spending are inconsistent with the aims of the Social Contract", for a mere 3 per cent failed to meet the rising cost of living. But those who expressed disagreement, notably Danny Crawford of D'Arcy's own union, concentrated his criticism on the motion's last clause; this was to instruct the GC to seek an early meeting with the Chancellor "to discuss what steps should be taken to get Britain out of the economic recession". Crawford thought

> the GC had been its usual presumptuous self in speaking on behalf of the

> British working class. I think there is a degree of audacity in saying that they want to meet the Chancellor to discuss the British economy.

It would merely give some people the opportunity to go to the British TUC "and say the STUC did it so we must do it too". Though he received some support from the Transport and General delegation the motion was carried by "an overwhelming majority".

When it came to the direct debate on incomes policy, two motions were covered. One sponsored by Kirkcaldy Trades Council and the Footplatemen condemned the Government's inability to control prices and instructed the GC to call a conference "to mount a public campaign against profiteering and high prices"; it was carried by a large majority. However, a major composite, in which two General Secretaries of London-based unions took part, was finally defeated on a card vote by 717 to 1049. It was made up from motions from the Miners, both the TASS and Construction Section of the Engineers, Local Government Officers and four trades councils. While it was warmly supported by Alan Fisher, General Secretary of the Public Employees, the main opposition came from the General Secretary of the Iron & Steel Trades Confederation, W Sirs, the General Secretary of the General & Municipal Workers, and the Shop Assistants.

Section (vi): **The Historic 80th Congress**

The worsening economic situation quite dominated proceedings next year in their 80th Congress at Rothesay. In the main discussions of economic problems there was full agreement; but on strategy and tactics of Government policy in new stages of the Social Contract delegates continued to express differences. But on one topic they returned to total unanimity; that was on the tax concession device. Before discussing pay policy delegates had heard Helen Liddell for the Scottish Labour Party and Bruce Millan, Secretary of State for Scotland, defending the Government's main policy, although Marie Patterson for the British TUC confined her remarks to the importance of technical education and to women's rights. Then Michael McGahey for the Miners moved the big composite aimed at stopping "the steady erosion of real wages" by ending any incomes policy which interfered with free collective bargaining. It insisted that only when an adequate public sector could ensure economic expansion and therefore move towards the aim of "fundamental and irreversible shift in power and wealth" would there be conditions for any planned policy on wages and incomes". He was supported by Dundee and Stirling Trades Councils, the Colliery Overmen, John Walker as Scottish Secretary of the Footplatemen, the Civil and Public Servants Society and the Fire Brigades Union. It was opposed by T Dougan as Regional Secretary of the Engineers, A H Mackie, General Secretary of the Scottish Bakers, and Danny Crawford of UCATT; Alex Donnet, Scottish Secretary of the General and Municipal Workers said it was being presented as an alternative to the British TUC's policy "for an orderly return to voluntary collective bargaining". It was narrowly lost by 967 to 1017. The General and Municipal Workers also opposed a composite calling for the restoration of differentials and reinstatement of suspended pay bargaining procedures. Moved by the Footplatemen it was supported by J Morton, General Secretary of the Musicians Union, A Dorrens, the Scottish Secretary of the Patternmakers, the Civil and Public Servants and Stirling Trades Council. Yet another composite from Paisley and Kirkcaldy Trades Councils and the Supervisory Staff of the Engineers, failed to win majority opinion. This asserted that the Government's "present economic policies" had in fact broken the Social Contract, and that no incomes policy could be successful "until an alternative strategy is initiated". But there was overwhelming approval for a Public Employees' motion, moved by its General Secretary, Alan Fisher, supported by the Supervisory Staffs, which described

> the attempt to force through a wages policy by linking it to projected tax concessions in the April Budget as an attempt to forestall democratic discussion.

It was not surprising that the next morning an Emergency Motion by the GC was carried unanimously when it denounced the same point in the new Budget by Healey. For it declared the Budget's tax change "conditional on agreement on the third stage of the Social Contract is utterly unacceptable". It could have no reflationary effect and would do nothing to reduce unemployment.

Apart from these doubts on Government strategy on the Social Contract there were an immense number of positive proposals put forward on which delegates showed outstanding agreement. Covering many topics they were virtually all carried unanimously.[6] Composites moved for the GC covered the three major topics: the first including motions from eight organisations was entitled Economic Policy. There followed a motion on Regional Policy; and a composite of nine, entitled Cuts in Public Expenditure. The first composite recording "its deep dismay at the steadily worsening economic situation over the past year", and declared the central problem as due to "serious underinvestment in British industry since the war" by private enterprise. It rejected the Government's attempt to "transfer resources from the public sector to the manufacturing sector" which it saw as leading to greater unemployment and giving no guarantee that private enterprise would invest. The motion therefore set out a nine-point programme, it included:

1. control on capital outflow;
2. expanding the public sector;
3. planning agreements with largest companies;
4. expanding social services;
5. selective import controls;
6. 35-hour week and retirement at 60;
7. lower taxation of lower income groups;
8. wealth tax and pension increases;
9. much reduced arms bill.

This was moved by A Bell, Divisional Officer of the Iron & Steel Trades Confederation, the incoming Chairman. Seconded by J Langan, National Officer of ASTMS, speakers supporting included three General Secretaries, Geoffrey Drain (NALGO), C D Grieve (Tobacco Workers) and R McClement (School Masters & Women Teachers). On regional policy the motion called for selective strengthening of current investment incentives together with revenues from oil and gas reserves to finance a Regional Development Fund. This was moved by Andy Forman, Shop Assistants, for the GC and seconded by Thurso Trades Council.

In the series on cuts in public expenditure, the main composite was moved by the GC by C C Drury, District Secretary of Local Government Officers. It rejected the Government's complaint that too much had been spent in the public sector. Cutbacks hit the social wage; meant price rises; caused unemployment and abandonment of promises to the trade union movement; and brought "an unacceptable reduction" in education, housing, and transport. It was "specifically opposed to the closure of the four Scottish colleges of education". Seconded by the Public Employees and supported by ASTMS, the Fire Brigades and the Civil Servants on health questions, trades councils came sharply into the picture. In addition to the delegates from Dumfries and Falkirk, Arnold Henderson, representing Clydebank, spoke very sharply on the effect of cuts on the handicapped, the very young and the elderly. Before the subject was concluded, C McKay for Paisley Trades Council, reinforced it by calling for

> broadly based action committees to fight unemployment and the cuts in the localities.

He added that their role "must not be seen in opposition to the official trade union but complementary to it". It was seconded by J Reidford, the Secretary of the Glasgow Trades Council, speaking of their campaign which they had carried on over the previous 18 months; he added "trades councils are the ideal vehicles for pursuing this particular campaign".

The very considerable extent of the debates on the economy at their 80th Congress in 1977 may well be regarded as an effective tribute to Jimmy Milne, his staff and the GC in their preparations for and conduct of the "Summit Dialogue" six months earlier. Clearly a record number of delegates and those they represented, from top brass to grass roots, had responded to the richness of that work. For as James Milne told Congress the "Summit" had discussed "almost every industry that concerns us in Scotland".

In her fraternal speech for the Scottish Council of the Labour Party on the first morning, Helen Liddell had said "in the space of the last year there has been a historic drawing together of the Labour Party in Scotland and the STUC". She thought they all owed "a tremendous debt of gratitude" for that to her immediate predecessor and to Jimmy Milne "who have made this possible". On the last morning of their 80th Congress this same feeling found further expression from Tony Wedgwood Benn, Secretary of State for Energy. He was speaking on the immense need for an integrated fuel policy, which was to be at the heart of the homeric battle nationally only six years later, when the defeat of Britain's miners could put the whole trade union and progressive movement in jeopardy. To reindustrialise Britain, Benn said a "successful Socialist energy policy" was essential. To achieve this he put first "strong trade union organisation in the energy industries", followed by full public ownership, real capacity to plan and a major investment programme. Paying tribute to the work of the STUC he added:

> There must be a continuous and continuing dialogue about the whole range of economic policies, including our policies on incomes and prices and jobs, and industrial policies and social policies. And it must be that we seek agreements acceptable to all, not just agreements acceptable at the top, but agreements that meet the needs of all our people, and I am deeply convinced that the whole future of Britain could hinge upon our success in doing that.

That was certainly the mood of Congress.

Although the Scots were disappointed in the hopes of devolution being forthcoming in the years that followed, from henceforward there was no question but that the STUC was to be seen as able to give a voice to the vast majority of Scottish people, and capable itself of calling an all-embracing Assembly whenever some specific issue made it necessary. In that they had no rival. Moreover, if the whole of Britain had learned the same lessons and worked on the same lines, there would quickly have developed an immensely strong Labour Government; and the "enemy within" would have been finally excluded from Number 10 Downing Street.

References

[1] His members referred to the new United Kingdom Association of Professional Engineers as "the UK Apes".

[2] At that time the GC included W McLean, General Secretary of the Miners, H D'Arcy, of the Builders, Enoch Humphries, Fire Brigades Union, Alex Day and W Niven of the Technical & Supervisory Staffs, with the Assistant Secretary, James Milne, always on hand to deputise for James Jack.

[3] This is reflected in the change in annual reports submitted to Conference for debate: that for 1977 was twice as long as that in 1974, with 520 pages to 259.

[4] These were in aircraft, steel, shipbuilding, off-shore rigs, oil production, vehicles, rail, Royal Ordnance work, computers, Telecom, nuclear reactors, the Gas Board, hosiery, tailoring and carpets.

[5] The figure of affiliations was 1,164,123; but only 297,833 were women, with only 36 amongst the delegates.

[6] They ranged from specific import controls; companies to be forced to reinvest from gross profits; direct labour schemes; guarding Scottish fishing limits and forestry; mandatory development area grants to prevent the rundown of steel; the spending cuts in many spheres, especially social services; unemployment; how to stimulate youth employment; proper economic and industrial balance in plans for Scottish economy.

APPENDIX 1

Delegates attending the First Congress of the Scottish Trades Union Congress held in the Berkeley Hall, Glasgow on 25th, 26th and 27th March, 1897.

Names and Addresses of the Delegates	*Name of Society Represented*
Charles Stuart, 43 King Street, Broughty Ferry.	Bleachfield Workers' Union, Scottish
John Hutton, 2 Moncrieff Terrace, Edinburgh.	Bookbinders and Machine Rulers
R. Crew, 19 Abbot Street, Arbroath	Boot and Shoe Operatives, National Union, Arbroath Branch
R. S. Aytoun, 574a Gallowgate, Glasgow	Boot and Shoe Operatives, National Union, Glasgow Branch, No. 2
William Greer, 118 McLelland Street, Glasgow.	Brassfinishers, West of Scotland
William Horn, 542 Rutherglen Road, Glasgow	Brass Moulders, Scottish
David Bole, 75 East Nelson Street, Glasgow.	Bricklayers' Association, Operative.
Daniel McKay, 23 Green Street, Bridgeton, Glasgow.	Bricklayers' Association, Operative.
David Drinnan, 103 Walkinshaw Street, Glasgow.	Carpet Trades, Scottish, Powerloom Protective and Provident Association
James Manielles, 32 Hopehill Road, Glasgow.	Coopers, Glasgow Union
Thomas Husband, 23 Langlands Road, Govan.	Engineers, Amalgamated Society, Govan, No. 3 Branch
William Smith, 3 Dixon Street, Edinburgh	Flint Glass Makers, Edinburgh
James Reilly, 8 Watson Street, Gallowgate, Glasgow.	Labourers, National Union
Bernard Havilan, 169 Finnieston Street, Glasgow.	Labourers, National Union of Dock, No. 1 Branch
C.P. Sadler, 169 Finnieston Street, Glasgow.	Labourers, National Union of Dock, No. 1 Branch
George Douglas, 28 McLean Street, Plantation, Govan.	Labourers, Glasgow Harbour
William Glen, 3 Broomhill Street, Port-Dundas, Glasgow	Labourers, Glasgow Harbour
William Jeffrey, 122 West Graham Street, Glasgow.	Life Assurance Agents, National Union of
John H. Elric, 130 Hutcheson Street, Aberdeen.	Masons and Granite Cutters, United Operative, Aberdeen
James Brough, 768 Garscube Road, Glasgow.	Masons, United Operatives' Association of Scotland.
John Wardrope, 96 Abington Street, Glasgow.	Masons, United Operatives' Association of Scotland.
Patrick Fitzpatrick, 21 Old Assembly Close, High Street, Edinburgh.	Masons, United Operatives' Association of Scotland.
William Hunter, 46 Peebles Street, Newton, Ayr.	Masons, United Operatives' Association of Scotland.
Alexander MacKenzie, Airlie Street, Alyth.	Mill and Factory Workers, Scottish Alyth Branch
John Torrance, 10 High Street, Kirkintilloch.	Miners Union, Kirkintilloch
James Murdoch, Bellshill.	Miners Association, Lanarkshire
Robert Smillie, Larkhall.	Miners Association, Lanarkshire
John Wilson, 3 Melville Cottages, Scotstoun.	Miners Association, West Lothian and Renfrewshire
R. Chisholm Robertson, 93 Hope Street, Glasgow.	Miners Association, Scottish Central
James P. Browne, 77 Jamaica Street, Glasgow.	Musicians Union, Amalgamated
George Galloway, 16 Wallace Grove Place, Shields Road, Glasgow.	Plumbers, United Operatives, Association of Scotland
Alexander Irvine, 2 St. Giles Street, Edinburgh	Press and Machinemen's Union, Edinburgh

Names and Addresses of the Delegates	*Name of Society Represented*
John Miller, 41 Salamanca Street, Parkhead, Glasgow.	Railway Servants, Amalgamated Society
James Moir, 38 Milton Street, Edinburgh.	Railway Servants, Amalgamated Society
Robert Harris, 6 Freer Street, Fountainbridge, Edinburgh	Railway Servants, Amalgamated Society, West End Edinburgh Branch
William Morrison, Comeley Road, Camelon, Falkirk.	Range, Stove, and Ornamental Fitters, Associated, Falkirk.
William G.S. Macleod, 35 Robertson Street, Glasgow.	Sawmill Operatives and Woodcutting Machinemen's Society.
Thomas Grady, 20 Merryland Street, Govan.	Ship Riggers' Association, Clyde, Federated
R. Handyside, 16 Firhill Street, Glasgow.	Spindle and Flyer Makers' Society, Glasgow Branch
Councillor John Cronin, 53 Waterloo Street, Glasgow	Steel and Iron Workers, Amalgamated Society
W. Johnson, 41 Crosshill Street, Motherwell.	Steel and Iron Workers, Amalgamated Society
Robert Marr, 108 Calder Street, Motherwell	Steel and Iron Workers, Amalgamated Society
Adam Carnegie, 10 Carrickarden Street, Glasgow	Tailors, National Scottish Operatives, Executive
Donald McLeay, 10 Carrickarden Street, Glasgow.	Tailors, National Scottish Operatives, Executive, Glasgow Branch
W. McBain, 186 High Street, Edinburgh.	Tailors, National Scottish Operatives, Executive Edinburgh Branch
James Smith, 62 Montgomery Street, Edinburgh.	Tailors, National Scottish Operatives, Executive Edinburgh Branch
John Hamilton, 19 Kilnside Road, Paisley.	Tailors, National Scottish Operatives, Executive, Paisley Branch
John R. McBain, 146 North Street, Aberdeen.	Tailors, Amalgamated Society, Aberdeen Branch
Thomas McBurney, 24 Creichton Street, Dundee.	Tailors, Amalgamated Society, Dundee Branch.
Alexander Robb, 148 Waddell Street, Glasgow.	Tailors, Amalgamated Society, Glasgow Branch
William Dunn, St. Crispins Buildings, Falkirk.	Tailors, Amalgamated Society, Falkirk Branch.
John Jack, Town Hall Buildings, Alva.	Textile Workers, Alva.
Joseph C. McLeod, 202 Carnegie Street, Edinburgh.	Tinplate Workers and Gas Meter Makers, Edinburgh and Leith
George Carson, 256 Cumberland Street, Glasgow.	Tinplate and Sheet Metal Workers' Association.
Robert Chambers, 156 Centre Street, Glasgow.	Tinplate and Sheet Metal Workers' Association.
John Keir, 168a Skene Street, Aberdeen.	Trades Council, Aberdeen.
David Liddell, 5 Parker Street, Dundee.	Trades Council, Dundee.
David A. Blackburn, 12 South Elgin Street, Edinburgh.	Trades Council, Edinburgh.
Hugh W. Stuart, 190 Rose Street, Edinburgh.	Trades Council, Edinburgh.
William Strang, Wallace Street, Falkirk.	Trades Council, Falkirk.
Councillor Boyd S. Brown, 119 Great Hamilton Street, Glasgow.	Trades Council, Glasgow.
John Brown, 93 New Road, Parkhead, Glasgow	Trades Council, Glasgow.
Duncan McPherson, 122 Henderson Street, Kinning Park, Glasgow.	Trades Council, Glasgow.
Peter Ross, 655 Govan Road, Govan.	Trades Council, Govan.
Robert Lemmon, 17 Brymner Street, Greenock.	Trades Council, Greenock.
John Henderson, 22 Dundonald Street, Dundee.	Typographical Society, Dundee.
William Chisholm, 1 Maxwell Place, Glasgow, S.S.	Typographical Society, Glasgow.
John Robertson, 66 Norfolk Street, Glasgow, S.S.	Typographical Society, Glasgow.
James Farquhar, 182 London Road, Glasgow.	Warpers' Society, Handmill and Horizontal, Glasgow and District
Andrew Ballantyne, 3 Queen Margaret Place, Glasgow.	Women's Trades' Council, National Federal, of Scotland
Baillie A. J. Hunter, 3 Springfield Terrace, Glasgow.	Women's Trades' Council, National Federal, of Scotland
Miss M. H. Irwin, 58 Renfield Street, Glasgow.	Women's Trades' Council, National Federal, of Scotland
Mrs. Galloway, 16 Wallace Grove Place, Glasgow.	Women's Protective and Provident League.

Delegates attending the First Congress of the Scottish Trades Union Congress held in the Berkeley Hall, Glasgow on 25, 26 and 27 March, 1897.

Margaret Harding Irwin, Secretary to the Parliamentary Committee, seated 3rd left in second row.

APPENDIX 2

Past Congresses

No.	*Date*	*Place of Meeting*	*Name of President*	*Secy. to P.C. or General Council*
1	1897	Glasgow	D. McPherson (Glasgow T.C.)	Andrew M. Ballantyne
2	1898	Aberdeen	John Keir (Aberdeen T.C.)	Miss M. Irwin
3	1899	Dundee	T. McBurney (Dundee T.C.)	Miss M. Irwin
4	1900	Edinburgh	T. Wilson (Edinburgh Bakers)	Miss M. Irwin
5	1901	Paisley	Coun. J. Kent (Typographical)	George Carson, J.P.
6	1902	Falkirk	Coun. W. Muirhead (Ironmoulders)	George Carson, J.P.
7	1903	Ayr	Robert Smillie (Miners)	George Carson, J.P.
8	1904	Perth	George Murdoch (Perth T.C.)	George Carson, J.P.
9	1905	Hawick	Robert Smillie (Miners)	George Carson, J.P.
10	1906	Greenock	Bailie W. Johnston (Aberdeen T.C.)	George Carson, J.P.
11	1907	Aberdeen	John T. Howden (Joiners)	George Carson, J.P.
12	1908	Edinburgh	James Gavin (Ironworkers)	George Carson, J.P.
13	1909	Dunfermline	James Gavin (Ironworkers)	George Carson, J.P.
14	1910	Kilmarnock	J. C. Hendry (Brechin Mill Workers)	George Carson, J.P.
15	1911	Dundee	James Brown (Miners)	George Carson J.P.
16	1912	Glasgow	D. Palmer (Aberdeen T.C.)	George Carson, J.P.
17	1913	Dumfries	Coun. A. R. Turner (Glasgow T.C.)	George Carson, J.P.
18	1914	Kirkcaldy	Bailie R. Climie (Ayrshire T.C.)	George Carson J.P.
–	1915		NO CONGRESS HELD	
19	1916	Glasgow	David Gilmour (Miners)	George Carson, J.P.
20	1917	Falkirk	Robert Allan (Edinburgh T.C.)	George Carson, J.P.
21	1918	Ayr	Hugh Lyon (Horse and Motormen)	Robert Allan
22	1919	Perth	Neil S. Beaton (Shop Assistants)	Robert Allan
23	1920	Dunfermline	William Shaw (G.T. and L.C.)	Robert Allan
24	1921	Aberdeen	Bailie J. Walker (I. and S.T.C.)	Robert Allan
25	1922	Edinburgh	C. N. Gallie (Railway Clerks)	D. Marshall (Interim)
26	1923	Dundee	J. Murdoch (Scot. Mineworkers)	William Elger, J.P.
27	1924	Ayr	Tom Wilson (Shop Assistants)	William Elger, J.P.
28	1925	Dumfries	W. Leonard (Furnishing Trades)	William Elger, J.P.
29	1926	Inverness	J. F. Duncan (Scot. Farm Servants)	William Elger, J.P.
30	1927	Galashiels	P. Webster (Horse and Motormen)	William Elger, J.P.
31	1928	Perth	J. Nairn (Textile W., Kirkcaldy)	William Elger, J.P.
32	1929	Aberdeen	George Kerr (Workers' Union)	William Elger, J.P.
33	1930	Edinburgh	R. Watson (Scot. Typo. Assoc.)	William Elger, J.P.
34	1931	Elgin	C. N. Gallie (Railway Clerks)	William Elger, J.P.
35	1932	Hawick	W. Leonard (Furnishing Trades)	William Elger, J.P.
36	1933	Ayr	James Crawford (Printers' Assist's)	William Elger, J.P.
37	1934	Stirling	Thomas Scollan (Glasgow T.C.)	William Elger, J.P.
38	1935	Montrose	Thomas Brown (Shop Assistants)	William Elger, J.P.
39	1936	St.Andrews	James Young (A.E.S.D.)	William Elger, J.P.
40	1937	Inverness	Bella Jobson (Scot. Farm Servants)	William Elger, J.P.
41	1938	Girvan	H. Ellison (Nat. U. of Railwaymen)	William Elger, J.P.
42	1939	Rothesay	R. Taylor (Scot. Horse & Motormen)	William Elger, J.P.
43	1940	Aberdeen	W. Quin, J.P. (N.U.G. and M.W.)	William Elger, J.P.
44	1941	Dunoon	J. Watson (N.U.D. and A.W.)	William Elger, J.P.
45	1942	Rothesay	C. Murdoch, J.P. (Scottish Bakers)	William Elger, J.P.
46	1943	Aberdeen	P. Henderson, J.P. (Scottish Miners)	William Elger, J.P.
47	1944	Dunoon	J. Crawford, J.P. (Printers' Assist's)	William Elger, J.P.
48	1945	Aberdeen	James Young (A.E.S.D.)	William Elger, J.P.
49	1946	Dunoon	Councillor J. Campbell (N.U.R.)	William Elger, J.P.

50	1947	St.Andrews	Coun. J. Duncan (Con. Engineers)	Charles Murdoch
51	1948	Perth	J. Sullivan (T. and G.W.U.)	Charles Murdoch
52	1949	Aberdeen	Coun. W. McGinniss (G. and M.W.)	George Middleton
53	1950	Rothesay	W. Pearson (N.U. Mineworkers)	George Middleton
54	1951	Dunoon	J. Lang, O.B.E. (I. and S.T.C.)	George Middleton
55	1952	Perth	J. Brannigan, M.B.E. (S.H.M.A.)	George Middleton
56	1953	Rothesay	A. D. McKellar, O.B.E. (A.E.S.D.)	George Middleton
57	1954	Aberdeen	J. G. Bothwell (T.S.S.A.)	George Middleton
58	1955	Rothesay	T. B. Meikle, O.B.E. (T. and G.W.U.)	George Middleton
59	1956	Perth	D. Currie, J.P. (C. and A.W.U.)	George Middleton
60	1957	Rothesay	F. Donachy (Nat. U. of Railwaymen)	George Middleton
61	1958	Aberdeen	W. Mowbray (Scot. U. of Bakers)	George Middleton
62	1959	Dunoon	A. Moffat (N.U. Mineworkers)	George Middleton
63	1960	Perth	Jas. Milne (Aberdeen Trades Coun.)	George Middleton
64	1961	Rothesay	Edward W. Craig (U.S.D.A.W.)	George Middleton
65	1962	Aberdeen	Patrick Conner (A.E.U.)	George Middleton
66	1963	Dunoon	David Lauder (N.U.R.)	George Middleton
67	1964	Perth	Frank H. Stephen (D.A.T.A.)	James Jack
68	1965	Rothesay	William Scholes (T. and G.W.U.)	James Jack
69	1966	Aberdeen	A.H. Kitson, J.P. (S.C.M.U.)	James Jack
70	1967	Dunoon	W. MacLean (N.U. Mineworkers)	James Jack
71	1968	Aberdeen	J. Irvine (I. and S.T.C.)	James Jack
72	1969	Rothesay	E Humphries (Fire Brigades Union)	James Jack
73	1970	Oban	J. A. Matheson (N.U.R.)	James Jack
74	1971	Aberdeen	A. M. Donnet (N.U.G.M.W.)	James Jack
75	1972	Dunoon	R. Macdonald (T. & G.W.U.)	James Jack
76	1973	Aberdeen	A. W. Day (A.S.T.M.S.)	James Jack
77	1974	Rothesay	Miss E. McIntyre (N.U.H. & K.W.)	James Jack
78	1975	Aberdeen	J. H. Dollan (N.U.J.)	James Jack
79	1976	Perth	A. Forman (U.S.D.A.W.)	James Milne
80	1977	Rothesay	H. D'Arcy (U.C.A.T.T.)	James Milne

APPENDIX 3

Members of the Parliamentary Committee (1897 to 1922)
and of the General Council of the
Scottish Trades Union Congress(1923 to 1977)

Name	*Service on PC and/or GC*	*Nominating Body*
ADAMSON William	1908, 1934 to 1935	Scottish Miners Federation
AIRLIE W T	1950 to 1951	Nat. Union of Printing, Bookbinding, Machine Ruling & Paper Workers
AITKEN W	1972, 1977	Amalgamated Union of Engineering Workers (Engineering Section)
ALLAN Robert	1899, 1912 to 1921	Edinburgh Trades Council
ANDERSON T W	1899 to 1900	Amalgamated Society of Carpenters & Joiners
BAIRD Daniel	1903 to 1904	Glasgow Operative Plasterers
BALLANTYNE Andrew	1897	National Federation Women's Trades Council
BARR Andrew	1976 to 1977	National Union of Railwaymen
BARRIE Izobel	1940 to 1942	Nat. Amalgamated Union of Shop Assistants, Warehousemen & Clerks
BALSILLIE David	1905	Edinburgh Trades Council
BEATON Neil	1914 to 1920	Amalgamated Union of Shop Assistants
BELL Arthur	1970 to 1977	Iron & Steel Trades Confederation
BLACKBURN David	1897	Edinburgh Trades Council
BLACKLOCK Isabella	1898	Glasgow Council for Women's Trades
BLAIRFORD W B	1969 to 1977	Electrical, Electronic, Telecommunication & Plumbing Union
BOTHWELL J G	1940, 1948 to 1959	Railway Clerks Association
BOYD James	1903 to 1904	Glasgow Trades Council
BOYLE William	1945 to 1946	Association of Engineering & Shipbuilding Draughtsmen
BRANNIGAN John	1947 to 1952	Scottish Horse & Motormen's Association
BRECKENRIDGE R	1920	National Union of Seamen & Firemen
BROWN James	1910	
BROWN John	1897	Glasgow Trades Council
BROWN Thomas	1931 to 1939, 1945, 1947 to 1954	Union of Shop Assistants, Warehousemen & Clerks
BROWN W I	1950	Scottish Union of Bakers, Confectioners & Bakery Workers
CAMERON Alexander	1943 to 1944	National Union of Scottish Mineworkers
CAMPBELL James	1942 to 1948	National Union of Railwaymen

APPENDIX

Name	*Service on PC and/or GC*	*Nominating Body*
CARLIN D	1942	Transport & General Workers Union
CARNEGIE Adam	1897	National Scottish Operative Tailors
CARR Joseph	1898	Dundee Trades Council
CARSON George	1898 to 1917	Association of Tinplate & Sheet Metal Workers
CATHCART Alexander	1932 to 1934	Scottish Horse & Motormen's Association
CHARLTON Robert	1909 to 1911	National Amalgamated Soc. of Enginemen & Cranemen
CLIMIE Robert	1910 to 1918, 1920 to 1923	Ayrshire Trades Council
CONNOR Patrick	1957 to 1967	Amalgamated Engineering Union
COOK James	1918 to 1919	National Union of Scottish Mineworkers
COYLE Owen	1930 to 1931	Iron & Steel Trades Confederation
CRAIG Edward W	1956 to 1968	Union of Shop Distributive & Allied Workers
CRAIG George B	1905	United Operative Masons Association
CRAWFORD James	1930 to 1944	National Society of Operative Printers & Assistants
CREW R W	1897	National Union of Boot & Shoe Operatives
CRONIN John	1897	Amalgamated Steel & Iron Workers Society
CURRAN R	1977	National Union of Public Employees
CURRIE David	1948 to 1966	Clerical & Administration Workers Union
D'ARCY Hugh	1969 to 1977	Union of Construction Allied Trades & Technicians
DAY Alexander	1966 to 1975	Association of Scientific Workers
DOLLAN James H	1969 to 1977	National Union of Journalists
DONACHY Frank	1949 to 1957	National Union of Railwaymen
DONNET Alexander	1964 to 1972	General & Municipal Workers Union
DOONAN James	1923 to 1925	National Union of Scottish Mineworkers
DOUGAN Thomas	1977	Amalgamated Union of Engineering Workers (Engineering Section)
DOUGAN William	1972 to 1977	Amalgamated Society of Boilermakers
DOUGHERTY John	1932 to 1933	Amalgamated Society of Dyers & Bleachers
DRUMMOND Thomas	1925 to 1926	Edinburgh & District Trades & Labour Council
DRURY Charles C	1971 to 1977	National & Local Government Officers Association
DUNCAN James R	1942 to 1949, 1953 to 1959	The Constructional Engineering Union
DUNCAN Joseph F	1923 to 1932	Scottish Farm Servants Union
EARSMAN W P	1940 to 1942	Edinburgh Trades Council
ELLISON Herbert	1934 to 1941	National Union of Railwaymen
ELRICK John H	1902	Aberdeen Trades Council
FITZPATRICK Patrick	1897	United Operatives Masons Association of Scotland
FORMAN Andrew	1969 to 1977	Union of Shop Distributive & Allied Workers

Name	*Service on PC and/or GC*	*Nominating Body*
GALLIE C N	1918 to 1939	Railway Clerks Association
GALLOWAY George	1901 to 1902	Glasgow Trades Council
GARDEN George	1907	Mason & Granite Cutters
GAVIN James	1904 to 1911, 1913 to 1915	Amalgamated Society of Sheet & Iron Workers
GILLESPIE Peter	1931	Transport & General Workers Union
GILMOUR David	1912 to 1915	Scottish Miners Federation
GILROY Agnes	1932 to 1934	National Union of Distributive & Allied Workers
GIRVAN Robert	1900 to 1904	Association of Tailors & Tailoresses
GREER William	1897 to 1900	West of Scotland Brass Finishers
GUTHRIE James	1902	Amalgamated Society of Railway Servants
HAMILTON Fred	1909 to 1910	Edinburgh Trades Council
HENDERSON Peter	1939 to 1946	National Union of Scottish Mineworkers
HENDRY John C	1908 to 1912, 1916 to 1921	Brechin Mill & Factory Workers
HENRY John	1971 to 1977	Edinburgh Trades Council
HIGGINS James D	1921 to 1922	Electrical Trades Union
HILL J C	1947	Clerical & Administrative Workers Union
HOUGHTON Joseph	1916 to 1919	Scottish Union of Dock Labourers
HOWDEN John	1904 to 1908	Amalgamated Society of Carpenters & Joiners
HUMPHRIES Enoch	1963 to 1977	Fire Brigades Union
HUNTER Alexander	1926 to 1927	National Union of Scottish Mineworkers
HUNTER W G	1913 to 1917	Operative Bakers and Confectioners of Scotland
HUTCHISON William	1968 to 1971	Amalgamated Union of Engineering Workers (Engineering Section)
IRVINE John	1961 to 1968	Iron & Steel Trades Confederation
IRWIN Margaret	1897 to 1901	National Federal Women's Trades Council of Scotland
INNES James	1898 to 1899	Amalgamated Society of Railway Servants
JACK James M	1900 to 1901	Association of Iron Moulders
JACKSON Charles	1902 to 1908, 1923	Scottish Typographical Association
JARVIE James	1960 to 1962	Associated Blacksmiths, Forge & Smithy Workers Society
JOBSON Bella	1933 to 1941	Scottish Farm Servants Section
JOHNSTONE William	1903 to 1906	Aberdeen Trades Council
KEIR John	1897 to 1901	Aberdeen Trades Council
KERR George	1924 to 1934	The Workers Union
KESSACK J O'Connor	1912 to 1915	National Union of Dock Workers
KIRKWOOD James	1972 to 1975	Post Office Engineering Union
KITSON Alexander	1960 to 1977	Scottish Horse & Motormen's Association
LAIRD Gavin	1973 to 1975	Amalgamated Union of Engineering Workers (Engineering Section)
LAMBIE George	1968	Society of Graphical & Allied Trades

APPENDIX

Name	*Service on PC and/or GC*	*Nominating Body*
LANG John	1947 to 1960	Iron & Steel Trades Confederation
LANGAN John	1976 to 1977	Association of Scientific, Technical & Managerial Staffs
LAUDER David M	1958 to 1963	National Union of Railwaymen
LAW Thomas	1923	National Union of Scottish Mineworkers
LEMMON Robert	1906 to 1908	Greenock Trades Council
LEONARD William	1921 to 1931	Glasgow Trades & Labour Council
LESLIE J R	1905 to 1908, 1911 to 1912	Amalgamated Union of Shop Assistants
LOGAN Archibald	1899	Association of Ironmoulders
LYON Hugh	1902, 1909, 1916 to 1919	Scottish Carters Association
McCALMONT Thomas	1968	Scottish Slaters Tilers Roofers & Cement Workers Society
MACDONALD Raymond	1966 to 1977	Transport & General Workers Union
McGINNIS William	1943 to 1946, 1948 to 1958	National Union of General & Municipal Workers
McINTYRE Elizabeth	1968 to 1977	National Union of Hosiery & Knitwear Workers
MACKAY A B	1941 to 1942	Scottish Bankers Association
MACKAY Angus	1901	Scottish Typographical Association
MACKELLAR A D	1947 to 1955	Association of Engineering & Shipbuilding Draughtsmen
McKELVIE J	1974 to 1975	National Union of Railwaymen
McKERRELL Thomas	1916	Scottish Union of Mineworkers
McLEAN Kate	1911 to 1913	National Federation of Women Workers
McLEAN William	1961 to 1977	National Union of Mineworkers
MACPHERSON Duncan	1897	Glasgow Trades Council
McPHERSON Hugh	1932 to 1935	Building & Monumental Workers Association of Scotland
MALLINSON John	1898 to 1899, 1906 to 1907	Edinburgh Trades Council
MARSHALL David	1920 to 1922	Scottish Union of Dock Workers
MATHESON John A	1964 to 1973	National Union of Railwaymen
MEIKLE T B	1948 to 1958	Transport & General Workers Union
MEWHORT Grace	1921	Edinburgh & District Trades Council
MIDDLETON George	1943 to 1948	Glasgow Trades Council
MILLER John	1900	Amalgamated Society of Railway Servants
MILNE James	1954 to 1968	Aberdeen Trades Council
MOFFAT Alexander	1954 to 1960	National Union of Mineworkers
MORRELL James	1973 to 1977	General Municipal Boilermakers & Allied Trade Union
MORRIS Griff	1940	Railway Clerks Association
MOWBRAY William	1952 to 1963	Scottish Union of Bakers, Confectioners, Biscuit Bakers and Biscuit Workers
MUIR Dr A G	1946	Association of Scientific Workers, Technical & Managerial Staffs
MUIRHEAD William	1913 to 1915	Central Ironmoulders of Scotland
MURDOCH Charles	1936 to 1946	Scottish Union of Bakers, Confectioners, & Bakery Workers

Name	*Service on PC and/or GC*	*Nominating Body*
MURDOCH Hugh	1904 to 1912	Central Ironmoulders Association of Scotland
MURDOCH James	1901, 1920 to 1922	Scottish Federation of Miners
NAIRN John	1923 to 1930	Scottish Textile Workers Union
NIVEN William	1970 to 1976	Amalgamated Union of Engineering Workers (Technical, Administrative and Supervisory Section)
O'HAGEN Joseph	1916 to 1919	Amalgamated Steel & Iron Workers Society
O'NAGAN M	1924 to 1926	National Union of Shale Miners & Oil Workers
O'REILLY J H	1975 to 1977	Confederation of Health Service Employees
PALMER David	1908 to 1915, 1917	Aberdeen Trades Council
PEARSON William	1945 to 1949	National Union of Scottish Mineworkers
PENMAN H K	1972 to 1974	National Union of Public Employees
POLLOCK John D	1975 to 1977	Educational Institute of Scotland
QUIN William	1935 to 1940	National Union of General & Municipal Workers
REILLY James	1900 to 1903	National Union of Labourers
ROBERTSON D	1941, 1943 to 1947	Railwaymen Clerks Association
ROBERTSON John	1909	Scottish Miners Federation
ROBERTSON John	1897 to 1898	Scottish Typographical Society
ROBERTSON R Chisholm	1907	Scottish Central Miners Association
ROSS Peter	1897 to 1899	Govan Trades Council
SCHOLES William	1959 to 1965	Transport & General Workers Union
SCOLLAN Thomas	1930 to 1939	Glasgow Trades Council
SHAW B H	1902 to 1904, 1909	National Amalgamated Union of Shop Assistants, Warehousemen and Clerks
SHAW William	1916 to 1920	Glasgow Trades Council
SHERRIFF J	1948	Amalgamated Union of Engineering Workers (Engineering Section)
SHIELDS William B	1977	Amalgamated Union of Engineering Workers (Technical, Administrative and Supervisory Section)
SHINWELL Emanuel	1922	Marine Workers
SIME J F	1931 to 1934	Dundee & District Union Jute and Flax Workers
SIMPSON Robert	1918 to 1919	Scottish Shale Miners
SMALL William B	1938 to 1939	National Union of Scottish Mineworkers
SMILLIE Robert	1897 to 1899, 1903 to 1907	Lanarkshire Miners Association
SMITH Alexander	1922 to 1924	Edinburgh Trades & Labour Council
SMITH Ben	1967 to 1970	National & Local Government Officers Association
SMITH Robert	1927 to 1928	National Union of Scottish Mineworkers

Name	*Service on PC and/or GC*	*Nominating Body*
SPENCE R	1920	Amalgamated Toolmakers Society
STEIN Dr Lily	1955 to 1956	Association of Scientific Workers
STEPHEN Frank	1959 to 1969	Association of Engineering and Shipbuilding Draughtsmen
STEWART Hugh W	1900	Edinburgh Trades Council
STEWART J J	1940 to 1953	Aberdeen Trades Council
STEWART James S	1949 to 1953	Edinburgh Trades Council
STEWART Charles	1901 to 1903, 1905 to 1907, 1909 to 1910	Federal Union of Mill, Factory & Bleachfield Workers
SULLIVAN John	1943 to 1947	Transport & General Workers Union
SWEENEY James	1940	Iron & Steel Trades Confederation
TAYLOR Robert	1935 to 1943	Scottish Horse & Motormen's Association
TAYLOR T	1972 to 1977	National Union of Vehicle Builders
TONNER James	1911	Scottish Miners Federation
TURNER Alexander	1908, 1910 to 1915	Glasgow Trades Council
TWEEDIE William J	1966 to 1971	Amalgamated Society of Boilermakers, Shipwrights, Blacksmiths & Structural Workers
VEITCH John	1929 to 1930	Transport & General Workers Union
WALKER James	1919 to 1926	Iron & Steel Trades Confederation
WALLACE S R	1977	Engineers & Managers Association
WATSON James	1935 to 1944	National Union of Distributive & Allied Workers
WATSON Robert	1924 to 1930	Scottish Typographical Association
WEBSTER Peter	1923 to 1928	Scottish Horse & Motormen's Association
WILLIAMSON William	1927 to 1929	Edinburgh District & Labour Council
WILSON John	1900	Scottish Federation of Miners
WILSON Thomas	1921 to 1930	National Amalgamated Union of Shop Assistants
WILSON Thomas	1901 to 1903, 1925	Edinburgh Trades Council
WOOD John	1947, 1951 to 1958	National Union of Mineworkers
WYPER Hugh	1969 to 1970	Glasgow District Trades Council
YOUNG James	1932 to 1944	Association of Engineering and Shipbuilding Draughtsmen

Index